The Struggle Over the Past

The Struggle Over the Past

FUNDAMENTALISM IN THE MODERN WORLD

EDITED BY

William M. Shea

THE ANNUAL PUBLICATION OF THE

COLLEGE THEOLOGY SOCIETY

1989

VOLUME 35

UNIVERSITY
PRESS OF
AMERICA

Lanham • New York • London

Annual Publication • 35

ISSN 0276-2064
ISBN 0-8191-7920-5 (pbk. : alk. paper)
ISBN 0-8191-7919-1 (cloth : alk. paper)

 The paper used in this publication meets the minimum requirements of American National Standard for Information Sciences—Permanence of Paper for Printed Library Materials, ANSI Z39.48–1984.

ACKNOWLEDGEMENTS

President Francis T. Borkowski and the President's Council of the University of South Florida generously donated research support funds that helped pay the bills while I edited these papers in the summer of 1989.

Ms Kandy Jill Lones and Ms Patricia Schuster of the College of Arts and Letters of the University of South Florida processed words with patience and humor.

Over seventy members of the CTS and a handful who are not on its list promptly contributed critical reviews of the papers, greatly lightening the editor's burden.

The Institute of Christian Ministries of University of San Diego provided several weeks of telephone use while manuscripts were collected and reviews arranged.

The National Conference of Catholic Bishops, Archbishop Oscar H. Liscomb of Mobile, the Fundamentalism Project, and Rev. Dr. James Montgomery Boice gave permission for the reproduction of the documents in the four appendices.

Helene Anne Lutz and our sons Nathanael and Christopher share their life with me and so make even editorial tasks worthwhile.

To them all I am grateful.

William M. Shea
University of South Florida
February 20, 1990

TABLE OF CONTENTS

PREFACE

It is said that the American fundamentalist political tide has turned. This may be so, but it does not mean that fundamentalist religiosity has lost or will lose its appeal. It is highly likely that fundamentalism is here to stay, and so it merits increased scholarly attention. It also seems that fundamentalism is not a phenomenon peculiar to American Christianity. Putting aside questions of terminological aptness, an issue taken up several times in the essays collected here, religious fundamentalism is an international phenomenon. This, too, should be a focus of academic concern. The existence of The Fundamentalist Project of the American Academy of Arts and Sciences, supported by the MacArthur Foundation, is evidence of that concern. So, too, is the fact that the College Theology Society devoted its annual meeting in 1989 at Nazareth College in Rochester, New York, to the topic "Religious Fundamentalism in the Modern World," and heard over forty papers read on it. The meeting and this volume which prints sixteen of the papers display the new interest of academics at large and the particular interest of a Roman Catholic community of scholars in fundamentalism, international, Christian, and even Catholic.

In the study of fundamentalism by religionists there are two dangers, and I hope it will be said that the essays here escape them. The first is the long-standing anti-fundamentalist bias of the academic community. The bias is not, of course, entirely undeserved, for American Christian fundamentalism, from its beginnings at the turn of the century to this day, has been suspicious of the clique of academics who presume to settle the status and meaning of its sacred books and to declare what is and what is not believable. With vigor fundamentalists have protested the unbelief of the academic world, most especially of its theologians. Academics and theologians have not turned the other cheek. The mutual antagonism is pervasive, and appears recently and bitterly in the ongoing war over seminary theology and the struggle for control of the public school curriculum. Alarums sound constantly. The antagonism takes its toll from the ideally disinterested nature of the academic quest for understanding, for that quest is all too easily muddied by the received political and cultural liberalism of the academic class.

There is a second bias that could well affect essays such as ours, and it, too, has its historical roots and explanation. American fundamentalists are evangelical Protestants, and there is no love lost between American evangelicals and the Catholic Church (indeed, there has been none between evangelicals and the mainline Protestant denominations). Sidney Ahlstrom, when asked several years ago to list the primary distinguishing characteristics of American evangelical Christianity, placed anti-Romanism high on it. This anti-Catholicism of American fundamentalists seems a distillation of historical Protestant worries about hierarchy, works-righteousness, and sacraments intensified by a peculiar dispensationalist apocalyptic imagination. American Catholics remember well the viciousness of Nativism and its effects on Catholic participation in the public life of the nation; they remember (at least members of my generation do) the fact that a Roman Catholic was denied the White House in 1928 by the desertion of the Democratic Party by American evangelicals. While that evangelical attitude may have softened somewhat in the past decade, the American fundamentalists carry on the evangelical tradition on this point with close to pristine purity. Catholic theologians, as the theologians of other Christian churches, do not approach the study of fundamentalism without scars.

Yet here the authors, while they do not leave that difficult history or its tensions behind, approach the topic with something close to equanimity. Four of the papers study aspects of fundamentalism in traditions other than the Christian, and so are perhaps less liable to the biases. The twelve which study aspects of Christian fundamentalism appear admirable in their commingling of respect with serious criticism. Fundamentalism's historical associations are treated, its ambiguities are explored, its shortcomings are weighed, but without rancor. Some of the essays are even irenic!

The work done by evangelical academic historians on fundamentalism is taken as reliable, and especially on one very important point, namely, that at the fundament of fundamentalism there is a curious and serious wrestling with modernity. This by itself connects it to Catholicism, insofar as much of Catholic history over the past two centuries is a match with that same antagonist. Thus, several authors point to the parallels between Protestant fundamentalism and Roman Catholic integralism, and perhaps both are forms of a single and well-placed, if badly expressed, Christian mistrust of the Enlightenment and its offspring. The general evangelical unease with modern politics and culture, with relativism and pluralism, is acutely mirrored in Catholic social teaching with its critique of modern political and economic arrangements. As Protestant fundamentalism's history in this regard should be of value to Catholic thinkers, so Catholic history ought to be instructive to evangelicals and even, could they but cool their anti-papist brows, to fundamentalists. As Catholics have unfortunately ignored them, so the fundamentalists and their evangelical cousins have ignored the Catholic struggle, for at least until recently neither has gone beyond Reformation stereotypes and rhetoric. But perhaps by now both communities have suffered such consequences of modern culture that their common interest is exposed and reinforced. These papers, refusing the cheap adoption and misuse of the term fundamentalist practiced by some of our academic colleagues and the media, make a serious and non-polemical attempt to ferret out the common unease and forward the possibilities of a common theological evaluation of modernity and its costs.

There are, of course, many issues that are not raised here but that remain prominent on the academic agenda, topics which are being addressed by the participants in The Fundamentalist Project. One of them, and my favorite, is the possibility that fundamentalism is not a specifically and solely *religious* phenomenon at all, but a form of the human engagement with cultural change which shows itself most prominently in religious movements. And so it should perhaps, for what else has the depth and power to resist what is seen to be evil than one's religion and its tradition?

But there are interesting parallels to fundamentalism in other cultural contexts. Political figures, educational theorists, legal scholars and literary critics, philosophers and high-flying academic humanists, famed interpreters of archaic myths, some Catholics theologians, and probably quite a few village atheists and drunks are in a broad sense fundamentalists. They think the world is gone haywire and that the solution lies in the texts (the Great Books and the Constitution strictly constructed), or in the old ways and the old stories, or in rational argument, or in a light lit by more dedicated and universal application of scientific method in opposition to religious obscurantism, or in a renewal of our obedience to the Pope. In this most general sense, William Jennings Bryan and Reverend

Jerry Falwell have company, even some they would not savor. In brief, while from one perspective there is an unbridgeable canyon between religious fundamentalists and philosophical positivists, from another there is but a hair. The atomist and the literalist are what these days our relativist colleagues call foundationalists.

But here is the point that needs exploration by evangelicals and Catholics, namely, whether modernity creates a *common* unease by conditions that destroy community, weaken belief, eviscerate hope, undercut values, eliminate faith and trust, shred texts, corrupt freedom, water the milk of human kindness, and transmute culture into a playground for pornographic and lupine human imagination. Most of us who have been through the secularist academic mill have felt what it is like to see a living tradition suffer "objectification" at the hands of an academic religionist, and most of us know first hand a variety of victims of what those academics call progress. We should sympathize readily with the fundamentalist Christian who with horror watches Carl Sagan waltz though the eons on "Cosmos." And these in turn should breed a sense of communion with the Muslim who has lived through decades of a Westernized political leadership that homogenizes, frightens, bullies, herds, despises, expertly organizes, and bureaucratizes the community, and sells his or her heritage for a billion in a Swiss account, an international airport, and a well-equipped military. On this the fundamentalist is correct, and the Catholic must, it seems to me, agree: the Enlightenment, whatever blessings it may have brought, has also poisoned us all. Many of the essays printed here make this point: the moral ambiguity of the legacy of the Enlightenment equals that of the medieval period, and the fundamentalist protest against its dark side is earned if not profound or intellectually well articulated.

Furthermore, in view of the need for a radical critique of modernity, which is felt on many sides today, the labels liberal and conservative are unhelpful, for the reevaluation of the Enlightenment underway cuts across the Western ideological spectrum. Even the terms themselves, like the terms capitalist and socialist, are spawn of the Enlightenment, and derive their connotations from the various and unfolding ages of the Enlightenment in which they are used. Several of the authors worry about the adequacy of the term fundamentalist as a description of international religious unease, and others are specifically wary of its use to describe protests against "liberalizing" tendencies presently at work in the Catholic community. Labels are being stretched thin. A new and more precise terminology is needed in our evalation of our heritage.

Three insights are made clear in the essays. Enormous numbers of people are very unhappy with the way the modern world is going; a not insignificant number of them find a vital alternative vision to the Enlightenment in their religious traditions; and, when Catholics meet fundamentalists they do not meet a total stranger. The third is only suggested here and needs badly a complete unfolding. When Catholicism faces contemporary Christian fundamentalism it finds more than a bit of its own reaction to the modern world, as it does when it faces New Age (as David Toolan has recently made out). There is an irony to the Bishops warning Catholics about biblical fundamentalism. It is odd indeed to find the leaders of that Western religious community which most vociferously and dogmatically opposed the Enlightenment and which was opposed by it now warning their flock about simplistic and dogmatic answers to the complex problems and stresses of the modern world! At any rate, both Catholics and fundamentalists have in common what George Kennan recently admitted about himself: that he has remained a "guest of one's time and not a member of its household."

I owe a special debt of gratitude to three noted evangelical scholars who answered my plea for brief statements on the religious signifi- cance of fundamentalism: Professors Bernard Ramm, Samuel Hill, and E. Glen Hinson. The work of each has, over the years, made a deep impression on me. Their penetrating essays in the "Editorial Forum" show that even those close to the intellectual and spiritual world of fundamentalism can be expected to disagree on its evalua- tion.

My hope is that the essays printed here will make a modest contribution to the academic work of this season and that they are tempered enough to add light rather than heat to this topic. To the authors I add my thanks for their cooperation and, should they find my editorial judgment less than they can approve, I suggest they heed the advice of the Apostle to his Corinthian friends in I Cor. 6:7.

William M. Shea
University of South Florida
February 20, 1990

FUNDAMENTALISM AS A GLOBAL PHENOMENON

RELIGIOUS FUNDAMENTALISM AS A GLOBAL
PHENOMENON

R. Scott Appleby

Introduction: Labellers Beware

The first Jewish radicals to settle in the lands inhabited by Palestinian Arabs and seized by Israel during the 1967 Six-Day War were forerunners of Gush Emunim—"the Block of the Faithful"—who moved onto the land precisely to provoke a confrontation with Israeli authorities and to widen the rift in the Israeli electorate, already divided on the question of policy toward the occupied territories. Established as an organization in 1974, Gush Emunim refers to the occupied territories by the biblical names Judea and Samaria, and believes that these lands are Israel's by divine promise. They seek to regain the "Whole Land of Israel" (their slogan) as demarcated in the ancient Hebrew scriptures. Gush members are currently active in the Israeli reprisals against the Palestinian *Intifada* (uprising) and have vandalized, harassed, and killed members of the Arab population on the West Bank and Gaza. In recent years, they backed political candidates in Israel who won seats in the Knesset. It was only eight years ago, however, that twenty-five Gush activists, including an army officer with expertise in explosives, were apprehended by the Israeli police and charged with conspiring to blow up the third holiest shrine of Islam, el-Aksa, a mosque situated on the site of the ancient Jewish temple and the Dome of the Rock, constructed to mark the place of Muhammad's ascent to heaven. The Gush is a politicized religious sect, a messianic religious movement, that sees the secular establishment in Israel as an unwitting ally in their own endeavors to expand the borders of Israel to

Biblical boundaries, to eliminate the Palestinian presence altogether, and, in so doing, to reinvigorate traditional Judaism from within.[1]

In the Northern Indian state of the Punjab, Sikh separatists agitate for a religiously pure homeland. Uncomfortable with the Indian charter of independence of 1947, which allowed for a pluralistic secular state, the *Khalsa* or *gursikh*, a radical sect of Sikhism, engages in periodic spasms of violence against Hindus, Muslims, and, at times, moderate Sikhs. Members of this sect were responsible for the assassination of Prime Minister Indira Gandhi in 1984. This assassination was in reprisal for Operation Blue Star of that same year in which the government of India ordered units of its regular army to storm the precincts of one of the holiest Sikh shrines, the Golden Temple at Amritsar, which was then the refuge for the charismatic leader of the sect, Jarnail Singh Bhindranwale. A fugitive from Indian justice charged with over a dozen acts of terrorism and murder, Bhindranwale was reputed to be the main organizer of a terrorist campaign that was responsible for the murder of several hundred innocent Hindus. He and one thousand others lost their lives in the raid. In the years since Operation Blue Star polarized the Sikh community, followers of Bhindranwale have continued to exact vengeance upon the Hindu and Muslim communities of Northern India.[2]

On February 1, 1979, Ayatollah Ruhollah Khomeini entered Iran triumphantly in the wake of a populist revolution which deposed Reza Shah Pahlavi and established the Islamic Republic of Iran. Playing on the Shi'ite insistence that only the authority of the Twelfth Imam (the Prophet's divinely inspired successor, who went into hiding in 874 C.E.) may serve as the basis for the establishment of a legitimate Islamic state, Khomeini proclaimed himself the representative of the Imam, thus becoming the supreme "source of emulation" (*marja-i taqlid*) and interpreter of Islamic law for the Shi'ite community. In the decade after the Iranian Revolution, Khomeini's regime attempted, with varying degrees of success, to

---

[1]Gideon Aran, "From Religious Zionism to Zionist Religion: The Roots of Gush Emunim," in Peter Meddling, ed., *Studies in Contemporary Jewry*, Institute of Contemporary Jewry, vol. 2 (Jerusalem: The Hebrew University, 1986), p. 116. Also, see Ian S. Lustick, *For the Land and the Lord: Jewish Fundamentalism in Israel* (New York: Council on Foreign Relations, 1988), pp. 1–16.

[2]Murry J. Leaf, "The Punjab Crisis," *Asian Survey* 25 (1985): 475–98; T. N. Madan, "The Double-Edged Sword: Fundamentalism and the Sikh Religious Tradition," a paper presented at the public conference "Fundamentalism Observed," University of Chicago, November 15–17, 1988.

export the Islamic revolution by sharing personnel, arms, funds, and ideology with a number of smaller Shi'ite radical groups, most prominently the Party of God (*Hizbollah*) in Lebanon.[3]

In 1981 members of the Islamic Jihad, a militant revivalist group of Sunni Muslims, assassinated President Anwar Sadat, and inspired riots in the Egyptian city of Assyut in an attempt to promote an agrarian revolt against the regime. In both operations the Jihad depended upon a network of Sunni radicals, the Takfir-wal-Hijra, for arms and personnel. These are splinter groups of the Ikhwan, the Muslim Brotherhood, founded in 1928 by Hasan al-Banna, a school teacher distressed by the ineffective opposition of the Islamic religious leaders to the decadence of life in Cairo. Whereas Shi'ite activists are ruled by a clerical elite, Sunni radicalism emerges from the non-ulama (laity); the militant groups are peopled by young university graduates with degrees in science and engineering, and by members of the armed forces. Stalled in bureaucratic backwaters with little hope for advancement, they are frustrated by the unfulfilled promises of westernization and modernization made by secular democratic and socialist governments of the post-colonial era.[4]

In December 1980 the northern Nigerian city of Kano experienced eleven days of bloody rioting which led to the loss of five thousand lives and millions of dollars in damages to public and private properties. The rioting was provoked by followers of a self-proclaimed Muslim prophet, Muhammadu Marwa, who had declared a "Holy War" against the modern Nigerian state, which, in its neo-colonial form, he charged, had promoted, and in turn become a hostage to, corrupt elements in the society. Although this charismatic leader was killed in the bloody confrontation in Kano, the movement went on to perpetuate large scale violence in other northern Nigerian cities in 1982 and again in 1984–85. The hostilities have been directed at Christians, at fellow Sunni Muslims considered tainted by compromises with unbelievers, and at governmental authorities deemed to be less than pure according to the

[3]Juan Cole and Nikki Keddie, eds., *Shi'ism and Social Protest* (New Haven: Yale University Press, 1986), pp. 6–9. Also, see Michael M.J. Fischer, "Imam Khomeini: Four Levels of Understanding," in John L. Esposito, ed., *Voices of Resurgent Islam* (New York: Oxford University Press, 1983), pp. 150–174.

[4]Adeed Dawisha, *The Arab Radicals* (New York: Council on Foreign Relations, 1986), pp. 16–26; Amira El-Azhary Sonbol, "Egypt," in Shireen T. Hunter, ed., *The Politics of Islamic Revivalism: Diversity and Unity* (Bloomington: Indiana University Press, 1988), pp. 23–38; John O. Voll, "Fundamentalism in the Sunni Arab World," a paper presented at the public conference "Fundamentalism Observed."

dictates of the Qur'an. Deteriorating political and economic conditions of Nigeria as a whole and of the northern states in particular
contributed to the downfall of the constitutional government and
the return to military rule in Nigeria by 1984. The battle for communal and national identity continued in the Constituent Assembly
established in 1988 to prepare an amended Constitution for a third
experiment in civilian government. At issue was a decade-old proposal for the establishment of a Federal Shari'a (Islamic law) court
of appeal which would serve as an intermediary body between the
Shari'a courts in the Northern states and the Supreme Court of
Nigeria. The court was opposed bitterly by the Christian members of
the Assembly as a symbol of potential Muslim domination in a
country which is 35% Christian. "At the core of this and other
controversies is the feeling among politically aware and religiously
active Muslims that in the so-called secular state of Nigeria their
Islamic culture and way of life are being constantly undermined by
the forces of Western secularism, while Christian leaders insist on
the retention of such secularism as the minimum condition for
ensuring the survival and continued existence of Nigeria."[5]

Finally, in the United States, from 1969 to 1989, the number of
Christian academies and day schools—privately owned church
schools, usually tied to an independent congregation—increased six
fold. The Christian School "movement" now includes twenty per
cent of the private school population in the United States. It is
difficult to determine how many Christian schools exist because in
many states they do not need and generally do not choose to be
accredited. However, estimates indicate that between fifteen thousand and eighteen thousand Christian schools exist, with an average
enrollment of between 100 and 150 students, but ranging from five
to 2,500 students. These academies and day schools feed into a
growing network of Christian colleges and universities. For students
they provide a "total world" created and regulated by teachers,
administrators, parents, and fellow students, who are encouraged to
report any deviations by their classmates from either the rules
governing conduct in school or the moral code guiding conduct at

---

[5]Ibrahim A. Gambari, "Nigeria and Islamic Revivalism: Home Grown or Externally
Induced?," a paper presented for the International Conference on "The Iranian
Revolution Ten Years Later: What Has Been Its Global Impact?" sponsored by the
Royal Institute of International Affairs, London, The Johns Hopkins School of Ad-
vanced International Studies, and The Middle East Institute, Washington, D.C.,
February 3–4, 1989. Quoted by permission of the author.

home and "in the world"—both of which are drawn directly from the Bible. The Bible also serves as the common text (although they would describe it neither as common nor as text) for all courses in the academy; Christian pedagogy is informed by the desire for "integration" of scriptural wisdom and academic material, a process by which economics becomes Christian economics (and, almost exclusively, of the laissez-faire capitalist sort), science becomes Christian science, and so on.[6]

The existence of such schools in the 1980s was made possible by the lobbying and legislative efforts on the state and federal level in the 1970s and early 80s by such organizations as the Moral Majority and the American Coalition for Traditional Values. Formed to repeal laws they felt had been established by secular humanists, these groups train candidates for office and retain today a very strong institutional base in the hundreds of independent fundamentalist churches that have sprung up in the South and the Southeast in the last fifty years. The success of televangelism has provided the financial means for the building of a formidable network of universities, seminaries, academies, publishing houses, and recreational parks designed to disseminate the ethos of "Christians," a designation these groups reserve solely for themselves. Political action groups on the Christian Right have sponsored legislation on issues ranging from drugs and pornography to the Panama Canal, each effort associated rhetorically with the all-encompassing goal of preserving the traditional family. Striving to protect the traditional family translates into active opposition to laws permitting abortion on demand, encouraging equal rights amendments of women, and offering comprehensive protection for women and abused children—protection from their husbands and fathers. Fundamentalists oppose these laws

---

[6]Alan Peshkin, who observed the activities of a Christian academy in downstate Illinois for eighteen months, recounts the Headmaster's opening charge to new pupils: "Our classes here reflect the Word of God. We believe that history, for example, is his story, the unfolding of the word of Jesus Christ on the center stage of the world. A man trying to write a history textbook that presents Jesus Christ as just another historical figure has no concept of real truth. We don't teach that way in our history classes. Math is a study of orderliness. The Word of God says, "Let everything be done decently using some order. Try to keep a checkbook sometimes without using some order and organization. Science is an understanding of God's handiwork. Men deny the Word of God and try to make us believe that all that we see about us has come about just through a series of events. Sometimes, the general term of evolution is used to apply to all this, but the Word of God is different on that. It clearly teaches that man was created from nothing: 'Out of nothing,' God states." See Alan Peshkin, *God's Choice: The Total World of a Fundamentalist Christian School* (Chicago: University of Chicago Press, 1986), pp. 49–50.

as an encroachment on the man's natural and divine right to dominance in the family.[7]

One could go on, perhaps indefinitely, with such examples simply by picking up today's headlines from Northern Ireland, Afghanistan, Sri Lanka, sub-Saharan Africa and dozens of other flashpoints around the world where religion forms at least the ideological basis (and often the cultural and social context) for complex and highly sophisticated movements of reaction against threatening features of the contemporary world. In *Studies in Religious Fundamentalism*, the first book to appear placing the movements in comparative focus, eleven contributors examined, among other cases, Wahhabism in West Africa, "incipient fundamentalism" among Sri Lankan Hindus in England, Christian fundamentalism as a counter-culture in urban South India, and Sikh radicalism in the Punjab.[8]

This volume was the first scholarly assault upon the common practice nowadays of clumping and clustering each of these very unique cases under the general inclusive term, "fundamentalism," without sufficient nuancing of that term, a tendency of journalists and scholars alike which has led to misperceptions, misunderstanding and, in many cases, to the exacerbation of tension and ill will either by those who have been labeled fundamentalists or by those who wish to categorize, objectify and thus reduce and dismiss their opponents by imposing the word as a term of opprobrium. Clumping and clustering is not a good idea in any comparative study or analysis that aims at genuine understanding, that hopes each group described therein would recognize itself in its distinctiveness. To flash a series of images taken from the headlines and to present these as episodes of an integrated or coordinated global phenomenon does not serve such understanding. We all rightly resist labeling and the reductionism which ensues, especially when our group , family, or individual identity is the victim.

While the word "fundamentalism" is not found in many of the cultures to which it is applied, some proudly accept the term or develop a cognate, and wear it as a badge of honor. First coined by evangelical Christians early in this century who boldly proclaimed their willingness to do "battle royal for the fundamentals," it has

---

[7]Robert Liebman and Robert Wuthnow, *The New Christian Right* (New York: Aldine, 1983), p. 2. See also Nancy T. Ammerman, "North American Protestant Fundamentalism," a paper presented at the public conference "Fundamentalism Observed."

[8]Lionel Caplan, ed., *Studies in Religious Fundamentalism* (Albany: State University of New York Press, 1987).

been taken up with renewed vigor in our own time by, among others, the Rev. Jerry Falwell, who has celebrated *The Fundamentalist Phenomenon* through all media, we believe, known to humankind. Falwell does not, however, wish to be associated in the mind's eye with the Ayatollah Khomeini, to whom the label has also been applied.[9] Indeed, those people and groups now known as fundamentalists emerge from different regions of the world, cite different Holy Books or have different interpretations of the same Holy Book or follow no Holy Book at all but, instead, a venerable tradition. They are not in cahoots globally, and would be bitterly opposed one to another on most central religious issues (while forming some interesting political coalitions on others—Falwell and the Gush Emunim, for example, each wishing, for different reasons, to return the Holy Land to the Jews).

Moreover, these images of violence on the West Bank and Gaza, of revolution in the streets of Iran, of assassinations and massacres in the Sikh Punjab, are misleading if they are not balanced with images of moderate Sikhs eschewing violence and condemning extremism, of Shi'ite refugees pinned helplessly in the Lebanese crossfire, of charismatic Christians such as those parents and teachers prominent in Susan Rose's study of evangelical schools who are, as they put it, determined to educate rather than to indoctrinate their children, and who attempt to develop in them the faculties of critical reasoning and a respect for diversity of viewpoints and interpretations which they feel to be vital to a democracy.[10] To see fundamentalists, or any segment of the larger whole for that matter, so consistently prominent in the headlines, lending ersatz substance to the charge of the cultured despisers of religion that *this* is what it all leads to, this is what it all *is* in one subtle or vulgar disguise or another, is particularly vexing for those of us in the academy who appreciate the diversity, strength, and beauty of religion in its various manifestations in history and throughout the contemporary human commu-

---

[9]"Many regard the term *Fundamentalist* as the ultimate in derogatory labels, conjuring up images of foreign madmen and domestic snake-handlers. The media are quick to call any wild-eyed fanatic a Fundamentalist. But the misuse of this term should not intimidate Fundamentalist Christians. . . . I am proud to call myself a Fundamentalist. . . . When I say I am a Fundamentalist, you know where I stand on the five fundamentals of the Christian faith." Jerry Falwell, "I am a Fundamentalist," *The Fundamentalist Journal* 8 (May 1989): 10. See also Jerry Falwell, ed., *The Fundamentalist Phenomenon* (Garden City, N.Y.: Doubleday-Galilee, 1981).

[10]Susan D. Rose, *Keeping Them Out of the Hands of Satan: Evangelical Schooling in America* (New York, N.Y.: Routledge, 1988), pp. 78–81.

nity. And even these qualifications do not begin to account for the fact that fundamentalists themselves are not, as individuals or as groups, undifferentiated in motives and strategies.

These considerations may well bring to mind a fair question: why use the word "fundamentalism" at all? The most direct answer is that there is no better term for the phenomenon or phenomena we are studying—no term, that is, which does not bring with it the same kind of problems, or create new ones. In 1987 William Shephard devoted much of a very insightful article in the journal *Religion* to a consideration of whether the term fundamentalism is an appropriate label for certain Islamic movements. His method in so considering was to undertake a detailed comparison with Protestant Christian fundamentalism for which the term was originally coined. He found a number of striking similarities but concluded that fundamentalism is not an appropriate common label due to the fact that Biblical inerrancy as understood by Protestant fundamentalists has little relevance to Islam. So he replaced "fundamentalism" with the term "radical neotraditionalism," which, as I shall indicate momentarily, is at least equally insufficient.[11]

Our own caution about applying the term beyond its original historical context would be supplanted by reluctance were we to follow Shephard's method of allowing the original case to dictate the content of the term. We begin, instead, by emptying the term of its culture-specific and tradition-specific content and context, and by examining cases across the board see if there are in fact, in Wittgenstein's term, "family resemblances" among these movements commonly perceived as "fundamentalist" which justify including them in this broad category. The goal, then, is not to label every movement "fundamentalist" but to observe fundamentalistic and fundamentalist-like movements and test the "family resemblances" hypothesis in as many cases as possible.

One promising way to stretch the parameters of the study is to explore cases that do not seem to belong to the family but come close enough to shed light on those which do. For example, Tu Wei-ming authored an essay on the Confucian revival in East Asia without feeling obliged to make it fit into the hypothetical family of fundamentalisms. Tu's reading of neo-Confucianism does evoke certain "family traits" in that he presents the phenomenon as a revival

---

[11]William Shephard, "Fundamentalism, Christian and Islamic," *Religion* 17 (1987): 355–378.

drawing upon what are perceived to be fundamentals of a religious tradition which has suffered erosion, or direct cultural ban, or manipulation, by secular forces in the modern age. Furthermore, these fundamentals are retrieved, privileged, and sanctioned as a means of protecting or forging anew an ethnic or national identity seeking validation in the post-colonial era. In this connection Tu writes of the complex feeling of "humiliation, remorse, regret, and hatred" shared by Koreans (han) and Chinese (chi) due to "their sense of crisis at confronting the West combined with a profound fear of annihilation and a powerful feeling of destiny." He sees the renewed religious impulse as offering an ideological and cultural basis for the shaping of a reformed social or political order through a Japanese-Korean-Chinese alliance, a united East Asia.[12]

On the other hand, it is not clear that the Confucian revivalists—primarily intellectual elites and presumably in small numbers—enjoy either an institutional base of their own or an identifiable following. Their political and social program remains skeletal and its coherence with the retrieved Confucianism seems unclear. These missing elements seem crucial to the common fundamentalist enterprise of transforming the world in light of and by application of the retrieved fundamentals. Thus the East Asian case provides both a fertile comparison and contrast to other movements of religious reaction in our era. As philosopher Morris Cohen wrote, "The absolutely unique, that which has no element in common with anything else, is indescribable—since all descriptions and all analyses are in terms of predicates, class concepts or repeatable relations." Historian Marc Bloch argued that comparative methods are necessary because history cannot be intelligible unless it can "succeed in establishing explanatory relationships between phenomena."[13] Such "explanatory relationships" may assist scholars in addressing the questions of diplomats, legislators, and other government officials who seek to account for the surprising rise of fundamentalisms—and fundamentalist-like Confucian revivals —in the late twentieth century.

The Fundamentalism Project

It will not be possible in this essay to indicate the scope and range of even the most important work currently being conducted in the

[12]Tu Wei-ming, "The 'Search for Roots' in Industrial East Asia: The Case of Confucian Revival," a paper presented at the public conference "Fundamentalism Observed."

[13]Quoted in Martin E. Marty, "Fundamentalism as a Social Phenomenon," *Bulletin of the American Academy of Arts and Sciences* 62 (November 1988): 23.

study of revivalism and fundamentalism, but a bit of background to our own project may indicate something of the direction of such scholarship. The Fundamentalism Project is a five-year, interdisciplinary public policy study funded by a grant from the MacArthur Foundation and conducted by the American Academy of Arts and Sciences, a group of approximately 3,200 scholars drawn from all academic disciplines with a long tradition of bringing an interdisciplinary focus to bear on complex policy issues. Fundamentalism seemed an appropriate subject, in large part because it indicates a sustained opposition to the secularist attempt to position religion alongside other ideologies and value-systems competing for a hearing in the marketplace of ideas. Fundamentalism resists, at least in principle, the reduction of religion to ideology, and provides a thoroughgoing system that does not readily yield to the compartmentalizing tendencies of the modern social sciences. So, on one hand, ours is not a religious studies project per se, for economists, social theorists, political scientists, cultural historians, anthropologists, legal scholars, and social psychologists will contribute. On the other hand, scholars of religion have been overlooked, by and large, in the formulation of American foreign policy, with undesirable results.[14]

The first of five volumes of essays published by the Project, *Fundamentalisms Observed* (University of Chicago Press, 1991), is, in part, an attempt to correct this imbalance by describing the

---

[14]Gary Sick, the principal White House aide for Iran on the National Security Council staff during the revolution and the Iranian hostage crisis laments the failure of American policymakers to comprehend the enduring appeal and motivational force of radical religion in the Third World: ". . . [There are] contradictions between Khomeini's Islamic, theocratic revolution and the Western tradition of secularizing revolutions. In my view, this tension between the secular and the religious was a major contributing factor to the failure of both Iranians and Westerners to recognize the revolution in its early stages and to gauge properly its actual course and eventual outcome. We are all prisoners of our own cultural assumptions, more than we care to admit. Those of us who are products of Western cultural tradition—even if our national origins are in Africa or Asia—share certain assumptions that are so firmly ingrained that they no longer require discussion but are regarded almost as natural law—inevitable and irrevocable. It is now two centuries since the first modern revolution in 1776, and over that span of time the world has grown accustomed to the most outlandish proposals for the revolutionary change of political, social and economic conditions. We may be difficult to persuade, but we are no longer easily surprised. Nevertheless, Khomeini's call for the establishment of a religious philosopher-king, the *vilayat-i faqih*, and clerical management of political institutions according to religious law was so unexpected, so alien to existing political traditions that it was less a surprise than an embarrassment". Gary Sick, *All Fall Down: America's Tragic Encounter With Iran* (New York: Viking Penguin, 1985), pp. 192–193.

religious character of various fundamentalist movements within the context of the particular social, political, and economic conditions in which they emerged or came to prominence in this century. Accordingly, the authors are historians of religion, cultural anthropologists, and sociologists of religion, several of whom have been participant-observers in the movements under consideration. Gideon Aran, for example, lived among the Gush Emunim in Israel for three years, hoping to document a doctoral thesis on the gradual secularization of such groups (convinced finally of the irreducibly religious character of the movement, he revised his thesis); Nancy Ammerman lived in a Protestant fundamentalist community in the Northeast for extended field research. In Tu Wei-ming and Abdulaziz Sachedina, we relied on scholars who were not only born and educated in the region under consideration but were also advocates or insiders to the process they describe. Accordingly, the essays in this volume reflect an empathy and, in some cases, a sympathy, with the groups under consideration, an important quality in a study purporting to provide readers with an insider's sense of group ideals, motivations, perceptions of history, and vision of a just order.

In 1990 six teams of scholars examined the effects or consequences of fundamentalist activity for two volumes to be published this year in the Chicago series. We retain an empathic voice but are concerned here to assess the influence of fundamentalism as it seeks to create alternatives to modern options or in fact to transform the modern world. The volume opens with a consideration of the points of disagreement between fundamentalist and non-fundamentalist world views, with particular attention to conflicts over modern science and the application of technologies. The inquiry then moves throughout zones of life from the most intimate to the most public, beginning with fundamentalist prescriptions for the family and interpersonal relationships. Scholars analyze economic systems and theories informed by fundamentalists' adherence to scriptural or traditional norms; the development of educational systems and the manipulation of media as means of transmitting fundamentalists' message; the various attempts to reshape polities through legal reform, political activism, and constitutional amendment; and the resort to militancy when polities break down or fail to satisfy expectations. Contributors include economists, military experts, anthropologists, historians of science, legal scholars, political scientists, and sociologists of education.

Under the direction of social psychologists, cultural historians, and sociologists, the working group of 1991 studied *The Dynamics of Fundamentalist Movements* (forthcoming, 1993). Is there a "fundamentalist temperament" or personality type? What motivates individuals to join such movements? What is the significance of the charismatic leader in attracting and retaining converts? What social and functional roles do women play in the various groups? How do fundamentalists transform or effect a community's cultural expressions, patterns of social interaction, ethical behaviors? Under this rubric scholars will also consider fundamentalism as a mass movement, and distinguish between "passive" and "active" forms, those that co-exist with democratic polities and those that would replace them or have done so. ·

Volumes Five and Six will synthesize findings and elaborate their implications for public policy formulation. Volume Five will draw upon the work of the three previous years in an attempt to make comparative and definitional statements about fundamentalism as a global phenomenon. Volume Six will give careful attention to the ways in which detailed scholarship on religious resurgence (and on other social and religious movements) may be most effectively disseminated among educators, mass communicators, politicians, diplomats, religious leaders, and others.

Such a collaborative enterprise begins with a set of hypotheses to be tested through careful scrutiny of those movements which seem to belong to the family of fundamentalisms. As Charles Liebman has pointed out, it is difficult if not impossible to identify any "pure form" of religious extremism. The precondition for the existence of a pure form of fundamentalism would be a movement totally differentiated from other forms of culture and independent of all social institutions. Religious extremism, then, "might be best described as an ideal typical impulse rather than as objectified in individuals or institutions" for "once extremism or extremists organize to attain their goals, the process of organization introduces the very communal type constraints from which extremism initially freed itself."[15] The following description of characteristics held in common by various fundamentalist groups is offered with Liebman's qualification in mind: as a public, reform-oriented manifestation of religious extremism, fundamentalism is of necessity a fluid and contingent phenomenon, quite possibly a discrete stage in a longer and more complex historical process.

---

[15]Charles S. Liebman, "Extremism as a Religious Norm," *Journal for the Scientific Study of Religion* 22 (1983): 79.

Family Traits: Fundamentalism as Reaction

First, fundamentalists are not simply conservative or orthodox or traditional believers. Steadfast religious beliefs, strict adherence to a moral code, and the practice of traditional pieties do not alone a fundamentalist make. Fundamentalists set themselves apart from others when, perceiving cherished traditions, values, and ways of life to be under attack, they engage in counterattack. Fundamentalism finds its initial expression in reaction. Often the first one in the line of fundamentalist fire is not the liberal or the moderate or the unbeliever, but the conservative or orthodox co-religionist who shares the right beliefs but has not followed the reactionary, confrontational strategy fundamentalists deem necessary to prevent erosion and preserve identity. To Jerry Falwell, the most dangerous man in America in the 1950s was Billy Graham. As an evangelical Christian, Graham affirmed the five fundamentals—the Virgin Birth of Jesus, His Blood Atonement on the Cross and bodily resurrection, the literal and imminent Second Coming, and most important, the inerrancy of the Bible which contains these teachings. But Graham also made his way into the mainstream of American religious life, leading millions of Protestant Christians to post-war respectability. Such participation in the culture requires connivance in a pluralist system, and Graham would share podiums and sit on boards with Catholic bishops, Lutheran pastors, and Jewish rabbis. To the separatist, non-compromising fundamentalist, as Falwell was at the time, such behavior bespoke compromise and betrayal of a code of purity. Yet, when Falwell himself abandoned his separatist posture and built effective political lobbies to "turn America around," he found it expedient to form coalitions with Catholic bishops against abortion, feminists against pornography, and other previously unsavory types. Gone was the anti-Catholic and racist rhetoric of his hard-line days. Bob Jones, Jr. reacted by denouncing Falwell as "the most dangerous man in America." Some hard-liners remain hard-liners.

The insidious enemy, then, is the insider who compromises or negotiates with outsiders. In their reaction against hostile Hindu and Muslim "invaders" in the Punjab, Sikh militants do violence, if necessary, to fellow Sikhs who are not, in their judgment, pure (gursikh). Similarly, the battles raged most bitterly in the Lebanese civil war are frequently between two competing Shi'ite militias—the AMAL and the fundamentalist Hizbollah. The Hizbollah in fact grew out of the AMAL militia and split when they deemed the AMAL too

accommodationist with both Sunni and Christian forces in Lebanon.[16] Similarly, Khomeini ousted his own hand-picked successor,
Ayatollah Montazeri, because his "beloved" protege suggested reforms in the application of Shari'a to the crumbling domestic economy.

In these examples of internecine strife, one is reminded of the
Roman Catholic phenomenon of integralism, the 1907 condemnation of modernism, and the Vatican suppression of "traitorous insiders," those priests who pursued the modernist synthesis. Because
the neo-scholastic system was so delicately coordinated, so tightly
woven, to loosen even one strand by obstreperous criticism was to
threaten the cohesion of the whole. Each block is a foundation piece;
remove one and the entire edifice may crumble. The lesson applies
to fundamentalisms today as well: the people most competent to
offer such criticism are elites within the system who have experienced its vulnerable spots. They know where the bodies are hidden—in many cases, this has the awful ring of literal truth—and this
renders them capable of the utmost in treachery. Here the communal
or group identity is experienced, if not acknowledged as, fragile,
vulnerable, and conditional.

Fundamentalists are not, then, traditionalists or conservatives. In
fact, they reject the clinging to tradition and the uncritical conser-
vation of all that has emerged in the tradition, for they view tradition
as a mosaic of compromises, as the body of accumulated adaptations
to the demands of specific historical, and thus contingent, circumstances. Fundamentalists do not grant human history and culture a
privileged status. God works redemptively not through the ordinary
but through the extraordinary, and fundamentalists thus act in an
extraordinary manner out of a sense of necessary disengagement
with the ordinary course of events. The salient point here, however,
is that the fundamentalists seem not to object to adaptation in
itself—as a traditionalist might—but to the elevation of these adaptations to a privileged status which in turn precludes the flexibility
fundamentalists require in crafting an effective, identity-preserving
reaction. Unlike traditionalists, fundamentalists view traditions thus
canonized as little more than accretions—casuistic means, often, of
softening the fervor and modifying the pristine vision of the founder
or the charismatic leader who realized the founder's dream.

---

[16]Robin Wright, "Lebanon," in Shireen T. Hunter, ed., The Politics of Islamic
Revivalism, pp. 63–64.

This is not to suggest that fundamentalists reject traditional elements altogether, for, as we shall see, they select carefully from among the plethora of doctrines, practices, and interpretations available in the tradition. But they are not, if you will, "traditional traditionalists," for they do not look nostalgically to the past and seek a return to a golden age or a time of origins. They are, on the contrary, thoroughly modern and future-oriented. The privileged past is defined with a keen eye on the particular challenges of the present and the opportunities of the future. Who can deny that Shariati and Khomeini were brilliant innovators who have reinterpreted and developed the Shi'ite doctrine of the "Guardianship of the Jurist" so as to support absolutist politics (theocratic-style) in Iran?[17]

On this point Judaism provides an interesting contrast between the Haredim and the Gush Emunim. The Haredim, or "Ultra-Orthodox," retain the traditional garb, language, and lifestyle of late-eighteenth and nineteenth-century, pre-Holocaust Diaspora Judaism of Eastern Europe and until recently have avoided conventional political involvement in favor of "Exile politics." Anxious to fulfill the thousands of rules contained within the halacha (the code of Jewish law), the Haredim (literally, the "anxious ones," the God-fearing) believe that no human effort, including the establishment of a Zionist state, can bring the deliverance promised by the Lord God. Until the Lord comes, they attempt to remain true to His Law and to the memory of their ancestors.[18] Meanwhile, the young Ashkenazic, upper-middle-class, university-educated settlers of the Gush Emunim recruit Jews who wear secular garb and, as a political and religious "strategy," allow a certain latitude in religious observance. In many ways these fundamentalists are closer to modernists than they are to traditionalists. Yet they reject the modernist shaping of modernity, and are envious of what they perceive as modernist cultural, political, and religious hegemony. In short, they wish to best modernists at their own game of adaptation—but without the identity-eroding consequences of such adaptation.[19]

---

[17]On this point, see Abdulaziz Sachedina, "Ali Shariati: The Ideologue of the Iranian Revolution," in John L. Esposito, ed., Voices of Resurgent Islam, pp. 191–212. Marvin Zonis and Daniel Brumberg analyze Khomeini's leadership in "Khomeini, the Islamic Republic of Iran, and the Arab World," Harvard Middle East Papers n. 5 (Cambridge, MA: Harvard Center for Middle Eastern Studies, 1987): 23–30.

[18]Menachem Friedman, "Religious Fundamentalism and Haredi Society," a paper presented at the public conference "Fundamentalism Observed."

[19]Gideon, Aran, "Jewish Zionist Fundamentalism: On the Bloc of the Faithful (Gush Emunim)," a paper presented at the public conference "Fundamentalism Observed."

The Nature of the Enemy

Fundamentalisms arise or come to prominence in times of crisis, actual or perceived. The crisis is one of identity experienced by a group of people who fear extinction *as a people* or absorption into an overarching syncretistic culture to such a degree that their distinctiveness is undermined in the rush to homogeneity. This larger threatening culture includes patterns of behavior and belief which fundamentalists oppose as exogenous rather than indigenous. In Eastern societies the enemy is thus called "Westernization"; in traditional societies, its name is "modernity"; in sacred societies it is perceived as "secularization." Indeed, if fundamentalism is, at least in its initial stage, compulsively reactive, it *requires* a well-defined enemy. In order to sustain the intense reactive character of fundamentalism in its unmodified form, fundamentalists enter into a kind of symbiotic relationship with the enemy, feeding off "the other," as it were, to maintain vigor. Accordingly, confrontation and opposition are essential to the fundamentalist dynamic. The enemy, whether described in the abstract or personified in a shah or a prime minister or an American Catholic theologian, is the force which poses a mortal threat to identity.

Thus fundamentalists, in the first stages of response, are susceptible to extremism, and are possessed of a siege mentality predicated upon ideas about the forces besieging and the counterforces necessary to defend from aggression. As they seek an identity and a role in the cosmos immune to absorption, fundamentalists oppose the relativizing force of historical consciousness, especially as it is interpreted and translated by modernists into the kinds of foundational principles of modernism. Among these principles are the assertions that we know and believe and have our being within time and space as the sole arena of human agency; that belief and practice are therefore historically conditioned and contingent; and that, accordingly, as all belief systems and religions are thus bound, no one of them holds an *a priori* advantage over any other in terms of cognitive truth-claims. Such principles threaten fundamentalist purchase on unassailable identity, as would any socio-moral system which proceeds from the post-Enlightenment notion that we cannot know revelation from a transcendent God, if such a God exists, except and only through the radically limited capacities of the human mind. Were fundamentalists to concede these points—which they do not—their cherished sense of identity would lose its transcendent, erosion-free source; and the ethos and behavior proceed from that identity would seem suddenly susceptible to reform, adaptation, traditionalizing, and to tests of relative adequacy.

Non-fundamentalists no doubt cherish, and perhaps embellish, their own self-description and identity no less than do fundamentalists. But, as modern people who accept both the burden and the promise of sincere religious belief, and who strive to translate that belief into comprehensive principles of action in the public order, fundamentalists adopt a strategy replete with potential ironies of its own. For example, in order to protect the cherished beliefs and behaviors from manipulation by outsiders, they often manipulate from the inside, in such a way as to avoid the darkest consequences of the process: atheism, materialism, cultural homogenization. While they resent the outsider's interpretation of, or neglect of, the sacred past, fundamentalists seem to recognize that the religious tradition alone is insufficient to the task. Of course the innovation and developments are seldom presented as such by fundamentalist leaders and followers, in part because the innovations are assumed to be mandated by a transcendent source of authority immune to the relativizing forces of history.

The logic of absolutism unfolds from this assumption. Once the relativizing forces of history reach too far into the inner sanctum, an absolutist response is deemed appropriate. Clifford Geertz makes the helpful distinction between being held by one's beliefs and holding one's beliefs. In times of cultural consensus about ultimate questions, in which assumptions about human knowing go unchallenged, orthodoxy is dominant. It is customary to proclaim the right praise; one need not be particularly cantankerous or contentious; one is held by one's beliefs. But in times of cultural upheaval and rapid transition from one epistemological model to another, or to a plurality of models, one must hold fiercely to one's beliefs. This is the métier of the fundamentalist. She holds on desperately to beliefs which, given prevailing cultural notions, seem outdated at best and simply ludicrous at worst. He who may have in gentler times been admired as an upholder of traditional values finds himself cast as an extremist when he resorts to the authoritarian and absolutist discourse of the fundamentalist.[20]

---

[20]On this point, see Clifford Geertz quoted in Nancy Ammerman, "North American Protestant Fundamentalism," p. 22.

During the first half of the twentieth century, for example, most Roman Catholics would not have thought to question the literal belief in the Virginity of Mary or the actual existence of a Communion of Saints, much less the epistemological foundations underlying such doctrines. Fundamentalism as a counter-cultural reaction which insists upon the literal truth of beliefs and asserts their centrality, becomes a possibility once those beliefs are challenged and a new model for understanding is introduced by the agents of modernization within the religious community. Faced with the disorientation resulting from the acceptance of a new model, reactionaries seek haven in the absolutism of dogma divinely sealed and delivered. In the decree *Lamentabili* (1907) condemning propositions taken from the writing of Alfred Loisy, Pope Pius X offered a defiant reaffirmation of supernaturalism as the appropriate response to any notion of doctrinal development. When Loisy suggested as much, Pius responded forcefully: he who holds that the truths of the Catholic faith are not fallen from heaven—let him be anathema![21]

The fundamentalist response, then, to the pluralism of creeds and the disintegration of communal identity is a *scandalous absolutism*. Fundamentalists say that outsiders cannot understand them and one suspects that they do not wish to be understood. To be thus comprehended would be to suffer reduction to the social, economic, or religious categories of outsiders—skeptics, professional analysts, credentialed unbelievers— disrespectful or ignorant of the "sacred spark" (a concept shared by, among others, Sikh, Jewish, and Hindu radicals) which animates and brings meaning to human existence. Fundamentalist identity is thus distinctive, irreducible, perhaps exotic, and thus scandalous in the Greek etymological sense (a stumbling block—a trip wire).[22] It may hinge on a dramatic doctrine like the imminent return of Hidden Imam or the Virgin Birth of Jesus, teachings which do not conform neatly, if at all, to the canons of post-Enlightenment rationality. These fundamentals are an adver-

---

[21]"The dogmas which the Church professes as revealed are not truths fallen from heaven, but they are a kind of interpretation of religious facts, which the human mind by laborious effort prepared for itself. . . . *Censure of the Holy Pontiff*: 'His Holiness has approved and confirmed the decree of the Most Eminent Fathers, and has ordered that all and every proposition enumerated above be held as condemned and proscribed.' " Quoted in Henry Denziger, *The Sources of Catholic Dogma*, translated by Roy J. Deferrari (St. Louis and London: B. Herder Book Co., 1957), pp. 509–510, 513. Originally published as *Enchiridion Symbolorum*, revised by Karl Rahner, S. J. (Freiburg: Herder and Co., 1954).

[22]Martin E. Marty, "Fundamentalism as a Social Phenomenon," p. 20.

tisement of distinctiveness and uniqueness, and function as a litmus test of the soul—a metaphysical marker separating the elect, who accept such assertions on faith, from the reprobate, who find God's ways incredible and hew instead to the ways of men. Because the singular claim to divine guidance lends an irrefutable legitimacy to the fundamentalist authorities and to the truths they proclaim, fundamentalists are wary of any notion of revelation or providence which admits of either many fonts of revelation or many hearers of the Word. Without such exclusivity, their assertiveness in coaxing the moderate across the line into extremism might be undermined.

In accord with this guardianship, fundamentalists reject the principles of hermeneutics as developed by the modern academy. Hallowed texts and traditions did not emerge through the complex stereotyping, transmission, and redaction of narrative accounts of human responses to the sacred. "In the fundamentalist view," Lloyd Averill has observed, "truth—whether about the human personality, human society, or even the phenomena that are the stuff of the natural sciences—is not something that is progressively realized through the course of history as a result of painstaking human digging, imagining, sifting, and assessing; truth is, rather, something that was 'once for all delivered' in the biblical record, so that the results of human investigation through time must be continually referred, for their validation, to that ancient norm."[23] It is not that fundamentalists deny the need to interpret the sacred text. Rather, they insist that the *principles* of interpretation are drawn from the text itself, apart from any particular needs or perceptions of the congregation; that these principles, if followed piously, allow in fact for only one "interpretation"; and that this one way of reading the text is perennially binding on the community. Enamored of apocalyptic visions of a deliverance within history, or at its culmination, fundamentalists value the sacred text as a repository of clues, privileged information provided to the elect, who seek to discern and act upon the esoteric knowledge withheld from unbelievers. Hal Lindsey's best-seller, *The Late Great Planet Earth*, rife with arcana, was the most popular of several such guidebooks to the End in the 1970s.[24] Fundamentalists believe themselves to be actors in an

[23]Lloyd J. Averill, *Religious Right, Religious Wrong: A Critique of the Fundamentalist Phenomenon* (New York: The Pilgrim Press, 1989), p. 9.

[24]On the community of interpretation, see Kathleen C. Boone, *The Bible Tells Them So: The Discourse of Protestant Fundamentalism* (Albany: State University of New York Press, 1989), esp. pp. 61–76. On the notion of divine sovereignty implied in the fundamentalist exegesis and apocalyptic discourse, see Peter Phan, "Might or Mystery: The Fundamentalist Concept of God," a paper printed in this volume.

apocalyptic drama, the outcomes of which are predetermined. In this view of sacred history, human agency is instrumental rather than determinative. The sense of drama empowering religious extremism of this sort is not provided by the creative dynamism of radical freedom shaping whatever brave new world is available to human enterprise; rather, to use Averill's expression, it unfolds out of a sense of a "fated freedom."

The response to this existential situation depends, in large part, on the eschatological vision of the particular group. In the Protestant case, for example, most claim to subscribe to a *premillennial* view of the end times which holds that Christ will return to earth to bring ordinary history to a close and inaugurate time of tribulation and struggle with the forces of Satan. Held in its pure form, this doctrine results in a passive withdrawal from the world as true believers attempt to preserve doctrinal and ethical uniformity and to remain vigilant in anticipation of the Jesus' coming. A *postmillennial* view places Jesus' triumphant return at the end of a protracted period of warfare between the forces of good and evil. Held in its pure form, this doctrine results in an activist, interventionist fundamentalism, in keeping with the notion that the Lord waits upon the agency of the elect.

Various fundamentalist groups hold positions along this spectrum, but all agree that God has a plan for history and a blueprint for society, the specifications for which are contained in the Bible. "Freedom" in this context is the freedom to devote one's God-given talents to the building of the Kingdom, or to the preparations for the return of the Master Builder. Freedom is *not* to be understood as the liberty to define one's self or to shape one's destiny, for these questions are closed, having been settled in advance. As Averill puts it, extremist movements of both left and right are not content to view history as a complex and ambiguous interaction of human freedom and forces beyond human control. Thus leftists posit of human nature a radical freedom to shape an absolute future, while rightists seize upon fate as the key to human destiny.[25] Fundamentalists, then, oppose philosophers and philosophies of history which would limit or eliminate divine providence, thereby jeopardizing the theocentric (and thus irreducible) foundations of communal and individual identity. Donning the guise of progressivism, the enemy takes the form of any political or religious system (from Marxism to

[25]Averill, pp. 1–13.

Pentecostalism) that proceeds from a developmentalist or evolutionary world view, or which simply looks to the future as radically open and thus malleable.

The Nature of the Reaction

Fundamentalism often emerges, then, from a social and cultural milieu in which progressivist models of history assume priority over religious claims that would delimit developmental and evolutionary processes or collapse them within an overarching, meticulous providence. In such a milieu, fundamentalists quickly conclude that mere ad hoc rebuttals and counter-arguments will not suffice. In each case fundamentalist reactions to offensive epistemologies, world views, educational systems, or social philosophies are multifaceted and coordinated, as if these were ingredients of a threatening cultural recipe concocted by a conspiracy of atheists, materialists, and secular humanists. Envious of modern know-how but scornful of its fissiparous tendencies, fundamentalists strive to create an alternate society, or to replace or remake an existing one.

In this effort fundamentalism reveals itself as totalistic: moving through states of compromise, it may choose to work within an existing system, but retains the ultimate aim of remaking the world anew on the foundation of the fundamentals. To do so, it reacts against the existing system by *selectively retrieving* concepts, behavioral norms, legal codes and other aspects of the religious heritage deemed useful in mounting a political struggle to reconstruct society along religio-moral lines. In this effort fundamentalism also reveals itself as a modern phenomenon, to be distinguished from its antecedents in eighteenth century Wahhabism (Sunni Islam), in the Bar Kochba Rebellion of the second century (Judaism), in the radical wing of the sixteenth century Protestant Reformation (Christian), or in the cadre of "purified" Sikhs baptized by Guru Gobind Gingh in 1699. For both the *circumstances to which* and the *means by which* today's extremists respond are unprecedented.[26]

To support this contention, one must begin with the fact that

---

[26]On this point, see Bruce Lawrence, *Defenders of God: The Fundamentalist Revolt Against the Modern Age* (New York: Harper and Row, 1989). Lawrence argues persuasively that fundamentalism is entirely a modern phenomenon, occasioned by the interaction of traditional religions and industrial culture. He makes use of Marshall Hodgson's description of the "Great Western Transmutation" in reviewing the profound cultural transformations brought about in the EuroAmerican colonies in the modern era.

eighty-four new nations, most of them in the Third World, have been created since the end of World War II. Modernity had intruded upon these autochthonous cultures at the hands of European and American colonizers of the eighteenth and nineteenth centuries who established their own bureaucracies and economic systems, codified laws based on western principles of jurisprudence, and transplanted, piecemeal, western cultural icons onto foreign soils. Though the colonizers withdrew, the colonial presence remained, in the form of institutions, policies, and educational systems imposed upon the native populations. Independence left these peoples with the daunting task of forging viable states amid a dizzying array of options. Should new constitutions be formulated after the example of western liberal democracies or eastern socialisms? Could the value-laden technologies of the imperialists be appropriated to different, locally-determined ends? What is to be the relationship between the new state and the established industrial and military powers of east and west? In this changing geo-political context, the age-old search for identity assumed epic proportions. Nation-builders adopted a mélange of political and religious ideologies in the hope of lifting the countries out of a back-breaking poverty, relieving the pressure on cities crammed with newly arrived rural migrants, and establishing a common heritage for competing ethnic factions. In Egypt, for example, experiments in liberal-democratic, then socialist, pan-Arabist systems led to the disillusion of the masses when they failed to feed the poor, care for the sick, pave the roads—and to crush the Israeli army.[27]

To further complicate the situation, political and religious elites in many of these new nations had been tainted by their identification with the occupying regime. In the ensuing crisis of leadership, the way was prepared for purists with the political savvy to build the kind of institutions capable of meeting these needs—under the banner of Islamic (or Hindu, or Sikh, or Buddhist) fundamentalism. The case of Pakistan reflects this dynamic and demonstrates the ways in which fundamentalism is itself susceptible to manipulation and co-optation at the hands of a shrewd political leader. The establishment of Pakistan as a separate homeland for Indian Muslims apart from the Hindu majority was accomplished in 1947 to the tune of the Muslim League's slogan, "Islam is in danger." As a justifica-

---

[27]For an analysis of the situation confronting the Islamic world in this regard, see Bassam Tibi, *The Crisis of Islam: A Preindustrial Culture in the Scientific-Technological Age*, trans. Judith von Sivers (Salt Lake City: University of Utah Press, 1988).

tion for the partition of India, the claim was made (on both sides) that Islam and Hinduism were not just religions but in fact were distinct social orders and could not evolve into a single nationality. Each of Pakistan's rulers have, in the decades since, attempted to cover coercive measures in the legitimating cloak of Islam. The early parliamentary regime used a "liberal-modernist Islam," Ayub Khan a "developmentalist Islam," Yahya Khan a "nationalist Islam," Bhutto a "socialist-populist Islam," and Zia a "revivalist-fundamentalist Islam."

Zia's use of Islam was masterful. To consolidate the political and moral support of the religiously motivated lower middle classes of the Punjab, the urban Sind, and the Northwest Frontier Province, the government sponsored religious festivals and rituals popular with the masses, and instituted a network of zakat (religious taxes to be distributed to the poor). By introducing Islamic reforms in consonance with the priorities of the ulama, the regime secured the participation of the religious sector in the state-sponsored Islamization by mobilizing the nonpolitical ulama and bringing them inside the orbit of the state in order to counterbalance the influence of the politically organized ulama. Zia presided over a number of measures in accord with the dictates of Islamic law, including the establishment of an interest-free banking and investment system, the introduction of legal restrictions on the appropriation of private property, the denationalization of certain business and industrial enterprises, the reintroduction of Islamic penal laws, the imposition of a strict sexual morality, the revision of school and college textbooks, the opening of an international Islamic university in Islamabad, and the introduction of obligatory prayer breaks during working hours. Such measures cost the regime little but reaped invaluable benefits in consolidating political control.[28]

As the case of Zia demonstrates, the fundamentalist seems attracted to, and vulnerable to manipulation by, an authoritarian leader who wields absolute power. This leadership appeals to true believers only if it is perceived as charismatic, its powers blessed by, derived from, or bequeathed by God. Thus, many groups are messianic (in Islam, mahdist): the saviour will arrive at any moment, the

---

[28]"When a regime equates itself with both the state and religion and then presents a particular version of religion as official dogma, any deviation from the official interpretation of the ideology becomes a religious heresy and treason against the state," Mumtaz Ahmad has noted. See Ahmad, "Pakistan," in The Politics of Islamic Revivalism, pp. 229–234.

violent destruction of our enemies is nigh. In his absence, awaiting his imminent appearance or return, a charismatic leader acts as his vicar, or more modestly, establishes himself as one in a line of gifted reformers sent perennially by God to reinvigorate the elect and to renew the faith.[29] This leader demands unquestioning obedience and usually arrogates to himself the final word of pivotal interpretations of sacred texts or traditions. He shapes and articulates the group's vision of a just order through a complex process involving both the selective retrieval and reinterpretation of fundamentals from the symbolic and conceptual repertoire of the tradition, and the formulation and elaboration of new supporting doctrines deemed necessary, given contemporary conditions, as supporting corollaries to the retrieved fundamentals.

Again, note that fundamentalists do not simply reaffirm the old doctrines; they subtly lift them from their original context, embellish and institutionalize them, and employ them as ideological weapons against a hostile world. The doctrine of biblical inerrancy is the nineteenth-century creation of Princeton theologians who deemed its formulation and development necessary, given the advent of the Higher Criticism, in order to preserve the traditional Christian belief in the divine origins of the Bible; the definition of papal infallibility is a like-minded child of the nineteenth century. In restoring the Khalsa Sikh, Bhindranwale added to the traditional symbols of Sikh identity (the beard, the sword, and short pants) the implements of the new revolutionary age (the revolver and the motorcycle).

The process of selective retrieval is hardly unique to fundamentalists and, isolated from other characteristics, is not a distinguishing mark of fundamentalist activism. Yet activists on all points of the spectrum acknowledge the need for a critical approach to the sources of communal wisdom, and seek to validate their conclusions by an appeal to those sources. The argument of Abdullahi Akmed An-Na'im is instructive on this point. A University of Khartoum professor and leader of an Islamic reform movement in the Sudan called the Republican Brothers, he was imprisoned without charge in 1984 by Sudanese President Numiery, who had wrapped his regime in the cloak of Islamic fundamentalism. An Na'im claims that the wave of Islamic fundamentalism sweeping Africa and the Middle East is a mistaken attempt to impose Shari'a in order to counteract Western

---

[29]For a helpful typology of Islamic charismatic leaders, see R. Hrair Dekmejian, *Islam in Revolution: Fundamentalism in the Arab World* (Syracuse, NY: Syracuse University Press, 1985).

neocolonialism and cultural domination. He argues that the prescriptions of Shari'a revealed to the Prophet Mohammed after his flight to Medina and stressed in contemporary fundamentalist regimes—those which deal with penal law, rights and civil liberties, and the treatment of minorities and women—promote an "historically dated Islamic self-identity that needs to be reformed." Islamic economic and social justice and the exercise of legitimate political power depend upon the retrieval of the wisdom of the Qur'an given to the Prophet in Mecca, which provided, in An Na'im's judgment, "the moral and ethical foundation" of that tradition. "The Medina message is not the fundamental, universal, eternal message of Islam. That founding message is from Mecca," he writes. "This counter-abrogation (of the Medina code) will result in the total conciliation between Islamic law and the modern development of human rights and civil liberties." Rare is the disputant in such a conflict who does not claim to be upholding "the fundamentals." Rather, the battle is often over what they are, where they are to be found, how and by whom they are to be interpreted. In demanding the retrieval of the Meccan prophecy, An-Na'im concludes, "we are the *super-fundamentalists*."[30]

Conclusion: Fundamentalism and Compromise

In contemplating the future of fundamentalism one should recognize a second way in which fundamentalists are shrewdly selective, namely, in their evaluations and appropriations of modernity. As should be clear by now, they are not naifs: they know how the game is played, and they play it with increasing sophistication. Drawn from the university educated middle and upper middle classes, many have backgrounds in engineering and the sciences. Be they members of the Gush Emunim adept in the use of finely calibrated explosive devices, or televangelists skilled in the manipulation of modern media, they appropriate the latest technologies to their own ends with remarkable success. The growth of fundamentalism among professionally mobile Jews, Muslims, and Christians, belies the stereotype of the fundamentalists as poor, uneducated rural folk. Fundamentalists are intelligent, and their perceptions are often accurate. To millions of people who cannot tolerate the complexity

---

[30]Abdullahi Ahmed An-Na'im, "The Reformation of Islam," *New Perspectives Quarterly* 4 (Fall, 1987): 51.

and seemingly random character of modern existence they offer satisfying diagnoses and explanations for society's ills—and complete and direct prescriptions for recovery.

Neither "outsiders" nor "insiders" will be able to overcome entirely the limitations of personal perspective in the attempt to portray and analyze accurately so complex and significant a phenomenon as fundamentalism. But a first step must be the acknowledgement that fundamentalists have about them a certain *gravitas*: whether or not one agrees with their analyses of the contemporary situation, the moral seriousness of their discourse and its appeal to millions of believers renders them a force to be reckoned with in the foreseeable future. To describe fundamentalists as *religious extremists*, as I have done in this paper, is consistent with a respectful recognition of their commitment to ultimate questions. A propensity to religious extremism may be considered a mark of authentic religious orientation: religion is, after all, teleological in character, holistic in orientation, catholic in scope.

As I have suggested above, however, extremism seems characteristic of only the initial stage or stages of fundamentalism. What happens when fundamentalism achieves partial victories, enjoys recognition within a pluralistic public order, or, as in Iran has the opportunity to muffle opposing voices and to proceed with societal reconstruction? In short, how may the fundamentalist dynamic be sustained once the fundamentalist is acting and shaping rather than reacting and opposing? The study of fundamentalism is, if not in its infancy, hardly mature, and answers to such questions remain speculative. But the key to assessing fundamentalism's future may, instead, lie in examining the historic factors contributing to the recurrent phenomena of *religious moderation* or religious liberalism, "the willingness of religious adherents to accommodate themselves to their environment, to adapt their behavioral and belief patterns to prevailing cultural norms, to make peace with the world." In other words, the truly interesting question, given the fact that extremism is a tendency to which every religiously oriented person is attracted, is not "why are there religious extremists?"; it is "why are not *all* religious people extremists?" What are some factors of major importance which have mitigated the natural propensity of religion toward extremism?[31]

In the answers to this question, in examining the historical asso-

---

[31]Charles Liebman, p. 79.

ciation of religion, culture and society for clues as to the incentives for religious moderation—the need for the approval of others, for economic collaboration for survival, for the small compromises incumbent upon evangelizing outsiders, for negotiation once the group begins to win acceptance—one may find a basis for projections about the future of religious fundamentalism in the early decades of the next century. But such speculation is for another time for the end, rather than the beginning, of a five-year study.

REVIVAL AND REFORM IN CONTEMPORARY ISLAM

John L. Esposito

The Middle East has been the home of three of the major world religions and civilizations: Judaism, Christianity, and Islam.[1] In recent years religion has resurfaced as a potent force in the politics of the Middle East: Iran's "Islamic" revolution, Israel's Gush Emunim (Block of the Faithful) and the religious right, Lebanon's civil war, Egypt's Muslim Brotherhood. The strength and pervasiveness of a resurgent Islam is evident in all areas of life from personal piety to international politics, from religious institutions to education, banking, and legal reform. This study will analyze the origins, causes, and manifestations of Islamic revivalism in the Middle East as well as examine several key issues that emerge regarding the development and interpretation of contemporary Islam.

Much of the reassertion of religion in politics and society has been subsumed under the term fundamentalism. Although fundamentalism is a common designation, in the press and increasingly among academics, it is used in a variety of ways. For a number of reasons, it tells us everything and yet, at the same time, tells us nothing. First, all those who call for a return to foundational beliefs or the fundamentals of a religion may be called fundamentalist. In a strict sense, this could include all practicing Muslims, who accept the Quran as the literal word of God and the Sunnah (example) of the Prophet Muhammad as a normative model for living. Second, our understanding and perceptions of fundamentalism are heavily influenced by American Protestantism. Webster's dictionary defines fundamen-

---

[1]This essay was prepared as a presentation to a plenary session of the annual convention of the College Theology Society, June 1989. It has been adapted in part from J. L. Esposito, *Islam and Politics*, 2nd rev. ed. (Syracuse, N.Y.: Syracuse University Press, 1987) and *Islam: The Straight Path* (New York: Oxford University Press, 1988).

talism as: "a movement in 20th century Protestantism emphasizing the literally interpreted Bible as fundamental to Christian life and teaching."[2] For many mainline or liberal Christians, fundamentalist is a pejorative or derogatory term applied rather indiscriminately to all those who advocate a literalist biblical position and thus are regarded as static, retrogressive, and extremist. As a result, fundamentalism often has been regarded popularly as referring to those who are literalists and wish to return to and replicate the past. In fact, few individuals or organizations in the Middle East fit such a stereotype. Indeed, many fundamentalist leaders have had the best educations, enjoy responsible positions in society, and are adept at harnessing the latest technology to propagate their views and create viable modern institutions such as schools, hospitals, and social service agencies. Third, the term fundamentalism is often equated with political activism, revolutionary radicalism, and anti-Americanism. Yet, while some engage in radical religio-politics, most, as we shall see, work within the established order.

Perhaps the best way to appreciate the facile use of the term fundamentalism and its inadequacy in capturing the many faces and postures of contemporary Islamic revivalism is to consider the following. Fundamentalism is a term applied in recent years to the governments of Libya, Saudi Arabia, Pakistan, and Iran. Yet, what does this tell us about these states other than the fact that their rulers have appealed to Islam to legitimate their rule or policies? Muammar Qaddafi has claimed the right to interpret Islam, questioned the authenticity of the traditions of the Prophet Muhammad, silenced the religious establishment as well as the Muslim Brotherhood, and advocated a populist state of the masses. The rulers of Saudi Arabia, by contrast, have aligned themselves with the clergy (the ulama), preached a more literalist and rigorous brand of Islam, and used religion to legitimate a conservative monarchy. Qaddafi's portrayal as an unpredictable, independent supporter of worldwide terrorism stands in sharp relief beside the image of the low-key conservative, pro-American King Fahd. Similarly, contrast the foreign policy of the clerically run Shii state of Iran with the military, lay regime which implemented Pakistan's Islamic system (*nizam-i-Islam*) under General Zia ul-Haq (1977–88). Iran under the Ayatollah Khomeini has been highly critical, even condemnatory of the West, often

---

[2]*Webster's New Collegiate Dictionary* (Springfield, MA: G. & C. Merriam Company, 1981), p. 461.

at odds with the international community, and regarded as a terrorist state while Pakistan under Zia ul-Haq was a close ally of the United States, with warm relations with the West and the international community, and generally regarded as moderate.

Because I regard the term fundamentalism as too laden with Christian presuppositions and western stereotypes as well as implying a unity that does not exist, I prefer the more general terms religious revivalism or religious resurgence. Indeed, Islam possesses a long tradition of revival (*tajdid*) and reform (*Islah*), stretching from the early Islamic centuries to the present day, which provides the historical context for current developments as well as a source of religious legitimacy.[3]

Revival and Reform in Islam

Contemporary Islamic revivalism is not a totally new phenomenon. Rather, it builds on a tradition of Islamic revival and reform. Throughout history Muslims faced the dichotomy between faith and practice, and therefore recognized the need to address this failure or crisis. Individuals (theologians, legal scholars and mystics) and movement arose to renew and reform Islamic society. Islamic activists today are particularly influenced by eighteenth century Islamic revivalism and, more recently, by modern reform movements.[4]

During the eighteenth century across the Islamic World, Islamic revivalist religio-political movements occurred from the Sudan to Sumatra. These movements responded to a sense of socio-moral decline diagnosed as due to a departure from the straight path of Islam. The political fragmentation of Muslim communities and their economic decline were viewed as side effects of this process. Revivalists concluded that if the debilitating disease was due to straying from the path of Islam, its cure was a return to a more faithful following of the Qur'an and Sunnah (example) of the Prophet. Islamic revivalist movements like the Fulani in Nigeria, the Mahidyyah in the Sudan, the Sanusiyyah in Libya, the Wahhabiyyah in Arabia and the Padri in Indonesia reasserted the belief that Islamic monotheism meant the unity and totality of God's will or law in all

---

[3]John O. Voll, "Renewal and Reform in Islamic History: *Tajdid* and *Islam*" in John L. Esposito, ed., *Voices of Resurgent Islam* (New York: Oxford University Press, 1983), ch. 2.

[4]John O. Voll, *Islam: Continuity and Change in the Modern World* (Boulder, CO: Westview Press, 1982), Chs. 3 & 4.

areas of life: political, social and moral. Revivalist movements established Islamic States in what is today the Sudan, Libya, Northern Nigeria, Saudi Arabia, Pakistan and Indonesia. These movements consisted of communities of the faithful, trained religiously and militarily, governed by Islamic law, waging a holy war, where necessary, to spread God's rule through the establishment of Islamic States based upon the restoration of true Islam. It is this legacy that contemporary Islamic revivalism has appropriated.

The second major influence on contemporary Islam is a series of Islamic reformist movement in the late nineteenth and the twentieth centuries. The first, commonly called Islamic modernism, included among its leaders; Jamal al-Din al-Afghani (1838–97) and Muhammad Abduh (1849–1905) from the Arab world and Sir Sayyid Ahmad Khan (1817–98) and Muhammad Iqbal (1875–1938) in South Asia. Islamic modernists tried to bridge the gap between their religious heritage and modernity by offering an Islamic rationale for modern political, legal, and social change. Theirs was a process of "Islamic" acculturation and synthesis. Asserting that Islam was a dynamic, creative, progressive religion, Islamic modernism sought to appropriate the best of Western science, technology and learning in order to revitalize the Muslim community. Although it inspired movements for educational and social reform and national independence, Islamic modernism remained in many ways attractive only to an intellectual elite. Failure to produce a systematic reinterpretation of Islam and to develop effective organizations to preserve and propagate its message more broadly in Muslim society limited the impact of Islamic modernism. It was this void which led to the emergence of modern Islamic organizations or societies like the Muslim Brotherhood and the Jamaat-i-Islami (The Islamic Society). Their influence as prototypes of contemporary Islamic groups cannot be overestimated. Hassan al-Banna (1906–49) and Sayyid Qutb (1906–66) of the Muslim Brotherhood and Mawlana Abul Ala Mawdudi (1903–79) of the Jamaat-i-Islami, are the forerunners and ideologies of contemporary Islamic revivalism.[5] They have contributed two im-

---

[5]John L. Esposito, *Islam & Politics*, pp. 130–150. For the definitive study of Hassah al-Banna and the formation of the Muslim Brotherhood, see Richard P. Mitchell, *The Society of Muslim Brothers* (New York: Oxford University Press, 1969). For Sayyed Qutb, see Yvonne Y. Haddad, "Sayyid Qutb: Ideologue of the Islamic Revival" in *Voices of Resurgent Islam*, ch. 6 and Giles Kepel, *Muslim Extremism in Egypt* (Berkeley: California: The University of California Press, 1984), ch. 2. For Mawlana Mawdudi, see Charles J. Adams "Mawdudi and the Islamic State" in *Voices of Resurgent Islam*, ch. 5.

portant dimensions: (1) the delineation of Islam as an ideology for all of life and the belief that Islam affects public policy as much as private worship; and (2) the establishment of effective organizations to implement an Islamic system of government and law through political action.

Unlike Islamic modernists, these neo-traditionalists (or neo-fundamentalists) were more critical of the West. Rejecting the tendency of Muslim societies to admire and follow the West, they emphasized the perfection and self-sufficiency of Islam. Rather than trying to show how Islam was or could be reinterpreted in order to be amenable to Western political and social thought, they delineated Islam's relevance to politics, law, economics, education, family life.

Despite the emergence of neo-revivalist groups, the post World War II period was dominated by political independence and the establishment of modern Muslim states. In general, nascent nations and their political leaders continued to be heavily influenced by the West in the development of national ideology and state institutions (parliamentary systems of government, legal codes, education), economics and the military. With few exceptions, nationalist leaders were more secular than religious in orientation. The United States and the Soviet Union emerged as superpowers; western capitalism, Marxism and socialism were contending forces in political development.

From the late 1950's to the early 1970's nationalist and socialist slogans prevailed in the discourse and politics of many Muslim states: the Arab nationalism/socialism of Egypt's Gamal Abd Al-Nasir which also inspired the revolutions of Libya's Muammar Qaddafi and Sudan's Jaffar al-Numayri in the late 1960's; the socialism of the Baath Party in Syria and Iraq, of the Algerian revolution, and of Zulfikar Ali Bhutto's Pakistan People's Party; local forms of nationalism in Turkey, Tunisia, Iran, and Afghanistan.

Contemporary Religious Revivalism

Religion remained a presence in Muslim societies; governments, sensitive to its potential force, sought to control, coopt, or restrict its role in society. However, in the 1970's what seemed to be an increasingly marginalized force in the public life of modernizing states, now reemerged often dramatically as a vibrant, dynamic socio-political reality. The resurgence of Islam in Muslim politics reflected a growing religious revivalism both in personal and public life which in time would sweep across much of the Muslim world. The indices of Islamic reawakening in personal or individual life are many: increased religious observance (mosque attendance, prayer, fasting), more emphasis upon Islamic dress and values, proliferation of religious programming and publications, the revitalization of Sufism (mysticism), and intensification of missionary activities. This broader based renewal has also been accompanied by the reassertion of Islam in public life: an increase in Islamically oriented governments, organizations, laws, banks, educational institutions, social welfare services.

Both governments and opposition movements have turned to Islam to enhance their authority and muster support. Government use of Islam has included Sudan's Jafar al-Numayri, Libya's Muammar Qaddafi, Egypt's Anwar Sadat, Iran's Ayatollah Khomeini, Pakistan's Zia ul-Haq, Bangladesh's Muhammad Ershad, Malaysia's Muhammad Mahathir.[6] Most rulers and governments, aware of the potential strength of Islam, have shown increased sensitivity to Islamic issues and concerns, including more secular states such as Turkey and Tunisia. Indeed, revivalism has often proven to be strongest in more westernized states like Egypt and Iran. At the same time, Islamic organizations and societies have mushroomed: most (the Muslim Brotherhoods of Egypt and the Sudan, the Jamaat-i-Islami in Pakistan and India, the Islamic Tendency Movement in Tunisia, the Islamic Youth Movement of Malaysia) working within the existing political system and some (Lebanon's Hizbollah and al-Jihad, Egypt's Takfir wal Hijra and Jamaat al-Jihad, the Afghan *mujahideen*) with revolutionary goals.

While contemporary Islamic revivalism is often associated with the Iranian Revolution of 1978–79, its seeds may be found in many parts of the Muslim world during the late 1960's and early 1970's. A combination of stunning setbacks, for example in 1967, 1969, 1971, and remarkable successes in 1973 and 1978-1979 served as important catalysts. The 1967 Arab-Israeli war proved a turning point in the Arab world. The decisive defeat of the combined Arab forces (Egypt, Jordan and Syria) by Israel in the Six Day War with its loss of

---

[6]For case studies, see *Islam and Politics*; Shireen T. Hunter, *The Politics of Islamic Revivalism* (Bloomington, Indiana: The University of Indiana Press, 1988); James P. Piscatori, *Islam in the Political Process* (Cambridge: Cambridge University Press, 1983); "Islam and Politics," a special issue of *Third World Quarterly* Vol. 10, No. 2 (April 1982); and John L. Esposito, ed., *Islam in Asia: Religion, Politics & Society* (New York: Oxford University Press, 1987).

the West Bank, Gaza, and the Sinai was a major blow to the charismatic leadership of Gamal Abd al-Nasir and the banner of Arab nationalism/socialism. The loss of Jerusalem, the third holiest city of Islam, rendered the defeat a worldwide Islamic, not just Palestinian, issue, remembered in Arab literature as the "catastrophe." For many, the magnitude of the defeat struck at the heart of their sense of pride, identity, and history. Despite several decades of independence and modernization, Arab forces proved impotent. In the midst of the soul searching and disillusionment, a common critique of the military, political, and socio-cultural failures of western-oriented development and a quest for a more authentic, indigenously rooted society and culture emerged.[7]

Similarly, Chinese-Malay communal riots in Malaysia in 1969 led the Malaysian government to address the socio-economic concerns of Malay Muslims who charged that the more urban based Chinese minority enjoyed disproportionate economic and educational advantages. This perceived threat to Malay status and identity fostered a government affirmation action plan (the *bhumiputra*, sons of the soil) to strengthen the economic and educational aspects of Malay Muslim life. Greater emphasis upon Malay identity, language, values, and community contributed to the attraction and growth of Islamic revivalism in a culture where many regard it as axiomatic that to be Malay is to be Muslim.[8] In Lebanon Shii Muslims, long a minority in a Christian dominated system, called for greater political representation and socio-economic reforms to better reflect the demographic changes which had resulted in a Muslim majority. The Imam Musa Sadr appealed to Shii identity, history, and symbols to organize and mobilize members of the Shii community into what would become in the mid 1970's the Movement for the Dispossessed, more commonly known today as AMAL.[9]

The Pakistan-Bangladesh civil war in 1971 changed the map of South Asia when the Islamic Republic of Pakistan, a country established as a Muslim homeland in 1947, lost its eastern wing in a bloody slaughter of Muslims by their fellow Muslims and once more

---

[7]John J. Donohue "Islam and the Search for Identity in the Arab World" in *Voices of Resurgent Islam*, ch. 3; Ali Merad, "The Ideologisation of Islam in the Contemporary Muslim World," *Islam in Power* eds. A. S. Cudsi and Ali E. Hillal Dessouki (Baltimore: Johns Hopkins University Press 1982), ch. 3.

[8]Fred R. von der Mehden, "Malaysia: Islam and Multiethnic Politics" in *Islam in Asia*, ch. 8.

[9]Augustus Richard Norton, *AMAL and the Shia: Struggle for the Soul of Lebanon* (Austin, Texas: The University of Texas Press, 1987); *Islam and Politics*, pp. 291–301.

faced the question: "Why Pakistan?" In reestablishing Pakistan's identity and seeking greater economic ties with the Arab oil countries, Zulfikar Ali Bhutto, a secular socialist, increasingly appealed to Islam to establish Pakistan's ties with their Arab Muslim brothers and mobilize domestic political support. This unleashed a process in which Islam moved from the periphery to center stage as both the government and the opposition used Islam to legitimate their claims and gain popular support.[10]

During the early 1970's, heads of state such as Muammar Qaddafi of Libya, who had seized power in a *coup d'etat*, and Egypt's Anwar Sadat, who struggled in the shadow of his dead predecessor Nasir, increasingly appealed to Islam to buttress their regimes. Qaddafi introduced Islamic laws and his Green Book to enhance his legitimacy and influence at home and abroad. Sadat attempted to control and use Islamic groups such as the Muslim Brotherhood and student organizations. Most significantly, he led Egypt in a "holy war" against Israel. In contrast to the 1967 Arab-Israeli war which was fought in the name of Arab socialism, the 1973 war was fought under the banner of Islam as Sadat generously employed Islamic symbols and history to rally his forces. Despite their loss of the war, the relative success of Egyptian forces led many Muslims to regard it as a moral victory since most believed that an Israel backed by the United States could not be beaten. Military vindication was accompanied by the economic power of the Arab oil boycott of 1973. For the first time since the dawn of colonialism, the power of the West had to contend with and acknowledge, albeit begrudgingly, its dependence on Middle Eastern powers. For many the new wealth, success and power of the oil rich countries seemed to be signs of a return of the power of Islam to a community whose rich history of centuries long political and cultural ascendence had been shattered by European colonialism and, despite independence, by second class status in a superpower dominated world.

A number of factors enhanced the Islamic character of oil power. Most of the oil wealth was located in the Arab heartland, where Muhammad had received the revelation of the Quran and established the first Islamic community-state; its largest deposits were in Saudi Arabia, a self-styled Islamic state, which had asserted its role as a leader in the Islamic world as keeper of the holy cities of Mecca and

---

[10]Kemal A. Faruki, "Pakistan: Islamic Government and Society" in *Islam in Asia*, ch. 3; and *Islam and Politics*, pp. 162 ff.

Medina and protector of the annual pilgrimage (*Hajj*). As su
used its oil wealth to establish numerous internationa_
organizations, promote the preaching and spread of Islam, support
Islamic causes, subsidize Islamic activities undertaken by Muslim
governments.

No events demonstrated more dramatically the power of resurgent
Islam than the Iranian Revolution of 1978–79. For many in the West
and the Muslim world the unthinkable became a reality. The powerful, modernizing and western oriented regime of the Shah came
crashing down. This was an oil rich Iran whose wealth had been
used to build the best equipped military in the Middle East and to
support an ambitious White revolution, a modernization program
that was supposed to bring Iran rapidly into the twenty-first century.
The Shah had long been regarded in the West as an enlightened, if
somewhat autocratic ruler, who with the strong support of the
United States and Europe and assisted by western trained elites and
advisers, governed the most stable western ally in the Muslim world.
The fact that for a variety of reasons a revolution was effectively
mounted in the name of Islam, organizing disparate groups under
the banner of Islam and relying upon the mullah-mosque network
for support, generated a euphoria among many in the Muslim world
and convinced Islamic activists that the lesson was there to be
emulated. Strength and victory would belong to those who pursued
change in the name of Islam whatever the odds and however formidable the regime.

Post-revolutionary Iran influenced Islamic activists from Egypt to
Malaysia.[11] In the aftermath of the revolution delegates visited Iran,
Sunni and Shii alike. Quiescent Shii minority communities in Sunni
dominated states like Saudi Arabia, the Gulf and Pakistan aggres-
sively asserted their Shii identity and rights. In 1979 riots broke out
among the 250,000 Shii in Saudi Arabia's oil rich Eastern Province.
In 1980 Iraq executed Muhammad Bani al-Sadr, paramount Shii
cleric and the ideological inspiration of Iraqi Shii activism, in
particular Hizb al-Dawa al-Islamiyya (Islamic Call Society). Bahrain
was rocked by a failed *coup d'etat* in 1981. In Lebanon Shii activism
was dramatically affected by both the example of Iran and the
exporting of its revolution.

---

[11]John L. Esposito and James P. Piscatori,"The Iranian Revolution Ten Years Later:
What has Been Its Global Impact" (Washington, D.C.: The Middle East Institute,
1989).

The Ideological Worldview of Revivalism

While there are distinctive differences of interpretation, the general or common ideological framework of Islamic revivalism includes the following beliefs:

(1) Islam is a total and comprehensive way of life. Religion is integral to politics, law, and society.

(2) The failure of Muslim societies is due to their departure from the straight path of Islam and following a Western secular path with its materialistic ideologies and values.

(3) The renewal of society requires a return to Islam, an Islamic religio-political and social reformation or revolution, that draws its inspiration from the Quran and from the first great Islamic movement led by the Prophet Muhammad.

(4) To restore God's rule and inaugurate a true Islamic social order, western-inspired civil codes must be replaced by Islamic law which is the only acceptable blueprint for Muslim society.

(5) Although the westernization of society is condemned, modernization as such is not. Science and technology are accepted, but they are to be subordinated to Islamic belief and values in order to guard against the westernization and secularization of Muslim society.

(6) The process of Islamization, or more accurately, re-Islamization, requires organizations or associations of dedicated and trained Muslims who, by their example and activities, call upon others to be more observant and who are willing to struggle (jihad) against corruption and social injustice.

Beneath the facade of Islamic revivalism is a richly textured reality whose seeming unity of purpose hides a diversity of expression or practice. The return to greater observance of Islam in private life and the reassertion of Islam in political life present a variety of common concerns and practices: Islamic laws, dress, behavior. However, while many speak of an Islamic alternative for state and society, what they mean and seek to implement may in fact be quite different. The implementation of Islam by governments and the agendas and methods of Islamic organizations span the political and ideological spectrum. While all may agree upon their commitment to Islam, the desire to live according to the Shariah (Islamic law), the obligation to struggle (jihad) to restore Islam to its rightful place in society, their interpretations, leadership, and methods vary widely. Both governments and opposition parties are often pitted against each other in the name of Islam. In 1979 the Grand Mosque in Mecca was seized by militants who called for the overthrow of an Islamically legitimated Saudi regime in the name of Islam. Islam also proved to be a two-edged sword in Egypt and Pakistan. After appealing to Islam to blunt his leftist opposition and legitimate policies such as the Camp David Accords, Anwar Sadat who had taken the title "the believer president," was judged by an Islamic yardstick and assassinated for his "unbelief." Similarly, Pakistan's Ali Bhutto soon found that his appeals to Islam resulted in an opposition, the Pakistan National Alliance, which untied a cross section of political parties who critiqued the government in the name of Islam and pledged themselves to the implementation of an Islamic system (nizam-i-Islam) of government. Bhutto's overthrow by General Muhammad Zia ul-Haq and subsequent execution were all justified by alleged failure to adhere to Islamic standards.

As noted previously, Islamically oriented governments (so called Islamic fundamentalist governments) themselves have proven to be quite diverse: from Libya's populist "people's state" (al-jamahiriya) to the conservative Saudi monarchy, from the clerically guided Islamic Republic of Iran to the martial law regime of Pakistan's Zia ul-Haq. The common Islamic orientation of regimes reveals little unity of purpose in interstate relationships. Indeed, the opposite has often occurred due to conflicting national priorities and foreign policies. Libya's Qadaffi was a bitter enemy of Egypt's Anwar Sadat and the Sudan's Jafar al-Numayri at the very time that all were projecting their "Islamic images." Khomeini's Islamic Iran has consistently called for the overthrow of the House of Saud on Islamic grounds, their rivalry even erupting during the annual pilgrimage to Mecca. Islamically identified governments also reflect differing relationships with the West. While much has been made of the confrontational relationship between Libya and Iran vis-à-vis the West, and the United States in particular, at the same time, the U.S. has had strong allies in Saudi Arabia, Pakistan, and the Sudan.

Islamic organizations and movements like Islamically oriented regimes vary widely, from moderate to radical, from traditionalist to modernizing. Their activities are rooted in the concepts of dawa, the "call" to Islam, and jihad, to strive or exert oneself on God's path, i.e. to be a good Muslim. Dawa not only means calling non-Muslims to the faith i.e. propagation of the faith, but also calling those who are born Muslim to be more observant Muslims. *Jihad* has two general meanings: (1) the self-exertion or struggle to be virtuous, (2) the willingness to make the ultimate sacrifice and engage in armed struggle when necessary to defend Islam. Both concepts provide the rationale for a host of diverse contemporary Islamic organizations and societies like the Muslim Brotherhood and the Jamaat-i-Islami which seek to create more Islamic states and societies. For the moderate majority, the implementation of an Islamic system will indeed require a religio-social revolution or reformation but one that is achieved through preaching, media, publishing, day-care clinics, hospitals, banks, youth centers, legal aid societies.

For a minority, armed struggle or revolution is seen as necessary and obligatory on theological and political grounds. Theologically, many would argue that an Islamic system is not simply an alternative but an imperative. If it is God's command, then it must be done now since God's will or command is for all times and places. The logic here would be similar to that of a Jew or Christian who might argue that the Ten Commandments must be obeyed at all times and that to postpone implementation or take a partial approach (eg. to postpone enforcement of the prohibition on adultery until the products of a permissive society have been properly prepared or reeducated) amounts to infidelity or heresy. Politically, radicals would maintain that the political reality in their countries requires armed struggle to defend Islam in the face of autocratic governments that repress and persecute those who advocate an Islamic alternative. They regard their governments as repressive and illegitimate and believe that all true believers have an obligation and duty to rise to the armed defense of Islam. Those Muslims who do not do so are not simply seen as sinners but apostates, enemies of God. This was the rationale of the assassins of Anwar Sadat for whom *jihad* as armed struggle was the sixth pillar of Islam, requiring the death of a president whose policies they regarded as anti-Islamic.

Contrary to many stereotypes, the leadership of both moderate and radical Islamic organizations are not uneducated, anti-modern reactionaries. With the exception of Shii Islam where the ulama are prominent, most organizations are predominantly lay rather than clerical. Many of the activists combine traditional backgrounds with modern educations at major national universities and international centers of learning. They are graduates of Khartoum, Cairo, Alexandria, Teheran, Bandung and Kuwait universities as well as Harvard, MIT, Indiana, Wisconsin, Temple, Sussex, London, and the Sorbonne. The majority are graduates of the faculties of science, engineering, law, and medicine rather than religion or the humanities. They come from lower middle class and middle class backgrounds, both village and city dwellers, are pious and highly motivated. They are professionals from every walk of life: teachers, university professors, engineers, lawyers, doctors, government bureaucrats, the military. What one expert has said about the profile of an Egyptian radical group might be said for most moderate as well as radical activists: "It is sometimes assumed in social science that recruits of 'radical movements' must be somehow alienated, marginal, anomic, or otherwise abnormal. Most of those we investigated would be considered model young Egyptians."[12]

Most are not simply victims of modernization, rejecting modernity and retreating to a seventh century haven. Unlike many of their peers, these are Muslims whose experience of modernization has not led them to embrace it wholesale but instead to criticize its political, economic, and religio-social excesses and espouse a more indigenously rooted, Islamically oriented alternative to prevailing Western forms of modernization.

Issues of Leadership and Interpretation

Among the major questions which have grown out of contemporary Islamic revivalism and which remain important issues for the foreseeable future are questions of leadership and interpretation: "Whose Islam?" and "What Islam?" If the state is to implement Islam, who shall do it and how? Is Islam to be imposed from above by monarchs, military leaders, the clergy? Or is Islamic government to come from below, to be the product of an electoral process? Many who have witnessed the use of Islam to ban political parties, to silence dissent, to impose unpopular laws and measures, increasingly emphasize the importance of traditional notions of consultation (shura) and community consensus (ijma). They regard these as safeguards against both secular and Islamically legitimated authoritarianism. While many Muslims remain wary of the excesses that have accompanied the reassertion of Islam in politics, their tendency is not to advocate secularism or secular forms of nationalism but

[12]Saad Eddin Ibrahim, "Egypt's Islamic Militants," MERIP Reports 103 (February 1982): 11 and Zainah Anwar, Islamic Revivalism in Malaysia: Dakwah Among the Students. (Selangor, Malaysia: Pelanduk Publications, 1987). My own research from the Sudan to Malaysia reached similar conclusions.

rather some kind of accommodation or synthesis of Islam and society. Most Muslims emphasize the role of representative bodies such as parliaments in charting an Islamic path for state and society.

The role of the ulama in this process remains unclear. In many Muslim societies the more established ulama are regarded as pawns of the state as well as retrogressive thinkers. Thus, in contrast to Shii Islam, in Sunni majority societies (85% of the world of Islam) the vast majority of Islamic movements and societies are run by the laity. At best the ulama are regarded as those who should play an advisory role to organizations and to parliamentary bodies. Indeed, some reform minded Muslims emphasize that Islam knows no clergy and that the ulama were merely a class of scholars who emerged during the early Islamic centuries. Thus, they stress that given the nature of many modern day political, social and economic problems, the notion of expert must be broadened to include those that possess the knowledge and experience required: economists, historians, lawyers, sociologists. All will be necessary to undertake necessary reforms.[13]

Islamic interpretation or orientation is the second major issue facing contemporary revivalists. Is a more authentic return to Islam to be a process of restoration or reformation? For many of the more traditional ulama and their followers, the renewal of Islamic society means a reimplementation of classical Islam, its laws and institutions. In contrast, Islamic reformers distinguished between the immutable sources of Islam and the forms and regulations developed by the ulama of the past and are thus socio-historically conditioned. Islamic reformers emphasize the need for reconstruction, substantial reinterpretation and reform. It should be emphasized that the issue is not change but how much change and what kind of change. To begin with, modernization as science and technology is not rejected; modernization as westernization of state and society is. The issue is one of culture and values. All Muslims accept much of modern technology; they differ as to how that technology is to be utilized. Those who paint pictures of retrogressive anti-modern fundamentalists forget that they travel by jet and automobile, rely heavily on modern communications (press, video and audiotapes, the telephone, telex and fax), and that most advocate parliamentary systems of government.

---

[13]See for example Hassan Turabi, "The Islamic State" in *Voices of Resurgent Islam*, ch. 12.

One way to appreciate the differing orientations towards change is to briefly consider the issue of Islamic law. The first think that Islamic revivalists demand, regardless of their differences, the implementation of Islamic law (the *shariah*), the ideal blueprint for the good society. However, they differ in what they wish to implement. Conservatives tend to regard much of the corpus of traditional Islamic law as binding. Reformers such as Sadiq al-Gahdi and Hasan al-Turabi of the Sudan, Hasan Hanafi of Egypt, Rashid Ghannoushi of Tunisia, and Anwar Ibrahim in Malaysia, note the law is a combination of revelation and human interpretation and that the latter is subject to reinterpretation (*ijtihad*) and reform. Many of the issues which have accompanied the revival of Islam spring from this difference of opinion: for example, the nature of the state, the scope of Islamic law, the status and role of women, relations between the sexes, and the rights of minorities.[14]

The contemporary revival of Islam has been a dynamic period of implementation and experimentation. Like all experiments, some succeed and many fail. The excesses have caused many to reject what they regard as a negative Islam, one which often seems to emphasize penalties, taxes, and restrictions rather than true liberation. However, while the retrogressive hold of tradition is often emphasized in reports on revivalism, a great deal of change is taking place often supported by both conservative and reform minded Muslims: Islamic banks, insurance companies, money markets, schools, social services and development projects have been introduced. The vast majority of Muslims, secularists and Islamic revivalists, abhor the exploitation of Islam by some governments and movements. A minority continue to espouse violence as the necessary means of change. They will continue to disrupt society from time to time. However, the strength of contemporary revivalism remains with a growing moderate majority whose activities have become part of mainstream Muslim life. These are the apolitical and political *dawa* organizations or Islamic "Call" societies which seek to call all to a religious renewal which combines prayer observances with social action. Their vision of Islam is holistic. They believe that a faithful, righteous Islamic community is one that observes God's mandate to worship Him and to create a socially just society. This

---

[14]*Islam and Politics*, pp. 220 ff. and James P. Piscatori, *Islam in a World of Nation-States* (Cambridge: Cambridge University Press, 1986) chs. 4–6.

long term process, which is weaving its way into Muslim political and social institutions, will have significance both for the development of the worldwide Islamic community and Muslim societies, as well as their relationship with the West.

FLEXIBLE FUNDAMENTALISM:
TOWARD A JAINA APPROACH
TO INTERRELIGIOUS DIALOGUE

Christopher Chapple

The Jaina religion is one of the most ancient traditions in the world and is particularly noted for its emphasis on nonviolence. It has been dated from the 8th century B.C.E. and its current doctrinal forms were articulated by the 6th century B.C.E. Since that time, the basic teachings have changed little or none. In this regard, the Jaina tradition may be considered "fundamentalist" in the sense that its cosmology and ethics have not been subject to revision. Other historical issues have resulted in the emergence of two groups within the tradition, the Digambaras and Svetambaras, but both exhibit a "remarkable unwillingness to depart from their basic doctrine and practices."[1] However, this fundamentalism is tempered by a fervent concern that the points of view held by others not be dismissed but rather that they be explored, understood, and then contextualized in the light of Jaina doctrine. In the following paper, some of the central tenets or fundamentals of Jainism will be discussed. We will then focus on Jaina attitudes toward traditions that do not share their world view. Though many texts have been devoted to this task, we will limit our comments to the *Syād-vāda-mañjarī*, written by Mal-liṣeṇa in 1292 C.E. This approach will be explored as providing a model for interreligious dialogue and then compared with models for dialogue outlined by Paul Knitter, Leonard Swidler, and Seyyed Hossein Nasr. This paper is preliminary to a larger study of indigenous Asian approaches to both fundamentalism and pluralism and

[1]Padmanabh s. Jaini, *The Jaina Path of Purification* (Berkeley: University of California Press, 1979), p. 88.

hence does not claim to be comprehensive in its dealing with this important and complex subject matter.

The traditional fundamentals of Jainism include a comprehensive cosmology and interrelated ethics. What one does as a Jaina committed to nonviolence prescinds from a comprehensive and unique view of the world. Specifically, for the Jainas, the world is seen as divided into three existents: the sentient, the material, and substance/principles. The first existent, the sentient life forms (jīva) will be discussed in greater detail below. The second, the material, includes atoms that are indivisible and infinite in number, each possessing form, taste, smell, and palpability. These atoms form the foundation for both physical and psychic or karmic realities. The third existent is fourfold: space, motion, rest, and time. These three existents, although seemingly equivalent to those found in classical Greek physics or the Hindu system of Vaiśeṣika, are distinguished by their first and most important component: that of the sentient life force or jīva.

Within space and continuous with atomic structures are located an infinite number of life forces that have existed since beginningless time. These jīvas are able to assume diverse dimensions, just as a piece of cloth can be rolled into a small ball or unfolded to occupy an extended space. Each jīva is in a state of flux; each is suffused with consciousness, energy, and bliss. However, this latter aspect is obscured due to each jīva being defiled by psychic atoms called karma which cause the jiva to be reborn repeatedly within a hierarchy or states ranging from that of the gods (devas), humans (manuṣya), hell beings (nārakī), to plants and animals (tiryañca), which includes several subcategories. The universe thus conceived is in the shape of a giant person, with hell beings occupying the lower realm, humans and tiryañca) occupying the middle, gods residing in the heavenly realms divided into sixteen abodes, and finally, in the siddhaloka dwell the liberated jīvas or kevalins who have been purged of all karma. This is the final goal, the telos of the cosmos to which those who have successfully and most likely repeatedly lived the life of a Jaina monk.

The animal and plant realm (tiryañca) is subdivided into a hierarchy dependent upon the number of senses the life forms possess. Tiny microorganisms possess only the sense of touch, as do the earth, water, fire, and air bodies and plant life. Worms add the sense of taste; crawling bugs add smell; flies and moths add seeing; water serpents add hearing. Mammals, reptiles, fish, and humans all possess six senses, adding mental capacity to the five senses listed above.[2] Gods and hell-beings likewise possess six faculties but also have special powers, arise spontaneously (without parents), and, if a god, continually experience pleasure and, if a demon, experience only anguish. Regardless of one's state of life, from a clod of earth to heavenly beings, repeated existence on the wheel of life is certain until one achieves human birth and begins the quest for liberation.

Discussions of karma in its ethical sense are not found in the Vedic texts of the early Hindu tradition nor are they systematically present within the Upanisads. The Dharmasastra material of Brahmanical phases of Hinduism and the Jataka stories told by the Buddha use aspects of karma theory to intimidate attentive listeners into socially acceptable behavior. By contrast, in addition to emphasizing karma as an effective tool for moral education, the Jainas, as stated earlier, see karma as integral to their cosmological view. The Jaina tradition presents a highly technical interpretation, regarding karma to be a genuine, sticky, colorful substance, composed of atoms, that adheres to the life force and prevents ascent to the siddhaloka. Through passion, desire, and hatred, the jīva attracts karma, which remains until its potency is exhausted. It is stated in the Sarvārthasiddhi that the jīva "has successively taken in and cast off every particle of karmic matter in the universe." Karma comes in no less then thirty forms, ranging from the destructive (which is productive of delusion, passions, sentiments and obscurations), to the nondestructive. In the eyes of the Jainas, all karma must be purged (nirjarā) for liberation to be attained.

In order to cast off the oppression of karma, human birth is essential. The jīva through its many incarnations has accrued significant karma; the human modality allows for its expedited expulsion. The energy of the jīva in human form explicitly allows for the diminution of karma in a process proceeding through fourteen stages of purification or guṇāsthānas.

The first stage, mithyādṛṣṭi, is when one suffers from wrong views, and is attached to both a sense of self and to things as they appear to be in the world. The second state is one that is similar to the first, but to which one falls to having previously reached a higher state. The third state is transitional, and arises after the fourth guṇāsthāna

---

[2]For a discussion of the ethical implications of this "biocosmology" see Christopher Chapple, "Noninjury to Animals: Jaina and Buddhist Perspectives" in Tom Regan, ed., Animal Sacrifices: Religious Perspectives on the Use of Animals in Science (Philadelphia: Temple University Press, 1986), pp. 213–236.

when a mixture of correct and incorrect views prevails. The fourth
state, *samyak darśana*, is pivotal; its significance is second only to
the attainment of *Jina* status. It may last a single instant up to a
maximum of forty-eight minutes. In it all obstructions of karma are
prevented from arising. In this state

> so great is the purity generated by this flash of insight that enormous
> numbers of bound karmas are driven out of the soul altogether, while
> future karmic influx is severely limited to both quantity and intensity.[3]

This suppression of karma is preliminary to total elimination, yet
it guarantees the *jīva's* "irreversible entry onto the path that leads to
mokṣa (liberation)." It heralds a leaving behind of preoccupation
with the body, psychological states, and possessions. The gross
forms of anger, pride, deceit, and greed are "rendered inoperative."
One "no longer perceives things as 'attractive' or 'desirable' but one
penetrates to the fact that every aspect of life is transitory and
mortal."[4] At this point a resolve sets in to change one's lifestyle and
adopt the rigors of Jaina renunciation. Additionally, tremendous
compassion arises, wherein all beings are seen as holding the potential to be liberated from the shackles of karma.

It is only after this insight experience that the widely known Jaina
lifestyle is purposefully adopted. It is first indicated in the fifth
guṇāsthāna, wherein the vows of a layperson are undertaken. These
include refraining from meat, alcohol, honey, and certain figs as
well as adherence to the five vows or *anuvratas*: nonviolence, truthfulness, not stealing, refraining from illicit sexual activities, and
non-possessiveness. In support of these primary vows, restrictions
on one's movement and range of experiences are also self-imposed,
along with meditation, fasting, and chastity. Following the "baptism" of insight in the fourth *guṇāsthāna*, one undoubtedly has
reverted to conventional "wrong views." These disciplines allow the
active cultivation of right views on the part of the practitioner,
advancing one forward again.

In the subsequent nine stages, stricter monastic vows are followed,
leading to the progressive elimination of karmas. First the passions
of anger, pride, deceit, and greed are eliminated, not merely suppressed (#6). Then carelessness is overcome (#7). Then the subsidiary passions (sentiments) are suppressed. These include laughter,

---

[3]Jaini, p. 144.
[4]Ibid., p. 149.

pleasure, displeasure, sorrow, fear, disgust, and sexual cravings (#8, 9, 10). After a hiatus wherein a fall from this state is expected (#11) one then proceeds to eliminate any smoldering passions (#12) and then the karmas that obscure knowledge and perception, and that restrict energy (#13). In this state, one has become an arhat, a *kevalin*, Jina or Tīrthaṅkara. The final state (#14) is obtained the instant before death and signifies the elimination of those karmas that keep one alive (feeling, name, life span, and family).[5]

These are the fundamental teachings of Jainism: that the world is divided into nonliving and living components; that life forms have existed since beginningless time in myriad forms, and that life can be liberated through a fourteen-fold process. These teachings, which date at least to 2500 B.C.E., have remained unchanged since their inception. They have not been influenced by Buddhism or Hinduism. Furthermore, the Jainas have exercised great care in articulating how their position differs from those of others, while not condemning alternate views as incorrect . . . only incomplete. This concern for understanding one's own position relative to that of others is extremely ancient. Record of it is found in the earliest texts of Jaina Canon. The *Sūtrakṛta*, included in the second section of Jaina canonical literature, critiques other systems of Indian thought in light of Jainism, specifically those that seem to advocate fatalism, eternalism, or vacuity. In the fifth century (C.E.), Siddhaṣeṇa Divakārā's *Sanmatisūtra* investigates various viewpoints as being nonvalid when asserted in an absolutist manner. And in the thirteenth century, Malliṣeṇa's *Syādvādamañjarī* offers a comprehensive critique of non-Jaina philosophical schools and religious practices.

In each of these texts, great care is shown that the positions of others be understood and respected. The Jainas were engaged in a form of dialogue with other traditions that broadened their knowledge without altering their own faith commitment. Buddhists and Hindus also are known for referring to positions of others in order to clearly articulate their own views.[6] However, these traditions have also developed new forms that integrate and synthesize pre-existing traditions. Hence, Mahāyāna Buddhism appropriates Hindu deity forms; the Buddhist mind-only teaching is found in medieval Hindu texts; Ch'an Buddhism in China adopts the language of Taoism.

---

[5]See Jagmanderlal Jaini, *Outlines of Jainism* (Cambridge: University Press, 1916), pp. 48–52 and 105–107.

[6]The many schools of Vedānta are well aware of the "competition," and Tibetan debate training focuses on learning various Buddhist and non-Buddhist traditions.

Jainism, by contrast, did not develop substantially new forms, holding fast to its teachings on karma, jīva, and ahiṁsa or nonviolence.

The well known Jaina commitment to nonviolence arose out of a concern that action in the world promotes violence, violence results in additional karma and karma obstructs one from liberation. In addition to minimizing violence through vegetarianism, sweeping one's path, and covering one's mouth, the Jainas also extended the nonviolent ethic to their logic as well. Rather than advancing a two pronged, wrong or right analysis of arguments in the style of Aristotle, and rather than stopping at the fourfold analysis of reality in the style of the Upaniṣads and Nāgārjuna,[7] the Jainas brought forth a sevenfold analysis of reality that specifically disallows the holding of any extreme view. Implicit in this approach is a recognition of the limitations imposed by linguistic structures and their ultimate irrelevance in light of the task and achievement of human liberation.

The seven views are outlined as follows:

1. In a certain way, a thing exists (syād asti eva)
2. In a certain way, a thing does not exist (syād nāsti eva)
3. In a certain way, a thing both exists and does not exist (sequentially) (syād astyeva syānnāstyeveti)
4. In a certain way, if existence and nonexistence are taken simultaneously, things are inexpressible (syād avaktavyaṁ)
5. Hence, existent and inexpressible
6. Nonexistent and irrepressible
7. Existent, nonexistent, and inexpressible

The first view acknowledges the existence of things within the world and speaks of the waking reality upon which we all presumably agree. The second view, familiar to students of Indian thought but not generally considered in Western analyses, reminds us that the very existence of a thing implies its nonexistence. This paper was not here before it was written, nor will it endure eternally. The third view combines the first two, pointing out that things exist as moments within time but are subject to arising and decay. To speak of a thing purely in its existent phase as if it were eternal would be

---

[7]Within the Upaniṣads we find a fourfold analysis of reality: waking, dreaming, deep sleep, and the "fourth" state (turiya), wherein one identifies with the highest self. Nāgārjuna's Mādhyamika school of Mahāyāna Buddhism outlines (and rejects) four "corners" of reality: existence, nonexistence, both existence and nonexistence, neither existence nor nonexistence.

incorrect; to speak of a thing disparagingly because it is bound for destruction would represent an equally incorrect nihilistic view. The fourth view points out that the true nature of a thing can never be expressed adequately; no matter how much I might want to say in order to describe someone dear to me, words fail to do more than denote particular and fragmentary aspects. Even to describe an apple becomes an impossibility. How can one speak of an apple without taking into account the tree from which it came, the person who planted the tree, the surface of the front of the apple, the surface (unseen) of the back of the apple, the nature of its interior, including its flesh, core, and seeds. "A rose by any other name is still a rose" becomes in the Jaina rendering "A rose has so many names it in fact is unspeakable." Consequently, once the paradox of ineffability is admitted, each of the earlier views is further qualified: existence is also unspeakable, nonexistence is unspeakable, and the joining of both is also unspeakable.

This logical construct makes all statements provisional. It is not skepticism in the strict sense of the word, but, in the words of H. R. Kapadia, it signifies that "every judgment that we pass in daily life is true only in reference to the standpoint occupied and the aspect of the object considered."[8]

In the Jaina system, each truth is a partial one (naya) and no one statement can ever account for the totality of reality (anekāntavāda). Kapadia relates this stance to the practice of nonviolence:

> When this ahimsa is allowed to play its role on an intellectual plane, it teaches us to examine and respect the opinions of others as they, too, are some of the angles of vision or pathways to reality which is many-sided and enable us to realize and practice truth in its entirety. This implies that ahiṁsa—the Jaina attitude of intellectual ahiṁsa—is the origin of anekantavada. In other words, the Jaina principle of 'respect for life' (ahiṁsa) is the origin of 'respect for the opinions of others' (anekāntavāda).[9]

For purposes of illustrating the syād-vāda method, we will now examine a few key passages from the Syādvādamañjarī of Malliṣeṇa, the thirteenth century work mentioned earlier as an

---

[8]H. R. Kapadia, Introduction to Haribhadra Sūri's Anekāntajāyapaṭaka with His Own Commentary and Municandra Sūri's Supercommentary (Baroda: Oriental Institute, 1947), p. cxviii.
[9]Ibid., p. cxiv.

example of the Jaina concern for investigating the religious and philosophical positions of non-Jainas. This text analyzes the views of the Vaiseśika "atomists," the Nyaya logicians, the Pūrvamīṁāmsā ritualists, the Vedantins, the adherents to the Samkhya system, various schools of Buddhism, and the Lokāyata materialists. Malli-ṣeṇa's text is ostensibly written as a commentary on verses written by his teacher Hemacandra.

Sections IV through IX of the text critique the Vaiśeṣika system. The Vaiśeṣikas are criticized for being inconsistent, on the one hand asserting that a lamp is noneternal while on the other, that space is eternal. Within the Jaina system, as we have seen, no such inconsistency is allowed due to the teachings of atoms and space both being eternal. Malliṣeṇa then explains the Vaiśeṣika doctrine of a world-creating god, justified by his omnipresence, self-dependence, and eternity. The Jainas do not assent to the argument that a thing's presence proves that it has been created; the maker of a pot can be seen, so why is this creator-god invisible? If he is truly the author of scripture, then why would he praise himself therein? Why would he compose scriptures that contradict one another on the utility of animal sacrifice and the necessity of a Brahman to have a son? The Jaina position considers the postulate of a creator-god to be unten-able logically and also that such a notion weakens the perceived efficacy of karma.

The Nyāya logicians are criticized for their vagueness; the Pūrva-mīṁāmsā is criticized for its support of sacrificial animal slaughter. Vedanta's position on the nonduality of Brahman and the nonreality of the world is examined and then attacked on the grounds that if the world is not real then how is it that the world is seen? "One is not both a mother and barren."[10] Sāṁkhya is criticized on four counts: its notion that consciousness can be devoid of object; that the *buddhi* (intellect) could be "non-intelligent," proclaiming that "I am not"; that sky is born from the subtle element of sound; and that the *puruṣa* is neither bound nor liberated. From the Jaina perspective, each of these is contradictory.

Three distinct schools of Buddhism are presented. The Mādhy-amika is dismissed as not adequately disproving the existence of either cogniser or cognition. The Sarvāstivādin doctrine of momen-tariness, wherein things come into existence, remain for a moment,

---

[10]F. W. Thomas, *The Flower Spray of the Quodammodo Doctrine: Śrī Malliṣeṇasūr-i's Syād-Vāda-Mañjarī* (Delhi: Motilal Banarsidass, 1958), p. 78.

go into decay, and then cease, is countermanded by the perdurance of memory. The Yogācāra approach to *vasana* (residues of karma) is deemed inadequate due to its being based on the doctrines of impermanence and no-self.

The final system critiqued by Malliṣeṇa is the Nāstikas or Nihilists who proclaim nothing has meaning or purpose. As a retort, the author notes that there is "purity of intelligence even on the part of one who has a body infected by leprosy,"[11] thus advancing an alternate, optimistic view of human potential. In each of the instances mentioned above, Malliṣeṇa has clearly understood and summarized the various schools examined. The critique he presents, while certainly not palatable from the perspective of those holding the respective views being discussed, holds true to Jain sevenfold analysis of reality and rejection of extreme views. Each system is acknowledged as a partial truth and hence validated, though not applauded.

The Jaina technique of rehearsing and then abrogating the "extreme" views of others illustrated above in our cursory assessment of non-Jaina systems provides an interesting contrast with the *Yogavāsiṣṭha*, a tenth or twelfth century syncretic Hindu text that explicitly integrates teachings of Buddhist momentariness with Vedāntin absolutism.[12] In both instances, it is made clear that India has long grappled with an issue that has come to the forefront in the West during the last thirty years: given the plurality of world religions that now come regularly into contact with one another, what hermeneutic approach is the most valid? Will the traditions more clearly define and maintain their integrity in light of their contact with other traditions? Will traditions begin to meld together, in the manner of late Hinduism absorbing aspects of Buddhism, to the point where a discrete Buddhism disappeared?

The history of Christianity is replete with instances of both tendencies: inward looking fundamentalism and outwardly-influenced syncretism. On the one hand, the councils of Nicea and Chalcedon were fundamentalist responses to movements within the Christian community that were considered suspect: Arianism, monophysitism, Nestorianism, etc. The creeds aim to establish a clear, unambiguous definition as the foundation for Christian faith. And yet even the Gospels themselves are clearly the product of two cultural

---

[11]Ibid., p. 128.

[12]See my introduction to *The Concise Yogavāsiṣṭha*, trans. Swami Venkatesananda (State University of New York Press, 1984).

sensibilities joined together, the Hebraic and the Hellenistic. Likewise, as with Augustine and then with Aquinas, the insights of other
cultures have shaped and reshaped the direction and orientation of
Western Christianity. With Augustine we see an ascendance of
personalistic, Neoplatonic Manichaean religious forms; with Aquinas, thanks to the Islāmic translations of Aristotle, we see yet another
rewriting of the tradition. In each of these examples, the Christian
faith seems less interested in maintaining fundamentals than accom-
modating to new thought forms and issues.

Since the advent of rationalism, European colonialism, the rise of
the academic study of world religion, and Vatican II, whole new
revelations have been made accessible to the Christian world. As
Thomas Berry has noted, the acknowledgment of and interest in
world traditions potentially signals an infused vigor within the
realm of theological discourse, unparalleled since the time of
Thomas Aquinas. With this new development has arisen great de-
bates over how best to proceed. In *No Other Name? A Critical Survey
of Christian Attitudes Toward the World Religions*, Paul Knitter offers
a comprehensive survey of how various Christian denominations
and thinkers have assessed this situation.[13] In some ways, this book,
which describes itself as a textbook, is not unlike Malliṣeṇa's *syād
vāda mañjarī* and hence provides a similarly concise summary of a
much larger body of literature. It surveys a host of positions, including that all religions are relative (Troeltsch), that all are essentially
the same (Toynbee), that all share a common psychic origin (Jung),
that Christianity is the only true religion (Barth), that revelation is
possible in other religions while salvation is not (Tillich), that all
religions are ways of salvation (Rahner). Knitter's own contribution
attempts a new synthesis, building on the theocentric model of Hick,
Panikkar, and Samartha.

Of the various models offered in Knitter's survey, the combined
positions of Jung, Barth, and Tillich are closest to that of the Jainas.
Like Jung, the Jainas see a commonality amongst *jīvas*: all hold the
potential for liberation (though some lack the ability to achieve it).
Like Barth, the Jainas are convinced of the sole effectiveness of their
own tradition in achieving their goal. Like Tillich, they agree that
partial truth is found elsewhere as well.

The solutions posed by Troeltsch, Toynbee, Rahner, and Knitter

---

[13]Paul F. Knitter, *No Other Name? A Critical Survey of Christian Attitudes Toward
the World Religions* (Maryknoll, New York: Orbis, 1985).

himself are more problematic from the Jaina perspective. Radical relativity would negate the efficacy of the Jaina system. Commonality of traditions (Toynbee) flies in the face of the perceived content of the respective traditions, as does the idea that all religions are ways of salvation (Rahner). Ultimately, however, the most troublesome of these viewpoints from a Jaina perspective would be that of theocentrism, which, in the eyes of the Jainas, would remove the religious process from human control; the Jainas refute the notion of any external divine force and assert that all religious experience prescinds due to one's own initiative.

In comparing the world view and method of contemporary ecumenists with that of the Jainas, there are both similarities and differences. Many ecumenists are searching for a unified truth, a basis for one's own belief that shares a ground of commonality with the religious life of others. For the Jainas, this quest for common ground is not the case. The Jainas are firm in their own belief structure: their cosmology, logic, and ethics have remained unaltered for nearly three thousand years and, as we have seen, Jainism clearly distinguishes itself from other traditions. In a sense, Jaina fundamentals are unshakable. However, accompanying this certitude is a driving concern to understand the beliefs of others, not to change themselves or even necessarily to convert others.

The work of contemporary Christian ecumenists, on the other hand, is often exploratory, creative, synthetic, and sometimes syncretic. However, this adventurousness carries with it the possibility of losing or altering one's own truths. As Seyyed Hossein Nasr has pointed out,

> Although based often on the positive intention of creating better understanding of other religions, most of the proponents of ecumenism place mutual understanding above the total integrity of a tradition to the extent that there are now those Christian theologians who claim that Christians should stop believing in the incarnation in order to understand Muslims and have Muslims understand them. One could only ask why they should remain Christians and not embrace Islam altogether.[14]

This is the inevitable conundrum of holding a logical system that seeks truth in monolithic terms. Nasr himself clearly and admittedly

---

[14]Seyyed Hossein Nasr, *Knowledge and the Sacred* (New York: Crossroad, 1981), p. 289.

operates out of a commitment to esoteric experience that assents to
the Vedāntic and Islamic vision of oneness; in his perspective, all
religions are seen through this prism. However, like the Jainas (and
unlike some ecumenists), Nasr defends holding strongly to one's
own perspective while simultaneously advocating the exploration of
other expressions of truth:

> The criticism that can be made against the religious exclusivists is not
> that they have strong faith in their religion. They possess faith but they
> lack principal knowledge, that kind of knowledge which can penetrate
> into foreign universes of form and bring out their inner meanings.[15]

In this instance, a more sympathetic eye is cast on the foundations
of other traditions than has been evidenced by the Jainas.

Another approach, similar to the quest for commonality, has been
suggested by Leonard Swidler. Unlike Nasr's emphasis on the divine
or sacred as fundamental, Swidler offers an architectonic, "universal
theology" that, as its ethos, allows "full human life" and "ultimate
meaning."[16] However, just as Nasr's solution may sound odd to the
nontheistic ears of a Jaina, so Swidler's appeal to a higher humanism
might offend a Muslim because of its avoidance of God-language.

In this brief survey of interreligious encounters, potential outcomes can be discerned: conversion, accommodationist syncretism,
often in the form of a super-inclusivistic metatheology, and renewed
or tolerant or flexible fundamentalism.

Conversion is one very real option: undoubtedly some ecumenists
have been converted unconsciously or in spite of themselves and
would protest such a label. As Ewert Cousins has commented, one
of the greatest challenges facing Christians who have had a genuine
experience of Islam is to be able to return to the Christian Trinitarian
tradition: the monotheism of the Islamic faith is very compelling
and convincing. Likewise, the emphasis on interiority found within
south and east Asian traditions has been very attractive and effective
for many.

Accommodationist syncretism has been a longstanding practice
throughout Asia, with the interpenetration of Taoism, Buddhism,
and Confucianism in China, Korea, and Japan, and the successive
religious adaptations made in India when the Śramāṇic and Vedic

---

[15]Ibid., p. 291.

[16]Leonard Swidler, ed., *Toward a Universal Theology of Religion* (Maryknoll, New
York: Orbis, 1987), pp. 30 and 36.

traditions merged, when Sankara infused Hinduism with Buddhism, when Guru Nānak brought Islāmic and Hindu ideas together, when Akbar formulated and instituted his Divine Wisdom religion, when Ram Mohan Roy began to integrate the Christian gospels with all of the above, and when Swami Vivekananda brought neo-Vedānta to the World Parliament of Religions in Chicago in 1893. Within the last decade, the New Age movement has introduced shamanic techniques into this mélange. One difficulty with a "tradition" of this sort (and this is meant to also include inclusive ideologies such as benevolent humanism), is that the rigorous study and logical consistency that characterizes the "great traditions" becomes tenuous, though, as Raimundo Panikkar has pointed out, these matters should not be the litmus test for spiritual experience: "a rationality does not exhaustively define the human being."[17]

Renewed or tolerant or flexible fundamentalism, preferred by the Jainas, allows and in fact requires that the religiously informed person be well acquainted with how different traditions have approached the basic issues of human limitation and transcendence. It encourages respect for others' perspectives and yet allows one's primary commitment to remain rooted in that with which one feels most authenticated.

There are several merits to the Jaina partial-truth view. The attack on religion by science as perceived by Creationists would be mitigated if we/they had access to a grammar that would allow us to say—"from a certain perspective, the world appears to be very ancient, and to have included many life forms. However, from the perspective of human suffering, this story can be read another way." This method allow various scenarios to be possibly the case, but does not deny or relativize the validity of one's own position. It also allows traditions and persons to discover commonalities without heralding those commonalities as absolutes. For instance, in regard to ethics, some aspects of liberation theology may be agreed upon by diverse faiths. The World Wild Life Fund has brought together religious leaders and scholars from various faiths to conceptually deal with the pressing problem of environmental decay. The solutions may proceed from diverse ideologies, perhaps often non-religious ones, yet there need be no assumption that the ideologies themselves need to be changed. A respect for the viewpoint of others and a willingness to accept its contribution is made possible through

---

[17]Ibid., p. 122.

the Jaina percept of *syād vāda*, that in a certain way and in a certain context, seemingly opposed or contradictory positions have value.

Fundamentalism is often viewed disparagingly as a blind devotion to a fixed set of beliefs to the point of excluding all other views. However, in order for a religious tradition to perform effectively, certain world views need to be agreed upon by its adherents; understandably these at times come into conflict. The Jaina solution to this dilemma is found in a logical structure that allows for and respects myriad positions yet holds to its own cosmological and ethical view. Jaina belief and precepts have not changed in over two and a half millennia, and yet Jainism survives with vigor in modern, industrial India. As various forms of Christianity, Buddhism, Hinduism, and Islām enter into dialogue with their own multiple forms and with one another, new structures are needed to identify what beliefs are essential and central to one's own subtradition and tradition and how these may best be articulated and then related to the traditions of others. The Jaina model of flexible fundamentalism offers one option for validating a fundamentalist devotion to basic teachings while still acknowledging the validity of divergent views within their own context.

THEISM FOR THE MASSES, NON-DUALISM FOR THE MONASTIC ELITE: A FRESH LOOK AT ŚAṂKARA'S TRANS-THEISTIC SPIRITUALITY

Lance Nelson

Sensitive and thoughtful Christians are today prone to anxious reflection on the fact that their tradition has spawned disquieting displays of exclusivism, intolerance, and—in the modern period—rigid fundamentalism. In such a mood, there is a tendency to look wistfully at the religions of the East, reputed to be peaceful reservoirs of tolerance and inclusivity. The Asian religions themselves, however, are not immune from strident revivalist and quasi-fundamentalist movements.[1] Nor are there classical traditions entirely free from elements of narrowness or exclusivity, even when espousing metaphysical outlooks stunningly universalistic in tone.

This paper will consider a graphic example of the latter tendency in the thought of the great seventh-century Hindu philosopher Śaṃkara.[2] This primary systematizer of Advaita (non-dualistic) Vedānta believed in the absolute oneness of all souls with the supreme Godhead, *Brahman*. This and other features of his philosophy, especially his doctrine of Māyā, are well known. Commonly ignored in philosophical treatments of Advaita, however, is his teaching that only male monastics of the elite Brahmin caste could study Vedānta, realize this truth, and thereby gain salvation.

Vedānta has been identified—and sometimes promoted—as the

---

[1] I think immediately of Nichiren Buddhism in Japan and the Arya Samaj and the Rashtriya Swayamsevak Sangh in India.

[2] On the date of Śaṃkara, see Karl H. Potter, ed., *Encyclopedia of Indian Philosophies*, Vol. III: *Advaita Vedānta up to Śaṃkara and his Pupils* (Princeton: Princeton University Press, 1981), pp. 115–116.

fount of the Asian universalistic outlook. Beginning at the end of the last century, Svāmī Vivekānanda challenged the West with his forceful presentation of Upanisadic thought. Advaita, for him, was a liberal, universalistic philosophy holding answers to the problem of religious diversity and conflict. A way of thought able to accommodate both science and religious plurality, it could provide a rationale for being religious in the modern world. Vedānta would enable the West to overcome its religious provincialism and spiritual bankruptcy. At the same time, it would liberate the Hindu masses from their dualistic customs and superstitions, giving them a new dignity and fearlessness. Under the aegis of Advaita, Vivekānanda declared, India would become the spiritual leader of a unified world culture. Later, during the first half of the present century, Sarvepalli Radhakrishnan presented Hindu non-dualism in a way that was more academically polished, but in real content much the same. The climax of human religious aspiration, the liberal vision of Advaita would be a basis of tolerance, accommodation of divergent worldviews, and world unity. It could supply Hinduism with a workable modern world view that would put the dogmatic, intolerant monotheisms of the West to shame.

The many exponents of this kind of thinking—most accurately termed "Neo-Vedānta"—look to Śaṃkara as the major classical exponent of their religious vision. Śaṃkara has therefore been presented as the primary thinker of the Hindu tradition, a philosopher of world standing offering solutions to both perennial spiritual dilemmas and contemporary world problems. No doubt, Śaṃkara remains one of the great thinkers of India and of the world. As with all creative thinkers, however, there are aspects of his thought that betray certain narrow emphases of his era and culture. In reflecting here on some of these, my aim is not to diminish Śaṃkara's contribution. It is rather to understand more adequately the origins and underlying assumptions of this thought, sometimes so enthusiastically presented as a corrective to Western religious narrowness.

It is instructive to see the extent to which Śaṃkara was a man limited by his place and time. Since he is hailed as the source of a universalistic vision, it is particularly important to be aware that he was neither a liberal nor even truly tolerant in any modern sense of the word. Like other Indian philosophers, he engaged in a vigorous polemic against all views other than his own. And, particularly important for the present discussion, he was deeply conditioned by Hindu hierarchical social thinking. Indeed, his work gives ample evidence that he embraced it wholeheartedly. Most accounts of Śaṃkara's life hold that he belonged to a high-caste Brahmin community of Kerala, the Nambūdiri Brahmins. His profound metaphysical vision arose thus in the context of an ancient spiritual tradition that was conservative, elitist, and thoroughly stratified.

The complex, multi-levelled Hindu world that Śaṃkara assumed saw all beings on a vast transmigratory pilgrimage. Many thousands—even millions—of lives were required for the soul to complete its long journey. Eventually it would earn birth in the highest human estate. Having attained Brahmin-hood (brāhmaṇatva), the soul could then aspire to direct awareness of the supreme spiritual truth and, thence, final salvation (mokṣa). In this mythic view of the world, the Brahmin caste represented the "earthly Brahman" (bhaumasya brahmaṇaḥ), a class of beings at the pinnacle of the transmigratory hierarchy, above even the gods.[3] Religious maturity—one's stage in the great cosmic pilgrimage—and social status were seamlessly interlocked. The result: a system, authored by an elite, in which social exclusivity exerted a controlling influence on soteriology.

We know Śaṃkara as a thinker who attempts to accommodate both theism and an impersonal, trans-theistic non-dualism. He accomplishes this by providing two interrelated but non-continuous views of the world. Ranked hierarchically, these two ways of thought (buddhi-dvaya) assume as their counter-parts two distinct and unequal spiritual paths (dve niṣṭhe) with two separate, and again unequal, spiritual goals. Graded linkages to the Hindu system of hereditary social class give these two spiritualities concrete sociological manifestations. Finally, the capstone of this socio-religious structure is formed by restrictions that deny access to salvation to all but those at its very highest level.

Levels of Being and World of Theism

Any reader of Śaṃkara quickly realizes that he has much to say about ordinary religious life and especially the personal God (Īśvara), the individual soul (jīva), and their relationship. He adapts such notions to his non-dualist scheme by his well-known strategy of dividing religious truth into two levels, the absolute and the

---

[3]See ŚGBh, intro., Śatapatha Brahmāṇa 2.2.2.6, 4.3.4.4., 12.4.6, Mānavadharmaśāstra 9.319.

provisional. Thus he distinguishes the *para* ("higher") and the *apara* ("lower") *Brahman*. Of these two forms of *Brahman*, it is the lower that *BS* 1.1.2 describes as the source, the support, and the end of the world; it is the lower that is, in a word, the personal God. *Īśvara*, as the personal God is termed, is the transcendent, supreme *Brahman* appearing as if conditioned and personalized by virtue of its relation to *māyā*, the principle of phenomenality.

Although *māyā* is commonly translated as "illusion," Śaṃkara does not teach that the world is such. Within the higher and lower *Brahman*, he defines three levels of being of reality (*sattā*). These are: (1) the truly illusory (*pratibhāṣika-sattā*), (2) the empirical (*vyāvahārika-sattā*), and (3) the supreme (*pāramārthika-satta*), the last identified with the *para Brahman*.[4] The empirical (*vyāvahārika*) world, experienced intersubjectively and consistently through time, is much more than a bare illusion. While the few rare souls that attain direct intuitive realization of the supreme see the world to be false, it remains in place for all others.

Śaṃkara emphasizes repeatedly that as long as we have not attained the realization of the supreme *Brahman*, which dissolves all experience of duality, we cannot avoid recognizing the pragmatic truth of the empirical (*vyāvahārika*) world and all its relationships. The *vyāvahārika* realm, then, with its undeniable empirical reality, becomes the setting in Śaṃkara's system for all the symbols, activities, and emotions of ordinary religion. Accepting, for practical purposes, the full functionality of the lower *Brahman* as supreme personal Deity, he writes of the religion of theism and *bhakti* (devotion) with serious respect, even reverence. It was not without reason that a Christian theologian such as Otto was able to recognize this great Advaitin's relationship to the theistic worldview of the *Gītā*, the epics, and the *Purāṇas* as an "inner one."[5] Indeed, as P. Hacker has shown, it is almost certain that the sectarian background of Śaṃkara and his early followers was one stressing theistic worship of Visnu.[6]

Śaṃkara's Devaluation of Devotional Theism

Why, then, is there such a long history of bitter opposition to Śaṃkara's thought from the side of Hindu theism? Highly erudite

[4]See his commentary on *BU* 3.5.1 and Eliot Deutsch, *Advaita Vedānta: A Philosophical Reconstruction* (Honolulu: East-West Center Press, 1969), chap. 3.
[5]Rudoloph Otto, *Mysticism East and West* (New York: The Macmillan Company, 1970), p. 123.
[6]Paul Hacker, "Relations of Early Advaitins to Vaiṣṇavism," *WZKSO*, IX (1965): 147–154.

Advaitins will assert that the criticism of Advaita offered by the proponents of the various theistic forms of Vedānta results from a misunderstanding. There is, they will say, really no conflict between non-dualism and devotion. Only a more careful and open-minded consideration of Śaṃkara's thought is needed. Many articulate representatives of the Hindu tradition cherish this belief; even as so-phisticated a philosopher-scholar as Radhakrisnan subscribes to it. He is convinced: "While S. [Śaṃkara] is an absolute non-dualist in his metaphysics, he had great faith in *bhakti* or devotion to a personal God."[7]

Proponents of the idea that Śaṃkara was a devotionalist as well as a non-dualist commonly seek support in the so-called "minor works" (*prakaraṇas*) and the many devotional hymns (*stotras*) attributed to him.[8] Unfortunately, critical scholarship suggests that these works were almost certainly not written by Śaṃkara himself.[9] An examination of Śaṃkara's commentaries on the Upaniṣads, the *BS*, and the *BhG*, and his independent *Upadeśasāhasrī*—works which we are sure were written by him[10]—reveals a rather different attitude toward theism and devotional religion.

The reason for theistic opposition to Advaita is, in fact, quite obvious: Advaita removes the sense of ultimacy from both the devotional experience and its object. It leaves *bhakti* religion in a precarious position, in danger of losing much of its compellingness. "The Lord's being a Lord," says Śaṃkara, "his omniscience, his omnipotence, etc. all depend on limitations caused by adjuncts which are products of ignorance."[11] This kind of thinking does not quite place *Īśvara* in the realm of *maya*, but it does effectively remove him from the sphere of final truth in a way that a true devotionalist could not tolerate.

---

[7]S. Radhakrishnan, *The Brahma Sūtra: The Philosophy of the Spiritual Life* (London: George Allen & Unwin Ltd., 1960), p. 37.

[8]See Radhakrishnan, *Brahma Sūtra*, pp. 37–38.

[9]Even as orthodox a Hindu scholar as the highly respected Mahamahopadhyaya Gopi Nath Kaviraj writes regarding the hymns: "No doubt, most of these stotras must have been written by the later Śaṃkarācāryas but all of them have been attributed to the first Saṃkarācārya." In reference to the treatises he says, "It is difficult to decide about the authorship and genuineness of these works" (translated from the Hindi by A. P. Mishra, *The Development and Place of Bhakti in Śaṃkara Vedānta* [Allahabad: The University of Allahabad, 1967], p. 128). Of the *prakaranas*, Hacker, Ingalls, and Mayeda recognize only the *Upadeśasāhasrī* as genuine (Karl H. Potter, ed., *Encyclopedia of Indian Philosophies*, III, pp. 116, 320.)

[10]Sengaku Mayeda, *A Thousand Teachings* (Tokyo: University of Tokyo Press, 1979), p. 6.

[11]*BSŚBh* 2.2.14.

The Subordination of Bhakti

If the Lord himself suffers from penultimacy in Advaita, all the more does *bhakti*. Though the Advaitins themselves vary in the importance they place on devotional religion, all accept that it is but a preliminary step to the acquisition of liberating knowledge (*jñāna*). In this respect, it is a complement to, and on the same spiritual level as, *karma-yoga*, the *yoga* of dedicated action. Indeed, these two paths, which in practice are often mingled, form the Hindu counterpart of the traditional Christian "active life." And like the medieval Christian monastic, Śaṃkara subordinates the active life to the contemplative.[12] The way of pious action and devotion is the purgative way; it purifies the mind and prepares it for the final intuitive knowledge of the identity of *jīva* and *Brahman*.

Both *karma* and *bhakti* are therefore insufficient in themselves. The final gain from practicing them is the purity of mind that will eventually lead the seeker to the path of knowledge. If practitioners of *karma* and *bhakti* make the transition to *jñāna*, realization of *Brahman* may perhaps occur in this life. More likely, however, such individuals will have to wait for another birth or attain the requisite saving knowledge through the process known as *krama-mukti* ("gradual liberation"). The latter consists in the attainment after death of *brahma-loka*, the highest celestial realm from which there is not rebirth. Inhabitants of this heavenly paradise attain knowledge of the unconditioned *Brahman*, and hence *mokṣa*, when the whole universe, including *brahma-loka*, is dissolved at the end of the present cosmic cycle (*kalpa*).[13]

Knowledge the Sole Means to Liberation

Śaṃkara thus envisions two distinct styles of spirituality, two ways of religious life that parallel his two levels of being. For reasons that will become apparent, he calls them the way of engagement (*pravṛtti-dharma*) and the way of cessation (*nivṛtti-dharma*). These paths are for him of unquestionable sanctity, for they were founded by the primal acts of the Creator.[14] The way of engaged action and

---

[12]See Thomas Aquinas, *Summa Theologica*, 2a2ae, q. 179–182.

[13]*Krama-mukti* is originally postulated as the state gained by those who are devoted to meditations on the conditioned Brahman through various symbols as described in the Upaniṣads. Śaṃkara discusses it in detail in his commentary on BS 4.3–4. See also *BSŚBh* 4.3.10–11, 4.4.22, and 1.3.13; *ŚGBh* 8.23–27; and Potter, *Advaita*, pp. 26–27.

[14]*ŚGBh*, intro.

devotion corresponds to the metaphysical lower *Brahman*, the world of the merely empirical (*vyāvahāra*). The way to the supreme, *Brahman*, the *pāramārthika* realm, is the path of cessation, which leads to saving knowledge.

Śaṃkara never tires of repeating that the sole means to liberation is knowledge (*jñāna*): "The attainment of *mokṣa* is only from knowledge of reality."[15] Since the *jīva's* identity with *Brahman* is an eternally accomplished fact (*nitya-siddha*), realization requires only the removal of the soul's primal Ignorance (*avidyā*) through intuitive awakening. The way of knowledge, therefore, is the path to which all others lead.

The Seeker of Knowledge Rejects Devotion

An important part of the Advaitic spiritual practice—the *jñāna-niṣṭhā* ("discipline of standing firm in knowledge")—is the effort to remove "contrary ideas" (*viparīta-bhāvanā*). These comprise all dualistic ways of thinking and perception that contradict scriptural teaching of the Self's oneness and total inactivity. To succeed in the task of uprooting separative consciousness and immersing himself in the idea of oneness, the contemplative who has entered the path of knowledge must abstain from activities and modes of thought or feeling which reinforce dualism.[16] The practitioner of *jñāna-yoga* is taught to regard the Self as an inactive witness. He should see "the whole world and all knowledge born of difference as mere ignorance, like night."[17]

Chapter 12 of the *Gītā* is entitled "The Yoga of Devotion" (*bhakti-yoga*). In verses 1–12, Kṛṣṇa clearly asserts the superiority of devotion to the way of meditation on the impersonal Absolute. Śaṃkara chooses not to take this teaching at its face value. To save embarrassment to his way of knowledge, he treats the Lord's statement as mere hortatory praise. It is designed, he says, to inspire Ārjuna, who is not fit for the path of knowledge, to persist in the path of action and devotion. The superiority of "those who are identical with the Blessed Lord" (*bhagavat-svarūpa*) is so obvious, he feels, as to be beyond discussion.[18] Then follows a crucial passage:

---

[15]*ŚGBh* 2.20; see also *ŚGBh* 18.66.
[16]See, for example, *ŚGBh* 2.69, *ŚGBh* 5.1.
[17]*ŚGBh* 2.69.
[18]*ŚGBh* 12.4.

Here, having assumed a distinction between the Lord and the Self (*ātmeśvara-bheda*), the *yoga* which consists of concentrating the mind on the Lord in his universal form and performing works for the sake of the Lord is declared. The verse "If you are not able to do even this" [BhG 12.11] indicates that *karma-yoga* is the result of ignorance. So the Blessed Lord teaches that it should not be performed by those who meditate on the Imperishable and who see no distinction (*abheda-darśin*) [between the Lord and the Self]. Likewise, He teaches that meditation on the Imperishable should not be performed by the *karma-yogins*. . . . Those who meditate on the Imperishable are independent (*svātantrya*) in the attainment of liberation, . . . [while] the others [the devotees] are dependent on another (*pāratantrya*), dependent on the Lord (*īśvarādhīna*) . . .

Because the Blessed Lord is exceedingly desirous of Ārjuna's well-being, He recommends to him only the *yoga* of action which is based on the cognition of distinction and unconnected with right knowledge. [But] no one who has definitively known himself to be the Lord would wish to become a subordinate (*guṇa-bhāva*) of anyone. That would be a contradiction [of his knowledge].[19]

Those who wish to portray Śaṃkara as a teacher and practitioner of *bhakti* invariably overlook this interesting paragraph. Its implications, however, are important and are worth some elaboration.

First, the paragraph clearly defines the mutually exclusive presuppositions of Śaṃkara's two ways. Action-devotion is based on the idea of the distinction between the Lord and the Self (*ātmeśvara-bheda*). Further, it involves dependence upon an outside power (*pāratantrya*), the Lord, for salvation or deliverance. The path of knowledge, on the other hand, is founded upon the idea of the identity of the Lord and the Self, which Śaṃkara regards as true knowledge. Its followers do not think of themselves as dependent upon an external power for liberation, for they must dwell upon the idea that God is none other than the *pratyag-ātman*, the Self within.

Second, the fact that these paths have contradictory assumptions explains why persons are restricted to one or another of them. To follow both seriously and intently at the same time would be, for obvious reasons, psychologically impossible.[20] "The Lord has declared two distinct paths," Śaṃkara reminds us, "seeing the impos-

---

[19]*ŚGBh* 12.12.

[20]The renunciate, especially the adept who has realized his identity with Brahman, may participate in activities associated with the lower path. If he follows Śaṃkara's ideal, however, he does so in a detached way, merely for the sake of setting an example to others. See my further discussion below.

sibility of combining at once in a single person both knowledge, which depends on ideas of non-agency and unity, and action, which depends upon ideas of active agency and multiplicity."[21]

Third, the passage makes it clear that, for Śaṃkara and his school, the two paths are not of equal value. One way is for the "enlightened," the other for the "unenlightened."[22] The mode of action-devotion is the effect of ignorance (ajñāna-kārya). It has no connection with right knowledge (samyag-darśanānānvita). The aspirant on the higher path of jñāna is gripped by the truth "I am Brahman" (BU 1.4.10). Aspiring for total freedom (svātantrya), he will find the ideas of duality and dependence—fundamental to theistic devotion—abhorrent. As Śaṃkara says at the beginning of his commentary on the Kena Upaniṣad: "He who, having been led to Brahman, is consecrated to sovereignty does not wish to bow to anybody."[23] Śaṃkara is saying, almost in so many words, that theism and devotion, based on the dualistic distinction of God and soul, are products of spiritual ignorance suitable only for the lesser aspirants.

The Problem of Adhikāra

The significance of Śaṃkara's bi-level stratification of truth and spiritual discipline is intensified by the fact that, in classical Hinduism, entrance into a spiritual path is not entirely a matter of individual choice. Persons also—along with truths and yogas—are hierarchically graded. The tradition assumes that souls are all at different stages on their long transmigratory pilgrimage to the Absolute, and thus at different levels of spiritual capacity.

We encounter at this point in our investigation the concept of adhikāra ("eligibility"). While it plays a significant role in Hindu religious thought in general,[24] the idea is especially important in Advaita Vedānta. Jñāna-yoga is a demanding contemplative discipline. Only certain persons are thought to be suited to it. In addition to important social qualifications, which will be considered below, a long process of moral and spiritual preparation, either in this life or in previous lives, is presupposed.

---

[21]ŚGBh 2.10.

[22]"The Blessed Lord Nārāyaṇa, having divided the enlightened (vidvān) Saṃkhyas from the unenlightened (avidvān) men of action, makes them take two paths," ŚGBh 2.21; see also ŚGBh 3.4.

[23]na hi svārājye 'bhikṣito brahmatvam gamitaḥ kamcana namitum icchati.

[24]At the beginning of their works, authors of all Hindu religious treatises are required by tradition to state, among other things, the adhikārin, the type of person qualified to study the work.

At the beginning of the *BSŚBh*, Śaṃkara specifies the nature of the proper *adhikārin* for Vedāntic study. He outlines the "four-fold means" (*sādhana-catuṣṭaya*) that an individual must have to·qualify for this discipline. The strict requirements include: (1) the capacity to discriminate between the eternal and the non-eternal; (2) indifference to the rewards of action in this world or the next; (3) the "six-fold endowment," which includes equanimity, self-control, withdrawal from sensual pursuits, concentration, patience, and faith; and (4) the intense desire for liberation.[25]

Śaṃkara presents an even more detailed outline of prerequisites for the study of Advaita at *Upadeśasāhasrī* 2.1.2. There he indicates that his teaching is truly intended only for the mendicant monk (*parivrājika*) who is a *paramahaṃsa* ("supreme swan"), a title reserved, at least in the later tradition, for the highest and most respected order of renunciates (*saṃnyāsins*).[26] Those possessed of such qualifications, the highest aspirants (*uttamadhi-karins*), are utterly detached from the world and so able to contemplate their identity with the impersonal *Brahman*. Single-minded in their quest, they seek to remain aloof from everything in the realm of process and becoming, including both religious works and religious emotionalism. Only such individuals qualify for the path of knowledge, which forms the direct means to immortality. Other individuals, not possessed of such virtues, are eligible only for the paths of selfless action and devotion. According to Śaṃkara, Ārjuna was a seeker of this second sort. *BhG* 2.47 reads, "Your *adhikāra* is for action alone,"[27] and Śaṃkara's gloss has Kṛṣṇa saying directly to Ārjuna: "You are qualified for works alone, not for the path of knowledge."

Social Dimensions

In the orthodox Hindu world religion and society are inextricably bound together. In addition to—or as an assumed objective index of—an individual's spiritual maturity, the tradition takes into account his or her place in the social hierarchy, stage of life, and so on, when determining *adhikāra*. A person's spiritual duties, style of worship, and so on are commonly, especially in more conservative circles, limited and channeled by social criteria. This being the case,

[25]*BSŚBh* 1.1.1; see also *BSSBh* 3.4.27 and *Vedāntasāra* 15–26.
[26]Mayeda, *A Thousand Teachings*, p. 211.
[27]*karmany evādhikāras te.*

it is not surprising that Śaṃkara's levels of truth and practice have concrete social correlates. The question for eligibility for the path of knowledge, in particular, has several important sociological valences.

Limited Access to the Essential Vedic Revelation

The first has to do with caste and gender restrictions on the study of the Veda, specifically its later portion, the Upaniṣads. According to the orthodox tradition, in which Śaṃkara firmly stands, only initiated ("twice-born") adult males of the three upper classes are eligible for Vedic study. This restriction has implications of the highest consequence, because Vedic study, according to Advaita, is essential for Brahman-realization and the attainment of mokṣa. Saving knowledge of one's identity with the Absolute is dependent on access to scripture. It is a realization mediated verbally, through one channel only: the words of Vedic revelation (śruti). Śaṃkara writes: "The relation of Brahman and Ātman, stated in the passage 'That thou art,' cannot be known without the aid of scripture."[28] The "great sayings" (mahāvākyas) of the Upaniṣads, when heard (śruta) by the qualified pupil from the mouth of the competent teacher, are the necessary final catalysts of knowledge.

The highest yogic intuition (yogi-pratyakṣa), according to Advaita, cannot reveal Brahman directly.[29] Prakāśātman, an important follower of Śaṃkara, declares that even the "divine eye" granted to Ārjuna in the eleventh chapter of the BhG had access, not to Brahman, but to sensible things. Indeed, even the gods themselves do not attain the final liberation without hearing the Upaniṣadic sayings.[30]

Classical Vedanta is a mīmāṃsā, an "inquiry" into the meaning of the Veda. As such, it is a sister system of the Pūrva Mīmāṃsā (the "Prior Inquiry"), the study of Vedic ritualism. Known also as the Uttara Mimamsa (the "Subsequent Inquiry"), ancient Vedanta presupposed the completion of one's education in the ritual texts. In the pre-Śaṃkara tradition the inquiry into Brahman required, therefore, not only access to the Veda, but a good knowledge of both the scripture and its ancillary texts, the Vedāṅgas. In practice this often excluded—not merely women and sudras—but all except the male

---

[28]BSŚBh 1.1.4, p. 11.
[29]BSŚBh 2.1.3.
[30]K. Satchidanada Murthy, Revelation and Reason in Advaita Vedānta (New York: Columbia University Press, 1959), p. 138.

Brahmin. Although Śaṃkara denied the necessity of ritual study and performance, he was essentially a conservative and did little to alter the Brahmanical elitism of the Vedānta.[31] Indeed, he added a restriction that made the tradition even more exclusive. For him, only a select few male Brahmins were eligible for the path of knowledge.

Brahman-knowledge Requires Saṃnyāsa

Śaṃkara insisted that Vedantic study, and hence direct access to *mokṣa*, was available only to those who have entered the path of world renunciation (*saṃnyāsa*). In this, he opposed both the Vedic ritualists, who exalted the householder's life-stage as the foundation of true religious existence, and the teachers of traditional Vedānta, who felt that the active and contemplative lives should be combined (*jñāna-karma-samuccaya*).

For Śaṃkara, in short, the *yoga* of knowledge and the path of world renunciation were one and the same. Knowledge, he says, is for "the Paramahaṃsa mendicants, whose life is focussed on Brahman only."[32] It involves a life of constant "abiding in *Brahman*" (*brahma-saṃstha*).[33] This means, says the master, utter immersion (*parisamāpti*) in Brahman and the absence of all other activity. Those in the active life have scripturally ordained duties to perform; to omit them would be to incur sin. A life of total contemplative absorption is impossible for them. The mendicant, on the other hand, has formally renounced all such action. "The duties that he does have—tranquility, restraint, etc.—are conducive to abiding in Brahman, not opposed to it."[34]

Although it implied the transcendence of all social ties, *saṃnyāsa* was itself a highly institutionalized state of life. It had to be entered through a prescribed rite, "according to rule" (*yathā-viddhi*), under the sponsorship of an established preceptor. While it pointed to a state beyond all social restriction, the institution as it developed in

---

[31]J. A. B. van Buitenen, "On the Archaism of the *Bhāgavata Purāṇa*," in *Krishna: Myths, Rites, and Attitudes*, ed. Milton Singer (Chicago: University of Chicago Press, 1968), p. 33.

[32]ŚGBh 3.3.

[33]BSSBh 3.4.20. The term comes from *CU* 3.23.1: "He who dwells in Brahman attains immortality" (*brāhmasaṃstho 'mṛtatvam eti*).

[34]BSŚBh 3.4.20. Śaṃkara reserves special praise for the *naiṣṭhika-brahmācārin* ("complete celibate") who, like the great Advaitin himself, has renounced directly from the student stage and has never been entirely caught up in the illusions of the world (ŚGBh 2.72).

orthodox circles did not avoid the spirit of Brahmanical elitism. According to the tradition of which Śaṃkara was a preeminent spokesman, only male Brahmins were eligible for saṃnyāsa.[35]

In his commentary on BU 3.5.1 and 4.5.15, Śaṃkara states bluntly that only Brahmins, not Kṣatriyas or Vaisyas, are qualified for renunciation. The medieval exponents of religious law (dharma-śāstra), for the most part, concur in this opinion. A widely circulated verse from the Vaikhānasadharmapraśna reads: "The four life-states are that of the student, the householder, the retiree, and the renunciate; Brahmins have four, Kṣatriyas have the first three, and Vaiśyas the first two."[36] This issue was not without controversy, however, and indeed Śaṃkara's own disciple Sureśvara left a record of his disagreement with his master on this point.[37] Nevertheless, Śaṃkara's order of renunciates, the daśanāmīs, followed this rule strictly until the late medieval period, when certain orders admitted members of the warrior caste to defend the monks against militant Muslims.[38] Even in the late 16th century, the great Advaitin Madhusūdana Sarasvatī was arguing strenuously and at length for the validity of this restriction.[39] Of the ten daśanāmī orders, four are today still open to Brahmins only.[40]

This restrictive thinking is in fact the primary basis for Śaṃkara's argument that Ārjuna is ineligible for renunciation. Lord Kṛṣṇa in the Bhagavadgītā uses wide-ranging and carefully marshalled arguments to convince Ārjuna that he should remain in the tragic Bhārata war and fight. Śaṃkara by-passes most of these, reducing the remainder to what is little more than a narrow legalism. Renunciation by a member of the warrior caste, he insists, is prohibited (pratiṣiddha).

[35]See his commentary on BU 3.5.1 and BU 4.5.15. According to Upadeśasahasrī 2.1.2, the student of Advaita should be both a Brahmin and a paramahaṃsa.

[36]Quoted by J. N. Farquhar, "The Organization of the Sannyasis of the Vedanta," Journal of the Royal Asiatic Society of Great Britain and Ireland (July 1925), pp. 480–481.

[37]See his Vārttika on Śaṃkara's commentary on BU 3.5.1. See also Patrick Olivelle, Vāsudevāśrama Yatidharmaprakāśa: A Treatise on World Renunciation (Vienna: Publications of the De Nobili Research Library, 1977), II, p. 33.

[38]Farquhar, pp. 482–484; on this question, see P. V. Kane, The History of Dharma-śāstra (2nd ed.; Poona: Bhandarkar Oriental Research Institute, 1974), vol. II, pt. 2, pp. 942–944.

[39]See his Gūdhārthadīpikā commentary BhG 3.20; 5.5–6; 18.56, 63, 66.

[40]The Sarasvatī, Tīrtha, Āśrama, and Bhāratī orders, though the last has subsection open to non-Brahmins. See Wade Dazey, "The Daśanāmī Order and Monastic Life" (Unpublished dissertation: University of California at Santa Barbara, 1987), p. 575. For a general discussion of this issue, see P. V. Kane, The History of Dharmaśāstra, 2nd ed. (Poona: Bhandarkar Oriental Research Institute, 1974), vol. II, part 2, pp. 942–944.

It is quite simply a violation of religious law. Only those of Brahmin ancestry are permitted to renounce the world and take up the contemplative life, and for Ārjuna as a Kṣatriya to do so would amount to embracing the prerogative of another caste (*paradharma*). The profound questions of metaphysics, morality, and human psychology raised by Kṛṣṇa, if not ignored here, become subsidiary. The critical point is that Ārjuna cannot drop out of the battle because he is not a Brahmin.[41]

Not much thought is required to see the results of such constraints. If *mokṣa* is attained only by knowledge, only *saṃnyāsins* are eligible for knowledge, and only male Brahmins are qualified for *saṃnyāsa*, then the circle of those who can acquire *mokṣa* in this life is very small indeed. It includes only the few male Brahmins who have attained utter indifference to the world and taken vows of renunciation. To my knowledge Śaṃkara never says this in so many words,[42] and the restriction does not apply to *krama-mukti*, the "gradual" liberation through rebirth in *brahma-loka* described above. Moreover, Śaṃkara does concede there may be some exceptions to this rule.[43] Nevertheless the implication is clear. Saving rare exceptions, liberation is available directly only to male Brahmins who have, through renunciation, taken to the path of knowledge. Those in the active life have two lesser options. One is to be satisfied with *karma-mukti* and a wait of countless thousands of years until the current world-cycle comes to an end. The other is to hope for rebirth as a male Brahmin.

---

[41]*ŚGBh* 2.10.

[42]Other writers, however, do. In the introduction to Bhaskara's commentary on the *Gītā*, for example, we read:
"If women and the Śūdras were qualified for release, the caste eminence of the Brahmin would serve no purpose. . . . The Blessed *dharma* is only for Brahmans a way to release. The Śūdra, etc., cannot be elevated . . . nor can iron be made into gold by heating it some more . . . . Even the Kṣatriya and the Vaiśya do not have the same qualification for release as the Brahman. Therefore, only the Brahman has it" (trans. by van Buitenen, "Archaism," p. 32).

[43]See his comments on, for example, *BSŚBh* 3.4.36 and *BhG* 9.32. These exceptions appear to be only such as were necessitated by scriptural passages suggestive of the more liberal attitude of an earlier age, and which therefore called the later restrictions into question. The *ŚGBh* twice (at 2.10 and 3.20) discusses the case of Janaka, a King famed for his enlightenment. In both cases, however, Śaṃkara is noncommittal as to whether or not Janaka is truly a knower of Brahman. The traditional Advaitic explanation for the spiritual attainments of non-Brahmins who have either not renounced or not had access to the Veda is that such persons have done so in previous lives.

Śaṃkara's Hierarchical Socio-Religious Vision

Śaṃkara's bi-level metaphysic, with its ability to accommodate both theism and a trans-theistic Absolute, has rightly been regarded as an important contribution to world thought. Enthusiasts, however, should be aware of the elitist dimensions of this outlook. It is not so much a means of integrating both theistic and impersonalistic views of ultimacy, as a way of placing them in ranked juxtaposition. Śaṃkara does not encourage the theist to anticipate his or her eventual transition to the trans-theistic stance by consciously recognizing the provisionality of devotional worship. This would undermine the practice of bhakti. Nor—despite later developments in his own tradition[44]—does he encourage the follower of the discipline of knowledge to think theistically, as if difference were real, for this would undermine the monk's practice. In actuality, he presents two distinct ways of relating to ultimacy. These become continuous only for the enlightened being who looks back to see what the rest of the world is doing. Indeed, the whole doctrine is articulated from the point of view of the monk who has left the world of theistic religion behind. It allows him to understand bhakti and its function for others, but also teaches him to disdain it for himself.

The tradition itself, of course, regards this exclusivism as benevolently intended. If too many individuals were intensely seeking liberation, the Advaitin might say, the delusive energies which kept the universe in motion would begin to dissipate. What would happen to society if more than a small minority took to the path of knowledge? Even if it were socially workable, the radical liminality imposed by renunciation and non-dualistic modes of thought would be psychologically disastrous for most.

The authentic Śaṃkara Advaitin does not, and cannot, accept the validity of theism or devotional action for himself. They contradict the basic assumptions of his discipline. But he recognizes that they are good for others, those whose minds are more encumbered with worldly desires and distinctions, i.e., less "pure," than his. Indeed, for the sake of setting an example to others and encouraging them in

---

[44]There is no denying that devotional and Tantric elements (stotras, pūjā, mantra, yantra, etc.) became incorporated into the discipline of the Śaṃkara maṭhas (monasteries), perhaps at a fairly early date. To what extent this is a valid expression of the Advaitic path, and to what extent it is a concession to the religious interests of the aspirants and the surrounding Hindu culture, is not clear. I tend to believe that the latter is the case.

their path, the enlightened sage may willingly fulfill certain outward religious observances associated with *bhakti*. He knows that, through their devotion, the less qualified aspirants will eventually attain fitness for knowledge and, at last, *mokṣa*. *BhG* 3.20–26 teaches the superior (*śreṣṭha*) persons who have attained perfection (*saṁsiddhi*) to engage in action for the well-being of the world (*lokasaṁgraha*) and to set an example for the ignorant (*ajña*). Śaṁkara comments:

> He should not create confusion in the minds of the ignorant, the undiscriminating, who are attached to action. What, then, should he do? He should encourage them to enjoy, to do, all actions, the wise man himself performing in a disciplined way the very action [required] of the ignorant.[45]

Peter Berger points out that the detached, "as if" observance of social and religious customs, "out of consideration for the weaker spirit of the masses that has a need of these," is a common feature of world-relativizing mystical religion.[46] By way of illustration, he cites a passage from the *Theologia Germanica* that parallels the attitude of the Advaitin almost exactly: "Perfect men accept the law along with such ignorant men as understand and know nothing other or better, and practice it with them, to the intent that thereby they may be kept from evil ways, or if it be possible, brought to something higher."[47] The Advaitins' idea of *noblesse oblige* likewise includes supporting others in their worship, even though it may be opposed to his understanding of the ultimate truth of non-duality.

The complexity of Advaitic thinking on devotional, theistic religion is suggested by the fact that Śaṁkara is regarded, not only as the originator of the Advaita system, but also as an important reformer of popular Hinduism. His distaste for the active life, we are told, did not prevent him from traveling widely to spread his views, correct religious abuses, and combat Buddhist, Jain, and other heresies. He is venerated as the founding teacher (*sthāpanācārya*) of the six schools of worship (*ṣaṇmata*) recognized by the Smārta Brahmins. Each school is connected with one of the six most popular

---

[45]*ŚGBh* 3.25–26; see also *ŚGBh* 2.11.

[46]*The Sacred Canopy* (Garden City: Doubleday & Company, Inc., 1969), p. 98.

[47]Joseph Bernhart, ed., *Theologia Germanica* (New York: Pantheon Books, 1949), p. 159; quoted by Berger, p. 98.

Hindu deities,[48] and devotion to the deities of course implies the whole complex of theistic Hindu worship, both in the home and in the temple.

Śaṃkara may himself have actually engaged in such missionary activities to uplift the masses. It does not seem necessary to doubt tradition on this score. The point is that, if he did, he would have done so knowing that he was speaking down to the ignorant, to those not prepared for the truth of Advaita. The way of action and devotion, the goal of auspicious rebirth or heavenly paradise—in short, the whole theistic outlook—was for him the proper religion of the masses. It was the way most suitable and beneficial for those in the earlier stages of the great transmigratory pilgrimage back to *Brahman*, those—women, *śūdras*, and others—who did not have the proper *adhikāra* for higher things. The non-dualistic vision of identity with Brahman was, in his mind, to be reserved for the monastic elite.

ABBREVIATIONS

BhG	Bhagavadgītā
BS	Brahmasūtra
BSsBh	Brahmasūtra Śaṃkara Bhāṣya
	(Śaṃkara's commentary on the BS)
BU	Bṛhādaranyaka Upaniṣad
CU	Chāndogya Upaniṣad
SGBh	Śaṃkara Gītābhāṣya (Śaṃkara's commentary
	on the BhG)
WZKSO	Wiener Zeitschrift für die Kunde
	Süd-und Ostasiens

---

[48]The Śaiva, the Vaiṣṇava, the Śākta (worship of the Goddess), the Saura (worship of the sun), the Gāṇapatya (worship of the elephant-faced Gaṇapati), and the Kaumāra (worship of Kumāra or Skanda, the son of Śiva).

AMERICAN PROTESTANT
FUNDAMENTALISM

MIGHT OR MYSTERY: THE FUNDAMENTALIST CONCEPT OF GOD

Peter Phan

After almost a half-century of exile from the mainstream of American life, fundamentalism has emerged as a formidable power in politics, economics, education and media of communication. To its adherents and admirers, fundamentalism is a divinely-backed movement to establish the kingdom of God whereas on liberal lips it is a term of opprobrium and represents the worst forms of social and religious bigotry.[1]

So multifaceted and controversial a phenomenon as fundamentalism resists any neat definition.[2] In this essay I take fundamentalism to refer to the "twentieth-century movement closely tied to the

---

[1]Among the fiercest attacks on fundamentalism or the Religious Right, see Daniel C. Maguire, *The New Subversives: Anti-Americanism of the Religious Right* (New York: Continuum, 1982). The members of the "New Right," a term coined in 1975, are called "born again Fascists" and include Jerry Falwell's Moral Majority, the Religious Roundtable, Christian Voice, The Library Court, the National Conservative Political Action Committee, the Committee for the Survival of a Free Congress, the Heritage Foundation, and others. Richard Hofstadter has documented the link between anti-intellectualism in America and the rise of evangelicalism. See his *Anti-intellectualism in American Life* (New York: Alfred A. Knopf, 1962), pp. 55–136. Robert W. Shinn argues that fundamentalism is "a case of arrested development" on the basis of James Fowler's *Stages of Faith*. See his article "Fundamentalism as a Case of Arrested Development," *Fundamentalism Today: What Makes It So Attractive?*, ed. Marla J. Selvidge (Elgin, Illinois: Brethren Press, 1984), pp. 91–98. Alvin J. Schmidt criticizes the sexist theology of fundamentalism in "Fundamentalism and Sexist Theology," *Fundamentalism Today*, pp. 99–105. For an account of fundamentalist views of socio-political involvement and their critique, see *Piety & Politics: Evangelicals and Fundamentalists Confront the World*, eds. Richard John Neuhaus and Michael Cromartie (Washington, D.C.: Ethics and Public Policy Center, 1987).

[2]One needs to heed the warning of Stuart Rothenberg: "Anyone who lumps together charismatics, strict Fundamentalists (Separatists), born agains, liberal Evangelicals, and radical Evangelicals obviously does not understand Evangelicalism." See "Evangelicals Are Politically Diverse," *Piety & Politics*, p. 323.

revivalist tradition of mainstream evangelical Protestantism that militantly opposed modernist theology and the cultural change associated with it."[3] George Marsden has pointed out that while sharing certain traits common with other movements, such as Pietism, Evangelicalism, Revivalism, Millenarianism, and even Holiness and Pentecostalism, fundamentalism must be distinguished from them by its militant opposition to modernism.[4]

It is generally acknowledged today that the fundamentalist movement received its name and *impetus* from the twelve volumes known as *The Fundamentals*, which were widely circulated between 1909 and 1919.[5] The doctrines of *The Fundamentals* are often summarized in five points as follows: 1. The inspiration and infallibility of Scripture; 2. the deity of Christ (including his virgin birth); 3. The substitutionary atonement of Christ's death; 4. The literal resurrection of Christ from the dead; 5. The literal return of Christ in the second advent.[6]

---

[3]George Marsden, "Fundamentalism as an American Phenomenon: A Comparison with English Evangelicalism," Church History 46 (June 1977): 215. The accuracy of this definition is attested by the fact that fundamentalists recognize themselves in it. See The Fundamentalist Phenomenon: The Resurgence of Conservative Christianity, ed. Jerry Falwell with Ed Dobson and Ed Hindson (Garden City, New York: Doubleday, 1981), pp. 3–4. In practice the fundamentalists I have in mind are the early leaders of fundamentalism such as Jonathan and Charles Blanchard, William Bell Riley, Dwight L. Moody, Reuben A. Torrey, C. I. Scofield, William Jennings Bryan, Arnes C. Gaebelin, Billy Sunday, and Frank Norris; contemporary fundamentalists such as Jerry Falwell, Jim Robinson, Jimmy Swaggart, Pat Robertson, Hal Lindsey, and Tim La Haye; and members of various right-wing organizations mentioned in footnote 1.

[4]See George M. Marsden, Fundamentalism and American Culture: The Shaping of Twentieth-Century Evangelicalism: 1870–1925 (New York: Oxford University Press, 1980), p. 231, n. 4. This is one of the best historical studies of American fundamentalism. Besides Marsden's book, other works very helpful in establishing the history of fundamentalism are: George Dollar, A History of Fundamentalism in America (Greenville, S.C.: Bob Jones University Press, 1973); Ernest Sandeen, The Roots of Fundamentalism: British and American Millenarianism 1800–1930 (Chicago: University of Chicago, 1970); James Davison Hunter, American Evangelicalism: Conservative Religion and the Quandary of Modernity (New Brunswick, N.J.: Rutgers University Press, 1983), and Evangelicalism: The Coming Generation (Chicago: The University of Chicago Press, 1987); Evangelicalism and Modern America, ed. George M. Marsden (Grand Rapids: Eerdmans, 1984); The Evangelical Tradition in America, ed. Leonard I. Sweet (Macon: Mercer University Press, 1984); and Piety & Politics. A short, helpful article is David A. Rausch's, "Fundamentalist Origins," Fundamentalism Today, pp. 11–20.

[5]The twelve volumes, entitled The Fundamentals: A Testimony to the Truth (Chicago, 1910–1915), contain 90 articles written by 64 authors. It was published as a whole by The Bible Institute of America, Los Angeles, 1917, and is currently printed by Baker Book House, Grand Rapids.

[6]See The Fundamentalist Phenomenon, p. 7. Note that these five points had been taught earlier with slight variations by the 1910 Presbyterian General Assembly. The

Given the fact that the doctrine of God does not directly appear in the list of the five fundamentals, it would seem to be inappropriate to question the fundamentalist doctrine of God. In fact, most of its opponents have chosen to attack its teaching on plenary, verbal inspiration, and biblical inerrancy which they consider to be the basic flaw of its doctrinal system.[7] In this essay, I propose to evaluate the theological stance of fundamentalism from a different angle. I shall attempt first of all to go behind the explicit theological teachings of fundamentalism and its socio-political praxis, and to discern the concept of God undergirding such theory and praxis. Secondly, I shall inquire whether that concept of God suffers from any inadequacies which may be remedied by a recourse to the traditional Christian teaching on God's incomprehensibility and our analogical knowledge of him as Holy Mystery.[8]

A further preliminary remark is in order. Though I restrict my considerations to the fundamentalist movement as an American Protestant phenomenon, fundamentalism as a militant opposition to modernism and cultural changes attendant upon it is also found in other religious traditions, for instance Roman Catholicism, Judaism, and Islam, at least in recent times. Hence, my critique of the fundamentalist concept of God applies *mutatis mutandis* to the theology of these religions as well, in particular of Roman Catholicism, with which fundamentalism will be compared in the second part of the essay, especially with regard to the concept of God as mystery.

Assembly adopted a five-point declaration of "essential" doctrines known as "the five points of fundamentalism." See Marsden, *Fundamentalism and American Culture*, p. 117. The five points of fundamentalism are sometimes expanded to fourteen. See S. G. Cole, *The History of Fundamentalism* (New York: Richard R. Smith, 1931), pp. 52–64.

[7]See, for instance, Daniel Maguire, *The New Subversives*, chapter three entitled "The Bible as Oracle and Ouija Board," pp. 57–86. Sociologist James D. Hunter, assessing the present trends of evangelicalism, also starts out with the doctrine of biblical inerrancy. See his *Evangelicalism: The Coming Generation*, pp. 20–25. For nuanced and respectful critique of fundamentalist understanding of biblical inspiration and inerrancy, see Vincent Branick, "The Attractiveness of Fundamentalism," *Fundamentalism Today*, pp. 21–30; Edgar A. Towne, "Fundamentalism's Theological Challenge to the Churches," ibid., pp. 31–45; and Adela Yarbro Collins, "Fundamentalist Interpretation of Biblical Symbols," ibid., pp. 107–114.

[8]Two works that attempt to grapple with fundamentalism's concept of God are Gabriel Fackre, *The Religious Right of Christian Faith* (Grand Rapids: Eerdmans, 1982) and Nicholas F. Gier, *God, Reason, and the Evangelicals: The Case Against Evangelical Rationalism* (Lanham: University Press of America, 1987). Fackre's treatment is helpful but too brief, focussing basically in God's holiness and love (pp. 98–103), whereas Gier's is shaped by his sympathy toward process theology (pp. 79–95).

The God of Fundamentalism:
Anti-intellectualism and Empirical Rationalism

Ever since the Scopes trial, partially as the result of Clarence Darrow's ridicule and H. L. Mencken's satire, the image of a fundamentalist as an anti-intellectual, obscurantist, rural, small-town Protestant is etched in the popular imagination. Perhaps the label is not entirely undeserved, since anti-intellectualism, together with its paranoid style, as the works of R. Hofstadter have shown, is a feature of American revivalism of which fundamentalism was a part.[9] The distrust of learning was expressed by Bryan in his memorable phrase: "It is better to trust in the Rock of Ages, than to know the age of the rocks; it is better for one to know that he is close to the Heavenly Father than to know how far the stars in the heavens are apart."[10] A similar spirit was shown by the famed preacher, Billy Sunday: "I don't know any more about theology than a jack-rabbit knows about ping-pong, but I'm on my way to glory."[11]

However justified the charge of anti-intellectualism may be, it must be pointed out, as Marsden has persuasively argued, that it is a mistake to regard the fundamentalist controversies as basically a conflict between science and religion and that the fundamentalists are opposed to science. The fundamentalists rejected evolution, not because it was a science but because it was, in their view, not scientific enough. For them science was the result of observation and classification of facts, and of demonstration based upon them. Darwinism, so far as they could see, was neither. The fundamentalists' model of science is based upon that of Bacon and Newton. Arthur T. Pierson, one of the leading representatives of dispensationalism, declared at a prophetic conference in 1895: "I like Biblical theology that does not start with the superficial Aristotelian methods of reason, that does not begin with an hypothesis, and then warp the facts and the philosophy to fit the crook of our dogma, but a Baconian system, which first gathers the teachings of the work of God, and then seeks to deduce some general law upon which the facts can be arranged."[12]

---

[9]See Hofstadter, *Anti-intellectualism in American Life*, pp. 117–136 and *The Paranoid Style in American Politics, and Other Essays* (New York: Alfred A. Knoff, 1963).

[10]Quoted in Marsden, *Fundamentalism and American Culture*, p. 212.

[11]Ibid., p. 130.

[12]Ibid., p. 55, with emphasis added. Marsden has well documented the popularity of Bacon as philosopher among many Protestant Americans and the commitment to

This acceptance of Baconian inductive scientific method and Newtonian physics was coupled with a thoroughgoing adoption of Scottish Common Sense Realism as developed by Thomas Reid. This philosophy rejects the theory of ideas developed by Locke and his followers according to which we know the real world by means of interposing ideas. We do not apprehend external things directly, but only through ideas of them in our minds. Reid, on the contrary, argues for the immediacy of perception, memory, and thought of external reality and affirms that any person possessed of common sense would recognize his point. This philosophy with its emphasis on common sense as the universal means to know the truth suited the nineteenth-century American anti-elitist and democratic temper. By means of common sense first principles are apprehended by all and sundry, the uneducated as well as the learned, and from these principles certain conclusions can be deduced to establish the religious, moral, political and economic orders.[13]

One cannot help notice here an ironical twist in the history of fundamentalism. Originally a militant repudiation of rationalistic modernity and often ridiculed as an obscurantist movement, fundamentalism ended up by accepting the thoroughly rationalistic presuppositions of empirical scientific methodology.[14] Its paradigm is still that of Bacon insofar as it regarded scientific progress as the result of a simple accumulation of new and more advanced theories as more facts are discovered by objective observation. Its science is, to use Thomas Kuhn's expression, a "normal science." Fundamentalists assume that the universe is governed by a rational system of laws, like Newton's laws of physics, guaranteed by an all-wise and benevolent Creator, and that the task of science is to discover such laws by means of careful observation, division, and classification. With Common Sense philosophy fundamentalism insists on the perspicuity of nature. The universe is conceived as an open book, with no hidden mysteries, that anyone with native common sense can decipher correctly. Human language about the world, therefore,

empirical scientific analysis in American colleges throughout the first two thirds of the nineteenth century. See ibid., pp. 55–62; 212–221. See also Theodore D. Bozeman, *Protestants in an Age of Science: The Baconian Ideal and Antebellum American Religious Thought* (Chapel Hill: University of North Carolina Press, 1977).

[13]Marsden has shown the influence of Scottish Common Sense philosophy in American fundamentalism. See ibid., pp. 14–17.

[14]This has been pointed out by several authors. See, for instance, Nicholas F. Gier, *God, Reason, and the Evangelicals*. The book is a sustained case against what the author calls "evangelical rationalism."

is basically univocal and unambiguous. And this is true not only of the visible world but of the Bible and the invisible sphere of divinity as well.

"The God of Power and Might: I Know Him Well"

The fundamentalist construal of divinity is rooted in the biblical source as seen through rationalistic lenses and mediated by a particular cultural setting. As Gabriel Fackre puts it, it is "characterized by a functional *perspective* drawn by human experience, routed through one segment of church life and tradition, and making selective use of Scripture to validate its secular *source* and sectarian *resource*."[15] The socio-cultural setting of fundamentalism is that of crisis, indeed one of cataclysmic proportion; its ecclesial resource is sectarian, separatist, and militant; its biblical source is predominantly apocalyptical.

The rich soil in which fundamentalism germinated and prospered is a time of crisis especially in the areas of politics, economics, and religion. Marsden writes: "Fundamentalists shared with the discontented intellectuals of the 1920s, if little else, a sense of the profound spiritual and cultural crisis of the twentieth century. Unlike their more disillusioned contemporaries, however, they had very definite ideas of where things had gone wrong. Modernism and the theory of evolution, they were convinced, had caused the catastrophe of undermining the Biblical foundations of American civilization."[16] In post-World War I America (1919–1920) an overwhelming atmosphere of crisis, fueled by demobilization, labor disputes and strikes, and the "Red Scare" of Bolshevism, gripped the mass and made it a ready audience for the prophecies of gloom and doom pronounced by fundamentalists such as Arno C. Gaebelein, Oliver W. Van Osdel, William B. Riley, David S. Kennedy, Curtis Lee Laws, A. C. Dixon, and Frank Norris. Contemporary fundamentalists on their part are determined not to be outdone by their predecessors in their predictions of impending disasters. Jerry Falwell, Tim La Haye, and Hal Lindsey have warned us of the imminent thermonuclear annihilation and universal conflagration.[17]

---

[15]*The Religious Right of Christian Faith*, p. 33.

[16]*Fundamentalism and American Culture*, p. 3. See also chapter 17.

[17]See Falwell's *Listen, America!* (New York: Doubleday, 1980); La Haye's *The Battle for the Mind* (Old Tappan, N.J.: Revell, 1980); Hal Lindsey's *The Late Great Planet Earth* (New York: Bantam Books, 1983).

In prophesying unprecedented disasters fundamentalists appeal of course to their only source, the Bible, in which they see literal and detailed predictions of the disasters. Lindsey asserts that the Bible contains at least five hundred predictions of the second coming of Christ which he associates with the destruction of the world.[18] But a careful study of the fundamentalists' use of the Scripture shows their overwhelmingly selective use of apocalyptic texts such as Ez 36–38; the books of Dan and Rev; Matt 24; 1 Thes 4; 2 Thes 2; 1 Cor 15; 2 Tim 3–4 and 2 Pet 2.[19]

Not only is the Scripture appealed to selectively but it is also used to foster a militant, sectarian, and separatist posture toward culture and the world. Earlier fundamentalists, especially those of premillennial persuasion, advocated withdrawal from the condemned age and social involvements ("The Great Reversal"), separation from other Churches they considered not sufficiently orthodox, and militancy in defense of the truth. Marsden suggests that fundamentalism may be seen as providing American Protestants of English and Scottish ancestry with an analogous immigrant experience of other ethnic groups as they created their own equivalent of the urban ghetto "subculture with institutions, mores, and social connections that would eventually provide acceptable alternatives to the dominant cultural ethos."[20] Even contemporary fundamentalists, who spend their energy and wealth to transform the world by means of preaching, communications media, and political pressure, are basically sectarian and separatist. In The Fundamentalist Phenomenon: The Resurgence of Conservative Christianity, Jerry Falwell, Ed Dobson, and Ed Hindson argue that what makes fundamentalism a strong and successful movement is, among other things, missionary zeal, absolutism, and separation.[21]

What image of God would be fashioned by this rationalistic reading of apocalyptic Scripture in sectarian, separatist, and militant fashion in a context of crisis? It is a God of power and might, a sectarian and triumphant God, a moral God who rewards the good and punishes the wicked, and above all a God who is holy but is no mystery at all.[22]

---

[18]The Late Great Planet Earth, pp. 159–160.

[19]See Gerald Grace and Stephen Bosso, "The Language of Fundamentalism," Proceedings of the Forty Second Annual Convention of the Catholic Theological Society of America 42 (Louisville: Bellarmine College, 1987), p. 127.

[20]Fundamentalism and American Culture, p. 204.

[21]The Fundamentalist Phenomenon, (Garden City, N.Y.: Doubleday, 1981), pp. 173–176.

[22]See H. J. Bridges, The God of Fundamentalism (New York: Scribners, 1925), pp. 3–58.

It is remarkable how often fundamentalists use royal and military metaphors to describe God. Marsden points out that military imagery pervades fundamentalist literature in the 1920s. T. T. Shields' pamphlet, an address delivered in New York City in 1925, was entitled "The Necessity of Declaring War on Modernism."[23] One of the most popular fundamentalist songs declares God to be king: "I am a stranger here, within a foreign land; my home is far away, upon a golden strand; Ambassador to be of realms beyond the sea—I am here on business for my King."[24] Two of the influential journals were named *The King's Business* and the *Sword of the Lord.* Contemporary fundamentalists also display a marked predilection for military titles for their works: *Capturing a Town for Christ* (Falwell), *The Battle of the Mind* (La Haye), *The Battle for the Bible* (Lindsell), and *Combat Faith* (Lindsey). They do not hesitate to describe their cause as a "holy war."

The God of fundamentalism is a warrior god. Falwell believes that God participated in the 1967 "miraculous six-day war" and suggests that Israel would not have won "had it not been for the intervention of God almighty."[25] Hal Lindsey finds in the Bible a detailed "countdown to Armageddon" and sees total destruction of the planet earth as part of God's providential plan in installing his kingdom. Jesus, who according to Lindsey, came the first time as a lamb will come back as a lion in the midst of earthquakes and thermonuclear blasts.

In order to vanquish the forces of Satan, the fundamentalist God must possess omniscience and omnipotence, the two divine attributes most frequently invoked by fundamentalist literature. God knows and ordains every single detail of the plan which he has communicated to his saints, and has the power to carry it out exactly as he intends. God's omnipotence is most clearly displayed in his ability to act in history by direct intervention without human collaboration. The absence of human agency is implicit in its doctrine of Scriptural inspiration, creationism, substitutionary atonement, and apocalyptic eschatology. This conception of God as the Omniscient and the Omnipotent is reflected in and influences the fundamentalist stance on national defense, law and order, and the family. The fundamentalists' lobbying for nuclear build-up as the best deterrent to war is, I suggest, linked up with their conception of God as the

---

[23]*Fundamentalism and American Culture*, p. 286, n. 26.
[24]Ibid., 205.
[25]*Listen, America!*, p. 97.

powerful warrior. The salvation of America lies in its powerful weapons because the powerful God stands only with the powerful.

The fundamentalists' stance for strong military build-up is matched by their policy of law and order in the state of which God the Remunerator is the ultimate guarantor. The strict connection between their concept of God and their politics of law and order was unwittingly affirmed by a statement of Moody Monthly in 1923 in reference to evolutionism and Bolshevism: "As a matter of fact," said the magazine, citing Frank Norris as an authority, "evolutionism is Bolshevism in the long run. . . . It eliminates the idea of a personal God, and with that goes all authority in government, all law and order."[26] Again, Falwell's objection to democracy ties law and order to Almighty God: "Today we find that America is more a democracy than a republic. Sometimes there is mob rule. In some cases a vocal minority prevails. Our Founding Fathers would not accept the tyranny of a democracy because they recognized that the only sovereign over men and nations was Almighty God. A republic is a government of law."[27]

The image of power and might, in fundamentalist imagination and ethos, is associated with maleness. It is only natural therefore that fundamentalists hold up the model of the traditional family in which the father and husband is regarded as the authority and the mother and wife as his helpmate as normatively ordained by (the male) God. Larry Christenson declares: "The family belongs to God. He created it. He determined its inner structure. He appointed for it its purpose and goal. . . . to bring glory and honor to God."[28] Of course, the family designed by God is one in which, Christenson continues, "a wife's primary responsibility is to give of herself, her time and her energy to her husband, children and home."[29] In day-to-day life, Don Meredith affirms, the husband has the "final say," though he should not abuse his power because it derives from "divine order and not natural superiority."[30] Dan Benson leaves no doubt as to where the husband's authority comes from: "God said it! It is your duty to 'take charge'—to maintain a home atmosphere where your wife and children have no question of who is watching out for them. You are responsible for the mood and direction of your

[26]Quoted in Marsden, Fundamentalism and American Culture, p. 209.
[27]Listen, America!, p. 44.
[28]The Christian Family (Minneapolis: Bethany Fellowship, 1970), p. 11.
[29]Ibid., p. 47.
[30]The Total Man (Wheaton, IL.: Tyndale, 1981), p. 144.

household."[31] Dorothy Pape, in her *In Search of God's Ideal Woman*, affirms that motherhood is for woman "a challenging career," her "unique and most obvious role."[32] A final witness to the intrinsic link between the fundamentalists' view of God as Power and Might and their conception of family: "What is the key to success for a married woman?" asks Don Meredith. "First it is constantly seeking God's perspective on life. Secondly, it is modeling a personal plan for utilizing herself and *serving* her husband, children and home. At last it is allowing God to meet her needs through her husband, children and opportunities found through the home."[33]

It is patent then that the God of fundamentalism is made to sustain and support a particular socio-political, economic, and ethical order. Conversely, the fundamentalist option for a strong national defense, law and order, and "traditional family" reflects a view of God as all-powerful and all-knowing, patriarchal and dominant.

This divine power, however, is not exercised for the benefit of all. The God of fundamentalism is highly sectarian and separatist. Of course separation and sectarianism are the hallmarks of any revivalist movement, but American fundamentalism grounds its separation and sectarianism in a worldview that is, as Gabriel Fackre and Nicholas Gier have persuasively argued, radically dualistic and Manichean.[34] This Manichean tendency is manifested in fundamentalism's pessimistic view of the body, the woman, sexuality, and the material world in general; its lack of ecological ethics; its emphasis on sin and the rule of Satan; its suspicion of government; and its premillenarian eschatology.

The God of fundamentalism, then, is presented as a holy deity who demands total conformity to a particular system of morality. Such an emphasis on God's holiness is certainly biblical. There is however another divine attribute which, in Fackre's judgment, fundamentalism has left in the shadow, and that is God's love. In Fackre's memorable phrase, for fundamentalism "while God *may* be loving, God *must* by holy."[35]

---

[31]*Becoming One* (Nashville: Thomas Nelson Publishers, n.d.), p. 130.

[32]*In Search of God's Ideal Woman* (Donners Grove, IL.: Inter-Varsity Press, 1976), p. 331.

[33]Don Meredith, *Becoming One*, p. 156. Emphasis added. There is some truth to Daniel Maguire's excessively caustic characterization of a fundamentalist family, "Blue Print for a Fascist Family," *The New Subversives*, pp. 114–137. For a critique see "Fundamentalism and Sexist Theology," *Fundamentalism Today*, pp. 99–105.

[34]See Fackre, *The Religious Right and Christian Faith*, pp. 42–44, 50–52; Nicholas Gier, *God, Reason, and the Evangelicals*, pp. 7–8.

[35]*The Religious Right of Christian Faith*, p. 100.

While agreeing with Fackre's assessment that fundamentalism neglects God's *suffering* love, I would like to point out that the fundamentalist conception of God's holiness is narrowly moralistic and misses the more basic biblical meaning of God's holiness, that is, God as the ontological mystery, as the *mysterium tremendum*. Such a defect in fundamentalist theology, I contend, is not accidental; rather it is rooted in its empirical rationalism derived from Scottish Common Sense philosophy and Baconian scientific methodology as has been discussed above. In a debate with other Christians a fundamentalist would say, to parody a famous retort: "Our God is the God of power and might. We know him well."

This utter lack of a sense of God as *mysterium tremendum* can be illustrated in two examples, one somewhat banal, the other central to millennial fundamentalism. When we were informed by Oral Roberts that God had told him to raise an exact amount of dollars, otherwise God would take him away, one possible reaction was to write him off as a religious con man out to extort money from poor, uninformed folks. But a more fundamental response, at least from the *theological* standpoint, is to ask: How on earth could he know that God has ordered him to raise money, and in that exact amount?

More importantly, fundamentalist eschatology is not content with answering the questions of *what* the end is and *why* it is the fulfillment of the divine promises, but as Fackre points out, it also wants to know (and thinks it knows) where, how, who; it supplies the "*timetable, map, blueprint,* and *playbill* of the end."[36] Eschatology becomes, to use Rahner's terminology, "apocalyptic," a technicolor preview of coming attractions, a reading of future events back into the present.[37]

The Radical Weakness of Fundamentalism: The Lack of Mystery

Sociologist James Davison Hunter, in his recent book *Evangelicalism: The Coming Generation*, has shown that younger members of evangelicalism (i.e., theologically conservative and orthodox Protestantism, not synonymous with but inclusive of fundamentalism) have to a certain degree moved away from the separatist, sectarian,

---

[36]Ibid., 88.

[37]See Karl Rahner, "The Hermeneutics of Eschatological Assertions," *Theological Investigations*, Vol. VI, trans. Kevin Smyth (New York: Crossroad, 1982), pp. 323–346. For a discussion of Rahner's eschatology, see my *Eternity in Time* (Selingsgrove: Susquehanna University Press, 1988).

and militant conservative posture of fundamentalism. In theological matters, for instance, there has been a "deghettoization" process regarding biblical inerrancy, salvation of non-Christians, and social activism.[38] Even Jerry Falwell and his associates Ed Dobson and Ed Hindson have acknowledged that fundamentalism suffers from such weaknesses as little capacity for self-criticism, over-emphasis on external spirituality, resistance to change, elevation of minor issues, the temptation to add to the gospel, over-dependence on dynamic leadership, excessive worry over labels and associations, absolutism, authoritarianism and exclusivism.[39] Such an honest confession demonstrates a commendable sense of realism.

Still, if religion is about ultimate concern, and if theology is a critical reflection on this experience of ultimate concern, then the strengths and weaknesses of a particular religion and theology ought to manifest themselves primarily in their doctrine about God, their *logos* about *theos*. It is my contention, therefore, that the various deficiencies of fundamentalism, which have been loudly and sometimes stridently castigated by its liberal opponents, are rooted in its doctrine of God. This doctrine, often not explicitly thematised, legitimates and in turn is corroborated by the socio-political, economic, and ethical choices fundamentalists made, especially since the late seventies.

The strengths of the fundamentalists conception of God, it must be acknowledged, are manifold. It conveys a clear message about God's sovereignty, both in knowledge and power, and God's providential actions in world history. Consequently it fosters in the believers a sense of purpose, confidence, and corporate identity.

---

[38]See *Evangelicalism: The Coming Generation*, (Chicago and London: The University of Chicago Press, 1984), pp. 19–49. "There is less sharpness, less boldness, and, accordingly, a measure of opaqueness in their theological vision that did not exist in previous generations (at least to their present extent)" (p. 46). As regards their views on work, morality, and the self, "far from being untouched by the cultural trends of post-World War II decades, the coming generation of Evangelicals, in their own distinct way, have come to participate fully in them" (p. 74). Concerning family, "the Evangelical family specialists . . . advocate and defend a model of the family that is said to be traditional but in fact has no real historical precedent . . . in the name of a constituency that has largely abandoned it in favor of an androgynous/quasi-androgynous model" (p. 114). In politics, most evangelicals "believed that the Moral Majority is politically ineffectual, that it will lose influence in the years to come, and that it overall harms the cause of religion in America" (p. 147). For essays on how fundamentalism attempts to come to grips with contemporary American culture, see *Evangelicalism and Modern America*, ed. George Marsden (Grand Rapids: Eerdmans, 1984).

[39]See *The Fundamentalist Phenomenon*, pp. 179–185.

Furthermore, the fundamentalist God is a just and moral deity who enacts moral laws and demands ethical behavior on the part of the faithful. God's retributive justice will unfailingly reward the good and punish the wicked. Though in principle God can carry out the divine plan without human cooperation, God's call to holiness evokes a deep and sincere commitment to live by what is perceived as divine commandments, especially in the sphere of sexual and family morality and retributive justice.[40]

Nevertheless, as has been pointed out above, the fundamentalist conception of God's holiness and justice is onesidedly moralistic, and ignores the more basic biblical meaning of God's justice as saving justice and of God's holiness as absolute transcendence. There are different resources in contemporary theology with which the fundamentalist doctrine of God can be corrected and enriched. Feminist theology can challenge it to incorporate an androgynous approach to divinity. Liberation theology can help it perceive the biblical God as defender and liberator of the poor and the oppressed. Process thought can complement its vision of the holy God with that of God as suffering love. Ecological theology can help it retrieve the idea of God as protector of creation.

I have chosen to concentrate on one strand of the Christian theology of God which, though very widespread and repeatedly taught by classical theologians, is absent in the fundamentalist concept of God. The tradition I refer to maintains that God is holy mystery, and as such incomprehensible. It should be obvious by now why such a tradition is ignored by fundamentalism. For one thing, fundamentalism, despite its occasional anti-intellectualist rhetoric, is rationalist through and through. Recall that fundamentalism rejected evolutionism because it was not scientific enough. Another reason is that fundamentalism regards human language about God as either merely metaphorical or basically univocal.

It may be objected that the fundamentalist notion of God as Power and Might highlights divine transcendence, and therefore God as the *mysterium tremendum*. Indeed, the point must be conceded. But the fundamentalist notion of mystery is a rationalist one, and is similar to that found in Roman Catholic neo-scholastic theology. The resemblance is not at all coincidental. Both reacted against and yet were profoundly indebted to German rationalism and the En-

---

[40]G. Fackre well explained the strengths of the fundamentalist conception of God. See his *The Religious Right of Christian Faith*.

lightenment. Karl Rahner, in his 1959 ground-breaking essay "The Concept of Mystery in Catholic Theology," has subjected that notion of mystery to a searching criticism. He notes that it has three features: mystery is regarded as the property of a statement; mysteries are seen as plural; and mysteries are thought of as *provisionally* incomprehensible.[41] It is not difficult to see how the fundamentalist notion of mystery fits this description. Its doctrine of revelation is propositional;[42] there are many—at least five—fundamental mysteries; and the divine mysteries, especially those concerning the end-time, are not only provisionally incomprehensible but also have already been revealed in detail to God's prophets and saints. This understanding of mystery is, in Rahner's judgment, defective for three reasons. First, it is based on an extremely narrow concept of *ratio* and therefore fails to see that mystery is the very goal at which reason arrives when it attains its perfection by becoming love. Secondly, it fails to show the religious and supernatural character of the strict mysteries of Christian revelation. And, thirdly, it is unable to exhibit the intrinsic connections of the Christian mysteries with each other in a coherent whole.

The point, then, is to retrieve a genuine concept of God as mystery. This involves at least an examination of the nature of our analogical language about God and the notion of God's incomprehensibility. It is out of the question here to provide even a cursory presentation of these two theological issues. However, drawing upon the teachings of Thomas Aquinas and Karl Rahner, I shall present some very brief suggestions as to how our language about God and God's incomprehensibility should be understood.[43]

Mystery and Analogy

The doctrines of God's incomprehensibility has a long and distinguished pedigree, from the apophatic theology of the Fathers (in

---

[41]See *Theological Investigations*, IV, pp. 38–48.

[42]See Avery Dulles, *Models of Revelation* (New York: Doubleday, 1983), pp. 36–52. Dulles points out the similarities between "conservative Evangelicalism" represented by such theologians as Benjamin B. Warfield, Gordon H. Clark, James I. Packer, John Warwick Montgomery, and Carl F. H. Henry and "Catholic Neo-Scholasticism" represented by authors such as Reginald Garrigou-Lagrange, Christian Pesch, and Hermann Dieckmann and such ecclesial documents as Vatican Council I's *Dei Filius*, the anti-Modernist documents, and Pius XII's *Humani Generis*.

[43]On Thomas I am indebted to Gregory Rocca's as yet unpublished doctoral dissertation "Analogy as Judgment and Faith in God's Incomprehensibility: A Study in the Theological Epistemology of Thomas Aquinas" (Washington, D.C.: The Catholic University of America, 1989). The work contains an extensive bibliography (some 40 pages).

particular Gregory of Nyssa) with its roots in Jewish (Philo) and Hellenistic (Plotinus) thought to Pseudo-Dionysius' *theologia negativa* to Thomas Aquinas' *via negativa*.[44] Thomas' teaching on God's incomprehensibility can be summarized in two theses: "no created intellect naturally possess a quidditative knowledge of God's essence; no created intellect can ever possess, in principle, a comprehensive knowledge of God's essence."[45] Thomas grounds God's incomprehensibility in his infinity, that is in his nature as *ipsum esse subsistens*. Because of his faith in the beatific vision Thomas agrees that the blessed possess a quidditative knowledge of God, but even this knowledge is not quidditative in Aristotle's sense, i.e. definitional or comprehensive. In heaven God is personally and immediately present to the blessed, but no truly Aristotelian quidditative, i.e., comprehensive, knowledge of God is ever possible, not even by grace. Making a distinction between *totum* and *totaliter* Thomas affirms that the blessed know God *totum* but not *totaliter*.[46]

As regards Thomas' threefold way to God (*causalitas, negatio,* and *eminentia*), it is important to note that the *via negationis* (Thomas' other terms for *negatio* are *remotio, segregatio, ablatio, separatio*) is not a step beyond affirmative or cataphatic theology but a *moment within it* qualifying and correcting its positive affirmations about God.[47] In other words, it is not the case that we first have a positive theology by way of *causalitas*, and then a negative theology by way of *negatio*; rather the *via negativa* corrects and qualifies the *via affirmativa* throughout. The root of the *via negativa*, for Thomas, is God's incomprehensibility, the fact that he is *ipsum esse subsistens*.

Rahner accepts Thomas' theology of God as incomprehensible mystery. Nevertheless he finds the neoscholastic textbook notion of

---

[44]For a brief and clear summary of the development of the theology of God's incomprehensibility before Thomas Aquinas, see Rocca's work, pp. 52–88.

[45]Ibid., p. 89.

[46]See Ibid., pp. 132–136.

[47]See Ibid., pp. 173–176. The *via negativa* can be effected in three distinct ways: qualitative negation, when something is denied of God absolutely because of its incompatibility with divine nature (e.g. God is not corporeal); objective modal negation, when a perfection (the *res significata*) is affirmed of God but its finite nature is denied of him; subjective modal negation, when perfection is denied of God because of our mode of signifying (the *modus significandi*) does not belong to God. Thus, when we say "God is not wise," this statement is true insofar as our *modus significandi* is concerned (subjective modal negation), but it is not true insofar as the *res significata* is concerned (objective modal negation). Qualitative negations are absolute denials while modal negations are relative denials; objective modal negations remove the finite mode of creature from God while subjective modal negations remove those imperfections arising from our manner of understanding and signifying.

mystery inadequate. I have already mentioned above Rahner's analysis of the three features of the neoscholastic notion: mystery as propositional, plural, and provisional. Of the three the last one is of special interest here. Neoscholasticism—and we may add fundamentalism—share the view that mysteries are provisionally incomprehensible because, Rahner argues, they hold a common understanding of what knowledge is. For them knowledge is intellectual penetration into and mastery of the object to be known. For knowledge so conceived the incomprehensibility of God appears as an unfortunate limitation, to be accepted with resignation perhaps, imposed by God's infinity and freedom upon the beatific vision of the blessed. Rahner argues that this understanding of God's incomprehensibility is seriously defective. First, it leads to a kind of 'practical atheism,' that is, indifference on the part of human beings toward the mystery of God since it is something that ultimately does not concern them, even in the beatific vision. Secondly, it does not show how the beatific vision can truly be a state of perfect fulfillment and happiness for humans since they are ultimately and forever trapped within their finite capacity of knowledge in the face of the incomprehensible God. Thirdly, it fails to preserve the incomprehensibility of God's freedom even though ostensibly it attempts to ground God's incomprehensibility in his freedom. For, if God's free decisions remain hidden only to the extent that they are not revealed in the history of salvation and are not intrinsically related to his incomprehensibility, then they possess no special hiddenness beyond that which belongs to any free personal decision before it is made known in history.[48]

Rahner's own understanding of mystery takes its point of departure from the self-transcendence of human beings in knowing and loving. On the basis of his transcendental Thomism he argues that the goal or 'Whither' of human transcendence in knowledge and love is the nameless, the indefinable, the unattainable, or the Holy Mystery. This Holy Mystery, which can never be grasped as an object, is nevertheless the condition of possibility for each act of knowing and loving of the finite subject. Human beings, in their knowledge and love, are inescapably directed toward this distant and elusive mystery. Of course, in revelation and grace, and ultimately in the beatific vision, this distant mystery has bestowed itself

_____

[48]See "The Hiddenness of God," _Theological Investigations_, Vol. XVI, trans. David Morland (New York: The Seabury Press, 1979), pp. 231–235.

on humanity as nearness and accessibility. However, Rahner reminds us, it is near and accessible as an abidingly incomprehensible mystery. Grace makes God accessible to us in the form of holy mystery and as the incomprehensible.[49]

The permanence of God's incomprehensibility in the beatific vision then is not an unfortunate limitation imposed upon the finite intellect which is incapable of mastering a residue of the intelligible. In comparison with the unthematic knowledge of the overwhelming mystery of the *deus absconditus*, the categorical mastery and comprehension of finite objects is but a secondary and derivative form of knowledge. Failure to understand this point will prevent one from ever grasping the nature of God's incomprehensibility. The following statement of Rahner will serve as a salutary caution against fundamentalism's "idolatrous" view of deity:

> As long as we measure the loftiness of knowledge by its perspicuity, and think that we know what clarity and insight are, though we do not really know them as they truly are; as long as we imagine that analytical, co-ordinating, deductive and masterful reason is more and not less than experience of the divine incomprehensibility; as long as we think that comprehension is greater than being overwhelmed by light inaccessible, which shows itself as inaccessible in the very moment of giving itself: we have understood nothing of the mystery and of the true nature of grace and glory.[50]

Rahner's doctrine of God as incomprehensible, infinite, indefinable, and ineffable Holy Mystery makes it clear that incomprehensibility is not to be thought of as *one* among the many attributes that can be predicated of God as God's 'names' despite divine simplicity. Rather it is the attribute in the light of which and by which all other statements about God must be understood and radically qualified. Our cataphatic theology of God (as well as our anthropology) must be subjected to a stringent critique by our transcendental knowledge of God as the incomprehensible infinity and the infinite incomprehensibility who has bestowed God's self precisely as infinitely in-

---

[49]See "The Concept of Mystery in Catholic Thought," *Theological Investigations*, Vol. IV, pp. 48–60.

[50]Ibid., p. 56. See also "An Investigation of the Incomprehensibility of God in St. Thomas Aquinas," *Theological Investigations*, Vol. XVI, pp. 244–254. For further elaborations of Rahner's view, see my *Eternity in Time*, pp. 142–149; and Paul Wess, "Die Inkomprehensibilität Gottes und ihre Konsequenzen für die Gotteserkennis bei Thomas von Aquin und Karl Rahner," Doctoral dissertation, University of Innsbruck, 1969.

comprehensible nearness and accessibility. This doctrine of divine incomprehensibility has ramifications for our entire theological enterprise; insofar as fundamentalism is concerned I would like to draw attention to three areas.

First of all, our language about God. It is a common teaching, at least among Catholic theologians, that our language about God is neither univocal nor equivocal but analogical. It predicates of God terms whose meanings, when compared with their usage in the realm of finite realities, are neither the same (univocal) nor totally different (equivocal).[51] There is danger, however, of thinking that analogy is a hybrid between univocation and equivocation[52] or that analogy is ultimately univocal because there is in it an element of similarity, a common logos, a cryptic core of univocity.[53] Fundamentalists implicitly hold the second view, and consequently they run the risk of destroying God's transcendence.

To understand analogy correctly, Rahner argues, one must take a clue from the relationship between Absolute Being and finite realities as manifested in what he calls "transcendental experience."[54] By it Rahner means the experience in which the human subject, in its acts of knowledge and love of a particular (categorical) object, is at the same time implicitly (unthematically, transcendentally) conscious of itself and open to the unlimited expanse of all possible reality. In other words, human beings insofar as they are incarnate spirits or spirits in the world, possess two characteristics: they are conscious of themselves in every act of knowing and loving a particular object (unthematic self-presence) and they are oriented toward being in general (self-transcendence). It is the second characteristic that is of interest here. Human beings in the process of abstraction to achieve universal knowledge form concepts from the sensation of particular things. The universal form that is arrived at by means of the abstractive process and represented in the concept

---

[51]See Gregory Rocca, "Analogy as Judgment and Faith in God's Incomprehensibility," pp. 9–50; 178–271.

[52]A simplified presentation of analogy, often found in neo-scholastic philosophy textbooks, may be guilty of the view that analogy is a subsequent midpoint between univocity and equivocity.

[53]This is the objection of Wolfhart Pannenberg to analogy. See his *Habilitationsschrift* "Analogie und Offenbarung: Ein kritische Untersuchung der Geschichte des Analogiebegriffs in der Gotteserkennis" (1955) and *Basic Questions in Theology*, Vol. II, trans. G. H. Kehm (Philadelphia: Fortress, 1970–71), pp. 171–173.

[54]For a brief definition of transcendental experience, see Karl Rahner, *Foundations of Christian Faith*, trans. William Dych (New York: The Seabury Press, 1978), pp. 20–21.

is shown to be more than or not to be exhausted by the sensible singulars that embody it. The individual objects are seen as limited, as not fulfilling all the possibilities of the essential form. But how can the intellect categorically or explicitly know that particular things are limited unless it also grasps unthematically or implicitly being in general as the background or horizon against which these things are known and loved? Rahner detects therefore in the human intellect and freedom an inborn dynamic movement toward being in general as the condition of possibility for every act of knowledge and love. This act of unobjective tension toward being Rahner calls *Vorgriff*, the anticipatory reaching out for Absolute Being or God without ever grasping it as an object.[55]

It is in the context of this self-transcendence toward the asymptotic goal of knowledge and love that analogy must be understood. It is not to be taken as a subsequent midpoint between univocation and equivocation, or a secondary, inexact middle position between clear concepts that are either affirmed or denied. Rather it is rooted in the tension or transcendence of the human spirit toward Holy Mystery as given in the transcendental experience. So says Rahner:

> . . . Because transcendental experience is the condition which makes possible all categorical knowledge of individual objects, it follows from the nature of transcendental experience that the analogous statement signifies what is most basic and original in our knowledge. Consequently, however familiar equivocal and univocal statements are to us from our scientific knowledge and from our everyday dealings with the realities of experience, they are deficient modes of that original relationship in which we are related to the term of our transcendence. And this original relationship is what we are calling analogy: the tension between a categorical starting point and the incomprehensibility of the holy mystery, namely, God. We ourselves, as we can put it, exist analogously in and though our being grounded in this holy mystery which always surpasses us.[56]

It is clear then that even our analogical affirmations about God bring us right back into the bosom of divine incomprehensibility. This essentially analogous character of our being and our knowledge

---

[55]For Rahner's philosophical explication of this metaphysics of knowledge, see *Spirit in the World*, trans. William V. Dych (New York: Herder and Herder, 1968). For an excellent exposition of Rahner's philosophy, see Thomas Sheehan's study, *Karl Rahner: The Philosophical Foundations* (Athens: Ohio University Press, 1987).

[56]*Foundations of Christian Faith*, pp. 72–73.

of God can serve as a corrective to fundamentalist hermeneutics which has absorbed from the Enlightenment a preference for clear, logical language in which words have one precise meaning and has lost sight of what Adela Yarbro Collins calls "its depth character, its plurality of meanings, and its soft focus in truth."[57] Such a corrective is particularly needed in fundamentalist rhetoric about God's omnipotence and maleness. Its predilection for royal metaphors and its image of God as an all-powerful warrior must be radically qualified by the concept of God as a weak and compassionate fellow-sufferer, such as found in kenosis Christology as well as in liberation and process theologies. Fundamentalist patriarchal imagery of divinity, escorted by its anti-woman ethos, must be purified by a more faithful adherence to the Bible which also portrays God in female images. But, more fundamentally, every attempt to capture God in a comprehensive definition must be firmly rejected by recourse to the mystics' experience of God as "neti neti" and as:

> Nothing, nothing, nothing,
> Nothing, nothing, nothing,
> And even on the mountain, nothing.[58]

The second area in which fundamentalism stands corrected in light of the doctrine of divine incomprehensibility is the theology of history. The God as Holy Mystery functions in history as the Absolute Future. Rahner holds that in contrast to intramundane future (or Moltmann's *Futurum* or *Futur*) the Absolute Future (or Moltmann's *Adventus* or *Zukunft*) cannot be known in advance or planned or controlled. Whereas the intramundane future, both that which comes about because of a predetermined evolutionary pattern and that which results from human creativity and freedom, is achieved in space and time by human efforts, the Absolute Future bestows itself freely and unexpectedly, as the incomprehensible and infinite mystery. This Absolute Future is God, or more precisely, God-with-humanity-and-world, a Future that cannot be dominated or manipulated.[59] This does not mean that Christians should not take an active part to make the world a better place for future

---

[57]"Fundamentalist Interpretation of Biblical Symbols," *Fundamentalism Today*, p. 112.

[58]*Vida y Obras de San Juan de la Cruz*, ed. Crisogono de Jesus, Lucino del SS. Sacramento and Matian del Niño Jesus, 3rd ed. (Madrid: Biblioteca de Autores Cristianos, 1955), p. 492.

[59]See my *Eternity in Time*, pp. 189–197.

generations by means of well-planned policies and concerted actions. On the contrary. For Christians, as Vatican II teaches, faith in the afterlife, far from inhibiting them from building up the world or making them uninterested in the well-being of their fellows, is an incentive to do these very things, for "it is here that the body of a new human family grows foreshadowing in some way the age which is to come."[60] What is to be strongly discouraged is the propensity, not rarely found among fundamentalist preachers, to invest a particular policy with the aura of divine sanction or appeal to some private communication with the deity for its justification. The God of fundamentalism is thus turned into a powerful lobbyist of pro-capitalism, pro-gun, pro-capital punishment, pro-nuclear weaponry, pro-Israel, pro-traditional family, pro-American nationalism and so on. These policies must be pragmatically evaluated on their own merits, and the Absolute Future should not be manipulated into their service.

The third area is eschatology. Fundamentalist apocalyptic requires extensive reconstruction. God as Holy Mystery forbids any kind of anticipatory report on what will transpire at the end-time. Eschatology, Rahner points out, deals with the *hidden* future; it does not give us an advance description of the after life. Just as protology is an etiological account of the present situation of sin and salvation and not a historical report on what occurred at the beginning, so too eschatology is an etiological interpretation from the present situation of grace projected forward into its future stage of fulfillment and not an anticipatory description of what will happen at the end of time and beyond. Further, eschatology should not be regarded as an *additional* and quite different revelation about the future which can be gauged by means of a contorted exegesis of certain biblical texts. Rather, it should be seen as christology and anthropology transposed into their future mode of fulfillment whose nature is concealed in the *deus absconditus*.[61]

In this respect fundamentalist apocalyptic, especially in its pre-millennial form, must be recognized for what it is. As Marsden has convincingly shown, premillennial dispensationalism as developed by John Nelson Darby, W. E. Blackstone, James H. Brookes, and C. I. Scofield, especially in their interpretation of the books of Daniel and

---

[60]See *Gaudium et Spes*, no. 39, in *Vatican Council II*, ed. Austin Flannery (Collegeville, MN: Liturgical Press, 1984), vol. 1, p. 938.

[61]See Rahner, "The Hermeneutics of Eschatological Assertions," *Theological Investigations*, Vol. IV, pp. 332–337 and my *Eternity in Time*, pp. 67–74.

Revelation (the "seventy weeks," the "anti-Christ," the "Beast," the "great tribulation," the "rapture," the "Armageddon") is the result of applying the old Baconian view of science and Common Sense philosophy to biblical texts. The Scripture is modeled after the Newtonian view of the physical universe: created by God, it is a self-contained unity governed by exact laws which can be deciphered by careful analysis and classification (the doctrine of "perspicuity of Scripture").[62] A *sanatio in radice* of such a rationalistic apocalyptic is possible only by a recourse to the doctrine of God as incomprehensible mystery.

In conclusion, to the claim of fundamentalists, "My God is the God of Power and Might, I know him well!" theologians whose thought is nurtured by the Christian tradition of apophaticism and mysticism can respond in doxology: "Our God is Holy Mystery; we only know what God is not, but God's incomprehensibility *is* our blessed happiness."

---

[62]See *Fundamentalism and American Culture*, pp. 48–55.

CREATION SCIENCE: RELIGION AND SCIENCE IN NORTH AMERICAN CULTURE

Anne Clifford

"Creation Science" is a North American phenomenon initiated by some fundamentalist Protestants in an attempt to preserve what they believe to be essential to the Christian character of the culture of the United States. The founders of creation science militantly oppose explanations of life and its origins in terms of natural development. Instead, they look for explanations that stress supernatural intervention in the origin of all things and are compatible with their emphasis on the inerrancy of the Bible.[1] Creation science is promoted as a theory of origins alternative to the biological evolutionary theories taught in our nation's public schools. The promotion of creation science textbooks represents one of the most recent of a series of battles waged by fundamentalists to exert influence on American culture in the twentieth century. The creation science battle has been waged most visibly in the 1980's in our nation's courts.

On June 19, 1987 the United States Supreme Court struck down the Louisiana Balanced Treatment Act,[2] which sought to require that creation science be given equal time with the teaching of evolution science in the state's public schools. By its action the highest court of the land agreed with two lower courts that the creation science law passed by the Louisiana legislature in 1981 violated the First

---

[1]For an analysis of the elements that characterize fundamentalist Protestantism see James Barr, *Fundamentalism* (Philadelphia: Westminster Press, 1978). For an analysis of the patterns this movement adopted for relating to American culture in its early years, see George M. Mardsen, *Fundamentalism and American Culture: The Shaping of Twentieth-Century Evangelicalism, 1870–1925* (New York: Oxford University Press, 1980).

[2]The full title of the act is: "The Balanced Treatment for Creation-Science and Evolution Science."

Amendment of the U. S. Constitution which prohibits the establishment of religion. The majority opinion of the court expressed the
judgment that creation science has as its primary purpose the advancement of a religious doctrine.[3]

The Louisiana act was based very closely on an Arkansas act with
the same title passed earlier in 1981. The latter was struck down by
the U.S. District Court in 1982. Both pieces of legislation signaled a
major shift in emphasis among fundamentalist Christians which can
be traced to the 1960's. Instead of trying to outlaw evolution on
religious grounds by direct appeal to the Bible, they developed a
new science, "creation science," and argued for equal time with
evolution in the public school curriculum.

There was a very practical reason for this tactical move. In 1968
the U.S. Supreme Court declared the 1928 Arkansas anti-evolution
law unconstitutional. This law was part of the ground swell of
legislation in the South after the Scopes-Monkey trial of 1925. In
1967 this law was tested by the Arkansas Education Association, an
affiliate of the National Education Association. In conjunction with
AEA, Susan Epperson, a first year biology teacher, chose a text
which included evolution. The judge ruled in favor of Epperson, but
the verdict was reversed by the Arkansas Supreme Court. In 1968
the United States Supreme Court ruled that the law violated the
establishment clause of the First Amendment of the Constitution.[4]
The creationists had good reason for suspecting that any legislation
that would argue that evolution should not be taught in the schools
would meet the same fate.

Creation science raises numerous questions abut the social forces
at work in North American culture. Often theologians fail to understand the ramifications of the creationists' positions for theology in
the North American context. In this paper some basic questions
about creation science will be addressed: what creation science is,
how creation science developed, and what creationists want included in the text books placed in the hands of our nation's children,
and very importantly, why. Finally, we will engage in an inquiry

---

[3]Colin Norman, "Supreme Court Strikes Down 'Creation Science' Law as Promotion
of Religion," *Science* 236 (June 1987): 1620.

[4]For a full explanation of the events that led to the U.S. Supreme Court decision see
Edward Larson, *Trial and Error: The American Controversy Over Creation and
Evolution* (New York: Oxford University Press, 1985), pp. 98–119. According to
Larson, the primary reason for the Arkansas Supreme Court decision was that the
anti-evolution law was "a valid exercise of the state's power to specify the curriculum
in its public schools" (p. 107).

into what creation science might be saying to the theologian about how our society views science and religion. Langdon Gilkey, theological witness at the trial which took the "Balanced Treatment Act" off the legislative books in Arkansas, will be our guide, not only because he gave testimony at this trial, but because the relationship of science and religion in our culture has been a recurring theme in his thirty years of theological writing.[5]

Creation Science: Its History and its Tenets

A succinct definition of "creation science" can be found in the Arkansas Balanced Treatment Act (#590). The act states:

"Creation science" means the scientific evidences for creation and inferences from those scientific evidences. Creation-science includes scientific evidences and related inferences that indicated (1) Sudden creation of the universe, energy, and life from nothing; (2) The insufficiency of mutation and natural selection in bringing about developments of all living kinds from a single organism; (3) Changes only within fixed limits of originally created kinds of plants and animals; (4) Separate ancestry for man and apes; (5) Explanation of the earth's geology by catastrophism, including the occurrence of a worldwide flood; and (6) A relatively recent inception of the earth and living kinds.[6]

---

[5]Gilkey, a theologian at the University of Chicago, served as a theological witness for the American Civil Liberties Union at the "Creation-Science" trial in Little Rock Arkansas, December 7–9, 1981. His account of this experience and his analysis of its theological implications are found in *Creationism on Trial: Evolution and God at Little Rock* (Minneapolis: Winston Press, 1985). In addition he has published the following articles on creation science: "Creationism: the Roots of the Conflict," in *Is God a Creationist?*, ed. Roland Mushat Frye (New York: Charles Scribner's Sons, 1983), pp. 56–67; an abbreviated version of the same article can be found in *Christianity and Crisis* 42 (1982): 108–15; "The Creationist Issue: A Theologian's View," in *Cosmology and Theology*, Concilium 166, eds. David Tracy and Nicholas Lash (New York: Seabury Press, 1983), pp. 55–69; "The Creationist Controversy: The Interrelation of Inquiry and Belief," *Science, Technology and Human Values* 7 (1982): 67–77; and "Religion and Science in an Advanced Scientific Culture," *Zygon* 22 (1987): 165–178. He first addressed this question in *Maker of Heaven and Earth* (Garden City, N.Y.: Doubleday and Company, 1959) and has frequently addressed it since.

[6]Section 4 of Arkansas Act #590; the full text of this act can be found in *Science, Technology and Human Values* 7 (1982): 11–13. In regard to #4, the act does not specify exactly how old the earth is supposed to be, but in court a span of 6,000 to 20,000 years was given in testimony. The age widely accepted by the scientific community is a minimum of 4 1/2 billion years.

To circumvent court rulings based on the First Amendment, creation science is presented without any reference to a Creator-God.
However, the list of postulates obviously has Genesis 1–11 as an
unmentioned reference. Without explicitly mentioning a Creator,
creation scientists believe that they have set forth a scientific model
which combines geological, paleontological and biological research
into a science which is an alternative model to evolution through
natural selection.

How did creation science develop into its 1981 form? The history
of creation science can be traced to the 1960's when, in the wake of
the Soviets' successful launch of "Sputnik" (1957), the U.S. government funded new "Biological Sciences Curriculum Study" texts
which used evolution as the unifying perspective. The materials
were widely adopted by school boards across the nation, but not
without protest. Since the 1968 U.S. Supreme Court rejection of the
Arkansas Law of 1928, it has been clear that it is impossible to argue
that the Genesis account be taught in public schools because of its
explicitly religious character. Therefore, a new strategy was devised,
namely to teach the elements of the Genesis account of origins as
science, as "creation science," and as an alternative to the evolutionary account.

The strategy for advancing creation science as an alternative to
evolution began in California. In the late 1960's parents of school-
aged children, Nell Segraves and Jean Sumrall, appealed to the
California School Board to require public school books in the state
to include creation along with evolution. Their crusade for creation
science in the public school curriculum was fueled by the U.S.
Supreme Court's ruling in the Madalyn Murray O'Hair case which
protected atheist students from required prayer in the public
schools. Segraves reasoned that if the rights of atheists could be
protected, surely the rights of Christians should also be honored.
This line of argument persuaded the California Board of Education.[7]

If creation science was to be taught in California schools, text
books and teachers educated in this science were needed. In 1970
the Christian Heritage College of San Diego was founded by Henry
Morris as an educational center explicitly committed to the concept

---

[7]These women were associated with the Creation Research Society which was
founded in 1963 to bring about the union of Evangelical Christianity and science.
Ronald L. Numbers, "The Creationists," Zygon 22 (1987): 153.

of creation science.[8] The college catalogue states that the faculty supports the inerrancy of Holy Scripture, especially in these areas: 1) special creation of the world in six days, 2) biblical account of the entrance of sin into the world, 3) the Noachian Flood, and 4) origins of nations and languages at the tower of Babel.[9]

In conjunction with the Christian Heritage College, the Creation-Science Research Center was founded in 1970 to lobby for the creation science cause, although later it became a separate entity. In 1972 the Institute of Creation Research was also started for scientists engaged in creationism research and educational writing.[10] Since its foundation the Institute has published numerous books and pamphlets.[11] In addition, the Institute has developed a creation science text book for use in high school.[12] Members of ICR not only reject evolution, they also completely reject "Biblical higher criticism."

A few highlights from a creationist high school text, *Biology: A Search for Order in Complexity*, shed light on how creation scientists view science and the relationship between science and religion.

---

[8]Morris, director of the Institute for Creation Research, has a doctorate from the University of Minnesota and was a professor of hydraulic engineering at Virginia Polytechnic Institute, Blacksburg Virginia for thirteen years.

[9]Cited in Warren D. Dolphin, "A Brief Critical Analysis of Scientific Creationism," in *Did the Devil Make Me Do It?: Modern Perspectives on the Creation-Evolution Controversy*, ed. David B. Wilson (Ames, Iowa: University of Iowa Press, 1983), p. 23.

[10]Ibid. According to Dolphin, the Creation Science Research center is directed by Kelly Segraves and is primarily engaged in political action. The Institute of Creation Research is at Christian Heritage College and includes 20 Ph.D.'s as staff or consultants. Some of the members of ICR have doctorates in the sciences earned at institutions such as Yale, the University of California at Berkeley and Ohio State.

[11]For a full account of the tenets of Creation Science see Henry M. Morris, *Scientific Creationism* (San Diego: Creation-Life Publishers, 1974). This book contains documentation for creation science viewpoints in biology and geology, particularly the geological processes following the "Flood of Noah." The flood is viewed as a global catastrophe and is explained by the concept "hydraulic cataclysm," a concept coined by Morris (pp. 117–18). See also Duane T. Gish, *Evolution? The Fossils Say No!* (San Diego: Creation-Life Publishers, 1973). In this book Gish disputes the evolution of humans from apes based on what he believes is the absence of transitional forms in the fossil records. Pamphlets from the Institute include, "Resolution for a Balanced Presention of Evolution and Creationism," and "A Two-Model Approach to Origins: A Curriculum Imperative." Creation science literature has been spread with missionary zeal throughout the globe. Many of the titles published by the Institute have been translated into Chinese, Czech, Dutch, French, German, Japanese, Korean, Portuguese, Russian and Spanish. See Ronald L. Numbers, "The Creationists," 157.

[12]John N. Moore and Harold Schultz Slusher, *Biology, A Search for Order in Complexity* (Grand Rapids, Michigan: Zondervan Publishing Co., 1970). This text was accepted for use in Indiana schools. However, in 1977 the Indiana Superior Court ruled that it was unacceptable because it promoted fundamentalist Christian doctrine. See Dolphin, p. 24.

In the first chapter, "The Scientist and His Methods," the goal of the scientist is presented:

> Scientists endeavor to establish a valid interpretation of *facts* that has not been previously known. A scientist is not satisfied with mere data or *facts*, which consist of observations and measurements, but he desires to find out the reason for the *facts* being what they are.[13]

The description of scientific method places emphasis on "the facts." The scientist begins by stating a problem and then "gathers *many facts*" that may have a bearing on the problem. The scientist then forms an hypothesis and "*more facts* are gathered" and if possible experiments are performed. If the facts gathered are consistent with the suggested hypothesis, the scientist concludes that the explanation is valid and he/she publishes the results.[14]

Later in the chapter the authors caution their readers about the distinction between observed facts and interpretations drawn from facts. They write:

> If the data cited is (sic) correct we are inclined to think that the hypothesis or theory based upon it is also correct. This seems logical, but at times it may not be true, for another hypothesis might explain the data more accurately. Another theory might be used to integrate and relate all the known facts.[15]

The reader is especially cautioned about the interpretation of origins and is directed to accept an explanation, not on the grounds that it is made by a famous man (i.e. Darwin), but on the basis of "what is demonstrated by the facts."[16]

According to George M. Marsden, creation scientists with their strong emphasis on facts are "in a broad sense Baconians." They adhere to the epistemology which stems largely from the writings of Francis Bacon, the seventeenth-century philosopher of science, who taught that science is an inductive process of observation and experimentation conducted to discover the *facts* of nature. In reaction to Aristotelian deductive science, Bacon stressed the accumulation of facts as opposed to the building of hypotheses and generally held hypotheses in disdain. Creation scientists hold that, while hypothe-

---

[13]*Dolphin*, p. 4. Emphasis added.
[14]Ibid., p. 5.
[15]Ibid., p. 8.
[16]Ibid., pp. 8–9.

ses might be used to guide experimentation, speculative hypotheses are beyond the realm of true science.[17]This emphasis on science as a branch of knowledge concerned with observed facts is not limited to high school text books. In an essay in *Scientific Studies in Special Creation*, Henry M. Morris writes:

> Science . . . involves facts which are observed and laws which have been demonstrated. The scientific method involves experimental reproductivity, with like causes producing like effects. It is *knowledge*, not inference or speculation or extrapolation.[18]

The line of argument provides Morris with a basis for arguing that, since science deals with data which can be verified in the present by observation, theories which extrapolate from these to data speculate about the distant past cannot be proved. Therefore, such speculations cannot be "properly included in the definition of science."[19]

On the basis of a Baconian perspective on science, *Biology: A Search for Order in Complexity* addresses the question of the limitations of science. By mutual consent scientists agree to deal only with sense observations and to limit themselves to those things that can be demonstrated. The limitations are further specified: "This excludes supernaturalism from scientific study. The scientist does not deal with God as a subject of science; he deals with the laws and principles God has established."[20]

The text also addresses theories of biological change, and begins by presenting evolution and creation as two opposing "doctrines" or

[17]George M. Marsden, "Understanding Fundamentalist Views of Science," in *Science and Creationism*, ed. Ashley Montagu (New York: Oxford University Press, 1984), p. 97. For more on Bacon's contribution to scientific method and to the earliest of the scientific revolutions see I. Bernard Cohen, *Revolution in Science* (Cambridge, Mass: Harvard University Press, 1985), pp. 147–60. In assessing Bacon's contribution to the development of modern science Cohen indicates that it lies in the concept of "crucial experiment." Its shortcoming lies in the stress on science as residing in facts. Cohen notes that while it is appropriate to stress the accumulation of facts, Bacon's procedure downplays the conceptual innovations that have proved to be even more important for the advancement of science than facts. "The real growth modes of science are conceptual and theoretical rather than merely factual" (pp. 149–150).

[18]The emphasis on knowledge is his. See Henry M. Morris, "Science versus Scientism in Historical Geology," in *Scientific Studies in Special Creation*, ed. Walter E. Lammerts (Phillipsburg, N.J.: Presbyterian and Reformed Publishing Co., 1971), p. 104.

[19]Ibid., p. 105.

[20]Moore and Slusher, *Biology*, p. 7.

"theories."[21] The implication is that creation science is no more religious or less scientific than evolution. By asserting that evolution is a theory, it gives the impression that, since it is not *fact* and is based on faith, evolution is every bit as religious as creation science.

Although evolution and creation are presented in the text book as alternatives for interpreting the facts, creation science is put forward as the superior explanation. The text gives a brief summary of Charles Darwin's *The Origin of Species* (1859) and highlights in particular Darwin on "natural selection."[22] No references are made to developments and modifications of Darwin's positions which scientists have made in the past century.[23]

The summary is immediately followed by a section entitled "Failures of Darwinian Theory," in which the authors argue that the theory of evolution cannot be proven but only supported indirectly. They write:

> To produce support for the doctrine of evolution, proponents must show today that one animal form, or kind is changing into another animal form or kind. . . . And they must show that such changes have taken place in the past by tracing the tree of life in the rocks.[24]

Moore and Slusher then spend eleven pages arguing that there is a lack of fossil support for the theory of evolution. By pointing out that evolutionists cannot provide thorough fossil evidence for the transition states between some species, Moore and Slusher imply that creation science provides a better explanation for the "facts" they have gathered. Obviously, to point out inadequacies in the theory of evolution is not to make creation science a more adequate explanation, yet it may open the door to consideration of the alternative.

The creation science explanation which Moore and Slusher set forth claims that in the past there were life zones, just as there are today. They suggest that extinct animals of lesser and greater complexity, such as trilobites and dinosaurs, lived in one life zone at the

---

[21]Ibid., p. 398.

[22]Ibid., p. 402. Darwin's theory of evolution is presented in one column of text and it is noted that Darwin himself had misgivings about "the mechanism of evolution.

[23]For example, natural selection is no longer thought of in terms of crude competition between individuals. Understanding of the success of individual species has been broadened to include behavioral adaption of populations of animals in complex eco-systems.

[24]Moore and Slusher, *Biology*, p. 403.

same time. They do point out that the data indicates that the deepest fossil layers contain less complex life forms than the more shallow layers. However, they account for this phenomenon on the basis of the flood of Noah. Neither kind of animal was taken onto the boat. They argue: "As the flood waters rose, less complex forms, being less able to escape, would be buried first. More complex forms could move to higher ground."[25] Thus their argument relies on the great cataclysm of the deluge at Noah's time, at the direct intervention of God. But no evidence is offered for a global flood.

This "cataclysmic" interpretation of the fossil data is employed also in Moore and Slusher's interpretation of geological data. They attempt to refute the geological theory of Sir Charles Lyell, (1797–1875).[26] They argue that Lyell's "principle of uniformitarianism" is not an adequate explanation for geological data. Lyell developed his position in the 1830's as a critique of the "cataclysmic geology" which accounted for major geological changes by attributing them to God's direct intervention. Lyell believed that the data showed that all geological change could be explained by natural forces operating over a long span of time. He wrote: "All former changes of the organic and inorganic creation are referable to one uninterrupted succession of physical events, governed by the laws now in operation."[27]

The dismissal of Darwin's biological evolution and Lyell's geological uniformitarianism hinge in large measure on arguments from "catastrophism," a position often shared by scientists and theologians alike in the late eighteenth century through the mid-nineteenth century. Catastrophists claimed that scientific findings could be accounted for on the basis of divine interventions. Such arguments were common prior to Lyell and Darwin, and represented a concordism between science and religion which called for continuity between revelation as the infallible word of God and the Enlightenment sciences.[28] Creation science sets forth a new concordism between

[25]Ibid., p. 405.

[26]Sir Charles Lyell, *Principles of Geology*, 3 vol. (London: J. M. Dent, 1830–33), Vol. I, p. 144. See Moore and Slusher, p. 410.

[27]Lyell, I, p. 144.

[28]The concordism of the early Enlightenment period commonly took the form of explanations which presented religion and science in harmony or in continuity. Belief in the biblical account of divine creation of the world provided scientists such as Newton, Priestley and Linnaeus with cosmological presuppositions for their scientific inquiry. See Langdon Gilkey, *Religion and the Scientific Future* (New York: Harper and Row, 1970), pp. 10–12. For a more thorough treatment of the relations of science and religion in the late eighteenth and early nineteenth centuries see Charles

science and religion, namely a science which subscribes to the epistemology and methodology of Francis Bacon, supplemented by contemporary research, and a religion which relies on a literalist interpretation of Genesis 1–11.

Creation science, therefore, does not subscribe to the science-religion warfare evident at the "The Monkey Trial." William Jennings Bryan made the movement to ban the teaching of evolution in public schools a crusade which he took to the people in order to insure the rightful role of religion (evangelical Protestantism) in American society. Bryan was not a scientist, but rather a Presbyterian layman and politician. He volunteered to defend Tennessee's anti-evolution law against the agnostic Clarence Darrow because he believed that Darwinism was un-Christian. He reasoned that the teaching of evolution in schools would cause students to lose faith in the Bible, first in the doctrine or creation and later in other Christian doctrines, and that the moral fabric of American society would be in jeopardy.[29]

Creation scientists differ from Byran. Rather than engage in a warfare against science, they use science in the service of their religious convictions. Henry M. Morris argues against liberal "neo-orthodox and neo-evangelical movements" which claim that the Bible contains "scientific misinformation" and that the Bible is a book of scientific merit. Morris believes his role as a scientist is to defend the biblical account of creation against "the fires of intellectual attack and ridicule" and to demonstrate that the Bible is undergirded by solid knowledge.[30] His response is not only an attack on evolution scientists, but also on "mainline" Protestantism and Catholicism.

Morris, however, does share Bryan's broad ethical concerns. The motivation for Bryan's stance was his concern about the effects of the study of evolution on American Society. According to Ronald Numbers' assessment, Bryan believed that Darwinism was contrib-

Coulston Gillespie's *Genesis and Geology: A Study in the Relations of Scientific Thought, Natural Theology and Social Opinion in Great Britain, 1790–1850* (New York: Harper and Row, 1959).

[29]For an account of Bryan's political career and the motivation for his crusade against the teaching of evolutions see C. Allyn Russell, *Voices of American Fundamentalism* (Philadelphia: Westminster Press, 1976), pp. 162–89.

[30]Henry M. Morris, *The Beginning of the World* (Denver: Accent Books, 1977), p. 7. Morris makes this argument for the reasonableness of creation science and therefore of the scientific reliability of the Bible in a somewhat different manner in *Scientific Creationism*, pp. 203–4.

uting to moral decay in America. The law of Christ was being replaced by the law of the jungle and this threatened the principles Bryan valued most; democracy and Christianity.[31] Like Bryan, creation scientists are convinced that evolution has contributed to moral decadence.

Creation scientists recognize that the success of Darwin's theory of evolution has led to the wide extension of the concept of evolution into other fields of study. One finds among the essays creation scientists have published an article entitled "Neo-Darwinism and Society."[32] The essay examines the degree to which evolution has infiltrated the areas of history, economic studies, and literature. The author indicates the main thesis of the article:

> . . . presentation of evolution as fact, as observable reality, in educational institutions at any level across the surface of the globe has been used by free thinking scholars to implement selected indoctrination of the intelligentsia of the various societies of Western civilization.[33]

Although the article treats the areas in question in a superficial manner by merely drawing attention to Marxism, the Fabian Society of England, and the novels of Jack London as examples of dangerous Darwinism, it does bear witness to the recognition of the power and importance of evolution by creation scientists. Among the aims of creation scientists is to counter the impact of evolution on other academic disciplines and on the culture as a whole.

Science and Religion in American Culture

What can theologians learn about science and religion in American culture from creation science? Creation science highlights the complexity of the relations of science and religion in America today. Creation science is not merely a new outbreak in the warfare of science and religion; it is an attempt to blend science and religion into a new union which will be taught in our nation's schools and have an impact on the American ethos.

Langdon Gilkey believes that an appropriate starting point for an analysis of creation science lies in a sociological phenomenon

---

[31]Ronald L. Numbers, "The Creationists," pp. 137–38.

[32]John N. Moore, "Neo-Darwinism and Society," in Walter J. Lammerts, ed., Why Not Creation? (Phillipsberg, NJ: Presbyterian & Reformed Publishing Co., 1970).

[33]Lammerts, p. 382.

unique to North America: the non-hierarchical nature of society. Gilkey believes that creation science represents the American tendency to resist the acceptance of the authority of those who are perceived to be elites. This is particularly true in religious circles. This phenomenon makes the United States distinct from Europe. While in Europe the theologians, "the elites," speak generally for all the churches and mold public interpretations of Christianity up and down the various levels of society, in North American by contrast they do not. Creation science is "typically American": a non-elitist, popular movement which deliberately distances itself from academic theology and established ecclesiastical authority.[34] Therefore, the controversy about creation science actually represents a contest between two different sorts of understandings of science and religion. On the one hand, there is an "elite form" made up of scientific organizations such as the American Association of the Advancement of Science, and the Christianity of the mainline denominations such as the National Council of Churches. On the other hand, there is a "popular form" which combines fundamentalist Christianity and a commonly held perception of science as "fact."[35]

The recent development of creation science represents more than an effort by fundamentalists to avoid the First Amendment test. Creation science signals the desire of fundamentalists to actively participate in and shape our scientific culture. It also underscores the extent to which our culture is an advanced scientific one. As Gilkey points out: science is the established "queen," the paradigmatic form of knowing which is deemed necessary for every aspect of American life. Since it represents the central form of knowledge that brings forth truth and well being, it has a sacral character.[36] It provides the theoretical basis for what the culture accepts as knowledge and what it views as the most valuable forms of praxis. Its dominance is manifested in the common belief that other disciplines depend on science while science depends only on itself. This results in the myth that the scientific community need not understand the rest of the culture, or even understand itself in relation to that culture.[37]

---

[34]Langdon Gilkey, "The Creationist Issue: A Theologian's View," p. 56. Gilkey indicates that the union of science and popular religious ideology is not foreign to Europe; he cites Nazism and Fascism as examples.

[35]Langdon Gilkey, "Religions and Science in an Advanced Scientific Culture," pp. 169–70.

[36]Ibid., p. 167, a somewhat different presentation of science as "queen" is found in Creationism on Trial, pp. 163–65.

[37]Ibid., p. 171.

Creation science in fact reflects the dominance of science in North American culture. Gilkey points out that one of the major difficulties with the creationists' appropriation of science is their conception of science as concerned with "facts." The presentation of science as fact represents the extreme of the popular misconception of science as an impersonal and objective mode of knowing. Against this conception Gilkey argues:

> Science is not located in facts: thus scientific theories do not represent merely 'sensible' or 'rational' explanations of scientific facts. On the contrary, science is located in its theories; it is the theoretical structure, the coherent system of theories, created by scientific inquiry, that constitutes science—not the facts associated with those theories. In other words, it is the way science explains facts, not the kinds of facts it explains that makes science science.[38]

Certainly in the era of theories such as relativity, quantum mechanics and the principle of indeterminacy, a Baconian understanding of science is inadequate. It is now widely recognized that what scientists count as factual, namely the objective value-neutral data of science, is open to conflicting interpretations. There is always a multiplicity of theoretical interpretations that can fit a set of facts.[39] One of the contributions of the scientific community to Western culture as a whole has been to make us realize that any claim to truth is always an approximation of the truth, an approximation that is provisional and open to being replaced by a more adequate theory.[40] In the scientific paradigm most widely accepted by the scientific community today, scientific theories are adjudicated on the basis of determinative rules or canons.[41] A scientific theory is more than a rational explanation. It must conform to the canons of the scientific community to be a science.

Gilkey uses three major scientific canons to analyze creation science. These canons are: 1) No supernatural force or agent can be appealed to in explanations. 2) Explanations of science must be in terms of natural laws, i.e., invariable and necessary forces and

---

[38]Gilkey, "The Creationist Issue . . . ," p. 59.

[39]For more on this point, see Mary Hesse, "Cosmology as Myth," in D. Tracy and N. Lash, pp. 49–50.

[40]Creationism on Trial, p. 70.

[41]Here scientific paradigm means a standard of scientific achievement in terms of which scientific work is conducted and evaluated. See Thomas Kuhn, The Structure of Scientific Revolutions (Chicago: University of Chicago, 1962).

factors. 3) Scientific theories must grow out of experimental evidence, and must be testable by further experiment.[42] In Gilkey's judgment, a theory or model that refers to the action of a transcendent creator establishing in a unique act at the beginning of time the entire realm of nature defies all of these canons. It appeals to a transcendent, divine power beyond the system of finite causes; it explains in terms of the power and purpose of the Creator, not in terms of natural laws; and being a unique and nonrepeatable act, it cannot be tested in the present since there are not similar processes available in present experience.[43] Therefore, creation science is religion, for all that is related to a Creator-God is religious. To speak of a Creator is to speak religiously and not scientifically, for *a priori* science cannot raise the question of God.[44] Talk about creation, even under the guise of science, is religious speech.

The creationists' attempt to substantiate their belief in the authority and inerrancy of Genesis 1–11 with "facts" (neutral data), and their claim that what results is scientific truth, represents not only an archaic understanding of science, but also a confused understanding of truth. It is Gilkey's judgment that the deepest level of error of creation science is the assumption that there is only one level of truth, that truth is factual, physical, and quantitative. It assumes that both science and revelation give the same type of information.[45] When the two seem to contradict, the truth of God's Word must prevail. In Gilkey's assessment this represents a misconception of the relation of personal religious belief to science and its theories.

Science and religion present very different forms of discourse. To ask whether there is scientific evidence to establish scientifically a religious doctrine is an empty question. There can be evidence for a religious view, but no amount of scientific evidence for a religious theory can make that theory a scientific theory. It remains religious if it speaks of God and is concerned with humans in relation to God.[46] In contrast, science deals with nature and its forces; it is secular. It cannot propose theories that go beyond the secular level,

---

[42]Gilkey, "The Creationist Issue . . . ," p. 60. On the canons of science, see his "Religion and Science in an Advanced Scientific Culture," pp. 172–173.
[43]Ibid., pp. 172–173.
[44]Ibid., p. 61.
[45]Ibid., p. 63; for a more extensive treatment of this point see *Creationism on Trial*. pp. 111–12.
[46]*Creationism on Trial*, p. 114.

because when it leaves the observable, sharable, quantitative, measurable natural level, it ceases to be science.[47]

One of the major manifestations of the dominance of science in North American culture is the belief that scientific explanations represent explanations of the totality of reality. In Gilkey's judgment this belief is found on both sides of the creationist controversy. The creationists assume it of their own doctrines—if creation is true, if the Genesis account is valid, then it is or must be science. In addition, they assume it of evolutionary science. If evolutionary science does not mention God or use God as a cause, then evolutionary science has excluded and so denied God, and it represents a form of atheistic religion.

The misconception of the relations of religion and science and a misconception of truth are not the exclusive purview of creationists alone. Gilkey points out that scientists and the participants in our scientific culture must bear in mind that science and its claims to truth have limits. The same rules that limit the creationists also limit scientific explanations. This means that the scientific question of origins can only question proximate origins. Science is limited to questions about how one process led to another one in the ongoing development of the world system. By its very nature it cannot ask questions about the ultimate ground of the processes themselves.

Science cannot provide a total explanation of our existence. Since scientific inquiry deals only with secondary causes, science should lead to no particular philosophical or religious world view. Still it is clearly possible for science to expand into a view of the whole of reality, into a naturalistic philosophy and a humanistic religion.[48] The forgetfulness of the limits of science and the presentation of scientific explanation of proximate origins as replacement for Genesis and the Judeo-Christian belief in creation are the major reasons for the religious backlash by creation science. Gilkey expresses this strongly:

> . . . by a movement from a methodological (heuristic) principle of inquiry to a metaphysical, substantive assertion about ultimate reality, we arrive at that philosophy, that "atheistic and humanistic religious perspective" of which science as such is accused by the Creationists.

[47]Ibid., p. 115.
[48]Gilkey notes that creationists have achieved much of their credibility by pointing out the relationship between evolution and naturalistic humanism; see "The Creationist Issue," p. 62.

That many in the scientific community have in fact participated in, witnessed to, and proclaimed as science this "expansion" into a religious perspective, there can be little doubt. All too many distinguished scientists had stated that "science now knows" that "the religious theories of the past are outmoded myths" and "the origins of all things lie in the material nature we find around us."[49]

The expansion of science as a reliable method into a speculative world view and humanistic faith with its own quasi-religious myths has led to the creation science controversy. It is to the religious dimension of evolutionary science that the creationists have reacted. This certainly is what is at stake when Henry Morris writes: "If man is a product of evolution, he is not a fallen creature in need of a Savior but a rising creature capable of saving himself."[50] Morris' words highlight that evolution has generated a powerful social and rhetorical myth, a secular common faith that has been highly persuasive in North American society.

A specific illustration of quasi-religious myths in North American culture is the vision of the future closely linked with the scientific theory of evolution, "the myth of progress." In Gilkey's assessment the myth of progress is used by members of the scientific community in interpreting historical processes as a whole. As a consequence, elements abstracted from this theory became the dominant theme in a vision of progress to be achieved through control, not only of natural evolution, but also of cultural evolution.[51] The possibility of control through knowledge has deeply affected our world, our society and ourselves. Gilkey explains how the acceleration in knowledge has been used to create a vision of control over human destiny:

> Through physical science and technology, men and women can make of their natural environment a place that serves them; through the biological and psychological sciences, they can remake themselves into more efficient instruments of their own ends; and through the social sciences and their development, they can reshape their economic and political environments into ones illustrating a rational society.[52]

---

[49]*Creationism on Trial*, p. 120. See also "Religion and Science in an Advanced Scientific Culture," p. 173.

[50]Henry M. Morris, *The Troubled Waters of Evolution* (San Diego: Creation-Life Publishers, 1974), p. 184.

[51]Gilkey, *Reaping the Whirlwind, A Christian Interpretation of History* (New York: Seabury Press, 1981), pp. 70–73.

[52]Ibid., 71.

Gilkey's criticism of the myth of progress is a recurring theme in his later writings. He points out that this myth has tended to serve as an instrument of redemption in modern history, a type of secular salvation myth. This myth of scientific progress has functioned in American social existence religiously, that is, as the ultimate formative symbolic structure of our culture.[53]

Conclusions

Creation science is an illustration of the fact that both science and religion are permanent and essential aspects of society. There is a great deal of ambiguity surrounding both, for each has the potential for being creative or destructive. In the case of the union of science and religion promoted by creationists, the latter is true. Creation science is a blend of a popular, positivistic model of science with a simplistic Biblical religion which misconstrues the meaning and purpose of revelation, a product of the pervasive influence of science on society, and a reaction to the dilemmas which science and technology have generated.

Creation science makes it obvious that efforts by some scientists to mix scientific theories with the doctrines of their own religious communities indicate that the question of the relationship between science and religion needs to be addressed. Without a recognition of the appropriate relationship of science and religion within the culture, the two can be easily united in aberrant forms which contribute to the disintegration of society, rather than its creative growth.

In many ways creation science is a product of the pervasive influence of science on society and a reaction to the dilemmas which have been generated by science and technology. Creation science's blend of science and religion teaches us the importance of a critical stance vis-à-vis the dominance of science within our culture. The peculiar union teaches us the importance of a critical stance vis-a-vis the dominance of science. Science easily expands from inquiry about what is observable in the natural world to the generation of

---

[53]Ibid., pp. 71–73; see also "Religious Dilemmas of a Scientific Culture," pp. 92–93 and "Is Religious Faith in a Scientific Age Possible?" in Society and the Sacred: Toward a Theology of Culture in Decline (New York: Crossroad, 1981). In the Society and the Sacred articles Gilkey argues that this myth is disintegrating because, although the levels of scientific knowledge and technology have steadily risen, contemporary life remains suffused with suffering and the ever present threat of self-destruction.

quasi-religious myths. When scientists equate science with their own naturalistic humanism, they are not acting as scientists, but rather they are expressing, without logical ground or empirical testing, a myth which has been generated in our scientific culture.

Creation science points to the need for the "religious elites" to develop more fruitful ways for communicating the rapprochement or concordat between natural science and the Judeo-Christian religious traditions that has been in effect among scholars and theologians and educated laypersons for well over a century. This rapprochement conceives of the relations of science neither as warfare nor as a concordism. It respects the distinct roles of each in society and views their relationship as one of mutuality. To prevent needless warfare and destructive concordism it is vital that the recognition by theologians of mutual interdependence of science and religion be effectively communicated to the wider public.

Theologians should draw attention not only to the blatantly religious uses of scientific theories, such as creation science, but also to the more subtle interpretations. For the good of society the logical limits of science should be maintained. If science in a scientific culture begins to define the extent of reality and of possibility for us all, then it can usurp the role of religion as the effective redemptive force in a culture.

Gilkey argues that science should not be allowed to replace religion, nor should religion claim competence in theories about the proximate causes in nature. Science and religion should maintain their independent spheres in our societal life in a relationship of mutuality. If this relationship of mutuality is to be part of the fabric of the culture, Gilkey proposes that theologians engage in conversations with scientists and philosophers of science.[54] Thus, theologians will at once become more knowledgeable about the presuppositions, methodologies and findings of science, and be in a position to remind the scientific community that its findings are not "value

---

[54]Gilkey calls for dialogue between scientists and theologians in "Religion and Science in an Advanced Scientific Culture," p. 178. He has engaged in dialogues with the scientific community himself. Among the more noteworthy is the 1975 Conference of Nobel Scientists at which he gave a paper entitled, "The Future of Science," published in The Future of Science, ed. Timothy C. L. Robinson (New York: John Wiley and Sons, 1977), pp. 105–28. He also delivered a paper entitled, "The Structure of Academic Revolutions," at a symposium sponsored by the Smithsonian Institution to mark the 500th anniversary of the birth of Nicholas Copernicus. This paper was published in The Nature of Scientific Discovery, ed. Owen Gingerich, (Washington, DC: Smithsonian Institution Press, 1975) pp. 538–45.

neutral," nor are its members "culture free." An understanding of science that ignores that science is a fully human activity affecting and affected by the broader cultural matrix is a dangerous one for the culture as a whole. If the scientific community is motivated primarily by the myth of progress and ignores its dependence on the moral and spiritual situation of the broader society, it is likely to be destructive of that culture and its people.

Gilkey also argues that a critique of the scientific community needs to be balanced by a similar critique of the leadership of the mainline Christian churches. Creation science points to the need for the "religious elites" to develop more fruitful ways for communicating the rapprochement or concordat between natural science and the mainline Christian traditions that has been in effect among scholars and theologians and many educated lay persons for well over a century.[55] The wider public needs to know that this rapprochement conceives of the relation of religion to science neither as warfare nor as concordism. It respects the distinct roles of each in society and views their relationship as one of mutuality. To prevent needless warfare and new forms of destructive union it is vital that the recognition by theologians of the mutual interdependence of science and religion be effectively communicated to the wider public.

One might ask, is Gilkey's call for the communication of the positions of the theologians of the mainline Christian denominations to the broader public sufficient? Such communication appears to be one sided. Is it not also important for the theologians of the mainline denominations to listen to the fundamentalists? What is needed is dialogue between the theologians of the mainline Christian churches and fundamentalist leaders. Gilkey seems to prefer dialogue with members of the scientific community. But to limit one's dialogue partners to scientists is to restrict one's conversation to "the elites" whom fundamentalists hold in suspect. For these elites to agree that creation science is both bad science and bad theology will not resolve the battles waged over what should be taught in our nation's public schools. Theologians of the mainline Christian denominations, both Protestant and Catholic, who ascribe to a rapprochement with the natural sciences, must seek out ways to engage in dialogue with fundamentalist Christians who do not accept it.

At a time in which mainline Christian denominations are experi-

---

[55]*Creationism on Trial*, pp. 185–86.

encing a decline in numbers, dialogue with fundamentalists is particularly desirable.[56] Such a dialogue is needed if mainline theology is to counter its elitist image and the perception that it is an activity of aloof academics who are out of touch with fundamentalist Christianity and its concerns.

Theological representatives of the mainline denominations who have accommodated their theology to the developments in science and to other forms of modernity must sit down with creation scientists and leaders of fundamentalist churches who hold these accommodations suspect. What is at stake is not merely the resolution of a contest between two opposing understandings of science and religion. The deeper and more important issue is concern about the disintegration of the moral fabric of American society voiced by those who oppose evolutionary science on religious grounds. Fundamentalists believe that the appropriate response for a Christian to the moral dilemmas of the secular humanism of modernity is to choose not to accommodate.

Such a dialogue will surely provide an opportunity for recognition that accommodation has taken place on both sides. Fundamentalists need to recognize that their critique of secular humanism and its values is a selective one. In many ways their theology is actually world affirming, particularly where capitalist values are concerned. On the other hand, theologians of the mainline Christian denomination have at times accommodated their theology to the values of secularity by adopting a moral relativism, particularly in questions dealing with personal or private life. Each needs to listen to the criticisms of the other, so that attention can be given to each other's anxieties and hopes. It is not likely that dialogue will eliminate the pluralism in views about the essentials of Christianity and the remedies for our societal problems. But such dialogue may lessen the polarization between fundamentalist and mainline Christians that now exists.

---

[56]For statistics and analysis of the decline of the mainline Christian Churches and of the increase in the numbers of the evangelical fundamentalists and non affiliates in the United States since 1950, see Wade Clark Roof and William McKinney, "Denominational America and the New Religious Pluralism," *The Annuals of the American Academy of Political and Social Science* 480 (1985): 24–38.

INSPIRATION AND TRUST: TOWARD NARROWING THE GAP BETWEEN FUNDAMENTALIST AND HIGHER BIBLICAL SCHOLARSHIP

John McCarthy

It is common within the academy to set fundamentalist biblical interpretation in opposition to historical and literary critical understanding, and often for good reason. Yet, no doubt, stereotypes play a role here also. The standard academic image of the local fundamentalist congregation is one in which assumptions about inerrancy, inspiration, literal interpretation and divine authorship either occasion or complement a program of biblical proof-texting, ominous prediction, social isolation or political reactionism. The standard fundamentalist image of the academic biblical scholar is one in which bible belief has not only been jettisoned in favor of historical and linguistic study, but also defiled by the assumption that the biblical text could be read as one would read any other text. Acrimonious exchange, suspicion or disdainful silence more often than not describe the exchange between the two positions. In this context, the purpose of what follows is twofold: 1) to suggest an analysis which brings fundamentalist biblical hermeneutics into a position of more fruitful exchange with critical biblical scholarship; 2) in light of this analysis to isolate more clearly significant points of hermeneutical convergence and divergence.

Hermeneutics of Inspiration

The first purpose will be addressed by formulating a fundamentalist hermeneutics of inspiration based on the work of theologians who have articulated a reflective fundamentalist perspective.[1] The basic claim put forth through this formulation is that inspiration, while seeming to be a category confined exclusively to the divinely intended meaning of the written word, in fact establishes what the adequate reception of the biblical text should include if one were to assume, as one should, the role of the implied reader/listener/ proclaimer of the Bible. Inspiration as a textual category is simultaneously one of authorship *and* implied reception.[2]

To begin, the suggested hermeneutic of inspiration is formulated as follows:

> The Bible should be trusted in its entirety as the privileged text for Christian discipleship. The Bible leads the reader to Christ and as such is a fundamental part of God's revelation from which it derives its authority. The Bible is the Word of God. In this context it is appropriate to say that the Holy Spirit is the author of the Bible, that the Bible is verbally inspired, inerrant and should be literally interpreted.

An explanation is called for, one which, in this case, takes up the formulation phrase by phrase.

"The Bible should be trusted."

The "Chicago Statement on Biblical Inerrancy" ends its first paragraph with this sentence: "Recognition of the textual truth and

---

[1]The texts chosen for consideration here include Benjamin Warfield, "The Real Problem of Inspiration" in *The Inspiration and Authority of the Bible* (Philadelphia: Presbyterian and Reformed Publications, 1948), pp. 169–226; Warfield, "Inspiration" in *International Standard Bible Encyclopedia*, vol. 2, ed. G. W. Bromiley, et. al. (Grand Rapids: William B. Eerdmans Publishing Co., 1982), pp. 839–849; G. W. Bromiley, "Inspiration, History of the Doctrine of" in *International Standard Bible Encyclopedia* 2, pp. 849–854, "The Chicago Statement on Biblical Inerrancy" in Carl F. H. Henry, *God, Revelation and Authority*, vol. 4 (Waco: Word Publication, 1979), pp. 211–219. By choosing texts such as these I recognize that I am focusing on a second order reflection on inspiration in a fundamentalist context. This is done to avoid any easy dismissal of the issues by viewing only popular instances of fundamentalism which clearly seem to need a critical view. By focusing on works at least partially shaped by the demands of the academy, common and fruitful engagement with the issues of inspiration may be possible.

[2]This is not to say that the reader of the text is inspired. Although Warfield extends the doctrine of the Holy Spirit to include the reader, he does not suggest that inspiration is properly attributed to the reader. The position maintained in this section of the paper is that inspiration is clearly a textual category in fundamentalism, but likewise there is an awareness that the text incorporates the reader as an implied reader within the text through a variety of literary means. Thus the boundary between the text and the reader is not an absolute one; the reception of the text is less the communication of information and more the assumption of a role in prayerful obedience.

trustworthiness of Holy Scripture is essential to a full grasp and adequate confession of its authority."[3] A fundamentalist hermeneutic of inspiration is characteristically assumed to be one of authority: the text is authoritative because it is the Word of God. The Chicago statement, as do all basically fundamentalist positions, clearly recognizes the authority of the Bible, and yet to reduce the understanding of inspiration to a logic of authority is premature.[4] The confession of authority is grounded in truth and trustworthiness. To say that the Bible is inspired places the reader in a position of trust before a text that is true. The implied reader of the inspired text affirms that the text is to be trusted because it is true, in the many ways that it may be true, and only because of this truth is it authoritative.

". . . in it entirety."

The presupposition of textual trustworthiness is not limited to any one type of text or religious position. Rather, the text as a whole, even in its apparent contradictions, is to be taken as trustworthy and true. This places the reader under a twin demand: 1) that she/he not reduce the understanding of the Bible to any one text, set of texts or religious positions within the scriptures; and 2) that she/he in light of the whole of the Bible attempt to understand textual meaning as the meaning of the whole. Benjamin Warfield criticizes Archdeacon Dr. Farrar precisely on this point in what he identifies as four, then contemporary, procedures for undermining a true understanding of biblical inspiration. Warfield writes:

It was the fault of the older dogmatists to depend too much on isolated proof-texts for the framing and defense of doctrine. Dr. Farrar would have us return to this method. The alternative, commended justly to us by the whole body of modern scholarship, is, as Schleiermacher put it, to seek "a form of Scripture proof on a larger scale than can be got from single texts," to build our systematic theology, in a word, on the basis, not of the occasional dogmatic statements of Scripture alone, taken separately and, as it were, in shreds, but on the basis of the theologies of the Scriptures—to reproduce first the theological thought of each writer or group of writers and then to combine these several theologies

---

[3]"The Chicago Statement," p. 211. Also, for example, see Warfield, "Inspiration," 841–842: Warfield, "Real Problem," pp. 210–212.
[4]Harold Lindsell, The Battle for the Bible (Grand Rapids: Zondervan, 1976), p. 39.

(each according to its due historical place) into the one consistent
system, consentaneous parts of which they are to be found.[5]

". . .as the privileged text."

Inspiration in the fundamentalist perspective is a category of the
text, not to be confused with any sense of artistic genius, either as
author or reader.[6] Further, it is the autographic text alone to which
inspiration may be attributed.[7] Properly speaking then there are no
inspired texts which are in our hands, although there is a high
degree of confidence in the accuracy of the transmission of the text,
and no texts other than the canonical Biblical texts (with the possible
exception of their component sources) can be accorded the privileged position of these texts. Yet for all this privilege accorded to
biblical texts as inspired, their inspiration cannot be severed from
the larger context of providence and grace. For a theologian like
Warfield this recognition allows for a consistent account of the
possibility of biblical texts being formed over long periods of time,
by multiple authors in various situations. Inspiration neither denies
nor opposes the conditions of textual historicity: production by
multiple authors, redactional process, linguistic idiosyncrasies, individual style, etc.[8] Yet inspiration differs from providence. Warfield
writes:

> For providence is guidance; and guidance can bring one only so far as
> his own powers can carry him. If heights are to be scaled above man's
> native power to achieve, then something more than guidance, however
> effective, is necessary. This is the reason for the superinduction at the
> end of the long process of the production of scripture, of the additional
> divine operation which we call technically, "inspiration." By it, the
> Spirit of God, flowing confluently in with the providentially and
> graciously determined work of men, spontaneously producing under
> the divine directions the writings appointed to them, gives the product
> a divine quality unattainable by human powers alone.[9]

This "end of the long process" can be understood as a linear
termination but to do so runs the risk of associating inspiration too

---

[5]Warfield, "Real Problem," pp. 198–199; on this issue of totality of the text, see the
"Chicago Statement," pp. 219.
[6]Lindsell, p. 33.
[7]"Chicago Statement," p. 213.
[8]Warfield, "Inspiration," p. 846.
[9]Warfield, "Inspiration," p. 847.

closely with a final random intervention. When located with and within the topics of providence, revelation and grace, and distinguished from incarnation, as indeed Warfield does,[10] then inspiration refers to an excess of the text beyond the competence, control or genius of the writer. Neither a social history, a language or individual human skill account for biblical inspiration, but neither does inspiration negate these. In such a context inspiration acts as a double limit concept: 1) the autographic text is a limit to any received biblical text as inspired; 2) inspiration is a limit to the control of the author over the meaning and truth of the text. For the reader, then, the authentication of the textual tradition is an important part of understanding the text and thus historical scholarship is not categorically excluded. Likewise any hermeneutic which seeks the intention of the original author becomes inadequate precisely because the text is not within the control of any human author, either in its process of production or in its meaning and truth.

> "... for Christian discipleship. The Bible leads
> the reader to Christ."

The second sentence of the "Chicago Statement" reads: "Those who profess faith in Jesus Christ as Lord and Savior are called to show the reality of their discipleship by humbly and faithfully obeying God's written word."[11] G. W. Bromiley shares this position when he writes:

> ... since Christian understanding rests upon the work of the Spirit, the Bible cannot be treated as a Euclid of Christian faith and conduct to be learned, schematized and applied by the ordinary ways of reason and scholarship. On the basis of a sound doctrine and inspiration, Biblical theology is always a venture of prayer, humility and obedience in the Spirit.[12]

The stance of the implied reader within a text which calls for discipleship is one in which the truth of the text shapes the identity of the reader in a process of humility and obedience to the text. Humility and obedience to the text is understood Christocentrically. The "Chicago Statement" is clear on this when it states:

---

[10]Warfield, "Inspiration," p. 848.
[11]"Chicago Statement," p. 211.
[12]Bromiley, p. 852.

As the prophesied Messiah, Jesus Christ is the central theme of Scripture. The Old Testament looked ahead to him: the New Testament looks back to His first coming and on to His second. Canonical scripture is the divinely inspired and therefore normative witness to Christ. No hermeneutic therefore of which this historical Christ (sic) is not the focal point is acceptable. Holy Scripture must be treated as what it essentially is—the witness of the Father to the incarnate Son.[13]

If the truth of the inspired text is so centered on Christ then the role of the reader extends beyond textual comprehension as accumulated knowledge. Discipleship is a correlate of inspiration as the active expression of trusting the text.[14]

". . . and as such is a fundamental part of God's revelation from which it derives its authority. The Bible is the Word of God."

Little more needs to be added to explain this. The authority of the scriptures rests on the revelation of truth which exceeds the control of the human author and makes the text trustworthy. It is not an alternative incarnation and thus not a replacement of the Christ event.[15] It is the Word of God yet not the Son of God. Only in light of this prior placement in the trustworthy "Word of God" can the consideration of verbal inspiration, inerrancy, and literal interpretation be properly understood. To begin the hermeneutics of inspiration with these topics is to lose the essential context, namely the revelation of a trustworthy truth.

"In this context it is appropriate to say that the Holy Spirit is the author of the Bible."

With this statement a fundamentalist position reaches the limit of religious language. The language attempts to maintain a complex logic that is constantly on the verge of paradox. The Spirit is the true author of the scriptures, and yet nothing is taken away from human authorship. The words are the words of God and at the same time

---

[13]"Chicago Statement," p. 216.

[14]Warfield supports this same position by suggesting that the purpose of inspiration is not to provide an accurate record of salvation but to play an integral part in redemption and thus to be a redemptive act itself. It has,as he says, "its own part to play in the great work of establishing and building up the Kingdom of God." "Inspiration," p. 848.

[15]Warfield, "Inspiration," p. 848.

the human sounds. Consistently dismissed as naive by fundamentalist theologians is an understanding of authorial inspiration which
hints of dictation. Rather, the term of choice, after a conscious
rejection of terms such as "guidance," "direction," "control," or
"lead," is that of "movement." The fundamentalist position ultimately chooses what it understands to be biblical language. At the
same time it recognizes that this is not an explanation but a confession linked to the core of inspiration. Warfield writes:

> Though spoken through the instrumentality of men, it is, by virtue of
> the fact that these men spoke as "moved by the Holy Spirit," an
> immediately divine word. The stress is laid here, not on the spiritual
> value of Scripture (though that too is seen in the background), but on
> the divine trustworthiness of Scripture.[16]

Entailed by the position that the text is to be trusted by the reader,
authorship becomes the action of the Spirit, for who can be trusted
if God cannot? This aspect of the hermeneutic of inspiration is
clearly less of an assertion than a confession. The "Chicago Statement" makes this clear when it notes: We affirm that inspiration was
the work in which God by His Spirit, through human writers gave us
his Word. The origin of Scripture is divine. The mode of divine
inspiration remains a mystery to us.[17]

> "... that the Bible is verbally inspired, inerrant and
> should be literally interpreted."

The discussion of verbal inspiration is carried out by Warfield in
response to two major issues: 1) if all of Scripture, down to the very
words, are not inspired, then the possibility of deciding how one
distinguishes between inspired ideas or doctrines and their words
cannot be convincingly made; 2) if all of Scripture, down to the very
words, are not inspired then the trustworthiness of the Bible as a
whole is jeopardized.[18] No attempt is made to explain how it is that
each word is chosen by God; indeed, that does not seem to be the
point of the position on verbal inspiration. Rather there is a confidence that the language as a whole is an adequate vehicle for

---

[16]Warfield, "Inspiration," p. 841.
[17]"Chicago Statement," p. 213.
[18]Warfield, "Real Problem," pp. 179–181.

religious truth.[19] With this confidence in language and a confessional claim that the Bible is the Word of God, each aspect of the language is understood to be involved in revelation. Verbal inspiration is thus the expression of the attempt to be maximally inclusive of the possibilities of linguistic meaning given the trustworthiness of the text.

Closely linked to the topic of verbal inspiration is the position on literal interpretation. It is, in fact, a demand upon the reader, given the maximalist understanding of the relation of revelation and language. Yet literal interpretation, like verbal inspiration, is not to be minimally understood. Literal interpretation is the interpretation of meaning fashioned in a literary genre and not essentially the interpretation of discrete words or phrases. The "Chicago Statement" makes clear this awareness of literary genres when it writes:

> In inspiration, God utilized the culture and conventions of his penman's milieu, a milieu that God controls in His sovereign providence; it is misinterpretation to imagine otherwise.
>
> So history must be treated as history, poetry as poetry, hyperbole and metaphor as hyperbole and metaphor, generalization and approximation as what they are, and so forth. Difference between literary conventions in Bible times and in our own times must also be observed: since, for instance, nonchronological narration and imprecise citation were conventional and acceptable and violated no expectations in those days, we must not regard these things as faults when we find them in Bible writers.[20]

Literal interpretation as a correlate of verbal inspiration within this fundamentalist hermeneutic is a role demand for the implied reader to maximize the awareness of the complex interaction of truth and language.

Inerrancy is likewise closely related to the topics of authorship, verbal inspiration and literal interpretation. As part of the confessional position of textual trustworthiness, the claim for inerrancy supports the reader's position of confidence in the text as the revelation of truth. The standard problems usually include instances of textual contradiction, bad science, inaccurate history and the like. In the face of these, inerrancy, at the level of data, is surely difficult to maintain. In general two options seem to be taken: 1) overwhelm-

---

[19]e.g. "Chicago Statement," p. 213.
[20]"Chicago Statement," p. 217.

ing trust in the truth of the text demands that, even if positions, especially religious ones, seem to be in opposition or contradictory, the problem lies in an incomplete understanding. Such an incomplete understanding may be remedied by further information but may just as well be an expression of human finitude.[21] 2) There may be a more nuanced sense of error and the level of error. Thus Lindsell notes variously on Scriptural inerrancy,

> Those who advocate inerrancy take the Bible in its plain and obvious sense. The charge that they are "wooden headed literalists" shows the bias of those who make the charge. All that is meant by saying that one takes the Bible literally is that one believes what it purports to say. This means that figures of speech are regarded as figures of speech. . . . To say that the sun rises and sets is illustrative. . . . To claim from its use in scripture that the ancients who wrote this were saying that sun revolves around the earth is nonsense. We who are supposed to know so much more than the ancients still use the same kind of language, and no one in his right mind would conclude that we teach that the sun revolves around the earth. . . . Another gross distortion of the evangelical view of biblical meaning is one that supposes everything in the Bible is true. This is not the case. There are statements in the Bible that are false. . . . But [these statements] too, like so many of the claims of error in the Bible, can be satisfactorily explained.[22]

Thus even as seemingly strong a claim as inerrancy, when placed in this larger hermeneutical structure, finds a conditioned and interdependent meaning it seems to lack when it stands alone. This meaning is an extension of the trust accorded to the text, a trust which even allows for the possibility of retrieving apparent error within a more adequate interpretation.

What might be said at the conclusion of this explanation? A fundamentalist hermeneutic of scripture based on an understanding of scripture as the inspired Word of God is first and foremost a hermeneutic of trust for the reader through a confessional description of the authorship and character of the text. Scripture is confessed to be the Word of God and thus to be true as the revelation of God. This confession establishes the true reader of the true text to be the one who fundamentally trusts that the language of the text is maximally utilized in revelation. The reader's response to the text is discipleship. The discipleship takes the form of humility before the

---

[21]E. G. Warfield, "Real Problem," pp. 225–226.
[22]Lindsell, pp. 37–38.

text and obedience to it. This does not necessarily issue in a reader whose identity is humble and obedient in conventional or socially acceptable ways. Rather the identity of the reader is humble and obedient to the text by engaging and interpreting the truth of the text which is itself beyond the authorship, interpretation and control of any individual or church, and lodged in God as Spirit. Obedience responds to truth rather than sheer authority; the reader is the one who trusts rather than cowers.

It is helpful at this point to recognize Warfield's admonition that ultimately inspiration as a religious topic is a consequence of scripture rather its presupposition. He writes:

> Were there no such thing as inspiration, Christianity would be true, and all its essential doctrines would be credibly witnessed to us in the generally trustworthy reports of the teaching of our Lord and of his authoritative agents in founding the church, preserved in the writings of the apostles and his first followers, and in the historical witness of the living Church. Inspiration is not the most fundamental of Christian doctrines, nor even the first thing we prove about the scripture. It is the last and crowning fact as to the Scriptures.[23]

The trust placed in the text by the reader is consequently a trust maintaining the truth of the text through interpretation, indeed through an interpretation which is secure in a confession that the Word of God and the words of humanity are not radically at odds.

Convergences and Divergences

The purpose of the above formation and explanation was to provide a position which brings fundamentalist and historical/literary biblical hermeneutics into conversational proximity. Some who identify themselves with fundamentalism would find this theological and hermeneutical reflection too permissive; some in the academy would find it too irenic. And yet by focusing on fundamentalist articulations within the context of the academy—fundamentalist scholars—rather than on fundamentalist congregations, a more productive albeit limited exchange might be initiated, one which tempers the excess of the stereotypes on both sides.

As a step in this direction I want to isolate three points of common

---

[23]Warfield, "Real Problem," p. 210.

hermeneutical interest and suggest how at each of these points there is room not only for divergence but also convergence.

Inspiration and the variety of biblical discourse.

Historical and literary criticism view inspiration as outside the reach of their methodological apparatus. Thus while open to it as a confessional or theological claim they are less willing to speak of inspiration as an historical or literary category precisely because it is often construed as a variation of the miraculous, a textual "deus ex machina." A fundamentalist hermeneutic recognizes the confessional basis of inspiration and yet is more willing on the theological grounds to accept an interventionist model. In a figure like Warfield, this is not crudely articulated. There is the recognition of historical, linguistic, social and literary individuality and development of each text and yet a privilege granted to the text as being "from God." Such a confessional position does not exclude critical study, at least if the confessional position recognizes a matrix in the doctrines of revelation, providence, grace and incarnation. And such convergence may indeed be fruitful. For example, a fundamentalist position tends to identify inspiration with a model of prophetic discourse and a structure of double authorship understood as one voice behind another. Paul Ricoeur offers a very helpful remark in this regard:

> When extended to all other forms of biblical discourse we are going to consider, this concept of revelation, taken as a synonym for revelation in general, leads to the idea of scripture as dictated, as something whispered in someone's ear. The idea of revelation is then confused with the idea of a double author of sacred texts, and access to a less subjective manner of understanding revelation is prematurely cut off. In turn, the very idea of inspiration, as arising from meditation on the Holy Spirit, is deprived of the enrichment it might receive from those forms of discourse which are less easily interpreted in terms of a voice behind a voice or of a double author of scripture.[24]

Ricoeur identifies other modes of biblical discourse, namely, narrative, prescriptive, wisdom and hymnic. Given this intra-biblical ground, a position which explicitly or assumptively confines inspiration to double authorship reduces biblical inspiration to the pro-

---

[24]Paul Ricoeur, "Toward a Hermeneutic of the Idea of Revelation" in *Essays in Biblical Interpretation*, ed. Lewis S. Mudge (Philadelphia: Fortress Press, 1980), p. 76.

phetic formula, "The word of Yahweh came to me." It is a reduction precisely because biblical discourse is not exhausted in prophecy. Rather than discarding the category of inspiration, literary and historical scholarship may in fact provide a corrective which expands the consideration of inspiration.

Hermeneutics of Trust/Hermeneutics of Certainty.

"Trust in the text" can cover a broad range of intentional positions. Lower criticism works to develop the trust-worthy text as the original. Higher criticism variously trusts the text as a privileged trace of historical or social events, the literary result of an identifiable process of production or even as a classic statement of the truth of a tradition. Again historical and literary criticism understand the phrase, "Word of God inspired by the Holy Spirit," as first order, confessional language and thus view the claims to trust at this level as outside their competence. A fundamentalist hermeneutic is more willing to admit textual trust not only in the authenticity of the text, or in the disclosure of religious truth, but in the text as the Word of God. Higher criticism is not fundamentally opposed to textual trust, even to trust in the text as religiously revelational. Where it does react is at that moment when a hermeneutic of trust turns into a hermeneutic of certainty. A certain sense of self-righteous interpretation seems often to go hand-in-hand with the immediate access to biblical meaning afforded through spirit filled, "literal" interpretation. A hermeneutics of trust need not entail a hermeneutics of certainty, for trust in a text and certainty, often exclusivity, of interpretation are not coterminous. Again an observation of Ricoeur is helpful here because he, like Warfield, would suggest that revelation is the proper context of inspiration; it is in fact the account of revelation which limits inspiration's potential for premature certainty.

> If one thing may be said unequivocally about all analogical forms of revelation, it is that in none of its modalities may revelations be included in and dominated by knowledge. In this regard the idea of something secret is the limit-idea of revelation. The idea of revelation is a twofold idea. The God who reveals himself is a hidden God and hidden things belong to him.[25]

---

[25]Ricoeur, "Revelation," p. 93.

When religious language begins to operate within a logic of certainty rather than that of testimony, then the appeal to inspiration becomes an appeal to heteronomous power. The danger is one in which the religious subject loses an openness to an identity shaped by the text in exchange for the false and destructive security of self-certainty. If inspiration fosters this authoritative certainty then it has lost focus on the nature of revelation and the discourse of testimony appropriate to it. Trust has been exchanged for certainty, revelation for knowledge, discipleship for security.

Inspiration, Certitude and Hope.

Ricoeur's previous comments on the relation of knowledge and revelation suggest a third hermeneutical commonplace. If a distinction can be maintained between a hermeneutic of trust and one of certainty then it is possible to inquire whether the trusted truth of the text is best intended in hope or certitude. A confessional position regarding the Bible is that it is the "true Word of God." Not only biblical criticism but even common reading can note contradictions, historical misplacements, contextually conditioned "science" and the like, all of which are candidates for the modern understanding of error. Fundamentalist hermeneutics can likewise recognize these modern candidates for error and suggest at least two strategies. The first is to maintain that a truly literal interpretation demands the recognition of figures of speech, irony, double meaning, etc., all of which resist confusing "literal" with univocal, surface or observational meaning. Being truly literal in fact decreases the possibility of error. The second strategy is to suggest a displacement of the resolution of the "errors" to a situation of better understanding. If this latter strategy is understood as one in which truly logical contradiction can be resolved by knowledge, then a hermeneutic of certainty is still lurking. If however the latter strategy is read as one of hope that the truth of the text will be not only maintained but understood as that which God reveals, then the hermeneutics of trust is maintained without the tyranny of certitude. As text of testimony to truth, the Bible proclaims something to be true and yet need not present this as knowledge achieved. Testimony issues in hope rather than in certainty. The one who hears and reads the testimony as testimony is the one who is willing to risk the incorporation of the truth into identity as a textual understanding which is self understanding. Ricoeur is willing to suggest that in the face of the limit to knowledge the proper stance before such textual interpretation may be summarized in the phrase, *spero ut intelligam*.[26] Likewise hope before the text maintains both an openness and a humility to the possibilities of truth which lie in front of the text. Certainly as much as unbelief is an impediment to interpretation so also is certainty precisely because both are premature closures to the truth of the text and a betrayal of the trust and hope demanded.

---

[26]Paul Ricoeur, "Hope and the Structure of Philosophical Systems," *Proceedings of the American Catholic Philosophical Society*, 14 (1970), pp. 55–69.

SOCIAL INSPIRATION: A RENEWED
CONSIDERATION

by Robert Gnuse

Introduction

For two millennia Christians have described the Scriptures as
inspired. Though there was some discussion concerning the nature
of this concept in the first eighteen hundred years, the vast bulk of
Christian discourse concerning the actual nature of inspiration has
arisen in the past two centuries. In a previous work this author
summarized briefly the various ways of defining inspiration which
have been proposed by Christians.[1] Theologians have debated
whether inspiration lay in the actual writings or the original spokespersons, whether inspiration extended to the ideas or both words
and ideas, and what the implications are for the veracity of the text:
is it infallible in matters of faith and morals only or does an
inerrancy extend to matters of history and science. In the most
simplistic terms the debate came down to two positions: one which
spoke very conservatively of a high degree of inspiration rendering
the text a valuable guide for faith and morals when interpreted and
obeyed quite literally, the other which spoke of a human element in
the creation of the text and a mode of inspiration which accommodated the revelation of God to human finitude and rendered the text
a source for theology along with other valuable resources, including
human reason. The different viewpoints expressed by theologians
occupied a wide range of options on a spectrum encompassing both
of these aforementioned positions.

The past generation has seen a renewed discussion of the nature

---

[1]Robert Gnuse, *The Authority of the Bible: Theories of Inspiration, Revelation and
the Canon of Scripture* (Mahwah, New Jersey: Paulist, 1985), pp. 14–65.

of inspiration, especially among Protestants. Conservative Protestants have been the most active in presenting a more sophisticated articulation of a high view of scriptural authority undergirded by the concept of inerrancy. Such spokespersons would call themselves Protestant evangelicals, though some of the most conservative members of the movement would even accept the label of fundamentalist, a term that the majority of authors would shun. Most of their literature has been put forth in the form of essays, so that no significant work has attained a central focus comparable to that of Benjamin Breckenridge Warfield's *The Inspiration and Authority of The Bible* in former generations. Central figures in the on-going evangelical discussion include John Warwick Montgomery, Clark Pinnock, David Carson, John Woodbridge, Roger Nicole, and several others.[2] Some of the theologians have taken a more moderate stance in their advocacy of the inerrancy position, so that within this group there is a degree of discussion concerning the articulation of a doctrine of Scripture.[3]

In distinction to this entire group some Protestant evangelicals have moved to a theological stance which no longer wishes to maintain inerrancy as an attribute of the Scriptures, especially in the affirmation that the text is perfect in matters of history and science. Rather, they prefer to maintain that Scriptures are infallible in matters of faith and morals alone, while historical and scientific matters are culturally relative and reflect the human knowledge of that era.[4] The tensions between those who hold to inerrancy and

---

[2]F. Benjamin B. Warfield, *The Inspiration and Authority of the Bible* (Philadelphia: Presbyterian and Reformed Publishing Co., 1948); Clark Pinnock, *Biblical Revelation: The Foundation of Christian Theology* (Chicago: Moody, 1971), pp. 53–106, 158–207; John Warwick Montgomery, ed., *God's Inerrant Word: An International Symposium on the Trustworthiness of Scripture* (Minneapolis: Bethany, 1974), especially the essay by Pinnock, "Limited Inerrancy: A Critical Appraisal and Constructive Alternative," pp. 143–158; Leon Morris, *I Believe in Revelation* (Grand Rapids: Eerdmans, 1976); Harold Lindsell, *The Battle for the Bible* (Grand Rapids: Eerdmans, 1976), a popular work for the laity which sharply attacked Protestant evangelicals who did not adhere to a sufficiently strict view of inspiration; James Montgomery Boice, ed., *The Foundations of Biblical Authority* (Grand Rapids: Zondervan, 1978); Norman Geisler, ed., *Inerrancy* (Grand Rapids: Zondervan, 1979); and D. A. Carson and John D. Woodbridge, eds., *Scripture and Truth* (Grand Rapids: Zondervan, 1983).

[3]Roger Nicole and Ramsey Michaels, eds., *Inerrancy and Common Sense* (Grand Rapids: Baker, 1980). It included a signal article by Nicole, "The Nature of Inerrancy," pp. 71–95, which defended a limited notion of inerrancy. See also Pinnock, *The Scripture Principle* (San Francisco: Harper and Row, 1984). In this he modifies his position.

[4]Gerrit Berkouwer, *Holy Scripture* (Grand Rapids: Eerdmans, 1975); Dewey Beegle, *The Inspiration of Scripture* (Philadelphia: Westminster, 1963) and *Scripture, Tradi-*

advocates of infallibility are great and often result in excommunications and job terminations of those who hold to the less stringent position of infallibility.

The more liberal Protestant position has likewise been reaffirmed in recent years. Traditionally, mainline Protestants have spoken of scriptural inspiration as pertaining to the ideas of the biblical text[5] or applying to the experience of the original spokespersons (prophets and apostles) but not to the words of the present text itself.[6] Recent articulations from the mainline Protestant stance or critical-scholarly viewpoint include work by Paul Achtemeier, James Barr, and others.[7] They seek to understand biblical authority in a more sensitive and complex way which takes into account modern critical-historical insights.

Generally, contemporary Roman Catholic discussions have leaned more in the direction of mainline Protestant viewpoints, if only for the reason that an extremely high degree of authority was not attributed to Scripture and the Scripture Principle was not the sole foundation for doing theology. Though Catholic scholars did debate whether the words or ideas of the text were inspired, especially during the nineteenth century,[8] nonetheless their positions were less stringent than the usual viewpoints of conservative Protestants, either of the traditional or the more recent vintage. Thus contemporary Protestant Evangelicals are not very receptive to Roman Catholic discussions on the issues of inspiration or biblical authority.[9] Nor

tion, and Infallibility (Grand Rapids: Eerdmans, 1973); Stephan Davis, The Debate about the Bible: Inerrancy versus Infallibility (Philadelphia: Westminster, 1977); and Jack Rogers and Donald McKim, The Authority and Interpretation of the Bible: An Historical Approach (New York: Harper and Row, 1979). Rogers and McKim recount the historical development of the concept of biblical authority and conclude that evangelicals ought to move toward the moderate position of infallibility.

[5]Harold DeWolf, A Theology of the Living Church (New York: Harper and Row, 1953), pp. 68–86 et passim.

[6]Harry Emerson Fosdick, The Modern Use of the Bible (New York: Macmillan, 1925) and A Guide to Understanding the Bible (New York: Harper and Brothers, 1938); and Charles Harold Dodd, The Authority of the Bible, rev. ed. (London: Fontana, 1960), pp. 27–28, 130, 264–270.

[7]Paul Achtemeier, The Inspiration of Scripture: Problems and Proposals, Biblical Perspectives on Current Issues (Philadelphia: Westminster, 1980); James Barr, The Scope and Authority of the Bible (Philadelphia: Westminster, 1980) and Holy Scripture: Canon, Authority, Criticism (Philadelphia: Westminster, 1983); also see William Countryman, Biblical Authority or Biblical Tyranny? Scripture and the Christian Pilgrimage (Philadelphia: Fortress, 1981) and David Barlett, The Shape of Scriptural Authority (Philadelphia: Fortress, 1983).

[8]James Tunstead Burtchaell, Catholic Theories of Inspiration since 1810: A Review and Critique (Cambridge, England: Cambridge University Press, 1969), pp. 58–163.

[9]Montgomery, "The Approach of New Shape Roman Catholicism to Scriptural Inerrancy: A Case Study," God's Inerrant Word, pp. 263–281.

were the Roman Catholic positions as polarized into liberal and fundamentalist/evangelical categories as has been the case among Protestants.

The recent sensitivity displayed by the Roman Catholic Church to the impact of conservative Protestants and fundamentalists upon its membership brings the debate concerning biblical authority and inspiration into consideration. The two positions, "word inspiration" and "idea inspiration," seem to be the poles between which one must hold to a theological stance. But this may not be the case.

Since World War II Roman Catholics have spoken of a new mode of inspiration which sidestepped the issue whether individual persons or written text were inspired and the extent of that inspiration. This new model was far more sensitive to the recent strides in biblical studies which enabled scholars to see Scripture as the result of a long process of development. Called "Social Inspiration" by advocates and critics alike, it posited that inspiration lay in the community of faith which produced the documents of the biblical text. This was a new way of viewing the debate, and it might yet prove to be a model acceptable to a wide range of biblical theologians both Roman Catholic and Protestant. The first person credited with raising the discussion was R. A. F. McKenzie whose presidential address before the Catholic Biblical Association raised the general question of how to assign inspiration when so many people were involved in the generation of the text.[10]

Fuel for the discussion was provided by the biblical scholar Pierre Benoit and the systematic theologian Karl Rahner.[11] Benoit's perception that different degrees of inspiration must be accorded to the many individuals involved in the process and Rahner's description

---

[10]R. A. F. McKenzie, "Some Problems in the Field of Inspiration," Catholic Biblical Quarterly 20 (1958): 1–8.

[11]Their contributions were assessed by: David Stanley, "The Concept of Inspiration," Proceedings of the Thirteenth Annual Convention of the Catholic Theological Society of America (Yonkers, New York: St. Joseph's Seminary, 1958), pp. 76–84; John L. McKenzie, "The Social Character of Inspiration," Myths and Realities: Studies in Biblical Theology (Milwaukee: Bruce, 1963), pp. 63–64, and "Inspiration," Dictionary of the Bible (New York: Macmillan, 1965), p. 392; John Topel, "Rahner and McKenzie on the Social Theory of Inspiration," Scripture 16 (1964): 34–40; Wilfrid Harrington, Record of Revelation: The Bible (Chicago: Priory, 1965), pp. 120–128; John Scullion, The Theology of Inspiration, Theology Today Series, vol. 10 (Notre Dame: Fides, 1970), pp. 36–44; Bruce Vawter, Biblical Inspiration, Theological Resources (Philadelphia: Westminster, 1972), p. 111. Stanley ("Concept," pp. 84–85) and J. McKenzie ("Inspiration," p. 392) both give credit to Bernhard Brinkmann, "Inspiration und Kanonizität der Heiligen Schrift in ihrem Verhältnis zur Kirche," Scholastik 33 (1958): 208–33, for contributing to the development of a social inspiration model.

of inspiration as a charism of the Apostolic Church and as a communal function were combined to articulate the notion of social inspiration. John McKenzie then provided the key essay which expressed this model.[12] Critical response from colleagues sought to refine the model, but since the 1960's the model has not received much attention.[13]

This brief essay seeks to raise the discussion once more and provide new impetus and new direction to the explication of the model. It builds upon previous work by this author wherein the model was described and evaluated in neutral fashion.[14] Let us first review the principals involved in the discussion, and then move to a critical re-articulation of the model of social inspiration.

Pierre Benoit

The noted French scholar Pierre Benoit helped lay the foundation for talk about social inspiration more than any other individual.[15] He defined inspiration in the broadest sense as an impulse from the Holy Spirit to act, speak, or write, since the creation of the biblical text involved all of these. Therefore he sought to redefine inspiration so as to include all the functions in the process of generating the Scriptures. Sensitive to the advances made by modern critical biblical studies, he was well aware of the significance of oral tradition

[12]"The Social Character of Inspiration" first appeared in *Catholic Biblical Quarterly* 24 (1962): 115–24 and was reprinted in *Myths and Realities*, pp. 59–69.

[13]Dennis McCarthy, "Personality, Society, and Inspiration," *Theological Studies* 24 (1963): 553–76; an abbreviated version of this article was reprinted under the same title in *Modern Biblical Studies*, eds. Dennis McCarthy and William Callen (Milwaukee: Bruce, 1967), pp. 18–30; Harrington, *Record*, p. 131; and Scullion, *Theology*, pp. 48–9.

[14]Gnuse, *Authority*, pp. 50–62.

[15]Paul Synave and Pierre Benoit, *Prophecy and Inspiration*, trans. Avery Dulles, French ed. 1947 (New York: Desclee, 1961), pp. 84–168; Benoit, "La Septante est-elle inspirée?," *Vom Wort des Lebens: Festschrift für M. Meinertz* (Münster: Westfalia, 1951), pp. 41–49; see also Benoit, "Inspiration," *Guide to the Bible*, eds. Andre Robert and A. Tricot, trans. Edward Arbez and Martin McGuire (New York: Desclée, 1960), I, pp. 9–52; "Note complémentaire sur l'inspiration," in *Revue Biblique* 63 (1956): 416–22; "The Analogies of Inspiration," *Aspects of Biblical Inspiration*, trans. Jerome Murphy-O'Connor and S. K. Ashe (Chicago: Priory, 1965), pp. 13–35; "Inspiration Biblique" and "Inerrance Biblique," *Catholicisme*, ed. G. Jacquemet (Paris: 1963), 5:1539–49, 1710–21; "L'inspiration des Septente d'après les Pères," *L'homme devant Dieu: Mélanges offerts au Père Henri du Lubac, S. J.*, 3 vols. (Paris: Aubier, 1963), I, pp. 169–87. "Revelation and Inspiration," *Aspects*, pp. 36–127; and "Inspiration and Revelation," *The Human Reality of Sacred Scripture*, Concilium, vol. 10 (New York: Paulist, 1965), pp. 6–24.

and its transmission and evolution in the hands of many anonymous spokespersons. Heretofore the doctrine of inspiration seemed to imply only the final writer or redactor was inspired, even though his or her efforts might be minimal in regard to the finished product.

Throughout his career Benoit used Thomistic categories to generate terms to describe the inspiration of the various stages in the evolution of the biblical text. Early in his career he spoke of dramatic, prophetic or apostolic, and hagiographic forms of inspiration to describe the Spirit's impulse to lead people to live a certain lifestyle, to speak orally, and to write, respectively (1947).[16] In other writings he used the categories of cognitive, oratorical, and scriptural inspiration to describe the initial illumination, oral proclamation, and writing (1958).[17] He preferred to combine the categories of speaking and writing, and define them as the result of "practical judgment," while the initial illumination resulted from "speculative judgment."[18] Though he did sometimes speak of "speculative judgment related to action" in reference to oral proclamation, which he called "prophetic inspiration."[19] The use of all these terms, of course, was artificial, since it was impossible to truly understand the dynamic of inspiration, and doubtless Benoit believed that. But these categories were pedagogically helpful and they impressed upon the reader that inspiration as a charism was visited upon more than just the writer of the text. Wilfred Harrington, for example, effectively utilized these categories in his textbook on the Bible.[20] Inspiration was a charism involved at many stages in the evolution of the text, a point reiterated by Benoit frequently.[21]

Inspiration "ceases to be the charisma of one isolated individual working in a vacuum."[22] But since the degree of contribution by individuals to the ongoing process of scripture formation was uneven, the degree of inspiration must be different, and therefore Benoit felt compelled to define different terms for inspiration at different stages of the process. The "charisma of inspiration may

---

[16]Synave and Benoit, Prophecy, pp. 126–27.

[17]Ibid., p. 127, and "Analogies," pp. 16–17.

[18]Synave and Benoit, Prophecy, pp. 103–19; "Inspiration," Guide, I, pp. 12–28; "Analogies," pp. 17–19, 30–31; and "Revelation," Aspects, pp. 101–21. See also Stanley, "Concept," pp. 76–79.

[19]Benoit, "Analogies," pp. 30–31; and "Revelation," Aspects, p. 111. See also Scullion, Theology, pp. 36–40.

[20]Harrington, Record, pp. 25–39.

[21]Synave and Benoit, Prophecy, pp. 123–37; "Inspiration," Guide, I, pp. 30–31; "Analogies," pp. 25–26, 34–35; and "Revelation," Aspects, p. 121.

[22]"Inspiration," Reality, p. 17.

have been shared by a large number of individuals, but in different degrees."[23]

Benoit's logical deduction, however useful the result, did lead to artificial categories. Though these categories are nice pedagogical tools, they may be considered dispensable, and perhaps to use the word inspiration in a generic fashion stripped of specifying nuances may now be the best direction in which to move.[24] Ultimately, logical deductions are symbolic statements conditioned by the philosophical presuppositions to which an author is indebted; they are not primary categories of the text. Primarily Benoit's purpose was to dethrone a definition of inspiration which viewed it merely as the impartation of propositional revelation, and to that end his definitions were useful and successful.

Benoit's most useful notion for the continued discussion was the emphasis on inspiration as a charism visited upon many people in a process. He especially emphasized that inspiration was given to specific individuals rather than the group as a whole. In fact, he criticized the notion of "collective inspiration," a concept which denied inspiration to individuals in favor of the greater community of faith.[25] This important distinction was lost in later expressions of social inspiration, which emphasized that the believing community was the source of the inspiration. Many of the criticisms levelled at the theory of social inspiration remarked on its undue emphasis upon the group and the denial of creative expression to individual authors.[26] Perhaps the demise of the model occurred for this reason more than any other. A return to Benoit's nuance and a re-emphasis upon the individual within the group as the recipient of the charism might re-invigorate the model.

Karl Rahner

Karl Rahner provided the theological basis for later advocates of social inspiration. His views on the subject of inspiration are found

---

[23]Synave and Benoit, Prophecy, p. 124.

[24]In Key to the Bible (Garden City, New York: Doubleday, 1976), pp. 41, 47, Harrington pointed out that many of the Thomistic categories have been abandoned.

[25]Benoit, "Analogies," pp. 25–26; and "Inspiration," Reality, p. 16.

[26]McCarthy, "Personality," p. 572; Scullion, Theology, pp. 45–49; William Heidt, Inspiration, Canonicity, Texts, Versions, Hermeneutics: A General Introduction to Sacred Scripture, Old Testament Reading Guide, vol. 31 (Collegeville, Minn: Liturgical Press, 1970), p. 36; and Luis Alonso-Schökel, The Inspired Word: Scripture in the Light of Language and Literature, trans. Francis Martin (New York: Herder and Herder, 1972), p. 224.

in several of his writings, but the most significant work was *Inspiration in the Bible*.[27] The result of his efforts was to focus attention on the community as the locus of inspiration.

Rahner addressed the question how God and a human author both could be the author of sacred Scripture.[28] He defined God as the creator or author of the Apostolic Church (*Urkirche*) which in turn authored the Scriptures through the agency of individual writers.[29] Thus inspiration was a unique function of the ancient Church and Scriptures were the articulation of that early community: " . . . this apostolic church . . . has objectified itself, has settled down, made itself concrete and has expressed itself in what we call Holy Scripture."[30] Scriptures are the deposit of an oral tradition produced in the Church, the normative precipitation of the earliest community.[31]

Rahner's emphasis upon the corporate *Ecclesia* highlighted a distinctive Roman Catholic agenda. His discussion of the relation of Scripture and Tradition led him to describe Scripture and the Church, or more particularly the Magisterium, as the co-terminus creation of God. God created the Church, which then created Scripture, which in turn remains "the concrete norm for the post-apostolic Church in its future understanding of the faith."[32] Scriptures are normative because they come from a crucial moment in the formation of the Church.[33] Rahner's response to the traditional

---

[27]Karl Rahner, "Über die Schriftinspiration," *Zeitschrift für Kirche* 78 (1956): 137–68, which was later expanded into *Inspiration in the Bible*, Quaestiones disputatae, vol. 1, trans. Charles Henkey, (New York: Herder and Herder, 1961), pp. 6–80; "Écriture et Tradition à propos du scheme conciliare sur la revelation divine," *L'homme devant Dieu*, III, pp. 209–21; "Exegesis and Dogmatic Theology," *Dogmatic vs. Biblical Theology*, ed. Herbert Vorgrimler (Baltimore: Helicon, 1964), pp. 31–65; "Observations on the Concept of Revelation," *Revelation and Tradition*, Quaestiones disputatae, vol. 17, trans. W. J. O'Hara, German ed. 1965 (New York: Herder and Herder, 1966), pp. 9–25; *Theological Investigations*, vol. 6: *Concerning Vatican II*, trans. Karl H. and Boniface Kruger (New York: Seabury, 1969), pp. 89–112; and *Foundations of Christian Faith*, trans. William Dych, (New York: Crossroad, 1978), pp. 369–78. His contributions in this regard have been evaluated by Topel, "Social Theory," pp. 33–44; Harrington, *Record*, pp. 119–28; Scullion, *Theology*, pp. 40–44; and Vawter, *Inspiration*, p. 111.

[28]Topel, "Social Theory," p. 35; Harrington, *Record*, pp. 120–22; Stanley, "Concept," pp. 71–75.

[29]Topel, "Social Theory," pp. 39–40; Harrington, *Record*, pp. 120–28; J. McKenzie, "Inspiration," p. 392; and Scullion, *Theology*, pp. 40–44.

[30]Rahner, *Theological Investigations*, p. 376. A similar expression can be found in *Foundations*, p. 102: "Scripture itself is the concrete process and the objectification of the original church's consiousness of the faith."

[31]Rahner, "Schriftinspiration," pp. 137–68; "Écriture," pp. 209–21; *Inspiration*, pp. 39–63; and *Foundations*, pp. 158–61.

[32]Rahner, *Foundations*, p. 363.

[33]Ibid., pp. 361, 373, and *Inspirations*, p. 74.

expression of the Two Source theory was to describe Scripture and Tradition in circular fashion, each one foundational for the other. Rahner concluded:

> Since Scripture is something derivative, it must be understood from the essential nature of the church. . . (God) is the inspirer and the author of scripture, although the inspiration of scripture is "only" a moment within God's primordial authorship of the church.[34]

Thus Rahner really wished to address the question of Scripture and Tradition as well as the nature of the Church rather than an actual doctrine of scriptural inspiration.[35] Hence, biblical exegetes who followed the direction provided by Rahner would naturally emphasize the corporate or collective nature of social inspiration, and this would lead them away from Benoit's nuance which stressed inspiration as a charism residing in many individuals.

Some problems arise with Rahner's thesis: 1) His emphasis upon the Apostolic Church as the origin of the charism relegated the entire Old Testament to a dependent status; it was not truly Scripture until the Church took it into the canon.[36] Few biblical scholars would accept this subordination of the Old Testament. It has been noted that John McKenzie's redefinition provided the correction by describing Israel at least as a society, if not a Church.[37] But such a redefinition may have vitiated the foundational presupposition of Rahner concerning the formative period which those later "social inspirationalists" built upon. 2) Rahner seems to have two levels of meaning for the concept of tradition. Tradition which is the oral proclamation or kerygma of the Apostolic Church did indeed generate Scripture. But there is a qualitative difference between that and the later traditions of the Church, over which the ecclesiastical officials preside and which is subordinate to Scripture. This distinction would ruin Rahner's view of the circularity of Scripture and Tradition as coequal pillars of the faith. The tight interrelationship in Rahner's thought between Scripture and Tradition led the discussion of social inspiration away from the process which generated scriptural texts to the thorny problem of ecclesiastical development. Perhaps the inclusion of this side issue may have led to the demise or disinterest in social inspiration.

---

[34]Rahner, Foundations, pp. 371, 375.
[35]Harrington, Record, pp. 119–20.
[36]Rahner, Inspiration, pp. 51–54.
[37]Vawter, Inspiration, p. 112.

John McKenzie

The classic form of the social inspiration theory was articulated by John L. McKenzie in his article, "The Social Character of Inspiration," where he indicated his dependence upon both Benoit and Rahner.[38] Observing that most biblical works were authored anonymously and by many individuals in a process of oral tradition, McKenzie concluded we cannot speak of individual authors in a modern sense, nor can we therefore speak of inspired individuals.[39] McKenzie spoke very strongly of how the writer lacked individual identity:

> I suggest that the ancient author was anonymous because he did not think of himself as an individual speaker, as the modern author does. He was anonymous because in writing he fulfilled a social function; through him the society of which he was a member wrote its thoughts. He was its spokesman and the society was the real author of the literature. . . . The modern author is an artist who feels a compulsion to express his individuality through his art; the ancient writer, if we can judge from what he wrote, was more interested in concealing his individuality. He wished to be the voice of Israel and of the Church, to produce in writing utterances which were not the expression of his own mind but of his society.[40]

Inspiration worked within the community to develop the Scriptures; God worked through the community to affect individuals to formulate particular insights.[41] But even though individuals were used, inspiration should not be limited to them any more than to the written books, for individuals were merely spokespersons for their society into which they were completely submerged. McKenzie noted: "In some sense Israel and the Church must be conceived as the real authors of the Bible."[42]

The biblical traditions reflect more than the sum of individual expressions, they reflect values of the entire community. Were an author lacking in knowledge, he or she would consult the community's traditions, the greater kerygma. The author has a religious experience only because the community provided the possibility for

---

[38]Topel, "Social Theory," pp. 41–42; Harrington, Record, pp. 129–32; Scullion, Theology, pp. 44–49.

[39]J. McKenzie, "Social," pp. 60–63.

[40]Ibid., pp. 64–65.

[41]Ibid., p. 68.

[42]"Inspiration," p. 392.

it with worship and piety. Authors are not inspired to write in isolation. Authors wrote and theologized as representatives of the community, and their work was designed to edify the community.[43] McKenzie paraphrased Rahner when he said that the authors of the New Testament books "wrote them as officers and representatives of the Church which is the real author of the New Testament."[44] Thus inspiration died as the oral tradition faded several generations after Jesus.[45]

McKenzie built upon the work of Benoit and Rahner by self-admission, but he seems to have interpreted Benoit through the theological lens of Rahner.[46] In his article he summarized what he believed to be Benoit's position, citing the articles in *Sacra Pagina* and *Guide to the Bible*, when he observed that "None of these charismata are properly understood if they are considered as communicated to the individual; they are primarily communicated to the Church within which they are expressed, and for which they are given."[47]

McKenzie has presented a highly nuanced version of Benoit's views. Benoit still maintained a strong emphasis upon the charism of inspiration as a gift bestowed upon the individual. McKenzie overlooked that theme in Benoit and emphasized the corporate dimension.

Critical Response

McKenzie's views were critiqued by several authors.[48] Dennis McCarthy took issue with the characterization of the ancient writer as lacking individuality. He noted: "The total submergence of the individual in a tradition of impersonal production is not, in fact, indicated by the ancient Oriental literature."[49] In particular, the

---

[43]McKenzie, "Social," pp. 66–67. Cf. Pierre Grelot, "Tradition as Source and Environment of Scripture," trans. Theodore Westow, *The Dynamism of Biblical Tradition*, Concilium, vol. 20 (New York: Paulist, 1967), p. 15; and Richard Smith, "Inspiration and Inerrancy," *Jerome Biblical Commentary*, eds. Raymond Brown, Joseph Fitzmyer, and Roland Murphy (Englewood-Cliffs, New Jersey: Prentice Hall, 1968), pp. 508–9.

[44]J. McKenzie, "Social," p. 64.

[45]Ibid., p. 68.

[46]Harrington, *Record*, pp. 129–32.

[47]J. McKenzie, "Social," p. 64.

[48]McCarthy, "Personality," pp. 553–76; Harrington, *Record*, pp. 129–32; Scullion, *Theology*, pp. 48–49; and Gnuse, *Authority*, pp. 57–62.

[49]McCarthy, "Personality," p. 554.

creative and self-critical growth of the literature in the Hebrew canon indicated that the authors did not exhibit a simple piety toward previous tradition, and their anonymity did not prevent the expression of individual and critical viewpoints over against received tradition.[50] The social origin of inspiration is inadequate as a concept, for "the great streams of Old Testament revelation are deeply marked by personalities."[51] Likewise, Wilfrid Harrington believed McKenzie to have overstated the case. From the New Testament perspective Paul and John appear to have communicated far more than what their religious community furnished them.[52] Essentially, the critics felt that McKenzie's approach did not give enough credit to the genius of individuals.

There are a number of strengths in the social inspiration model which recommend it, however. The model places the charism of inspiration clearly upon people rather than upon the literature. The model recognizes the process of oral tradition and transmission from which written Scripture finally arose. The modern mind with its orientation toward the empirical and social sciences is more receptive to a model which uses social categories in some way, especially one which seeks to accept seriously the cultural background to the literature. Problems with other theories of inspiration are avoided in some way: whether inspiration extends to ideas or to both the words and the ideas, whether there are degrees of inspiration, and whether only the final writer was inspired.[53] The model has enough strengths to merit retaining it in the discussion of inspiration.

But criticisms levelled against McKenzie's approach and the subsequent discussion indicated revisions were necessary. In particular, there were several weaknesses. Even if inspiration was a community charism, the significance of individuals could not be overlooked, otherwise inspiration was rendered amorphous. Great literature is not produced by "everybody"; specially gifted individuals arise to generate artistic expressions superior to those of their contemporaries.[54] If literature only reflects the understanding of the group, how does a creative advance occur? The traditio-historical development of literature seems to imply a growth attributed to insightful theologians, such as the prophets and Paul, rather than the entire group.[55]

---

[50]Ibid., pp. 569–70.
[51]Ibid., p. 572.
[52]Harrington, Record, p. 131.
[53]Gnuse, Authority, pp. 57–59.
[54]Ibid., p. 59; see also Scullion, Theology, p. 45; Alonso-Schökel, Word, p. 224.
[55]McCarthy, "Personality," p. 572; Scullion, Theology, pp. 46–49; and Gnuse, Authority, p. 59.

Above all, the dynamic of dissent in the generation of literature may be overlooked. Job, for instance, challenged traditional views of retribution, expressed previously in Deuteronomy. Deuteronomy clarified existing notions of covenant found in the Sinaitic traditions and the royal Psalms. Koheleth challenged the optimism expressed in Proverbs concerning the human ability to grasp wisdom and discover meaning in life. Finally, Paul challenged traditional Jewish-Christian values. Where would the community of faith be without the courageous manifestos of insightful individuals? Books of the Bible arose from "the repeated, centuries-long confrontation by individuals raised up to denounce the infidelity and immorality of the social group."[56]

New Directions for the Model

What is needed, therefore, is a clarification and modification of the model which takes these criticisms into account. Several of McKenzie's colleagues moved in this direction with their critique of his position. McCarthy stressed how individual identity and community must be held in tension as we articulate the model of inspiration.[57] Scullion likewise spoke of this tension between community tradition and individual genius.[58] Vawter pointed out that the creative words of individuals were filtered through the medium of the community's faith.[59] This filtration would have affected the shape of the oral tradition received by the individual genius, but the community filter was also responsible for transmitting and preserving the contributions of the creative individual. Harrington could speak of the inspiration process as God working through the community to affect a spokesperson, or as a community charism exercised by individuals.[60] Thus the subsequent consensus among Roman Catholic biblical exegetes declared the need to re-emphasize the importance of the individual in the community of faith.

The creation of any piece of literature involves a subtle interplay between an author and his or her cultural tradition. In turn the community relies upon benefits conferred by the creative genius of

---

[56]Heidt, Introduction, p. 15.
[57]McCarthy, "Personality," pp. 553–76. See Scullion, Theology, p. 48, for a comment upon McCarthy's views.
[58]Scullion, Theology, p. 49.
[59]Vawter, Inspiration, pp. 106–7.
[60]Harrington, Key, pp. 47–48.

such individuals. As this is true for all literature, it is especially true for religious literature. The observation of Benoit in this regard is an apt starting point: "(inspiration) illuminates and directs a structured society through individuals chosen and personally endowed with charisms to serve the group."[61]

The model of social inspiration is more sensitive to the biblical text than any other model of inspiration, yet it seems to have been forgotten after the initial flurry of discussion in Roman Catholic circles twenty years ago. The reasons for this are hard to discern, since the overall interest in discussing models of inspiration has increased in the past generation, especially in Protestant circles. Protestant awareness of the social inspiration model (and Roman Catholic discussions in general) appears to be minimal; among evangelicals in particular, where extensive discussion of this topic occurs, response to social inspiration is rather limited and fails to adequately comprehend the dynamics of the model.[62] Perhaps because the Roman Catholic discussions, especially in the writings of Rahner, addressed ecclesial matters and the relation of Scripture to Tradition, many Protestants failed to pay attention to the discussions. Often Protestants fail to read Roman Catholic systematic theology so as to develop a fuller sensitivity to the naunces of the discussion.

Yet Protestant theologians and biblical scholars have voiced sentiments quite similar to their Roman Catholic counterparts. For example, James Barr would say:

> If there is inspiration at all, then it must extend over the entire process of production that has led to the final text. Inspiration therefore must attach not to a small number of exceptional persons . . . it must extend over a larger number of anonymous persons . . . it must be considered to belong more to the community as a whole.[63]

Likewise Paul Achtemeier observed:

---

[61]Synave and Benoit, *Prophecy*, p. 127.

[62]John Warwick Montgomery, "The Approach of New Shape Roman Catholicism to Scriptural Inerrancy: A Case Study," *God's Inerrant Word*; pp. 263–81. His invective was bitter but ineffective, since he maintained that the discussions only reproduced traditional Roman Catholic views with some liberal Protestant nuances and he failed to note the new directions provided by the concept of social inspiration.

[63]James Barr, *Holy Scripture*, p. 27; he made similar observations in *Fundamentalism* (Philadelphia: Westminster, 1978), pp. 288–9, and *The Scope and Authority of the Bible*, pp. 124–5.

Inspiration, in short, occurs within the community of faith and must be located at least as much within that community as it is with an individual author. . . . nameless people who formulated, retold, and adopted the traditions that went into the sources (are inspired) . . . inspiration must be understood to be at work in all who shaped, preserved, and assembled portions of the traditions contained in the several books.[64]

Like his Roman Catholic counterparts Achtemeier repeatedly stressed that inspiration must reside in the process of oral tradition which results from the interplay of communal need and reflection upon the traditions which address those needs, for herein is the most dynamic part of the process.[65] But Achtemeier emphasized how the process is one of critique upon the various traditions and the community which produced the traditions.[66] In short, there is a dialectic involved in producing the text, the values of which arise by way of critique of the community of faith from which they arise.

It would seem that under the aegis of contemporary critical biblical scholarship the model of social inspiration has a chance to flower. But it must be articulated in more ecumenical fashion, embodying concepts from the Protestant perspective. To begin we should return to Benoit's stress upon many inspired individuals in the process endowed with a special charism, for this is the common notion shared with Protestant theologians, as well as the corrective to McKenzie's model. It might be best to drop the various distinctions proposed by Benoit to describe inspiration, since we are attempting to describe a reality beyond our comprehension. Rather, we should speak of inspiration in a generic sense applying to bards, prophets, transmitters of oral torah and legends, collectors, redactors, and scribes.

Furthermore, the critics of McKenzie who stressed the tension between individuals and the community have focused upon a second significant tenet. What remains is a better definition of the nature of that tension and especially a better definition of the concept of "community." A chief weakness of the Roman Catholic discussion was a facile definition of community, which could allow a naive equation of community with institutional leaders, or as Rahner called them, "officers of the Church." Institutional leaders

---

[64]Paul Achtemeier, *The Inspiration of Scripture*, pp. 116, 132, 133.
[65]Ibid., pp. 90–2; 102–3; 123, 134.
[66]Ibid., pp. 92, 115–18.

in the Old Testament and New Testament were not the source of the charism of inspiration; they were too often the targets of critique by those individuals of genius who directly generated the oral traditions and the sacred literature. Certainly Benoit would not have made such a naive equation, nor even perhaps Rahner and Mc-Kenzie, but their language could permit the equation of community with its leaders. In his early writings Benoit even suggested that the levels of inspiration operative in his definitions could form the basis for distinctions among ecclesiastical leaders of the structured Church.[67] This was the great unconscious leap of Roman Catholic scholars: to move too quickly from describing a Scripture generating process to the evolution of ecclesiastical structures. Protestants analogs would be far less liable to this *faux pas*, for obvious reasons.

How then should we define the community which is inspired and which produced the inspired individual? There is a community of believers within the greater community of the faithful which produces the context out of which the individual genius will arise to articulate new insight. For example, the prophetic movement and the Deuteronomic reform were ideological movements which constituted a clear minority in pre-exilic Israel. These movements drew all Israelites ultimately toward a monotheistic and ethical religion. But they cannot be equated with the greater community of Israel, which was to a great extent syncretistic. Nor were their theological leaders the institutional leaders of the Israelite faithful; rather, movement leaders stood in opposition to the established priestly and royal leadership, until eventually their position of dissent became the norm. Then again a later wisdom circle had to protest Deuteronomic and prophetic notions of retribution, and out of this circle arose the inspired genius who created the book of Job.

Likewise in the New Testament Paul was a dynamic and revolutionary individual, but he did not stand alone. Presumably he arose in theological circles who gave him initial insight which he took to new heights. Then his writings were subsequently preserved in Paulinist circles until they become our written text. But the Paulinists were not the Church; they were a component part of it, much as the Pauline literature is now a part of the New Testament but certainly not the totality of it. Paul stood in clear opposition to the greater structures of his age, the Jewish-Christian leadership in Jerusalem, exemplified in the person of James. James likewise epito-

---

[67]Synave and Benoit, *Prophesy*, p. 127.

mized a community which had its viewpoints re-called in some Christian texts (e.g. Matthew, Hebrews, and James). These examples demonstrate the naiveté of speaking so simply of the community which supports the individual. We rather have communities within the greater community.

If we use the social inspiration model we must speak of the inspired community as that specific movement which supports the inspired genius, for it, and not the greater community of all believers be it Israel or the Church, provides the ideas and preserves the literature. Attributing inspiration to the greater community renders the concept of inspiration amorphous and makes it impossible to discern how change occurs. For the community that supports the individual is often a community of dissent which perceives more clearly the direction of the greater religious tradition and arises to voice an inspired proclamation for which inspired individuals become the spokespersons. Rahner's description of inspiration residing in the Apostolic Church must be refined to speak of inspiration residing in the spearhead movements of the Apostolic Church.

This leads to another observation: the necessity of acknowledging that inspiration generates change, development, or a process. The greater community of believers does not reside with a static theological position. If the notion of tradition is a meaningful concept, it implies that the teachings of the Church evolve. Faithful to the core of the Gospel, the teachings of the Church evolve in every generation to proclaim the old message in new form.

The early advocates of social inspiration models did not stress the notion of change sufficiently. Social inspiration refers to the creative surge of the Spirit leading Israel or the Church forward in thought and social values. This reiterates the emphasis upon how the individual may counter the commonly held beliefs of his or her religious contemporaries. The smaller support group behind the individual is also in the process of developing, and this places the group in a position of critique over against the greater religious tradition. In essence, inspiration as a charism visited upon the community is a force which promotes change, re-adaptation, and new insight. The individual is the focal point through which the ideas are expressed. Even such a solitary figure as Jeremiah is really the quintessential result of the greater prophetic movement. Inspiration is not a static charism which leads the genius merely to summarize the thoughts of a community in systematic fashion; rather, it causes change, disruption, insight, but above all, creative advance.

Early Roman Catholic advocates of social inspiration knew this, but to vocalize it clearly would have been a concession to an image of inspired authors as reformers or revolutionaries within a greater religious-social matrix. To assume such an evolutionary paradigm implies that every Christian generation must be ready to correct, adapt, or reform the teachings of an earlier generation. That is painful, for it acknowledges that the respected and beloved teachings and piety of our forebears might be at times inadequate, and that some day our most profound articulations may equally become insufficient for human needs. Yet clearly this is implied by the evolution of tradition manifest within the Scriptures themselves. Such an acknowledgement might be easier for Protestant theologians than for Roman Catholic theologians of a former generation; hence, the concept of social inspiration may be developed in the future only with the addition of Protestant perspectives.

Conclusion

Where have we come? Roman Catholic biblical theologians made a significant contribution to biblical theology with the presentation of the model of social inspiration. If the model is to be revived and given a broader base for the consideration of a wider range of theologians, certain nuances need to be made: 1) The tension between community and individual must be maintained, lest the significance of the individual genius be lost. 2) The contributions of various people in the process of generating Scripture should not be characterized by different terms for each function. Granted, the nature of the genius involved at each level of development may be different, but we are not capable of defining the symbol of inspiration. 3) The community which provides the charism of inspiration to an individual ought not be defined as the entire religious tradition, but rather as that specific school of thought, movement, or social-religious group which nurtures the spokesperson and preserves the traditions and the literature. 4) The aspect of dissent or critique is an important function of the inspired movement which produces the spokesperson. For the dialectic of critique is what ultimately enables the entire religious community to move creatively forward in the process of generating a true tradition. 5) Social inspiration must be seen as involved in a dynamic process of change, not simply in a static mode of preserving what had been said in the past. The process promotes reform, and only in this way may we explain the "growth" of Scripture or Tradition. In these ways the model of social inspiration may become a healthy mode of discourse among biblical and systematic theologians.

REASON, FAITH, AND AUTHENTIC RELIGION

Cynthia Crysdale

Sandra's Dilemma: Reason and Faith in Conflict

Let us begin by recounting a story. Imagine, if you will, a young girl of age 14. She is an average student, somewhat shy, but eager to join in group activities and a spirited participant once she has loosened up. This girl has been raised in a nominal Christian home in which God, like sexuality, is something everyone knows exists but about which no one ever speaks openly. Our young girl, let us call her Sandra, often lies awake at night, talking or crying or complaining to the empty darkness, not sure if she is talking to God or just musing to herself.

Now put yourself in Sandra's shoes on a damp December night on a church retreat in the woods of West Virginia. After a day of hilarity, adventure, and competitive play, a large assembly of teenagers sits enthralled as an energetic and handsome young man begins talking about God in a way that Sandra has never heard before. He tells stories about Jesus, stories that take place in her high school corridors, that speak of fears she has never admitted to anyone and of love she has barely dared to hope for. At the end of the man's moving speech everyone exits in silence. Sandra too walks out into the damp night and wanders in the rain, wondering if the empty darkness is just empty or if there is something more to be reached, to be spoken to, to be loved. When finally she is chilled to the bone she creeps back to her cabin, silently takes off her sodden clothes, slips into her pajamas, and shyly joins the circle of girls sitting on their beds crying and talking about Jesus. With her heart pounding in her throat Sandra finally gets up enough courage to ask whether, when she talks to the darkness, there is really Someone listening. The others encourage her to realize that, yes, there is Someone out there and that this Someone is Jesus, who can be her friend and companion. Sandra slowly admits that the experience everyone has been talking about, that is, the experience of meeting and accepting Jesus, has happened to her. With hugs and tears the group accepts her and she is counted among those who have "made a commitment" on this weekend retreat.

This is the story of Sandra's conversion: but the story does not end at the camp in West Virginia. Sandra returns home and, though she does not have the courage to mention her conversion to her family, she does start attending the Fellowship Bible Study for girls. She is fascinated by the Bible and longs to understand it but she is treated as a bit odd when, instead of gossiping and crying about boyfriends as the other girls do, she actually wants to talk about God. In spite of the fact that the Fellowship insists on the Bible as the sole source of faith, whenever she raises questions about the truth of the Bible her questions are dismissed as the queries of an unbeliever. Her companions in the Fellowship fail to encourage her intellectual pursuits and, in fact, exhort her to be very careful about what sorts of books she reads and the kinds of courses she takes. In spite of her growing faith and maturity she is never asked to give public talks at the Fellowship meetings but is always relegated to reciting inspirational messages to new converts in the backrooms. When her high school education ends she ignores the warnings of her spiritual brethren and attends a secular university where she enrolls in numerous religious studies courses. With both fear and excitement she discovers the complexity of the Bible and encounters advocates of critical Bible interpretation as well as experts in the sociology of religion. Other Christians on campus criticize these courses as heretical and dangerous to faith. Sandra finds herself confused and once again begins questioning the empty darkness. The certainty, relief, and love of the damp December night in West Virginia now seem far removed as conflicting voices challenge, on the one hand, the validity of her critical intellectual pursuit and, on the other hand, the reality of a conversion that now seems childish.

Sandra's story is a story that belongs to many within the Christian faith. It is the story of those who have grown to the point of adding critical thought to religious experience. The actual particulars of one's conversion and the issues around which one's intellectual questions arise may differ from tradition to tradition. One may come to question the authority of the magisterium in teaching doctrinal truth or one may come to view scripture from a critical distance.

From this new perspective one may mock one's previous devotion to the Sacred Heart of Jesus, or come to view a dramatic conversion experience as merely emotional immaturity. Whatever the form religious conversion may have taken, and whatever the experiences and insights that cause one to challenge this conversion, the crisis of faith that results from being introduced to innovative and critical ideas is a difficult, but perhaps not uncommon, experience.

Because Sandra's story strikes a common chord in the experience of many who have tried to make faith critical but no less "faithful," let me explore some dimensions of Sandra's dilemma in an effort to clarify what is at stake here. My analysis relies on the work of Bernard Lonergan and his position on human knowing.[1] I will draw out as well the implications of this position for moral and emotional life, based on Lonergan's discussion of moral conversion and Robert Doran's presentation of psychic conversion. In doing this I hope to provide some clarifications that will help to distinguish authentic from unauthentic routes that Sandra (indeed, all of us) could take out of her crisis.

The problem that Sandra faces can be conceived as a conflict between reason and faith. Sandra has come to a point at which to be reasonable means to jettison much of the spiritual, symbolic, and emotional truth that she had previously embraced. The people who encourage her to use her critical reasoning skills have also put her religious tradition in such a new light as to make it seem fraudulent. The sources she used to rely on for spiritual sustenance are now seen to be highly ambiguous: a mixed bag of varying perspectives rather than a single voice of truth. Reason demands that she face these contradictions and accept the facts that are now revealed. On the other hand, her own faith requires that she not reduce transcendent truth to merely that which is within the domain of reason. Her religious friends caution her against making her subjective reason the arbiter of faith. A dichotomy emerges in which reason is associated with hard core facts whereas faith is relegated to matters of mere opinion or, at best, a mediator of some reality that is not subject to critical questioning.

Bernard Lonergan's philosophical method reveals that this dichotomy is not as severe as it first appears. The opposition between reason and faith is not ultimately contradictory but is a complemen-

---

[1]See Bernard Lonergan, *Insight: A Study of Human Understanding* (London: Harper and Row, 1957) and *Method in Theology* (New York: Seabury Press, 1972).

tary interaction between two ways of gaining knowledge. But grasping this complementarity is only possible if we examine some false assumptions about both reason and faith. The first issue is whether knowing the facts is quite as simple as just taking a good look (even if that "look" is a highly technical literary or scientific endeavor). The second issue has to do with the role of belief in our knowledge. We tend to assume that believing involves only moral maxims or religious opinions and has nothing to do with facts or with reality.

Let me try to deal with the second assumption first by asking you, the reader, to distinguish between what you know because you have discovered it yourself and what you know because you trust someone else's knowledge. The mechanic tells us what is wrong with our car. The doctor explains the possible side effects of a certain drug as well as the risks of not taking the drug. Experts explain why hurricane Hugo took the path that it did. In all these cases we have gained some knowledge: we understand why our car doesn't work, we know about Drug X, we can explain what happened to hurricane Hugo. But in none of these circumstances did we ourselves undertake the experimentation, the postulation of possible theories, the verification of one theory over another, that would be involved in discovering these facts for ourselves. In other words, most of what we know we have not discovered for ourselves.

At the same time there is in each of us a persistent drive to understand things for ourselves, to raise questions, to look for evidence, to verify our hunches. There are some questions we do pursue in an effort to discover for ourselves what the facts of the matter are. Perhaps we don't trust the mechanic, or are skilled enough to do our own tinkering under the car until we figure out the problem. Each of us has some area of expertise in which we have made our own discoveries through struggling with a problem until an insight arises.[2]

The point is that knowing involves two different but complementary movements. There is the way of belief, what Lonergan calls "the way down," in which we accept others' discoveries. There is also

---

[2]One way to grasp the difference between having an insight oneself and accepting the judgments of others is to reflect on the experience of "getting" or "not-getting" a joke. Someone may tell you a joke at which others laugh but which misses you entirely. This person may explain the punch line to you. You may even tell the joke to others and make them laugh. You know the joke and can perhaps repeat the explanation of the punch line. But until you have "gotten" the joke, that is, had an insight into the meaning of the joke, you haven't discovered the humor of the joke for yourself.

the way of discovery, "from below upwards," when we begin with a problem and work with it until we have an insight, test and verify our hunch, and conclude with an answer. These two ways of gaining knowledge are distinct but not contradictory. Our knowledge will always be some mixture of that which we know through trusting others and that which we have discovered for ourselves.

The important thing here is to recognize that our knowledge of facts has as much to do with belief as it does with discovery.[3] The maps we use, the medicines we take, all rely on believing certain facts. In fact, science itself couldn't go forward without trusting previously discovered facts. If every scientist were to verify for herself each fact that underlies her current experiment, science would amount to nothing more than perpetually re-inventing the wheel. Instead, scientists try out new theories based on previous discoveries of other scientists. If these earlier discoveries are erroneous, these errors emerge in the current research and the scientist backtracks to correct what he had simply accepted on faith.

This puts the dichotomy between reason and faith in a new light. It is not the case, as is often assumed, that reason discovers facts while faith accepts opinions. A large portion of the facts that we know, we know through faith in others' expertise. While it is quite possible that these other people are mistaken, this does not mean that we should jettison belief altogether. The issue is not one of belief versus knowledge but of whom one believes and why. One needs to distinguish, not between the hard facts of reason and the questionable opinions of belief, but between valid believing and mere credulity. One need not rail against reason as the enemy of faith, but against critical thought that is inconsistent with its own inherent norms.[4]

---

[3]For more on the role of belief in knowing, see Lonergan, Method, pp. 41–47, and "Belief: Today's Issue," in A Second Collection, eds. W. F. J. Ryan and B. J. Tyrell (London: Darton, Longman, and Todd, 1974).

[4]I am equating "faith" and "belief" in a somewhat imprecise manner. I mean faith both as the deposit of faith and as the process of believing. In using the word this way I am clearly associating it with the "way down," with inheriting faith through faith in others. In doing this I do not mean to convey that faith has nothing to do with the "way up." Indeed, faith is part of the orientation toward intelligibility, truth, and value. In fact, Lonergan distinguishes between faith as an orientation to divine mystery that is fulfilled in receiving the gift of God's love, and beliefs which are formulations of faith. In equating faith and belief here I do not mean to say that faith is simply a matter of receiving truth or of trusting others. Indeed, I am saying just the opposite, that faith involves both a journey of discovery and trusting those who have gone before. For more on this topic, see Lonergan, Method, pp. 115–119 and 326–330.

This brings us to the first issue mentioned above: false assumptions about the process of discovery. Many people assume that we discover things for ourselves simply by taking a good look at them. Facts are there to be grasped if we just turn our attention in the right direction. When it comes to historical interpretation, as is the case in a theological endeavor to know the truth of scripture or tradition, taking a good look becomes a mental rather than a physical look. Nevertheless, the truth is obvious if we manage to "look" carefully enough.

In contrast to this assumption, Bernard Lonergan has pointed out that the process of discovery involves, not just looking, but a series of operations. In fact, there are four distinct types of operations that all persons use recurrently in their knowing and doing. At a primary level we all have experiences: of sight, sound, touch, taste, smell, or of ourselves as conscious. This experiencing is the occasion of our questioning: we spontaneously want to know what it is that we experience, why it has happened, what caused it. If our car suddenly sputters to a halt we seek to understand what has happened. But we do not merely postulate coherent explanations, we go on to make judgments, to determine which of the myriad possibilities has in fact caused our car to stop. Is it overheated, are we out of gas, is there something wrong with the transmission? So from **experience** we seek to **understand**, and out of many potentially correct explanations we make a **judgment** as to which is the case here and now. Yet having determined the facts we shift to a fourth level of **deciding** what to do. And clearly the levels, though distinct, are interrelated. A different set of experiences would lead to a different judgment. (Smoke pouring out from under the hood is evidence weighing strongly against the car merely being out of gas.) And the action one takes relies heavily on how one judges the facts. (Should one call the nearest gas station or the local fire department?)

Thus, the process of discovery involves more than merely "looking." It involves an invariant and recurrent pattern of operations that moves beyond mere looking to understanding, judgment, and decision. How is this pattern related to the way of belief? Towards the end of his life, Lonergan hinted that perhaps the "way down" had a parallel structure. Just as development from below upwards begins in experience and moves through understanding, judgment, and the apprehension of value in decision, so the handing on of development ". . . begins in the affectivity of the infant, the child, the son, the pupil, the follower. On affectivity rests the apprehension of values;

on the apprehension of values rests belief; on belief follows the growth in understanding of one who has found a genuine teacher and has been initiated into the study of the masters of the past. Then, to confirm one's growth in understanding comes experience made mature and perceptive by one's developed understanding . . ."[5]

In other words, just as the way of discovery involves a recurrent pattern of experience, understanding, judgment, and decision, so also the way of belief, or heritage, involves these four elements but works in the opposite direction. Because of this affective connection the learner apprehends certain **values**, accepts as correct certain ways of behaving. **Judgments of fact** are then adopted by reflecting on these values or simply received by believing the trusted source. Questions for **understanding** then arise: persons want to grasp the intelligibility of what they have accepted as true. As understanding increases, **experience** itself changes to become more mature and perceptive.

Furthermore, this way of heritage is the chronologically prior phase. The ability to ask questions, to make discoveries for ourselves, is a mere potential in the child. Experiences must accumulate, understanding of accepted beliefs and values must expand, before one can even ask questions for oneself. The spirit of inquiry is there from the start, but the actuation of capabilities is a slow process. How can one develop the right attitudes, habits, the skills of inquiry if one does not already have them? The answer, of course, is that one has a teacher who guides the way, who initially exhorts the child not to touch the hot stove, and only later explains why. Prior to the slow road of achievement, and contributing to it, is the way of heritage, of accepting as given the knowledge and values of others.

The structure of reason and faith could be portrayed as follows:

THE WAY OF DISCOVERY	THE WAY OF BELIEF
(Loving)	(Loving)
Deciding	Values received
Judging	Beliefs accepted
Understanding	Explanations adopted
Experience	Experience molded

---

[5]Lonergan, "Natural Right and Historical Mindedness," in *A Third Collection: Papers by Bernard J. F. Lonergan, S. J.*, ed. Frederick E. Crowe (New York: Paulist Press, 1985), pp. 180–181. Frederick E. Crowe develops this idea of two directions of knowing in his discussion of the "way of achievement" and the "way of heritage" in *Old Things and New: A Strategy for Education* (Atlanta: Scholars Press, 1985).

Notice that the relationship between these two ways of knowing is not ultimately contradictory. There is a dialectical interaction between the two, an on-going revision and critique of both types of knowledge. The way of heritage and belief comes first. When one is able to think for himself he begins questioning what he has been told. He may unearth errors, factual or moral, in the fund of knowledge he has received. Indeed, discovery advances not only from ignorance to truth, but also from error to truth.[6] This is not to say that immanently generated knowledge is always right and received knowledge always wrong. Many errors are made in the way of discovery, through oversight, human limitations, or bias. It is the fund of common knowledge that often corrects these errors, or at least becomes the occasion for re-examining one's discoveries. New discoveries or revisions of old ones are passed on to others, thus becoming themselves part of the common fund of belief.

So it is that the pursuit of truth and authentic living is an ongoing interaction between knowledge as received and knowledge as discovered. Neither faith nor reason has a monopoly on the truth. Rather, each is part of a self-correcting process of learning in which faith is challenged and enriched by creative discovery and reason is held accountable by the common fund of knowledge and its canons of accuracy.

Objectivity and Authentic Subjectivity

Let us return to Sandra for a moment. Given the foregoing explanation of belief and discovery, we can understand Sandra as caught in a shift between the way of heritage and her own critical creativity. Indeed, her own journey began within the depths of her affectivity, through her longing for connection with something beyond herself and her attraction to those who had found such a transcendent fulfillment. She accepted the values of those whom she loved and admired. Her own love for God issued in obedient acceptance of a certain lifestyle. She accepted by belief the judgments of her faith community and adopted their doctrinal positions. In attempting to make sense of these doctrines she grasped the coherence of the explanations of her teachers. All of this confirmed her experience and molded it towards greater depth of perception.

This increased perception and maturity, however, has brought her

---

[6]See Lonergan, *Method*, p. 44.

to the point of raising questions about the tradition itself, about the grounds on which its claims are made. Accepting the beliefs of others no longer satisfies her curiosity. She is on the verge of moving out of a conventional acceptance of her religious faith to a more critical grasp of her religious heritage.[7] Her religious heritage has now become data for the process of discovery. She wants to know that what she believes is really true. She wants to judge for herself.

Now it is quite possible that Sandra's dilemma will remain at the level of questioning *what* it is that she believes. She may decide that her university professors are correct, that their judgments and values are well-grounded and should be embraced.[8] Or she may decide in favor of her previous faith community, having analyzed and grasped for herself the insights and judgments on which its beliefs are founded. She may create her own personally held set of beliefs and/ or find a community that endorses some such mixture of beliefs.

It is also possible, and I would suspect most likely, that Sandra's questions go deeper than just *what* it is she believes. She is also implicitly questioning *how* it is that she believes and *why*. It may not be only religious doctrines she is questioning but the very grounds on which any religious doctrine is founded. In her case, the issue at hand has to do with scripture: what is its authority and how does Sandra know it is true?[9] But underlying this question is an even

---

[7]In developmental terms, perhaps Sandra is involved in a shift from what James Fowler calls "Synthetic-Conventional Faith" (Stage 3) to "Individuative-Reflective Faith" (State 4). See *Stages of Faith: The Psychology of Human Development and the Quest for Meaning* (San Francisco: Harper and Row, 1981). This move away from conventionally accepted faith to individual, critical faith at times results is a complete rejection of what one had accepted through the way of belief. There are others who remain perpetually in this transition and never really resolve it (see Fowler, 179). My exposition here of reason and faith and of objectivity is an attempt to lay a groundwork by which persons can transform and re-integrate much of their traditional religion rather than rejecting it altogether.

[8]Note that there is no guarantee that Sandra's university professors will be any clearer on the relationship between reason and faith or objectivity and subjectivity than members of her Fellowship are. These are issues that underlie not only theology but all disciplines, inasmuch as these disciplines involve knowing and there are a host of ways in which people conceive what their knowing involves. Note also that the intellectual conversion I am advocating will not necessarily promote authentic faith. It could lead to a rationalism or idealism that is antithetical to faith. This is one reason why Robert Doran developed his position on psychic conversion: psychic conversion re-connects thought to the sensitive flow of living and mediates between religious conversion and intellectual conversion. See my discussion of this below and Doran's article, "Psychic Conversion," *The Thomist* 41 (1977): 200–36.

[9]My experience as a Protestant studying theology at a Roman Catholic institution was that the crisis of faith is often the same though it differs in the locus of the issues. In our Foundations of Theology course I became quite agitated when we discussed

more fundamental one: how does she know anything is true? Challenging the authority of her faith as mediated through a particular tradition leads Sandra to ask: How do I know my faith and this tradition are authentic? How do I know anything?

It is precisely this question that Bernard Lonergan spent his life addressing and that I began to deal with above. It is a question in which the process of knowing becomes a matter for discovery. By attending to one's own operations of knowing, one realizes that, in making a discovery, one does more than just "look" at the data. This discovery is what Lonergan calls "intellectual conversion":

> Intellectual conversion is a radical clarification and, consequently, the elimination of an exceedingly stubborn and misleading myth that knowing is like looking, that objectivity is seeing what is there to be seen and not seeing what is not there, and that the real is what is out there now to be looked at. Now this myth overlooks the distinction between the world of immediacy, say, the world of the infant and, on the other hand, the world mediated by meaning. The world of immediacy is the sum of what is seen, heard, touched, tasted, smelt, felt. It conforms well enough to the myth's view of reality, objectivity, knowledge. But it is but a tiny fragment of the world mediated by meaning. For the world mediated by meaning is a world known not by the sense experience of an individual but by the external and internal experience of a cultural community, and by the continuously checked and rechecked judgments of the community. Knowing, accordingly, is not just seeing; it is experiencing, understanding, judging, and believing. The criteria of objectivity are not just the criteria of ocular vision; they are the compounded criteria of experiencing, of understanding, of judging, and of believing. The reality known is not just looked at; it is given in experience, organized and extrapolated by understanding, posited by judgment and belief.[10]

Note that you can grasp this fact only if you attend to yourself as a subject. You take the proposition that knowing is not just looking (that is, is not just sense experience) but also involves understanding sense experience, judging that certain propositions are correct, mak-

---

the "mediation of revelation" through Scripture, while my Roman Catholic friends found my questions somewhat incidental. The situation reversed itself, however, when we got to the "mediation of revelation" through the Church. The class erupted with questions and criticisms while I looked blankly on. I finally realized that their questions were exactly the same as mine—How can I know the truth of this source of theology?—but centered around a different source.

[10]Lonergan, Method, p. 238.

ing decisions to pursue the truth, and accepting the discoveries of others. You then come to a judgment on this proposition (about knowing) by checking the evidence. But the evidence you must refer to is the evidence presented by yourself as an operating subject. You must attend to, understand, and make a judgment about your own process of attending, understanding, judging, deciding, and believing. In other words, the only way to make an accurate judgment about knowing is to pay attention to yourself as a knower.

The key to intellectual conversion is thus the self-appropriation that is not the result of any particular theological position but the foundation of all authentic theological positions.[11] What prevents this self-appropriation and its consequent theological claims from the indictment of being "merely subjective" is the recognition that the operations of the subject include their own norms of objectivity. These norms are constituted by the native orientation we all have toward discovering intelligibility, ascertaining the truth, and knowing and creating a good beyond criticism. They are operative in us before we can name them, they exist without being inculcated through education.[12] It is our inherent orientation to intelligibility, truth, and value that provides the impetus for questioning and for creative living. It is this native orientation that lets us know when we have arrived at correct answers. Hence the norms of objectivity are within us, not in some external authority that we merely accept or obey. Being objective lies within the realm of authentic subjectivity.

Let me emphasize this last phrase, "authentic subjectivity." If one begins with the assumption that knowing involves getting out of one's mind in order to have access to what is "already out there now real" then the terms "objective" and "subjective" come to be equated with reliable external facts over against arbitrary internal feelings or opinions. However, if one comes to the discovery that knowing involves creative insights and discerning judgments, that one contributes a good deal more to the knowing process than merely sensing, then one must begin to recognize that there are norms

---

[11]For Lonergan self-appropriation is foundational to any theological enterprise. It is something the theologian does as an integral part of her theologizing. It is not an addendum or a conclusion to her theological positions. See Lonergan's discussion of method in *Method*, chap. 1.

[12]What education does is to train us in how to skillfully use and develop an orientation that already exists. The key factor in education is whether an educational approach encourages recognition and pursuit of the transcendental notions or not. See Crowe, *Old Things and New*.

within the subject that contribute to the objectivity of knowledge.[13] Then the question of objectivity asks, not whether one is adhering to some standard "out there," but whether one is authentically adhering to the internal exigence to understand clearly, to verify the truth, to know and create value. The criterion of objectivity is thus authentic subjectivity.[14] Vernon Gregson puts it as follows:

> Whenever we use the full capacity of our subjectivity, all of our levels of consciousness, all of our desire to experience, our desire to under-stand, and our desire to find the truth, then our conclusions have a claim to objectivity. If we don't use all that we are, then our conclusions are merely arbitrary and "subjective" in the pejorative sense. Lonergan makes the point of the relationship between objectivity and subjectivity quite strikingly in his statement: "Objectivity is the fruit of authentic subjectivity." The full use of all of our capacities leads to objectivity, and nothing less than that leads to objectivity. Intellectual conversion is the recognition that that is true.[15]

The Distrust of Subjectivity

I have used Sandra's story as a means of illustrating a dilemma that is prevalent today. It is a dilemma that underlies many crises in religious living as well as pervading many theological controversies. I have tried to show that the dilemma itself is often conceived inaccurately as a dichotomy between "hard facts" and "mere opinions," that gaining both moral and factual knowledge comes by believing others and by discovering things for oneself. Most of all, I have emphasized that discovery involves more than merely "looking" and, hence, that objectivity is not a matter of comparing inner pictures to outer reality but of adhering authentically to certain inherent norms.

I would now like to relate this position to a trend in Christian religious circles to distrust anything "subjective." I am not referring to any specific Christian tradition but to groups of believers within a

---

[13]Of course one of the internal norms that contributes to objectivity is the impera-tive to pay attention to what is "out there." My point is not that objective knowing is a totally internal or intuitive process. Sense experience, attention to the data "out there" is an important and integral part of making judgments of fact. But it is not the only operation involved in objective knowing and to think that it is to distort the issues of objectivity. See Lonergan, *Insight*, chap. 13.

[14]On the terms "subjective" and "objective," see Lonergan, *Method*, pp. 265, 292.

[15]Vernon Gregson, "The Desire to Know: Intellectual Conversion," in *The Desires of the Human Heart*, ed., V. Gregson (New York, Paulist Press, 1988), p. 27.

variety of denominations. The common thread amongst these persons and groups is that they implicitly adopt a solution to the modern crisis of faith that overlooks the operations of the subject and that misconstrues the problem as an issue of adherence to external authorities and/or doctrines.

Perhaps the best way to discuss this is to portray Sandra's Fellowship group as typical of the trend to which I am referring. In contrast to my presentation of the complementarity between critical reason and the knowledge of faith, members of this Fellowship regard critical thinking with great suspicion. Because so much of the higher criticism and the modernist trends of the twentieth century have seemed to undermine what is most precious to Christian believers, groups like Sandra's Fellowship feel the need to protect the fundamentals of the faith; and to protect them specifically by presenting critical thought as the enemy of faith. Michael Fahey describes this trend as fundamentalist:

> Fundamentalists, whatever their church, tend to regard critical awareness and questioning in regard to the faith with high distrust. For them, faith is a matter of conviction expressed in the heart-felt rhetoric of revivalism (a very common form of Protestant fundamentalism) or in the rooting of one's faith in the pronouncements of authority (the more usual Catholic form). Both forms are what theologians call types of "fideism," that is to say, an expression of religious faith which does not regard itself accountable to the faculty of reason. The true fundamentalist sees openness to change as a kind of infidelity.[16]

From this perspective it is clear why the Fellowship tries to dissuade Sandra from developing her questions on the authority of the Bible or other matters of faith. The assumption is clear that endeavors of this kind are dangerous to authentic faith, and that faith is retained by remaining within clearly defined parameters of safe teaching.

Implicit in this stance is the related distrust of the operations of the subject as "merely subjective." Rather than recognize the exigence to discover truth for oneself as inherently normative, members of the Fellowship adopt an erroneous dichotomy between objectivity and subjectivity. Objective truth is something outside that one looks at, albeit with the look of faith. Subjective process is always rendered suspect. The notion that being objective requires one to be authenti-

---

[16]Michael Fahey, "What Makes a Fundamentalist?" in *Ecumenism* 91 (1988): 7.

cally subjective—that is, to follow an internal exigence to be intelligent, reasonable, and responsible—is rejected. What is required for objectivity is adherence to some external standard. James Barr puts it as follows:

> Nothing is more marked in that [mental] structure than the sense of need for objectivity. Non-conservative theological arguments might be attractive, but in the last resort they are subjective, that is, they depend on the arguments of this man or that man, while some other man will have a different argument. Critical scholarship studying the Bible is also subjective: someone says that the J passages in Genesis are different from the P passages, but how can one be sure of this, especially when some other scholar will come along and make a different separation? How can one escape from this subjectivity? The only way is to make it clear that the centre of authority lies beyond the range of human opinion altogether. The inspiration of the Bible means that, though it is a product of identifiable human authors, it lies beyond the range of human subjectivity. . . . The fundamentalist thus thinks that he has a standard of absolute truth which stands entirely outside of himself and thus lends objectivity to his position as accepter of this standard.[17]

The net result of this viewpoint is that persons cannot be relied upon as communicators of the truth. Rather, the Bible (or the magisterium, or some dogma or set of doctrines) becomes reified into a reliable object "out there" which is not subject to the whims and fancies of human opinion. Any attention to the subject, any hint that truth involves the participation of a human subject, is immediately treated with suspicion.[18] Barr concludes:

> Objectivity thus comes to mean that the truth is not in people. Persons cannot be relied on. The only thing upon which you can rely is something objective in the sense that it stands beyond the realm of human personal life. . . . Objectivity in religion means that man must have something that 'confronts him as something outside of himself.'[19]

I am not claiming that there is no role in authentic faith for external sources: remember that the way of heritage often guides and

---

[17]James Barr, *Fundamentalism* (London: SCM Press, 1981), pp. 311–312.

[18]There is of course a contradiction here since both the Bible and the teachings of the magisterium emerge from human authors. But the reification of these authorities removes their human subjectivity from them and makes them reliable and objective sources. See Barr's discussion of the Bible, pp. 312–313.

[19]Ibid.

corrects the process of discovery. What I am concerned about is the tendency to reify truth and leave the human subject out altogether. What begins as a valid attempt to establish the fundamentals of faith deteriorates into an entrenched insistence that truth lies in certain doctrines or sources themselves, and that valid faith consists of adhering uncritically to these doctrines or sources. The two go hand in hand: the notion that truth is external to human subjectivity and that faith means obedience to external authority. When these are combined any advertence to subjective process is dismissed as "merely subjective" and therefore dangerous to faith.

In and of itself, this faulty epistemology could be innocuous enough. Indeed, there are many, in the present and the past, who have lived lives of authentic faith without being able to explain the knowing process and/or the grounds of objectivity. Nevertheless, the misconstrual of the dilemma of reason and faith and mistaken assumptions about objectivity can have dangerous implications for the authenticity of faith. Let me elaborate.

First of all, the viewpoint I have described above rests on an erroneous view of what it means to be human. As I have tried to point out, to be human is to be inherently oriented toward asking questions, questions that are themselves normative. To be human also means to accept certain facts and values as a heritage received through belief. To deny any of this is to put oneself in a position of performative self-contradiction. In the very act of denying that one performs certain operations, one will perform them. In the very act of denying that there are norms operative in human consciousness, one will appeal to these norms.[20]

When this performative self-contradiction gets translated into a community of faith, the result is a disjunction between what is promulgated as authentically human and how people actually operate. The fact is that people spontaneously ask questions; the want to understand, to judge truth from error, to discern values and make decisions. They attempt to do these because they are responding to internal norms that point beyond themselves toward self-transcendence. To label this subjective process as the enemy of truth and authentic faith is to ask people to live a contradiction, to deny the very orientation that is the source of their pursuit of truth and good living. Rather than creating persons or communities of enriched human life, this results in stifling the best of human nature. It is like telling people that breathing oxygen is at the root of human illness.

---

[20]See Lonergan, *Method*, pp. 16–17.

Secondly, this stance is all in favor of the truth of heritage and very critical of critical reasoning. This means that the self-correcting process of learning by individuals and in communities never takes place. The critical distance on tradition that arises out of the way of discovery is stifled on the assumption that the tradition is always correct.[21] The healthy dialectical tension in which discovery weeds out unauthentic elements in the way of heritage and in which tradition challenges new discoveries is stifled.

The counterpart of this lack of balance is that the carriers of the tradition, that is, those in positions of authority, become the arbiters of truth and the sole instigators of any change that comes about. Any bias or inauthenticity on the part of these carriers of tradition is never subject to open scrutiny. In and of itself, this is not always bad, as long as those whom one believes are living authentically religious lives. But if they are not, the silencing of creative discovery is also the stifling of truth and authenticity. Then learning in the way of belief means faithfully adhering to an unauthentic faith.[22]

In sum, the misconstrual of the modern crisis of faith as a conflict between "subjective" critical inquiry and the "objective" contents of faith runs the severe risk of hampering and not promoting authentic faith. This solution to the modern problem is a solution that not only stifles Sandra's individual religious growth but hampers the faith community itself, holding it within the confines of a select set of doctrines and practices without any critical reflection or revision. It is only by self-appropriation, by attending to the operations of oneself as a knower, that one grasps the inherent normativity of one's own subjectivity. By excluding this self-appropriation from the start, through ignoring or even denigrating the role of the subject in knowing, these Christians overlook the very source required for making modern faith authentic faith.[23] Ironically, their very attempt

---

[21]Let me also point out that the appeal to tradition here is often selective. That is to say, it is not the tradition as a whole that is held up as authoritative but particular teachings within the tradition. This can be true whether one appeals to Biblical teaching or certain doctrines. The point is that the critical distance provided by the way of discovery is never allowed to provide the corrective to this selective interpretation of belief, a corrective that would return tradition to its "catholic" stance.

[22]Lonergan speaks of major and minor authenticity or inauthenticity. Minor authenticity has to do with the subject in response to the tradition that nurtures her. Major authenticity involves the justification or condemnation of the tradition itself. To the degree that the tradition itself has become unauthentic, minor authenticity means authentically realizing inauthenticity. See Lonergan, *Method*, pp. 79–81.

[23]Another way of saying this is in terms of different realms of meaning, that is, the worlds of common sense, of theory, and of interiority. While many believers function

to protect authentic religion results in cutting off authentic religious growth.

Moral and Emotional Dimensions of the Problem

So far I have focussed on issues of how we know truth, how we discover whether what we believe is valid or not. But this entire discussion of objectivity and subjectivity has implications as well for moral and emotional life. I would like to draw these out by discussing Bernard Lonergan's position on *moral conversion* and Robert Doran's analysis of *psychic conversion.*

Moral conversion involves changing the criterion of one's choices from satisfactions to values. It also involves coming to a recognition of the role one plays in creating the values one lives by. It is part of an ongoing moral development in which one gradually lays aside the imposed rules of others and more and more claims freedom to make one's own choices.[24] In referring to this moral development Lonergan says:

> So we move to the existential moment when we discover for ourselves that our choosing affects ourselves no less than the chosen or rejected

with an authentic faith arising from the world of common sense, contemporary culture has moved beyond common sense to theory and is now struggling to move beyond mere theorizing to questioning realms of interiority: the modern "turn to the subject." While there are many modern answers to questions about interiority, with varying degrees of adequacy, a position that rejects the questions themselves, hoping to return to a world of common sense in which no one wonders how we know, amounts to burying one's head in the sand. While religious conversion may be authentic without intellectual conversion, in our day and age it is hard to imagine how religious development can go forward without at some point confronting the crisis of belief that the turn to the subject has brought about. Furthermore, while religious living may be authentic without cognitive self-appropriation, the task of reflecting on religion, of theologizing, requires such a self-appropriation if it is to avoid a jungle of errors. To the degree that Sandra's Fellowship (or its Theologians) accept the role of the subject in knowing it will encourage her to pursue her questions, even if she herself never objectifies the process of knowing. On realms of meaning, see Lonergan, *Method,* pp. 81–85. On the modern exigence for intellectual conversion, see Doran, "Psychic Conversion," p. 211.

[24]Those who have worked extensively on Bernard Lonergan's notion of conversion have come to distinguish uncritical moral and religious conversion from critical moral and religious conversion. The distinction has to do with whether one has actually stepped back and reflected on what one is doing in opting for value over satisfaction and/or in falling in love with God. While moral conversion may be a genuine and uncritical adherence to a set of rules that define the difference between value and satisfaction, my discussion of moral conversion here has more to do with the critical recognition of the role one plays in creating oneself as moral person. For a fuller discussion of this, see Walter E. Conn, *Conscience: Development and Self-Transcendence* (Birmingham: Religious Education Press, 1981), pp. 190–194.

objects, and that it is up to each of us to decide for himself what he is to make of himself. Then is the time for the exercise of vertical freedom and then moral conversion consists in opting for the truly good, even for value against satisfaction when value and satisfaction conflict.[25]

This discovery is a discovery of moral autonomy. It may not be explained in philosophical terms of authenticity and self-appropriation, but it nevertheless involves a shift from accepting values in the way of belief to realizing that we can discover and create values on our own. Walter Conn describes it as follows:

> In such a discovery we recognize ourselves as originators of value who create ourselves in every deed, decision, and discovery of our lives, for the subjective effects of these personal acts accumulate as habits, tendencies, and dispositions determining the concrete shape of our very selves. Such a discovery demands that we take hold of and in radical freedom, responsibly choose ourselves precisely as the originating values we have recognized ourselves to be. . . . The essential point of moral conversion is that after it occurs, our creation of ourselves is open-eyed and deliberate.[26]

This recognition that we participate in creating our own moral standards is not, as some might fear, equal to a submission to ethical relativity. It is in fact quite the opposite, because it involves acknowledging the transcendental notion of value that underlies and orients all our moral deliberations. The essential question becomes not whether we will obey an external and therefore objective and reliable moral standard but whether we will authentically pursue questions of deliberation and consistently act on the answers at which we arrive. Once again, moral objectivity in knowing and moral rectitude in living depend on authentic subjectivity.

The dangers of missing this point are that moral norms are reified and never subject to individual or communal scrutiny. Sandra's Fellowship may make a clear distinction between acting for mere satisfaction and acting on the basis of value. But if the values advocated are determined solely by external authorities, then obedience, not creative discovery, is the norm. In this case the values of self-discovery, of autonomy, and of critical reflection are discredited in favor of conformity, certainty, and avoiding the tension of inquiry.

[25]Lonergan, *Method*, p. 240.
[26]Walter E. Conn, "The Desire of Authenticity: Conscience and Moral Conversion," in Gregson, *Desires*, p. 49.

Moral discernment then comes to mean checking to see whether one's behavior matches the prescriptions of some external source, not a self-reflective effort to determine what is right to do in this situation. At its worst, the good can be reified in a way that, rather than preserving the integrity of the individual or the community, merely heightens the role of the collective ego.

An important aspect of moral conversion has to do with the role of feelings in moral judgments. Lonergan insists that values are apprehended in feelings; not in just any feelings, not just in feelings which are the result of a physiological discomfort, but in feelings that are oriented to an object and that move one beyond oneself. These are feelings oriented to objects of value not just objects of pleasure. It is in these feelings that one discerns the value of a certain action. Feelings *apprehend* values. In judgments of value we *affirm* what the correct action is. In decision and action we *create* the value apprehended and affirmed. But feelings, like our consciences, are nurtured and directed: first, by those who are responsible for our upbringing and, then, by ourselves. To the extent that moral conversion involves the critical recognition that we play a role in creating ourselves as moral persons it will also involve a recognition of affective autonomy. That is to say, we will come to accept the role we play in encouraging certain feelings and curtailing others, and we will take responsibility for our affective development.[27]

This brings us to a discussion of what Robert Doran calls psychic conversion. Intellectual conversion involves a self-appropriation of the acts of understanding and judging. Critical moral conversion occurs when one discovers what one does in making decisions. Psychic conversion has to do with the self-appropriation of feelings and their symbol systems as they arise in consciousness and contribute to decision making. Doran says:

> . . . [T]he primordial entry of the subject onto this fourth level [of decision making] is affective, "the intentional response of feelings to values." Furthermore, affective response for Lonergan is symbolically certifiable, in that a symbol is "an image of a real or imaginary object that evokes a feeling or is evoked by a feeling." Thus moral self-appropriation will be to a large extent the negotiation of the symbols interlocked with one's affective responses to values. It will be psychic self-appropriation.[28]

---

[27]For more on Lonergan's position on the role of feelings in moral judgment, see *Method*, pp. 30–34 and 36–41.

[28]Doran, "Psychic Conversion," p. 228.

In other words, parallel to the cognitive self-appropriation that takes place when one discovers how one knows truth or value, there is a dispositional self-appropriation that takes place when one objectifies how one feels, when one discovers the process by which one's psychic life unfolds. Through the interpretation of dreams, through active imagination, or through other therapeutic techniques, feelings which have become disassociated from the images that originally were connected to them can be rediscovered. The energy that had been usurped in the service of repressing unwanted memories, feelings, or images can be released again in the service of constructive living. Not all the materials of sensitive living can be dealt with at one time: some sort of censor is needed to prevent overload. Psychic conversion is simply an objectification of our feelings in a manner that changes this censorship from a repressive role to a constructive one.

Furthermore, this negotiation of feeling complexes elucidates the complexity of moral discernment. It reveals the one-sidedness of outer oriented ego life and unveils the flip side of one's personality. One confronts the violence, the bad feelings, the forgotten dreams, the ignored strengths that dramatic, productive, extraverted living has neglected. One discovers that, not only are the criteria of good and evil left up to one's judgment, but that this moral task is neither straightforward nor easy. One must move from the simple answers of conventional moral expectations to an intra-psychic League of Nations in which destructive and constructive elements co-exist:

> As the dark and unfamiliar, the "inferior function," is granted freedom and a share in the life of the ego, identification of the ego-persons with collective value orientation ceases. "The individual is driven by his personal crisis into deep waters where he would usually never have entered if left to his own free will. The old idealized image of the ego has to go, and its place is taken by a perilous insight into the ambiguity and many-sidedness on one's own nature." Only the total personality is accepted as the basis of ethical conduct. No longer is St. Augustine's prayer of gratitude to God possible that he is not responsible for his dreams.[29]

This extension of ethical responsibility into the realm of the unconscious can be devastating as one confronts many evils within. But it can also be an occasion of healing, in which psychic conver-

---

[29]Ibid., p. 219.

sion intersects not only with moral conversion but with the religious conversion of an "other-worldly falling in love."[30] Indeed, it is only as one's inner horrors and powers of destruction are met by forgiving love that darkness can be embraced and transformed. "For it is only at the summit of moral self-transcendence in the love of God that wholeness becomes something of a possibility for man. There alone, 'values are whatever one loves, and evils are whatever one hates,' because there alone 'affectivity is of a single piece.'"[31]

In this manner psychic self-appropriation becomes the vehicle by which intellectual, moral, and religious conversion are completed. The intellectual grasp of how we know is filled out and re-connected to the sensitive flow which undergirds it. Moral autonomy is refined from arbitrary rebellion to nuanced inner discernment. Religious love becomes not only an outward consent but also an inner journey. Forgiveness is not only the cancelling of outer deeds but the healing of inner wounds and the transformation of an inner destructiveness.[32]

In this essay I have tried to show that some groups within the Christian faith function with a false diagnosis of the modern crisis of faith and that their failure to advert to the normativity of subjective process has some potentially dangerous implications. If this is the case with regard to cognitional process so much more is it the case with regard to dispositional process. Just as truth and value are assumed to be entities outside of oneself that one accepts by belief rather than creatively discovers, so also one's affective life is assumed to be governed by external interpretation and admonition. The inner movements of one's heart are considered suspect whereas the interpretations and directives of external authorities are considered reliable. One directs how one feels not by inward discernment

---

[30]See Lonergan, *Method*, pp. 240ff.

[31]Doran, "Psychic Conversion," p. 222. He is quoting Lonergan, *Method*, p. 39.

[32]Doran develops Lonergan's position on the relationship between intellectual, moral, and religious conversion. Lonergan says that, in the general case, intellectual conversion is preceded by and sublated by religious conversion. Doran expands this by suggesting that the conversions that precede intellectual conversion are pre-critical and set the existential stage for the questions dealt with in cognitive self-appropriation. Intellectual conversion then precipitates a revision of our understanding of our moral and religious lives in light of a new understanding of knowing. Thus the moral and religious conversions that precede intellectual conversion are pre-critical while the moral and religious conversions that sublate intellectual conversion are critical. Psychic conversion permeates all three and facilitates the working unity among them. It also assures a re-connection to sensitive living and prevents an intellectualism that could result from a merely cognitive self-appropriation. See Doran, "Psychic Conversion," pp. 206–209, 234ff.

but by outward conformity. In sum, the criterion of authentic feelings is not the self-transcendence of the subject but the degree to which one's feelings match those prescribed by authority.[33]

The danger in this is that believers will not take responsibility for their inner lives. They will not "own" their own feelings but will allow external monitors to interpret and guide these feelings. Rather than creating a community of affective integrity this can result in a community of collective affectivity, in which the mood, disposition, or feeling of the group determines the psychic life of the individual. Here the personal cost is extreme: it is not only conscious discovery that is silenced but sensitive emotion that is forced into deceit. What may begin as a healthy formation of affective life can result in individual and communal projections of evil onto others:

> The initial phases of the development of an autonomous ego must be sustained by the demands of the collective and its sanctions, by its juridical structures and dogmas, its imperatives and prohibitions, even its suppressions and attendant sufferings. But soon enough identification with the ethical values of the collective leads to the formation of a facade personality, the *persona*, and to repression of everything dark, strange, unfamiliar, and unlived, the *shadow*. The ego is cumulatively identified with the facade and the shadow is projected upon various scapegoats.[34]

Conclusion

I have presented Sandra's dilemma as typical of a modern crisis of faith. I have advocated a solution to this dilemma that is based on the self-appropriation of the knowing subject. This self-appropriation would lead to the recognition that knowing involves both believing the discoveries of others and making discoveries for oneself. Believing includes accepting facts and values of those one admires and allowing one's affective life to be formed by them. The way of discovery involves not just looking at the world but experiencing, understanding, judging, and deciding. While all of this can

---

[33]This amounts to a kind of emotional empiricism, in which the operations of understanding and judging what one's feelings are and of deciding which feelings are to be encouraged and which discouraged are overlooked. Moral control of feelings thus becomes, not understanding, judging, and deciding what to do with one's emotional reactions, but admitting or negating feelings at the very level of their occurrence at the threshold of consciousness. This can only promote a censorship that is repressive rather than self-conscious and constructive.

[34]Doran, "Psychic Conversion," pp. 218–219.

go on without explicit objectification of the knowing process, such objectification can provide a great deal of insight, freedom, and greater control over the road to self-transcendence. Recognizing that the norms of objectivity lie within subjective process allows one to attend more explicitly to these as one engages in the on-going self-correcting process of becoming an authentically religious person. While God is beyond the grasp of critical reason and religious tradition, God is both the ultimate source of the love and grace that carry the faith community forward and the ultimate objective that critical inquiry pursues. Authentic religion is the open-ended search in which the individual and the community remain receptive to new insights and to continual conversion. The community can guide the individual toward authentic adherence to subjective norms while the on-going pursuit of truth and value by believers will correct bias in the church and become part of the tradition passed on to the next generation.

In contrast to this I have presented a perspective in which Sandra's dilemma is solved through adhering to some set of external doctrines or prescriptions. In this view, "subjectivity" is the problem, to be solved by reference to "objective" sources of knowledge: scripture, tradition itself, the magisterium, some set of fundamental doctrines. The appeal to these objective sources overlooks the fact that they themselves are interpreted by some person using his own operations as a human subject. The danger of this reification of truth and value is that it will lead to personal and communal disjunction in which the best of the human spirit (its desire for intelligibility, truth, and value) is deemed to be the enemy of human authenticity. There is the further danger that the healthy dialectic of criticism between creative discovery and the beliefs and practices of tradition will be cut off. The objectification of truth becomes tied to acceptance of external authority, such that any bias or inauthenticity of the author-ities themselves is overlooked. Rather than subjecting itself to a creative and open-ended process of renewal, such a community confines its renewals within a closed set of "safe" parameters. The problem here is not the appeal to authority of tradition per se, but the antecedent restriction set to any answers that might emerge in the way of discovery.

Let us return once again to Sandra's story. We met her in the midst of an intellectual crisis, a crisis with implications for her religious faith and her existential being in the world. The questions she struggles with are questions about how she knows truth, about the criteria by which she can accept or reject what she is taught. But we could have met her also in the midst of a moral crisis, in which she is confused about what to do and about how to determine what she should do. Or we might have discovered Sandra caught in an emotional crisis, not sure what she feels or how to figure out what is authentic or unauthentic in what she does feel. All of these of course are related and will affect Sandra's religious faith and living. But the happy resolution of these crises does not depend alone on whether Sandra accepts or rejects the answers given by the Fellowship that engendered her religious faith. It depends also on whether Sandra accepts or rejects herself as a questioning, struggling, honest inquirer. And the authenticity of the Fellowship will manifest itself not in the answers and advice it offers as much as in the confidence and hope with which it encourages Sandra on her journey of inquiry.

REFORMED EPISTEMOLOGY AND RELIGIOUS FUNDAMENTALISM: HOW BASIC ARE OUR BASIC BELIEFS?

Terrence W. Tilley

This paper explores the work of contemporary reformed episte-mologists by using their approach to philosophy of religion in analyzing the discourse of Protestant fundamentalism. "Reformed epistemology" is at the center of the most vigorous movement in contemporary American philosophy of religion. The formation of the very active Society of Christian Philosophers (with its journal *Faith and Philosophy*) provides an organization (and an organ) for the movement. Its most noted member, Alvin Plantinga, is recog-nized throughout the academy for his work in epistemology, logic, possible world semantics, and for (decisively, in my view) solving the *logical* problem of evil by formalizing the Free Will Defense. He holds a chair at Notre Dame, has been honored by a *festschrift*,[1] has been honored with the Gifford Lectureship. Numerous other philo-sophers, including William Alston, Thomas Morris, Philip Quinn, Nicholas Wolterstorff, Eleanore Stump, and George Mavrodes, are recognized as both important philosophers and "fellow-travellers" in this movement which has grown out of the analytical tradition in philosophy.

The thesis of this paper is that contemporary reformed epistemol-ogists' accounts offer no help in showing that any basic or properly derived religious belief is more justified than any other basic or properly derived religious belief. In the first section of the paper I describe the religious epistemologists' understanding of the justifi-cation of religious belief. In the second section of the paper I apply

---

[1] J. E. Tomberlin and P. van Inwagen, eds., *Alvin Plantinga*, (Dordrecht: Reidel, 1985).

this to fundamentalism and argue that, on the reformed epistemologists' account, no religious discursive practice has been shown to be
more reliable or justifiable than fundamentalism because the fundamentalists' basic beliefs are as reliable or justified as others' basic or
derived beliefs. In the final part I use some recent analyses of
fundamentalism to bring out some problems for which contemporary reformed epistemology does not account. The reader may take
this as an argument in support either of the rationality of fundamentalism as a religious discourse, or of the irrationality of all religious
discourse, or of the failure of reformed epistemology to provide any
material help to theologians of any stripe, depending on other beliefs
the reader holds.

Reformed Epistemology and the Issue of Epistemic Entitlement

The first task is to examine epistemic entitlement, an area explored by contemporary epistemologists and extended by "reformed
epistemologists to religious epistemology.[2]

One can describe two sorts of beliefs in a person's noetic structure:
basic and non-basic. "Basic beliefs" can be defined as those beliefs
which an indivdual has and which are not based on other beliefs
which that individual holds.[3] They are those beliefs in the founda-

---

[2]This paper addresses issues as formulated by Alston and Plantinga. However,
similar arguments could be applied to Wolterstorff, Mavrodes and other reformed
epistemologists, insofar as they walk similar paths.

[3]It is crucial to understand that basic beliefs are defined not by their source, but by
their status in an individual's noetic structure. Any belief not based on another belief
the individual holds is basic. The grounds another individual has for the belief are
irrelevant to its place in my noetic structure. An individual's basic belief may be
based on self-evidence, or sense evidence. Or it may be based on other causes or
grounds. For example, my belief that my name is Terrence Tilley is not groundless
(pace Norman Malcolm, "The Groundlessness of Belief," Reason and Religion, edited
by Stuart C. Brown [Ithaca: Cornell University Press, 1977], pp. 143–157), but is
grounded on the facts (not the belief) that that is what my parents named me and
called me. Supposedly sophisticated theological beliefs, e.g., "Jesus Christ is really
present in the Eucharist," can be basic for some people (in terminology developed
below, it is an "I-belief" self-evidently entailed by an "M-belief" such as "Jesus
comes to me in the bread and wine") even though such beliefs might not be basic for
others. If I accept the real presence of Jesus in the Eucharist because I am told that is
the right way to talk about the Eucharist in which I devoutly participate does not
count against its being basic any more than I accept my name to be Terrence Tilley
because my mother and father told me that is my name.
   The individualistic emphasis of reformed epistemology, at least in Plantinga's
version, makes it quite possible that what is a derived belief for another can be a basic
belief for me. The key question in this area is not whether a belief is basic, but
whether that belief is properly basic, whether it is proper for an individual to have

tions (if one is a foundation-layer) or at the edge (if one is a raft-builder or web-spinner) of one's noetic structure. Non-basic beliefs are defined as those beliefs an individual has which are derived from or based on other beliefs that individual holds.

Normatively, one's beliefs can be proper or improper. Proper basic beliefs are those beliefs which one is justified in holding on grounds other than one's other beliefs. Proper derived beliefs are those beliefs which one is justified in holding on the basis of other beliefs. Improper basic beliefs are those basic beliefs which one holds and which one is not justified in holding. Improper non-basic beliefs are those which one holds on the basis of other beliefs and which are either not properly warranted or are warranted only by improper beliefs.

One focus of contemporary epistemological debate is how to distinguish improper from proper basic beliefs. Two approaches have emerged for defining criteria for proper basic beliefs: methodist and particularist.[4] A methodist argues from criteria for proper basicality to support or undermine the propriety of holding specific basic beliefs or types of basic beliefs. A particularist argues from beliefs or types of beliefs which cannot but be proper when formed in certain circumstances to "frame hypotheses as to the necessary and sufficient conditions of proper basicality and test these hypotheses by reference"[5] to the exemplary proper basic beliefs.

Modern epistemologists from Descartes to the logical positivists exemplify the methodistic approach. They construct a priori, inductive, or transcendental arguments for their criteria. They then use those criteria both to defeat skepticism and to identify and prune improper beliefs. However, no epistemologist has been able to mount an argument which demonstrates either the necessity or the sufficiency of a criterion or set of criteria for proper basicality.[6]

---

this belief as basic in her or his noetic structure. If one neglects this individualism when attempting to understand Plantinga's work, one may mistakenly think that because a belief is derived for one person it cannot be basic for another. That's simply wrong.

[4]See Roderick M. Chisholm, The Foundations of Knowing (Minneapolis: University of Minnesota, 1982), p. 65.

[5]Alvin Plantinga, "Reason and Belief in God," Faith and Rationality, eds. A. Plantinga and N. Wolterstorff (Notre Dame: University of Notre Dame, 1983), p. 76.

[6]Compare Plantinga, p. 78. Anthony M. Matteo is wrong in suggesting Plantinga rejects "all forms of foundationalism as such" in "Can Belief in God Be Basic?" Horizons 15 (Fall, 1988): 272. Basic beliefs are foundational; the question is whether theistic ones are proper. The question cannot be resolved by the methodistic approach of "natural theology," which allegedly 'proves' the necessity of some formal princi-

Diagnoses for the methodists' failures to resolve this epistemolog-ical *agon* have ranged from wholesale rejections of epistemology as a discursive practice, e.g., by the deconstructionists and Richard Rorty, to retail refutations of specific methodological proposals by more common philosophical argument, e.g., by discovering the dreaded unassimilable counter-example. But rather than abandoning epistemology, particularists reverse the methodists' procedure.

Particularists begin with beliefs which cannot but be properly basic. "I am being appeared to redly here and now," "I have a pain in my chest," and other first-person avowals can be analyzed to derive a criterion of proper basicality: those beliefs which are inde-feasibly evident to the senses or self-evident. Such first person avowals, which express A-beliefs (A for avowal), are indefeasible.[7] Of course, people can be hypnotized into feeling chest pain or deceived about color appearances by being placed in a room bathed in red light. In such circumstances someone could be wrong about the cause and significance of her chest pain or the color of objects he sees. But neither would be wrong in holding an A-belief, but in holding what we can call an I-belief. An "I-belief" is a belief ordinarily taken as basic because it is "self-evidently entailed" by proper basic beliefs such as A-beliefs.[8]

Inferring I-beliefs from A-beliefs is a generally reliable epistemic practice. Unless I have good reason to believe otherwise, I am justified in believing that what seems red to me is red, or that the pain I feel in my chest is there (and may even be a warning of disease). However, even inferences from A-beliefs to I-beliefs which seem warranted by self-evident entailment are defeasible in certain circumstances. An argument that such circumstances obtain is a "defeater."

---

ples (Matteo, p. 281). Formal epistemic principles not only provide no material religious content, but arguments for them are highly controversial. The issue is not the formal and general one of the scope of reason or the principle of intelligibility (which non-theists can flesh out in their own ways), but the material and particular one of the reality of the God of Christians. And there is no non-controversial route from the formal principles to the material beliefs.

[7]See Chisholm, p. 11. A-beliefs are indubitable and incorrigible, at least at the time they are acquired. They also are apparently indefeasible, for they are not so much *retracted* if found false as *reinterpreted* ("I thought I saw . . . , but what I really saw was . . ." or "I thought I had a pain in my . . . , but I now know it was . . .)." What is defeasible, as discussed below, are the I-beliefs which often are not distinguished from the A-beliefs which warrant them. Nonetheless, this does not entail their truth. Even proper basic beliefs can be false.

[8]See Plantinga, pp. 81–82. Plantinga also argues that there is no argument to sustain a claim that properly basic beliefs can or should be limited to beliefs which are self-evident or evident to the senses.

A-beliefs are insufficient to be the basis of any well-developed noetic structure. But we can't simply add to our noetic structures all the I-beliefs self-evidently entailed by A-beliefs. Not only would they be insufficient for the job, but not all I-beliefs are reliable. We could add indefeasible I-beliefs or perhaps even undefeated I-beliefs. But that requires a criterion of proper I-belief formation which must be either methodistically or particularistically developed. A method-based criterion will run into the same difficulties as the method-based criterion for basic beliefs. Either we must prune our noetic structures drastically (as skeptics would urge), or abandon any attempts at justifying what we believe (as ironic deconstructionists have done), or find more examples of proper basic beliefs and inferential practices until we can justify beliefs other than A-beliefs in our noetic structure.[9]

The particularist assembles more examples of beliefs which seem both basic and proper. Among the reformed epistemologists' examples are expressions of what Alston has happily labeled "manifestation beliefs" or "M-beliefs," such as "God is speaking to me now."[10] Plantinga has argued that in certain conditions such belief is, even for mature theists, an exemplary proper basic belief. He also writes that belief that there is a God, because it is self-evidently entailed by "God is speaking to me now," is also a proper basic belief. Hence, he finds that theists are epistemically entitled to believe in God. As he put it:

There are therefore many conditions and circumstances that call forth belief in God: guilt, gratitude, danger, a sense of God's presence, a sense that he speaks, perception of various parts of the universe. A

[9]Gerald D. McCarthy has objected that the dichotomy between particularists and methodists is phony. He suggests that what happens is that in epistemology we reach a "reflective equilibrium" of principles and cases, as Rawls suggests we do in morality. Sometimes we reject a case that contradicts a principle, sometimes we revise a principle in light of a case. But what McCarthy fails to note is the extension of the "we" in these examples. Who is qualified to participate in the discussion? The problem becomes acute in the issues of religious beliefs, as discussed below. For even if McCarthy is correct and we do resolve general epistemic issues in a Rawlsian weighing process, it is not clear that this applies in religious epistemology. The claim that religious beliefs are properly basic is one that is unsettled—and perhaps cannot be settled. No equilibrium seems to be emerging, but only a continued violent oscillation of claims and counter-claims from various epistemological and religious positions.

[10]William P. Alston, "Religious Experience as a Ground of Religious Belief," *Religious Experience and Religious Belief*, eds. J. Runzo and C. K. Ihara (Washington, DC: University Press of America, 1986), p. 33.

complete job would explore the phenomenology of all these conditions and of more besides. This is a large and important topic; but here I can only point to the existence of these conditions.[11]

These "unexplored conditions" lead to the question of how Plantinga can find *any* M-belief—even belief that the Great Pumpkin is about to land in this pumpkin patch—improper, as he has not formulated a criterion of proper basicality. He answers formally by reiterating that particularists work from examples and that there is no reason to assume either that everyone will agree on the range of examples or that the criteria developed from those examples in the Christian community must conform to examples valorized in non-Christian discourse. More specifically, Plantinga sees that there is a *difference* between belief in God and belief in the Great Pumpkin. The former is held as an exemplary rational belief by Christians and Jews, and is basic for at least some of them. The latter is held as proper only by Linus in *Peanuts*—if even he holds his belief to be proper.

Plantinga takes the "Great Pumpkin" objection to get its force from the methodists' claim that the particularists both need and lack a proper criterion of proper basicality. Given the problems methodists have in formulating a criterion, Plantinga rightly dismisses this objection *from the methodists*. However, two *particularist* questions which Plantinga cannot dismiss so easily also lurk in this vicinity.[12]

First, there is the extent of the "community." Plantinga arbitrarily rules out those who are not of the "Christian community.[13] Not only is this, as Alston says, rather "hard-nosed,"[14] but we don't know materially and particularly *which* Christian community Plantinga means. For there are many Christian communities and the issue here is *materially* which community he means. The various Christian communities simply differ on essential beliefs. For instance, some Catholic Christians see Christ present in the Eucharist, body and blood, soul and divinity. Other Christians, especially some reformed

---

[11]Plantinga, p. 81. Some sophisticated believers might take these beliefs as non-basic because they could construct arguments for them. Yet that does not mean that those beliefs could not be basic for some "simple" believers, while being "derivative" for some theologically sophisticated believers, even the teachers of those "simple" believers.

[12]Compare Axel D. Steuer, "The Epistemic Status of Theistic Belief," *Journal of the American Academy of Religion* 55 (Summer, 1987): 254.

[13]Plantinga, p. 77.

[14]William P. Alston, "Plantinga's Epistemology of Religious Belief," *Alvin Plantinga*, p. 301.

Christians, don't. Disagreements about this belief can symbolize or effect apparently intractable schism between Christian communities.

For many Catholic Christians, literal belief in Real Presence is basic. Obviously, these people were taught to see Christ in the Eucharist by authorities in their community or by more 'sophisticated' believers who think they have arguments from scripture and tradition which justify such a belief. But that does not make the belief any less basic for them, *for the same can be said about the manifestation beliefs that Plantinga cites.* Unless Plantinga's favorite manifestation beliefs also fail to be basic because they were brought about by a person's accepting the authority of a leader of her or his religious community, the manifestation of the Real Presence in the Eucharist cannot fail to be basic because it was brought about by a person's accepting an authority. Indeed, a person who is not taught how to exercise her or his propensity to see God in natural phenomena or the Eucharist will be unable to form such beliefs. And many of those believers were taught by those who believed there were arguments which grounded such vision. I see no reason to reject the claim that those who hold such a belief in the Real Presence cannot be on an epistemic par with those who hold a belief that God is speaking to me now.[15] I also see no reason to accept the claim that

---

[15]See Ronald J. Feenstra, "Natural Theology, Epistemic Parity, and Unbelief," *Modern Theology* 5 (October, 1988): 1–12. Feenstra argued that Penelhum's attempt in *God and Skepticism* (Dordrecht: Reidel, 1983) to show that Plantinga has constructed a "permissive parity" argument fails. Feenstra writes that Plantinga "affirms that belief in God is grounded in the design of the world along with certain triggering conditions" (p. 4). Therefore, Plantinga can coherently affirm that failure to develop a belief in God is the result of human sin, and that failure to believe in God is not on an epistemic par with belief in God.

Feenstra helpfully shows that Plantinga does not construct a "permissive parity argument" in the sense that in certain conditions it is optional to develop a belief in God. If "believers and unbelievers" (p. 10) met God in a burning bush as Moses' encounter is portrayed in C. B. DeMille's "The Ten Commandments," belief in God would not be optional for them any more than for Moses. Plantinga is not arguing for the permissibility of their not believing in God.

However, the real issue is not between the positively characterized believer and the negatively characterized straw person, the unbeliever, but between two believers with contrary M-beliefs, generated by (possibly) different stimuli in different triggering conditions. Of course, it is possibly true that (1) refusal to believe in God is due to sin; but it may be that (2) refusal to believe in the Real Presence is due to intellectual pride and separation from the One True Roman Catholic Church, or (3) inability due to failure to be enlightened, etc. (1), (2), and (3) are each possibly true, may be inscribed in the nature of things, and are incompatible. There are no criteria available to adjudicate which is correct, certainly not formal ones established by natural theology for which Matteo argues. Therefore, so far as we can tell, they are on an epistemic par with each other. Now we might restrict the membership of the epistemic

the Eucharistic belief is somehow less fundamental than belief in God. Clearly, there can be Christians for whom it is basic and fundamental. The question is whether such belief is proper. The latter group of reformed Christians can be seen as doubting whether such a belief is proper.

But how would such a disagreement be resolved? Which community of believers is the proper provider of examples for "the Christian community"? Appeal to "the Christian community" does not resolve the problem of which members of that community are to provide authoritative examples when the members of that community do not agree on the examples. Plantinga's claim is far too facile.

Second, that Christians, or a subset of Christians, form a distinct and unique epistemic peer group, is unproven at best. One might accept rather high-level Calvinist doctrines about the total depravity of the sin-darkened intellect and the availability of enlightening grace only to believing Christians. But one can only justify these doctrines if they are properly derivable from proper basic beliefs or are themselves proper basic beliefs. But using these doctrines to establish the membership of the relevant epistemic community for establishing the criteria of proper basicality seems either circular or mistaken. If these are taken to be proper basic beliefs, then we have a narrowly stipulative definition of Christianity: "When I say 'Christian,' I mean only those Christians who are Reformed." That is surely arbitrary. If these are properly derived beliefs, to be justified they must be derivable, at least indirectly, from proper basic beliefs. But since examples of what are proper basic beliefs are what is at issue, such an argument is ignoratio elenchi, and must be rejected.[16] The issue is not the formal and methodistic one of whether one can be justified in limiting a community of exemplars, but the material and particularist one of whether reformed epistemologists can delimit and have rightly delimited the epistemic peer community.

What Chisholm has identified as the problem of the criterion

community ("we" in "so far as we can tell") establishing the criteria of propriety to only those who share our M-beliefs. But that is just the problem that needs to be resolved.

Beliefs may not be "optional" for individual believers. Those beliefs are not on an epistemic par with their negations for those believers. But individual believers with possibly true, but contrary, beliefs are on an epistemic par with each other. That is the real point of the parity argument.

[16]The reformed epistemologist might respond that the issue is not one of being able to give a justification of the belief, but rather one of being justified in holding that belief. Even if one cannot do the former, one can be the latter. While this is clearly true, it is not relevant here.

appears transformed in Plantinga's work: now we don't have the problem of the criterion of proper basicality, but of the criterion for limiting the community which provides the examples for establishing a criterion of proper basicality. Plantinga has not shown how a particularist can justifiably equate the relevant epistemic community with a religious tradition. He has not shown why his position is not arbitrary or making the mistake of presuming what is at issue. If the criterion is, "just because it is my community," then he needs to show why such a response does not lead to a vicious relativistic communitarianism (for, after all, if you make the community small enough, you can be entitled to believe almost anything). The reformed epistemologist must bear a burden of proof here, one which Plantinga has not borne.

One possibility is to consider the epistemic *practices* which yield M-beliefs, a strategy employed by William Alston to respond to this problem. Alston draws two key conclusions. First, one cannot show that "the practice of accepting M-beliefs in conditions of certain types," which he labels "theistic practice"[17] or "religious experience"[18] is unreliable, for it cannot be shown that people who participate in the practice develop beliefs randomly or develop false beliefs. Thus, participation in such practices is not unjustified. Second, one cannot show that M-beliefs have an epistemic status inferior to perceptual beliefs. Alston considers the fact that participants in different religious traditions have incompatible basic M-beliefs, but finds that this gives no reason to find religious experience epistemically unreliable.[19]

I will not contest Alston's meticulous analysis here; indeed, insofar as it goes, it seems to me valid. However, careful consideration shows that it may not 'save' reformed epistemology in any useful sense. Alston does not show that I-beliefs self-evidently entailed by the M-beliefs derived from religious experience are not unreliable. In short, the M-belief, "God is speaking to me now," may well be a proper basic belief, but that does not reliably imply that an I-belief, "God exists," is a proper basic belief or a proper derived belief. For "God exists" is not a type of M-belief, but an I-belief, a belief self-evidently entailed by a properly basic belief. The question is whether this *specific* belief is a properly derived I-belief. Given that

---

[17]Alston, "Plantinga's Epistemology," p. 303.

[18]Alston, "Religious Experience," p. 33.

[19]Alston, "Plantinga's Epistemology," p. 308; "Religious Experience," pp. 47–48.

particularists have not shown what is a proper way to derive I-beliefs, we simply don't know whether it is or not.

Alston has argued that the disagreements about basic beliefs among religious traditions does not mean that religious experience or practice is unreliable *as a practice or type of practice*. However, this point seems directed against the methodists who would exclude religious experience on methodistic grounds. But the key practical issues are not methodistic, but particularistic. The question is which *particular* I-beliefs are proper, not whether the *practice* is proper.

There are two possibilities here. Either the adherents of the various traditions who hold incompatible I-beliefs are engaging in the same practice or they are engaging in different practices when they have religious experiences. I shall explore both possibilities.

First, if they are both properly engaging in the same reliable practice, then properly engaging in the practice is not sufficient to yield reliable I-beliefs. Something is bringing it about that a certain Hindu sitting under the Bo tree and coming to know the Four Noble Truths, a certain Christian beholding the starry skies above and coming to know the reality of God, a certain rabbi after Auschwitz coming to believe that omnipotent nothingness is lord of creation, and a certain agnostic observing his best friend's wife in intractable pain and coming to see the ultimate meaninglessness of everything, all properly engage in a practice of forming M-beliefs, but come to different basic M-beliefs and derived different, even contradictory, I-beliefs from those M-beliefs. If we accept a normative account of epistemic justification, even a relatively permissive one as reformed epistemologists do, then we need to explain why the fact that a properly-engaged-in practice yields such various results does not constitute a *defeater*, a good reason for doubting the reliability of the practice, for *pace* Alston, it seems either that these beliefs are generated randomly or that some of those who properly engage in the practice develop false beliefs.

Now of course, it might be argued that some of these practitioners are not properly engaging in the practice. But then we need a criterion of propriety. And it will be established either methodistically or particularistically. Such an argument would only move the issue back another step, not resolve it. And the problem would have the same shape as it does here, so such a move does not get the reformed epistemologist any further forward. Hence, I propose to examine the reliability of the practice.

Alston suggests that the following sort of response, a "defeater defeater," is sufficient to defeat the proposed *defeater*:

It may be that the attempt to discern God's presence and activity from religious experience is in the state that the attempt to discern the basic nature of the physical world, by reasoning from what we learn from perception, was in for the first 1600 years of our era. And if God is as hard for us to discern as all the great religious traditions suggest, we may be in that position for an indefinitely long period of time in the future.[20]

Thus Alston introduces a possibility which seems to show the defeater unreliable.

But if Alston's response is accepted, then *we* must see *our* status as religious believers as *we* see *the medievals'* status as scientists: as they were in no position to tell which of the contradictory beliefs their scientific practice yielded was most reliable, so are we in no position to tell which of the contradictory beliefs our religious practice yields is most reliable. The practice may be reliable as a practice, but at this point we can't know *which* exercises of the practice are proper and *which* beliefs they yield are reliable.

Alston claims that it is permissible to participate in a practice unless there is good reason to doubt the reliability of the practice. And he has argued that there is no good reason to doubt the reliability of what he calls "theistic practice." But this reliable practice yields varying M-beliefs which in turn self-evidently entail incompatible I-beliefs. But if there be no reason to doubt the reliability of the practice of religious experience, then there must be reason to doubt the reliability of moving from M-beliefs to I-beliefs. In sum, if engaging in a reliable epistemic practice yields varying M- or A-beliefs which "self-evidently entail incompatible I-beliefs, is that not good reason to think that the practice of inferring I-beliefs from A- or M-beliefs on the basis of self-evident entailment is unreliable as a move in the context of this specific epistemic practice? However that question may be answered in the future, it is insoluble now. Indeed we don't know if it can or will be resolved. Future practitioners may have an answer to that question. Or they may not. But we don't. Hence, there is *some* reason *now* to doubt the reliability of the practice. But whether this is a sufficient reason, a good reason, to either participate in or avoid the practice, is arguable.

---

[20]Alston, "Plantinga's Epistemology," p. 308.

Second, let's presume that the practitioners engage in different practices. Now the issue is to discern which of the practices, if any, is the most reliable. This is like a debate concerning whether the use of a telescope or the naked eye is a more reliable epistemic practice for discerning the heavens. Each way of viewing gives varying A-beliefs which self-evidently entail varying, perhaps contradictory, I-beliefs. Which practice is more likely to give reliable or useful I-beliefs? Obviously, for examining the stars scientifically, the question can be—has been—solved, but *at one time it could not be settled.* Similarly, is the more reliable practice for forming basic beliefs about the ultimate to engage in meditation as Gautama did, to espy the stars as Kant did, to feel the *tremendum* of the Holocaust as Rubinstein did, or to respond empathetically as Russell did? The question is not whether only one practice is reliable. They may all be reliable for forming M-beliefs. The key question is *which practice is most reliable for forming I-beliefs.* On Alston's account, it is theoretically possible to resolve the problem, but at the present time it remains unsolved and may be practically insoluble. Even if we are engaging in reliable practices, we have no way now to discern *which* religious practice is most reliable for yielding I-beliefs or which I-beliefs religious practice or practices yield are reliable, even though all of them may yield reliable—and proper—basic M-beliefs. If we take religious experiencing as multiple epistemic practices, Alston's suggestion raises the question of the criterion again. Hence, whether we take religious experience as a single or multiple epistemic practice, the question of the reliability of deriving I-beliefs from M-beliefs is unresolved.

At this stage we are in a muddle. We are like nineteenth century physicians who are confronted with many possibilities for treating a disease and trying to find one or more therapies which work. But unlike them, we cannot identify what "working" consists in. They could tell the difference between surviving and succumbing to a disease, and construe the former as a criterion of a therapy which works. But we don't even know what counts as "working," what the *telos* or the *teloi* of the practice or practices would be. As far as we can tell, the practice or practices and the I-beliefs they yield have epistemic parity (see note eight). A permissive epistemologist would say that many could be justifiable. A rigorist might argue that none are justifiable. Alston's move does not solve the problem. Moreover, it leaves us with some suspicion that there may be good reason to doubt the reliability of the practice.

However, what the reformed epistemologists neglect to analyze is the ways in which communities of discourse shape the very beliefs we take to be basic. Plantinga acknowledged this when he noted that he had not done a "complete job" of exploring the conditions and circumstances which produce basic religious belief.[21] A more complete job has been done, at least in regards to American Protestant fundamentalism, by Kathleen Boone.[22] The following section examines some basic beliefs of fundamentalism in light of both her analysis and that of the reformed epistemologists.

Protestant Fundamentalism as a Discourse Practice

The single distinctive belief which marks fundamentalism off from other forms of Christianity is an epistemically basic belief that the Bible is the literally true, inerrant word of God.[23] The single distinctive practice of fundamentalism is their commitment to separate themselves from the world insofar as they can.[24] Beyond the *combination* of biblical inerrantism with ecclesio-political separatism, there is little, if anything, which definitively distinguishes fundamentalists from other Evangelicals. Following Barr (whose analysis they generally oppose), Ed Dobson and Ed Hindson, two pastoral associates of Jerry Falwell, write: "This point is exactly what contemporary Evangelicalism needs to face—the fact that it is not intrinsically different from the mainstream of Fundamentalism."[25] From the fundamentalists' viewpoint, the differences between them and Evangelicals is not in the realm of theological belief, but in that of tactics in approaching non-believers.

Fundamentalists believe that the inerrancy of Scripture is simply the traditional basic belief of Christianity. The tragedy is that Scriptural inerrancy is a doctrine abandoned by liberal churches.[26] Once

---

[21]Plantinga, p. 81.

[22]Kathleen C. Boone, *The Bible Tells Them So: The Discourse of Protestant Fundamentalism* (Albany: State University of New York Press, 1989).

[23]Compare Boone, p. 9.

[24]Compare Nancy Tatom Ammerman, *Bible Believers: Fundamentalists in the Modern World* (New Brunswick: Rutgers University Press, 1987), pp. 3–4 and William C. Ringenberg, *The Christian College: A History of Protestant Higher Education in America* (Grand Rapids: Christian University Press and Wm. B. Eerdmans, 1984), p. 176.

[25]Jerry Falwell et al., eds., *The Fundamentalist Phenomenon* (Garden City: Doubleday, 1981), p. 7. Whose pen wrote which portions of this book is unclear. Apparently it was composed mostly by Ed Hindson and Ed Dobson under the plenary inspiration of Falwell.

[26]Falwell, p. 8.

this basic belief in inerrancy is given, fundamentalism builds a belief system "marked by an unrelenting rationalism, rather than the irrationalism or emotionalism with which fundamentalism has so often been identified."[27]

The Bible is also the final word on all matters, a standard against which all other beliefs and practices must be measured. Barr well described the importance of the doctrine of biblical inerrancy for the fundamentalist:

> [I]t is an absolutely central and pivotal doctrine, without which, it is supposed, nothing can be positively believed. It is a keystone of the arch of faith, without which the entire structure will collapse. For the fundamentalist, to say anything that questions his idea of biblical inspiration will seem to be totally negative, to be an attack upon the whole essence of religious faith.[28]

If an experience or belief contradicts the Bible, then that experience is *not* of and from God. The Bible becomes not only the basis of fundamentalists' noetic structure, but also the *criterion* by which fundamentalists judge all beliefs and practices.

But the obvious question is how the fundamentalist establishes that criterion. If fundamentalist belief is "unrelentingly rationalist," then the fundamentalist must be able to show how this criterion is a proper criterion. Dobson and Hindson suggest the structure of fundamentalist belief in the following:

> Fundamentalists and Evangelicals alike hold to a *basic belief in the inerrancy of Scriptures in their original autographs.* To Fundamentalists, the inerrancy of Scripture is ultimately linked to the legitimacy and authority of the Bible. They view the Bible as being God-breathed and thus as possessing the quality of being free from error in all of its statements and affirmations. Robert Lightner asks: "How can an errant Bible be God's revelation? How can it be God-breathed? How can it possibly be authoritative and therefore trustworthy? How can Scripture possibly be inerrant in some parts and errant in others at the same time? In a book which claims God as its author, inspiration must extend to all its parts. If it does not, how does one go about determining what is and what is not God-breathed and therefore free from error?" He rightly observes that the trend among radical Evangelicals away

---

[27]Boone, p. 7.
[28]James Barr, *Beyond Fundamentalism* (Philadelphia: Westminster, 1984), p. 124.

from the total inerrancy of the Scriptures is really nothing more than an intellectual accommodation to contemporary society.[29]

Although Dobson and Hindson were, presumably, not using the technical terminology of reformed epistemology in their exposition, but intending "basic" to mean "central, distinctive, and foundational," their discussion shows that they also take belief in the inerrancy of the Scripture as basic in the *epistemic* sense, as an "I-belief." Indeed, using the reformed epistemologists' approach can reveal just what shape the "rationalism" of fundamentalism takes.

To be *epistemically* basic, a belief would have to be an M-belief, such as "God speaks to me through this book," or self-evidently entailed by such an M-belief. Assertions which refer things to God are M-beliefs frequently articulated by fundamentalists. For instance, consider Frances Fitzgerald's report on her encounters with some members of Falwell's Thomas Road Baptist Church: "If you ask a Thomas Road member 'what brought you to Lynchburg?' or 'How did you find this house?' the answer will be 'God brought me here' or 'God found this house for us'—and only after that will come some mention of the family's desire for a warmer climate or of the intervention of a real-estate agent."[30] The fundamentalist Christian has learned to refer all things to God and to use M-beliefs generated by this practice as responses to questions. Surely the *first* thing to refer to God is the Scripture through which God speaks. Hence, a belief formulated as "God speaks to me through this book" (or something similar) expresses a fundamentalist's basic M-belief.

For the fundamentalist, the move from "God speaks to me through Scripture" (a possible "M-belief") to "Scripture is inerrant" (an "I-belief") is as 'self-evident' as the inference from "This wall seems red to me here and now" to "This wall is red" is to me. For the fundamentalist, the inerrancy of the Scripture is what I have identi-

---

[29]Falwell, p. 8; emphasis added. Boone finds that the "attribution of inerrancy only to lost autographs renders the inerrancy claim imponderable, because of the impossibility of verification, and useless because there is no practical value to the interpreter. It further seems obvious that the autographs serve as a convenient dodge, allowing the fundamentalist to uphold the doctrine in the face of textual evidence to the contrary" (pp. 34–35). Yet Boone also notes the real function and practical value of the doctrine: it reserves the fault of misinterpretation to the interpreter and exonerates the text of any possible fault. It thus preserves the "absolute authority" of the text. Fundamentalists also claim that the content of that text "in the providence of God can be ascertained from available manuscripts with great accuracy (p. 33). Hence, in practice the AV becomes an inerrant text.

[30]Boone, p. 94.

fied above as an I-belief, a belief self-evidently entailed from an A- or M-belief. The force of Lightner's argument cited above is thus to give a *defense*[31] of the propriety of the derivation of Scriptural inerrancy (for those of us for whom it is not self-evident). To make the logic of the defense explicit: If God speaks to me through the Bible, then I am both entitled to believe in God and can call the Bible inspired or "God-breathed," (cf. II Tim. 3:16–17: "All scripture is inspired by God [literally "God-breathed" in Greek: theópneustos] and profitable for teaching, for reproof, for correction, and for training in righteousness, that the man of God may be complete, equipped for every good work" [AV]). But the Bible, the defender argues, may be either errant or inerrant. But if it were errant in part or whole, then it could not be *intrinsically* authoritative, for the interpreting individual or community would have to decide which parts were inerrant and which parts were errant, which parts carried God's message and which parts were humanly given. Therefore, to be the authoritative and trustworthy revelation, a quality which is manifest to the fundamentalist, the Word of God must be inerrant. Hence, the belief that the Scripture is inerrant can be understood as a basic belief, in Plantinga's sense, for the fundamentalist. It is an I-belief self-evidently entailed by an M-belief, and the defense shows the propriety of making the entailment.

But is it a *proper* basic belief? At this point, we are in the position in which Alston left us. The fundamentalists' way of understanding Scripture is one form of theistic practice or one of many religious practices. Any of them may or may not be reliable ways of forming beliefs. Various participants, holding varied I-beliefs, including one who believes in the inerrancy of Scripture, are on an epistemic par. On the reformed epistemologists' grounds, there is no good reason to believe that the fundamentalists' practice is unreliable or beliefs are unjustified. Therefore, a fundamentalist is as justified as any other religious practitioner in her or his basic beliefs. Moreover,

---

[31]A defense is not a proof meant to convince opponents, but a rational justification of the individual's right to hold a belief or set of beliefs. For the significance of this distinction, see T. W. Tilley, "The Use and Abuse of Theodicy," *Horizons* 11 (Fall, 1984): 304–319. The fundamentalist is not attempting to convince outsiders of the truth of her or his belief, but only of the permissibility of holding it, that is, that the belief does not violate any clear standards of rationality. Their practice is obviously analogous to Plantinga's standard move of showing that there is no clear criterion for proper basicality, in the absence of which a Christian's M-beliefs cannot be shown not to be properly basic. The fundamentalist is here deploying a *defeater defeater*, an argument which shows that an argument against their view is invalid or unsound.

construed as theological belief systems, there is no difference between the fundamentalists' and the evangelicals' beliefs. Epistemically, they are on a par with each other. Hence, given the distance
which the reformed epistemologists have taken us, there is no reason
not to accept a claim that fundamentalists are as justified as others
who engage in religious practices from which M-beliefs and I-beliefs
are developed.

Religious Fundamentalism: Beyond Reformed Epistemology

Yet there *is* a question about whether there is a way to resolve the
suspicion noted above that some of these practices or the beliefs
they yield are unreliable. Two questions are considered in this
section. First, if there is an inconsistency between a practice and the
beliefs triggered by that practice, is that practice unreliable? Second,
if the beliefs delivered by the practice are inconsistent and thus
jointly necessarily false, is that practice unreliable? I argue that
Protestant fundamentalism fulfills both conditions and that reformed epistemologists would nonetheless not find the practices
unreliable.

First, reformed epistemologists privilege specific beliefs in individuals' noetic structures. However, those beliefs may not be privileged or basic in the discourse practices in which the participant is
taught that those specific beliefs are epistemically basic. This may
not be a problem for most practices or for epistemology in general.
However, if participating in a discourse practice triggers beliefs
which deny the role of the practice in triggering those beliefs,
participating in that practice may be deceptive, i.e., the very participation generates beliefs inconsistent with the practice participated
in. Reformed epistemologists have not yet, to my knowledge, considered this issue, although fundamentalism is a paradigm case.

Boone's analysis of fundamentalism as a discursive practice brings
out aspects of the epistemology of fundamentalism that the Christian
philosophers' generic analyses of religious epistemology ignore. As
she put it:

> The authority of fundamentalism arises in the 'reciprocal relations' of
> text, preachers, commentators, and ordinary readers. And in studying
> these relations, one confronts the compelling power of the closed
> system, a power which cannot be localized but is of one cloth, a power
> woven in and through every thread.[32]

---

[32]Boone, pp. 2–3.

In epistemic terms, even if belief in the *inerrant* text as a foundational authority is a basic belief for individual fundamentalists, that
text is not "basic" to the discourse practice, but rather supported by
and supportive of other strands in the web of the practice. There is
an inconsistency between the practice engaged in and the beliefs the
practice triggers.

Reformed epistemologists do not give much consideration to the
discourse practices which trigger individuals' basic beliefs. While
they spill much ink over issues about the proper basicality of beliefs,
even Alston, who has begun to explore theistic practice, does not
consider the reliability of concrete discourse practices. Yet the connections between communities' discourse practices and individuals'
noetic structures are crucial.

A discourse practice can be analyzed into its constituents, but no
one of those constituents can be separated out as basic or privileged
and all the other constituents as somehow derivative. A person who
enters a discourse practice (for instance, "is converted" to Christianity or "becomes an intern" in a hospital) learns not only to hold
some beliefs as basic or fundamental. The participant also learns
how to take some texts (in the former case, the Bible, usually the AV;
in the latter, medical textbooks) and persons (the pastor; the attending physician) as authoritative. The participant recognizes some
practices (drinking liquor, dancing, gambling; fee kickbacks, ambu-
lance chasing, euthanasia) as forbidden and other practices (referring all things to God, attending church; professional courtesy,
diagnosing), as expected. The participant can take an institutionally
determined place (worshipper in the church, parent and supporter
of the Christian school; physician in the hospital, diagnostician in
the clinic), which gives the participant a status in the discursive
community. In short, the beliefs, persons, texts, practices, and even
institutions in a discourse practice or system mutually affect and
reinforce each other.[33]

We have already examined the role of the text through which God
speaks to the fundamentalist. But it is the preachers and commentators who say what the text means. Their place in the community and
their status with the fundamentalists' discourse practice cannot be
neglected. Boone's summary deserves quotation:

---

[33]Given the sketch in the first paragraph of this paper, "Christian philosophy"
could well constitute a delineable discourse practice. To explore that issue would
take us far beyond the scope of the present paper.

Fundamentalists are caught in the very trap they want to avoid. They must resort to some form of institutional authority, unless they want to grant authority to the interpretations of any reader whatsoever who espouses the inerrancy doctrine. The ultimate difficulty with textual inerrancy is that it necessarily requires an inerrant reader. . . . Try as they might to be humble, to avoid the pitfalls of intellectual pride—largely because the Bible tells them to, perhaps—fundamentalists are dogmatic and doctrinalistic because their doctrine of the text forces them to be. They are reading an inerrant text; what they read, and therefore by definition what they *interpret*, must be inerrant.

We are now at a difficult crossroads, one which many fundamentalists do not even recognize. The sole authority of the text is subverted by the very nature of texts. How does the fundamentalist control interpretation, while claiming at the same time that nothing but the text itself is authoritative?[34]

In point of fact, fundamentalists cannot both control interpretation of the text and allow people to read the text freely, "controlled" only by the text itself. As Plantinga has shown in his brilliant Free Will Defense, even God cannot *make* another agent *freely* perform an act. There is an inconsistency between the claim that the Bible is a self-standing inerrant text and the actual discourse practice of fundamentalism.

In the claim that preachers and commentators merely read, but do not interpret, the Biblical text in its plain and literal sense, typical of fundamentalism, the function of commentators who control how the text is interpreted is obscured. Boone's analysis of the function of the Scofield Reference Bibles among fundamentalists and of the intimate and inevitable connection of pastors' authority with textual authority, and Barr's analysis of the status of the Scofield text and of the fundamentalists' understanding of inspiration shows that *materially* what the Bible tells fundamentalists is, in fact, controlled by a set of extra-textual authorities.[35] Ammerman summarized historical beginning of this practice clearly:

Around the turn of the century, conservative leaders began to make formal statements of the beliefs they saw as central to the Christian

---

[34]Boone, pp. 72–73. In some ways Boone retrieves a traditional Catholic critique of the principle of "*sola scriptura*" For example, Orestes Brownson, writing in 1843, put it this way: "The Bible . . . is too inflexible to be received as the authoritative rule, unless there be a co-ordinate authority to interpret it and apply it" (Patrick W. Carey, ed., *American Catholic Religious Thought* (Mahwah: Paulist Press, 1987), p. 120. Brownson's attack on the sufficiency of scripture parallels Boone's.

[35]Boone, pp. 49–55, 79–82, 85–88; Barr, pp. 6, 124–130.

faith. In 1890, at the Niagara Bible Conference, J. H. Brookes's "Fourteen Points" were endorsed. At about the same time, at Princeton Theological Seminary, Charles Hodge and B. B. Warfield were fashioning a scholarly defense for inerrancy and orthodoxy. C. I. Scofield's premillenially annotated version of the King James Bible was published in 1909. And from 1910 to 1915, A. C. Dixon edited a series of booklets called *The Fundamentals*, which defended the Bible, conservative doctrine, and the Second Coming. Taken together, such publications began to provide a body of dogma that was distinct from the beliefs of the rest of Protestantism and that circulated in unique organizational channels.[36]

Not only do individual interpreters become authoritative interpreters, but texts other than the Bible, especially the Scofield notes, also become accepted as the standard for interpreting the Bible. By becoming the standard interpretation in the discourse practice, the interpreters and the notes acquired the authority of the Biblical text. Hence, those who would deviate from these touchstones of orthodoxy are anathematized from the community by the authoritative interpreters, the preachers who constitute authorities in the discourse practice.

The claim that the text of the Bible is the inerrant word of God is *formally* and *abstractly* the center of fundamentalism. But to flesh that claim out and make it operative in the life of believers requires *concrete* and *material* explication of the inerrant words uttered by the God who neither deceives nor can be deceived. And this is what the commentators and preachers who work within the discourse of fundamentalism do. The authority preachers have is practically equivalent to the authority of the text. But this authority can be exercised only so long as the preachers conform to their proper role. Neither the preacher nor the individual believer controls the practices which given them or the text authority, but each participates in them. And when fundamentalist preachers transgress the rules of the practices, e.g., by violating sexual mores forbidding homosexual and extramarital activity, or by distancing themselves from fundamentalist orthodoxy (as more moderate evangelicals do), they lose their authority. Non-conformity to the practice strips them of their ability to participate in their customary role in the discourse practice.[37]

---

[36]Ammerman, p. 21.
[37]Boone, pp. 110, 113–114.

What is significant here is not that there *are* authorities in the discourse practice, but rather that these are both *necessary* for the discourse practice to continue and either explicitly or implicitly *denied* being authorities by *individuals* who participate in the practice. The participants in the discourse of fundamentalism *cannot* recognize the authority of the interpreters, whether individuals like Falwell or texts like Scofield, without contradicting their own individual basic belief in the sole authority of the inerrant biblical text. Crucial to fundamentalism is its refusal to recognize a web of multiple authorities. Indeed, if it did recognize such a web, then the sort of argument Lightner made (as analyzed above) would be superfluous.

Although Boone uses "true" and "false" rather than the epistemologists' "justified" and "unjustified," her key point is correct: Fundamentalism's "central claim—the sole authority of the Bible—is both true and false, true at the level of personal belief, false at the level of general discourse."[38] In epistemological terms, an individual believer may be entitled to hold that central claim, because the discourse practice reliably triggers that belief, even though that belief is inconsistent with the discourse practice. Reformed epistemologists do not investigate particular discourse practices in which differing religious believers participate. At least to this time, their account of the generation of individuals' beliefs does not notice the significance of an inconsistency between individuals' beliefs and shared practices. In sum, even if there is an inconsistency between the practice engaged in and the beliefs delivered by the practice, the reformed epistemologists have neither claimed nor shown why such inconsistency would count against the practice.[39]

Second, there seems to be inconsistency not only between the discourse practice and the beliefs generated, but also among the beliefs fundamentalists hold. This can be shown by analyzing the fundamentalists' practice of *separation*. Ammerman summarizes this practice nicely:

---

[38]Boone, p. 2.

[39]If the beliefs of fundamentalists and more moderate evangelicals are as similar as Falwell and Barr maintain, and if those evangelicals also have a basic belief in the Bible as the inerrant foundational text, then there may also be a problem of inconsistency between the discourse of evangelicalism and the beliefs of individual evangelicals. Exploring that problem is beyond the scope of this paper, but the present analysis suggests that it is possible that *any* claim for the unquestionable reliability of a foundational authority is necessarily deceptive.

As we have seen, the people of Southside [a Fundamentalist Baptist Church] have created a world of home and church and school that supports and confirms their ideas about life. Many withdraw from the outside world almost entirely, while others learn to manage their encounters with outsiders so as to minimize psychic and social conflict. The establishment of such an alternative social world has come as Fundamentalists have encountered modernity and found it wanting. As modernity has refused to yield ground to the onslaughts of Fundamentalists, they have responded by creating a territory of their own, existing alongside and in continuing reaction to the institutions and assumptions of modernity.[40]

And as Ammerman also notes, they will continue to nourish the institutions and practices in which "clear rules and authority can take the place of subjectivity, and in which truth is truth without compromise" so long as "the world" is hostile to them.[41]

But part of the world from which fundamentalists assiduously separate themselves are the more moderate evangelicals. Ringenberg has analyzed the difference *separation* makes in practice for fundamentalists and evangelicals:

The major factor distinguishing recent fundamentalists from more moderate evangelicals was the degree to which the former chose to separate from liberal Protestants and, in some cases, from other orthodox Protestants. The evangelicals did not insist that orthodox Protestants withdraw from the large, theologically mixed, denominations. Rather, they thought it appropriate to win the denominations back to their earlier orthodoxy. The fundamentalists, by contrast, thought it a violation of the separation commandment in 2 Corinthians 6:14 for an orthodox Christian to be associated with a denomination or any other group that was not completely administered and populated by fellow orthodox believers.[42]

For fundamentalists, if secular humanism is the bugbear outside the camp, evangelicals are the traitors within the camp. In the fundamentalists' view, the evangelicals are not to try to convert those liberals "outside the camp," but are to separate themselves from the world—or be cast out of the camp of bible-believing Christians.

---

[40]Ammerman, p. 212.
[41]Ibid.
[42]Ringenberg, p. 176.

Yet, even as Falwell and his associates accept the claim that their beliefs are substantially identical to the "evangelicals," they castigate the evangelicals for succumbing to worldly lures. In the concluding section of his book, Falwell himself appeals to *evangelicals* to "reaffirm the foundation. Come back to the fundamentals of the Christian faith and stand firm on that which is essential. Throw down the anchor of truth and stop drifting with every new wave of religious fad that comes along. Stop trying to accommodate the Gospel to the pitiful philosophies of unregenerate humankind."[43] Such an appeal presumes that his evangelical hearers have *left* the essentials of the faith, *drift* with fads, and *compromise* with sinners. The fundamentalists' principle of separation evidently requires them to separate even from those with whom they agree on fundamentals. As this principle of separation—and its application—is read in the inerrant Scripture, so it has an absolute authority.

At the same time as they label the evangelicals drifting compromisers, Dobson and Hindson dissociate themselves from "hyperfundamentalists."[44] The doctrine of separation from sinners and from the world leads fundamentalists to label those who agree on doctrine but differ on degree of separation on the "right" as derogatorily as they do the evangelicals to their "left." For example, Dobson and Hindson conclude a section on "Associational Separation" with the claim that "*we* must not allow *them* to categorize and label everyone to death.[45] The "them" from which they distance themselves are neither "worldly evangelicals" nor "secular humanists," but fundamentalists they categorize and label "hyper-fundamentalists." The practice of associational separation requires that the enemies be identified and cut out of the flock. But to identify them requires that they be labeled. So in castigating fellow-fundamentalists for doing just this, Dobson and Hindson marginalize preachers with whom they share fundamentalist beliefs. They write the hyperfundamentalists out of their own "real fundamentalist majority."[46] The discourse of fundamentalism requires the practice of separation, a practice that is necessarily divisive even among those who agree on fundamentals. And in following the practice of separation, Dobson and Hindson categorically label others categorical labellers. They derogate others for derogating and label others as labellers. Yet

---

[43]Falwell, p. 223.
[44]Falwell, pp. 155–162.
[45]Falwell, p. 163; emphasis added.
[46]Falwell, p. 163.

they fail to recognize not only that derogation and labelling are necessary for the practice of separation, but also that they actually do—and must do—what they condemn other fundamentalists—the "hyper-fundamentalists"—for doing.

At this point, the inconsistency in fundamentalists' practices— and beliefs—should be obvious. One would expect such inconsistency to count against the rationality not merely of fundamentalism as a practice, but against the rationality of individual fundamentalists. However, according to some reformed epistemologists, such inconsistency in a noetic structure, even when a person recognizes it, does not make it irrational for that person to hold those beliefs.[47] It is not clear that even if a discourse practice which regularly triggered an inconsistent belief set would be found unreliable on the reformed epistemologists' account, since they do not consider discourse practices, and since holding inconsistent beliefs is not necessarily irrational for a person. In short, the practice of separation is characteristic of fundamentalism, but it implies at least rejecting some with whom they agree on fundamentals and at most the inconsistent practices of derogating "labellers" and "labelling." The beliefs delivered by the practice are inconsistent and thus, jointly necessarily false, yet a reformed epistemological position cannot find the practices unreliable.

Conclusions

If one takes the reformed epistemologists' approach as it has developed to this point, not only is there no reason to find fundamentalists' basic beliefs any less justified than any other religious believers', there is no reason to find the discourse practice of fundamentalism unrealiable or irrational. Moreover, although some beliefs in fundamentalists' noetic structures are incompatible with others,

---

[47]Feenstra, pp. 8–9, citing Mavrodes, "The Prospects for Natural Theology," unpublished paper presented at a Workshop on Skepticism and Fideism, University of Notre Dame, May 1986. In his response to an earlier version of this paper, Thomas B. Ommen pointed out that "this may be true for some Reformed epistemologists, but Alston, at least, specifically recognizes that 'ineradicable internal inconsistency' would count against the legitimacy of theistic practice." But what "ineradicable" means in practice needs to be specified—would a theory of "eschatological eradication" count to show that a belief might appear ineradicably inconsistent now but that fact would not count against the practice which generated it? Such inconsistency would also *not* necessarily count against the individual practitioner's entitlement to hold her or his beliefs unless it were shown that holding contradictory beliefs was irrational—the point Mavrodes argues has *not* been made.

it is not clear that the reformed epistemologists would find that they are irrational in holding them. If the analysis here is accurate, one possible conclusion is that the (ir)rationality of fundamentalism is sufficient to show the (ir)rationality of religious belief in general.

Yet perhaps a different conclusion can be drawn. We need to ask the reformed epistemologists if our basic beliefs are *basic* enough to support a noetic structure such as they describe. Reformed epistemologists may show how individuals are justified in believing. Yet they neglect to examine how concrete practices which trigger participants' basic beliefs may be reliable belief-forming structures. Rather than accepting fundamentalism as the test case of religious rationality—and finding it rational, as the reformed epistemologists must—an alternative conclusion is that reformed epistemology, as it is presently understood, cannot properly account for the shape of religious belief.

Either fundamentalists with their evident inconsistencies are as rational as any religious believers or reformed epistemology needs vastly to expand its analytical horizons. As I find the basic approach of reformed epistemology attractive, my own preference is to grab the latter horn of the dilemma. It may indeed, as Mavrodes has argued, be rational for a person who finds her or himself with an inconsistent belief set to hold all those beliefs until further analysis or revision can make them consistent, or until further work makes it clear that one must drop one or more of the beliefs to be consistent. However, it does seem irrational to *take up* a practice which triggers individuals to hold either beliefs demonstrably inconsistent with the practice or inconsistent as a belief set. If a religious discourse practice can be shown to have the problems discussed in the previous section, then it seems imprudent to enter the practice and perhaps even immoral to get others to enter the practice. However, working out this claim goes far beyond the bounds of the present essay.[48]

Reformed epistemologists need to enlarge the account of religious epistemology. They do not need to take a transcendental and universal turn as Matteo argues, but to turn 180 from his path. They need to become more particular and concrete, to compare particular discourse practices, and to argue not against the straw person "atheist" or "unbeliever," but with believers of various stripes. Thus far,

---

[48]I attempt to deal with part of this question in "The Prudence of Religious Commitment," *Horizons* 16 (Spring, 1989): 45–64.

reformed epistemologists have tended to practice their own form of "separationism" by refusing to recognize the apparent epistemic parity between participants in various traditions and by simply ignoring them. They have also refused to consider at any length other forms of manifestation beliefs and have analyzed only those basic to forms of Christian theism. This leads to the problems revealed in the third section of this essay and the dilemma described above. But that dilemma is avoidable if the account of religious belief is enlarged to include not only the individual believers' entitlement to believe, but also the social practices which trigger those beliefs. But then our basic beliefs will be shown to be based on others' beliefs and the practices we share with them. The focus of epistemological investigation must then shift from the individual's noetic structure and the justification of the individual's beliefs to the actual communities and practices which are the basis of the "basic beliefs" the individual holds.[49]

---

[49]An earlier version of the first section of this essay formed part of a paper read to the Philosophy of Religion Section at the Annual Meeting of the American Academy of Religion in November, 1988. An earlier version of the whole was read to the Philosophy of Religion Section at the Annual Convention of the College Theology Society in May, 1989. A slightly shorter version appears in Modern Theology 6:2 (April, 1990). I am grateful to Kenneth Surin, the editor of Modern Theology, for permission to use the paper in this volume and to Gerald McCarthy, Thomas Ommen, Nancy Frankenberry, L. Gregory Jones, and an anonymous referee for suggestions for improvements.

AN EDITORIAL FORUM

THE SPIRIT OF AMERICAN FUNDAMENTALISM

Samuel S. Hill

"Fundamentalism" is a term recognized by nearly all Americans. For most, it conjures up a negative image and elicits a censorious response. Our aim here is to examine the reasons for fundamentalism's reputation and to ask whether that appraisal is justified. Why is this movement, that comprises some five million devout Christians, a puzzle to the majority and a source of worry for a great many?

Any suitable explanation must accord with what fundamentalists preach and teach, and with the political and social positions they advocate. That is not all a critical analysis must do, but those are issues that must be reckoned with. What animates this movement? What does it stand for? What impels or energizes these people? What are the movement's goals and what are the means it employs to attain these goals? What are its ethical standards? What are its attitudes towards other people, those who claim to be Christians and those who live without any religious commitment? How do fundamentalists view cooperation or negotiation in a pluralistic society? As a theological enterprise, how does fundamentalism rank and coordinate various aspects of living toward God, toward the society, toward neighbors?

Americans have been hearing about fundamentalism for quite a long time, actually since early in this century. But the phenomenon, a movement and a people, has acquired an enlarged significance since the mid-1970s. Fundamentalists have "gone public." Earlier devoted to a purity that required them to repudiate participation in public matters, especially politics, a large company of these conservative Evangelical Protestants has emerged from their arks of salvation into the general society. From their earlier identity as "come-outers," they have shifted to the strategy of being "in but not of the world." In some cases they have gone even farther than that, seeking to transform "the world" to accord with God's plan.[1] Since their spirit is a vital force in American public life, it is more important than ever that other Americans, academic theologians among them, understand the movement.

Fundamentalism is one form of evangelical Protestantism. The familiar formula runs: all fundamentalists are evangelicals but most evangelicals are not fundamentalists. The movement developed in the 1880s and 1890s and acquired a notable identity and strength by the 1920s. By the 1930s it had formed its own networks of Bible institutes, foreign missions efforts, summer camps and conferences, favorite preachers on the circuit, and the like. As part of the consequences of these occurrences during the same two decades, several new branches of Presbyterian and Baptist life appeared, directly and indirectly, to carry out the Fundamentalist program: the General Association of Regular Baptists and the Conservative Baptist Association of America, and the Bible Presbyterian Church and the Orthodox Presbyterian Church, among them. George M. Marsden has sought to describe this highly diverse and many-faced movement as a "patchwork coalition" that was a "militantly anti-modernist Protestant evangelicalism." Although it gradually took on its own identity, it bore some resemblance to a number of other conservative Protestant positions: "evangelicalism, revivalism, pietism, the holiness movements, millenarianism, Reformed confessionalism, Baptist traditionalism, and other denominational orthodoxies."[2]

In the subsequent half-century, a small proportion of fundamentalists have retained their hard-line separatist stance, the Bob Jones and Carl McIntire orbits being the most famous instances. But most by the 1970s had been influenced by mainline evangelicalism's adaptation from strict separatism to greater participation in the general society's activities, in education and politics most visibly. Still distinctive in that they continued to treasure their own heritage, build their own schools, and (later) television enterprises, they nevertheless ventured outside their own walls to challenge the dangerous drift of American life. Several mounted vigorous crusades against and for: against "secular humanism" and the nation's aban-

---

[1]See James Davison Hunter, *Evangelicalism: The Coming Generation* (Chicago: University of Chicago Press, 1988).

[2]George M. Marsden, *Fundamentalism in American Culture* (New York: Oxford University Press, 1980), p. 4.

donment of its Christian heritage and destiny; for a return to conservative values in family life, national morality, and public policy.

It is indeed more a form than a family. By nature, fundamentalists
are not cooperative or family-like—or at the least they do not prize
cooperation. Being correct outranks being amiable. Nothing justifies
the negotiation and compromise that seem always to accompany
cooperative efforts, not even getting along with others.[3] Noting this
quality introduces us to the character of fundamentalism. It is a
position and movement that believes purity and perfection are
requisite and virtually possible. God's truth is perfect and complete
and must be preached and practiced accordingly. His people are
called out of the sin-wracked world to purity and perfection in their
manner of living as individuals and congregations. That such practice is a possibility is as important as its being a requirement, we
must take care to note.

It follows that fundamentalists think in contrarieties: God is ar-
rayed against Satan, truth against error, faithful Christians against
secularists, authentic congregations against self-deceived churches.
Theirs is a black and white world. Genuine fundamentalism requires
enemies. These show such faces as false doctrine and worldly
society. But fundamentalism is *for* as well as *against*; indeed *against*
because it is *for*. Best known for reacting—a reputation often de-
served—its intention is always to be active in proclaiming God's
truth. That commitment issues in attacks on error and evil and to
standing in judgment on perversity wherever it appears. In a struggle
so urgent, no holds should be barred, and usually none are.

Its foreign policy and its domestic concerns are thus briefly indicated; that is to say, it lives by rules and perspectives that determine
what churches preach and teach and what individuals must believe
and how they are required to live. In fact, "home rule" is the
energizing and direction-setting force for its policy toward the world
outside. What happens in the church and with the individual (and
family) is constant and basic. External relations are derivative from
that. As a matter of fact, this movement that for so long only rejected

---

[3]While Fundamentalism is properly a movement within Protestantism, the term
has some applicability to the Roman Catholic Church. John A. Coleman has recently
suggested that historic integralism is a "kind of Catholic fundamentalism." Briefly, it
"appeals to a literal, a historical, and nonhermeneutical reading of papal or curial
pronouncements as a sure bulwark against the tides of relativism, the claims of
science, and other inroads of modernity." John A. Coleman, "Who Are the Catholic
'Fundamentalists'?" *Commonweal* 116 (January 27, 1989): 42–46.

"the world" and was alienated from it, might return to that practice again. We cannot be sure that it will not.

In their internal life, fundamentalist churches give highest priority to correct belief. What distinguishes them from other Christians is their inerrant reading of the inerrant and infallible biblical text and their perfect rendering of its meaning in preaching and theological formulation. Other Christians, evangelicals included, may exercise modesty in their claims for the total reliability of the Bible, acknowledging mystery and human limitation. Not so the fundamentalists.

It does not follow, however, that all, or even most, fundamentalists are arrogant people. Instead, they are simply taking God at his word. God—perfect, absolute; the one thing such a being would not do to human creatures is present them with an ambiguous message, a mine-strewn path to the truth. God is not a risk-running being. They are claiming nothing for themselves or on their own authority. Repeating: they are simply taking God at God's word.

What they are is rationalists. A venerable epistemic tradition in the Church, rationalism has taken a number of forms. Fundamentalists are hardly Thomists or seventeenth century Anglican divines— or even latter day B. B. Warfields and Charles Hodges. They are propositional rationalists with regard to textuality. The Bible is a collection of equally true, effectively discrete truth-sayings. It is not allegorical or dramatic-poetic. Its contents are not events, stories, and parables which readers perceive or hear for themselves. Rather, everything in the text is truth, propositional truth. This epistemic approach has no affinity for irony or drama or subtlety or mystical experience or even private devotional apperceptions.

The fundamentalists' rationalism sees precise correspondence between text and truth. Truth is understood as THE TRUTH. It is not subject to interpretation. It is not seen as pictures or as images that evoke, but rather as definition. The God whose truth it is is not portrayed as a being who feels or lures but as one who defines. God knows, God promulgates. Figuratively speaking, the truth has the status not of being something within God's being but of something flung into existence to which even God is subject.

Whenever human beings view truth as having such a firm and irrefutable quality, they are certain to be confident in their assertions about it and tough in their defense of it. More deeply still, they are apt to be preoccupied with message, teaching, and doctrinal position. They do well, by their lights, to see it so. Fundamentalists' preoccupation with their central theme, authority, leads to a slighting of other themes. Service to people sometimes is glossed over. Participation in aspects of human civilization, the creative arts, sophisticated learning, and public affairs often are assessed as secondary. Fundamentalism is so busy with its mandate to honor authority and defend the truth that it ingests a limited diet and contributes to only a limited number of areas of civilization.

Fundamentalism's view of authority and its attitude toward the truth reveals a great deal about its nature and spirit. That view takes three forms: 1) Absolute assent to absolute teachings is required. 2) An exclusivist attitude is implied and is quite common. 3) The doctrines are deployed serially and arranged hierarchically.

This third point refers to the preference for discrete or unit-focused thinking over systematic formulation. What is believed and what beliefs are required are specified doctrines rather than a system of thought. Of course, logic correlates the list of teachings and makes for some kind of coherence. But in this case, the demands help determine the content. That is to say, it is far easier to check on propriety when doctrines A, B, C, and D are at issue than when a whole system of thought is held to be inviolate. Checking on propriety by testing and proving true faithfulness is a standard procedure.

Fundamentalism deals in pieces more than wholes. Characteristically, some of the pieces, specified doctrines, will rank ahead of others in a sort of "first among equals" design on the span of constituent parts. Well known for holding fast to the five "fundamentals" in doctrine, fundamentalism actually teaches much more and sets these in a large framework. Just the same, holding up a short list of absolute teachings illustrates its penchant for serial and hierarchical thinking. Convictions about the infallible Bible and the divine Christ do not exhaust its repertoire, but they stand at the head of doctrines taught. Fundamentalism has no admiration for "balanced" or "well-rounded" or dialectical modes of thinking. Fundamentalism rates some doctrines higher than others, and correct belief ahead of cooperation and amiability. Thus, distinction by contrariety is joined by distinction by priority. Drawing distinctions is a characteristic function of the fundamentalist mentality. Differentiation, both side-by-side and higher-lower, is a standard mode of conceptualization.

A recent study by historian David H. Bennett, *The Party of Fear: From Nativist Movements to the New Right in American History*, sheds light on latter day fundamentalism. He achieves this by setting it alongside nineteenth century American movements in which the dominant fear of enemies in our cultural midst pertained to foreign peoples and foreign movements: Catholicism, Asians, Irish and German immigrants, and radicals, among others. By contrast, those Americans of the 1970s and 1980s who fear the ravages wrought by the enemies of noble ideals locate those enemies within our society. In fact, the enemies are the establishment people, policies, and values; their leaders abound in the media and the universities. This "secular humanism" promotes such dangerous positions as the welfare state, abortion rights, eliminating prayer from the public school classroom, and treating homosexuality as tolerable.[4]

At first glance, one may be impressed with the great differences between the two forms of fear, the older nativist movements and the new religious-political right. Yet they bear resemblances. In both cases, there are menacing enemies to be overcome and expunged. Let us remember that fundamentalism by its nature needs and always has enemies; that it is given to differentiation between proper, healthy causes and forces that disrupt and destroy. The fundamentalists of the 1970s and 1980s locate the enemy close at hand, as mistaken and insidious insiders, native born elites (not religious and ethnic outsiders). It goes without elaboration that communism remains a perennial threat against which constant vigil must be exercised.

Today's public-minded fundamentalists exhibit much the same spirit that we noted as characteristic of the early come-outer, world-repudiating religious movement. In the early case, anti-modernism in matters theological provided the occasion. In the recent case, broadly ethical concerns like anti-liberalism and anti-humanism have provoked the resistance and galvanized the cause around which several million Americans have rallied.

So, while things inevitably change, some remain much the same under different guises. Fundamentalist convictions and commitment are constant, but they deal with divergent issues depending on the times. Originally, purity was the ranking priority, almost the only concern of consequence. The New Christian Right has dedicated itself to conquest, in the interest of purity,to be sure. Straightening out America—purifying it—for all Americans is its calling. There is surprise, and a trace of irony, in the fact that the troops from the most conservative army within evangelical Protestantism

---

[4]See David H. Bennett, *The Party of Fear: From Nativist Movements to the Far Right in American History* (Chapel Hill: University of North Carolina Press, 1988).

are willing to devote themselves to making the whole society righteous even though such activites may deflect their vision and diminish their energies from their classic mission, evangelism. The cost,
whether great or small, is not too large since God has laid upon them
the burden to straighten out America, a nation that is faltering badly
in carrying out its special destiny.

Fundamentalism's application of its religious teachings to public
morality and governmental policy is quite consistent with its mentality concerning those religious teachings. "Order" is the basic
concept in both cases. Truth is order, orderly, and ordered. It is not
ambiguous or subjective or relative. It is issued from on high and is
changeless. Analogously, the moral regulations that govern a society
are firm and unchanging. They have authority because they are
permanently and fundamentally true, not because the majority ap-
proves of them at any time or all the time. Authentic moral life of
individuals, families, and societies accords to solid standards, fixed
principles, and transcendent norms. Social reality is not plastic,
awaiting the application of values that may suit the times or the
electorate. Instead it must be ruled by principles that grow out of the
ordered truth on which our universe is based and without which
order cannot be implemented. Relativism is public enemy number
one—just as in the religious sphere, the denial of truth claims is the
severest threat of all.

Recent public-minded fundamentalism also exhibits a keen sociological sense. Taking Jerry Falwell as an example, we observe his
clear-headed acknowledgment that a religious public policy must
take into account the family, the school, and the state. Teachings
about family life are spelled out: mothers should not work outside
the home; the family must look to its head, the father; the gender
roles and behavior have a specifiable pattern. In the school: prayer
in the classroom is appropriate and legal; creation science should be
taught alongside evolutionary theory; and teachers should demonstrate the highest standards and, among other traits, be normal
heterosexuals. The state should function as a republic not as a
democracy; America must defend itself against all foreign powers;
and it should raise itself high as a beacon of political and economic
freedom for the entire world.

It thus turns out that a fundamentalist religious program issues in
a consistent, coherent, and rather comprehensive political program.
Public order is meant to be in place, naturally. The Falwellian theory
of public order fills in the details. Other Americans too readily

caricature and even pillory fundamentalist theology and political philosophy. Some of the views and attitudes we have mentioned here help account for that response: exclusiveness, dogmatism, a sense of singular correctness and divine calling, a negative attitude toward cooperation. Thinking about fundamentalists and acting toward them in such harsh ways is unfair and accomplishes nothing positive. Many do judge it their responsibility to guard against fundamentalist incursions into church life and American political life. Be that as it may, understanding the fundamentalist spirit is essential for people who believe in the sanctity of a pluralist society. This commentary is offered with that goal in mind.

THE ETHOS OF THE FUNDAMENTALIST MOVEMENT

Bernard Ramm

The word fundamentalist or fundamentalism shall be used to refer to that movement which sprung up in the United States (and elsewhere) in opposition to the encroaching liberalism in denominations, in theological seminaries, and in denominational colleges.[1] The word *ethos* refers to the inner spiritual life, to the pattern of daily life, to a group's "spiritual formation" (to use the current buzz word). Fundamentalist characteristics are to be found in other groups but it is the peculiar combination of them which constitutes the fundamentalist ethos. The literature of fundamentalism usually spends time in tracing its origin or setting out its beliefs but rarely discusses its ethos. There is a paradoxical relationship between the theology of fundamentalists and their ethos. Much of their ethos is not the sort of thing one would expect from fundamentalist dogmatism or their inherent legalism in ethics. In this brief essay I shall present the elements which form this ethos and an assessment of its strengths and weaknesses.

(1) One would think from the manner in which the fundamentalists understand the Bible that their sole use of the Bible is to deduce from it fundamentalist theological propositions. However, in agreement with the Pietists the fundamentalists read the Bible devotionally much more than they read it for its theology. Every Christian is to read his or her Bible every day from the devotional standpoint as expressed in the quip "no Bible, no breakfast." Fundamentalist families have family devotions which center on reading a passage of Scripture for the day. Others go further and expect specific guidance

---

[1] The word today is often used with reference to the televangelists but this is an extended use of the term. Historic fundamentalism was very critical of the Pentecostal movement and other charismatic groups.

in some matter for that day in their reading of Scripture. The paradox here is that this subjective reading of Scripture is practiced by the same people who think that the allegorical interpretation of Scripture is subjective trifling with the Word of God.

(2) One of the aftermaths of the revival meetings held in England by the American team of Moody and Sankey (1873–74) was to kindle a new interest in personal spirituality. Eventually this led to the formation of the Keswick Movement. Keswick is in Northern England in the lake country made famous by the number of poets who lived there. Each year since 1875 Christians have come together for one week pitching a tent city for accommodations. The theme of the daily sermon centers on some specific issue of the spiritual life. At the end of the week the anticipated goal is the Spirit-filled life. Upon returning home the Christians are to maintain a serious devotional life consisting of daily Bible reading and prayer as well as reading through some classic of Christian spirituality. Some make a list of prayer petitions to aid the memory. Others expect to have the Lord speak to them through the reading of Scripture a word of specific guidance for that day.

The Keswick Movement, by name and by imitation, has spread through other parts of the world (even Beirut!). Other movements have arisen with different names but maintaining the same sort of spirituality as the Keswick Movement. Fundamentalism has been influenced by Keswick spirituality.[2] Fundamentalists hold summer Bible conferences in which much attention is given to spirituality in the mode of the Keswick movement.

There is a small but important number of fundamentalists who are Christomystics (similar to James Stewart of Edinburgh). The writings of the Quaker mystic Rufus Jones and those of A. C. Tozer have encouraged such a spirituality. The Christomystics are marginally interested in eschatology or controversial theology and hence do not make the headlines.

(3) Another aspect of the fundamentalist ethos is the use of codes. Codes are lists of matters prohibited. In other Christian circles many of these items are usually left to individual conscience. However, to fundamentalists there are things Christians cannot approve, e.g., dancing, drinking, alcohol, mixed bathing, membership in a secret society. There is no official list, for the codes differ from group to

---

[2]The great Princeton theologian of former years, B. B. Warfield (d. 1921), wrote in sharp criticism of these movements and other charismatic movements labeling all under Perfectionism.

group as well as changing with a changing culture, but specific codes are enforced in fundamentalist denominations, churches, mission societies, and parachurch movements.

Closely related to code-regulated behavior is the separated life (cf. 2 Cor. 6:13). The Christian is called upon to separate from all ungodly associations. This is usually stipulated as "the world" but also includes separation from apostate denominations.

(4) There is a magical element in the fundamentalist ethos, although they would be quick to deny it. The magic lies in they way the use such terms as *word* or *blood* in their conversations, in their prayers, in their sermons, and in their daily conversations. Their use of *word* is an extension of their particular doctrine of inspiration. The magical use of *word* surfaces in specific contexts. A Christian in devotions may receive a *word* from the Lord. Or one Christian may have a *word* for another Christian. Or a pastor is a person deep in the *word*. Citation of a scripture text may have an effect like David's smooth stone which struck down Goliath.

There is also a measure of magic in the fundamentalist use of the word *blood*. One of its favorite hymns is *There is Power in the Blood of Jesus*. In the New Testament the word *blood* is shorthand for a sacrifice. Fundamentalists talk of pleading the blood of Jesus or restricting Satan by the blood. This magical note is far more in the ethos of fundamentalism than in its formal theology. Fundamentalists would be straight forward in repudiating anything magical, for all magic in religious ceremonies they would attribute to demons.

(5) There is a specific fundamentalist ethos in the theory of backsliding. It is believed that any defection from the faith or lifestyle or morality can be traced to a failure in personal devotions. Contributing factors are recognized but the initial step can be traced to a weakening of the devotional life. Therefore, the way back is not intellectual but spiritual. This is the meaning of the expression "to get right with the Lord."

(6) The fundamentalists believe that a church's or denomination's spiritual status can be judged by the measure of its commitment to missions. The fundamentalists themselves carry on a very energetic program in missions and support many parachurch organizations. This, too, derives its strength from the inner ethos and is not a matter of ecclesiastical policy.

(7) Lastly, the fundamentalist ethos includes a strong eschatological feeling. It is true that they speak much of the plan of the ages. They publish books and charts outlining the unfolding of events.

Beneath this interest in a detailed eschatology is something deeper, a sense of the nearness of Christ. It is part of their ethos and not so much of their theology. Not able to articulate it in traditional language they express it in eschatological terms.

We now turn to the positive assessment of the fundamentalist ethos:

(1) If spirituality can be measured in numbers, the fundamentalist do have a remarkable record. Studies in the sociology of religion reveals that fundamentalists go to church more often, give more money and support a diversity of parachurch groups. Statistics also reveal that the more sophisticated people become, the less they engage in the measurable activities. No doubt spirituality cannot be readily quantified, but the numbers show the vitality of those governed by the fundamentalist ethos.

(2) Another commentary on the vitality of their ethos is the remarkable record of fundamentalists in the purchase of air time and recently of television time. Mainline groups get on the air waves or the TV channels on free time. Only the fundamentalists have supported national and international radio time, and in recent years have bought TV time to the tune of millions of dollars.

(3) Another word of commendation is the strength that a daily disciplined spiritual exercise can give to the Christian. General calls to an unstructured spirituality are usually failures. Of course structured spirituality is not new with the fundamentalists. The mystics of the middle ages had their ladders of union. Loyola had his spiritual exercises.

(4) The story of fundamentalists and missions is an unusual one. They organized their various "faith missions" and have sent their young people with only Bible institute training to the mission fields of the world. These young people, male and female, accepted the challenge and went to these lands with a miserably small salary, with no pension, with no medical plan, and with no professionally qualified board to handle the details of money, visas, policies of these distant lands, etc. The mission boards are far more realistic today, but when many denominations are retreating from mission fields, fundamentalists remain agressively missionary.

(5) As misguided as their codes may be in the particulars, nevertheless the codes reveal the moral seriousness of fundamentalism. The great Dutch theologian of the past generation, Abraham Kuyper, believed in such codes for they represent a visible line that marks out the difference of the Christian mind from the non-Christian.

We now turn to a critical assessment:

(1) The fundamentalists have been accused of preaching a gospel of full and free grace while teaching a legalistic ethic. In brief, the error of legalism is that it puts laws or rules above persons. If there is one lesson to be learned from Situational Ethics it is that care for persons prevents us from insensitively subjecting persons to rules. Furthermore, in that the code is an external matter, forced compliance with rules does not guarantee a high level of spirituality and in fact may provoke disobedience.

(2) At times the effort to be spiritual in public as well as in private can degenerate into silliness. For example, to judge that a man may have a moustache but not a beard and so be free form the charge of being a hippie is one such instance. A dean of women who ordered that women's dresses must be long enough to touch the top of a text in theology is another instance. Fortunately common sense contributes to the early demise of such rules.

(3) There is a long history of spirituality going back to Antony of Egypt (251–356) which is a storehouse of spiritual wisdom. In either not knowing of this history of spirituality or ignoring it the fundamentalists deprive themselves of all the treasures that are in that history. Without this history there is little to correct the parochialness of fundamentalist spirituality.

(4) Finally, fundamentalists in their ethos have not come to terms with the complexity of the human personality and the paradoxical character of Christian experience. Martin Luther's study of Romans 7 led him to state the most basic character of Christian existence. This he expressed in his famous dictum: at the same time justified and a sinner (*simul iustus et peccator*). The Christian is not a pardoned criminal but a new-born person, a justified person. But at the same time, in the same person, a Christian finds himself to be yet a sinner. Paul says the civil war is so great he cannot understand himself and concludes his exposition with a wail that is almost unChristian—"oh wretched man that I am." This inability to assess the paradoxical nature of Christian experience is echoed in the fundamentalists' inability to assess modern psychiatry and the healing processes at work in psychotherapy.

We can learn two things from the ethos of fundamentalism. The first is their devotional approach to Scripture. I find some modern movements ("spiritual formation," small groups or T-groups, autobiographical reading of a text) are but playing catch-up ball with the earlier pietist and fundamentalist personal and devotional reading of the Scriptures. The second is their moral seriousness. It is true that in too many cases sophistication in spiritual matters means dilution of moral seriousness—the tepid, lukewarm spirit of the Laodicean Church of Rev. 3:14–22.

The most serious flaw is fundamentalism's inherent legalism which mainfests itself in so many ways. The canonicity of the story of the woman taken in adultery (John 7:53–8:11) was debated in the early church. The legalists opposed it on the grounds that to include it would foster moral laxity in the church. Others maintained that it was a great witness to the grace of God and should so be retained in the text. Thank God that grace won the day.

FUNDAMENTALISM AND WORLD CONSCIOUSNESS

E. Glenn Hinson

Some would say that American Christian fundamentalism is a reaction to modernity. Another way to view it, however, is as a reaction to a religious "awakening" going on since the sixties in the West and perhaps throughout the world. America, according to historian William G. McLoughlin, has experienced three such "awakenings" since our forbears came to these shores. The first was the "Great Awakening," ca. 1720–1760, which revitalized religion after it died away during the Puritan era. The second was the frontier revival, ca. 1790–1820, which responded to new problems generated by the westward expansion. The third was the "Social Gospel Movement," ca. 1890–1920, which aroused concern about the plight of urban masses crowded into inner city ghettoes and working in those "dark satanic mills." Others have posited an awakening during the mid-to-late nineteenth century, but McLoughlin excludes that on the basis of the definition of awakening as revitalization.[1] If McLoughlin is right, we are now in our fourth "awakening," which began in the Vietnam War years and will continue through the nineties.

"Awakenings" proceed through three stages. First, there is a period of disorientation and despair, as in the sixties. This is followed by a deepened religious search, as in the seventies and eighties. Finally and gradually a change of consciousness emerges. McLoughlin did not conjecture what would eventuate from the present "awakening," but I suspect it has something to do with *world-consciousness*, the transcending of narrow nationalisms and petty particularism, the sensitizing and tenderizing of consciences to the world.

---

[1]William G. McLoughlin, *Revivals, Awakenings, and Reform* (Chicago: University of Chicago Press, 1978), pp. 141ff.

Fundamentalism is a reaction against the swing of the pendulum toward world consciousness. It is an instinctive reaction of masses to rapid and dramatic change. The trauma of the Vietnam War forced Americans to search their souls. Soul searching touched on many other sore spots in America's inner life—urban ghettos, racial prejudices, poverty, inequalities, injustices, poor education. Some made radical proposals and engaged in radical protests. Leaders, secular and religious alike, did not know how to respond as the country reached a state of near-anarchy. Some persons such as Thomas Merton and Martin Luther King, Jr. spoke as prophets of the awakening, but no one seemed to be in control.

Lack of control is a fearful experience. Political absolutists lay down a set of laws and proceed to enforce them rigorously by whatever means they have at their disposal. They use fear to gain and foster control. As Hannah Arendt has pointed out in her brilliant study *The Origins of Totalitarianism*, absolutists create the illusion of perfect and complete knowledge through skillful propaganda.[2] Fundamentalism is about control. By laying down absolutes, unshakable certainties, fundamentalists are convinced they can bring life under control.

Not all fundamentalists, to be sure, share the same perspective on things. A key principle of Protestant fundamentalism that developed in the early twentieth century was separationism, not only from the world but from other churches not "doctrinally pure." Reacting against Protestant liberal thought, the early fundamentalists scorned politics as a corrupting phenomenon that true believers should scrupulously avoid. Although fundamentalists of that stripe are still around, for instance, at Bob Jones University, the dominant fundamentalism today is a very different creature. The new breed of Protestant fundamentalists will give lip service to the five "fundamentals" of an earlier day (plenary verbal inspiration of the Bible, literal virgin birth, substitutionary atonement, physical resurrection, and literal second coming); but, thanks perhaps to the scare they got in the sixties, they have made politics their main concern. The surprising thing is not that this sort of twist occurred but that it has fascinated enough people to become a powerful force for right wing politics in the 1980's.

Political fundamentalism does have earlier roots in the McCarthy

---

[2]Hannah Arendt, *The Origins of Totalitarianism*. 2nd Ed. (New York: Harcourt Brace Jovanovich, 1973).

era, when Billy James Hargis and Carl McEntire staged small but loud crusades on behalf of American free enterprise and against communism. Cold war mania notwithstanding, not many Americans took either of them seriously. Hargis damaged his reputation beyond repair when discovered having sexual relations with both boys and girls in a school he operated. McEntire continued his strident campaign but found more support in Latin America than in the U.S.

Current political fundamentalism has enjoyed a success none of its antecedents dreamed of. Analysis of trends like this is always difficult, but I suspect fundamentalists such as Billy Graham, Jerry Falwell, Pat Robertson, Charles Stanley, Jim Bakker, Jimmy Swaggart, and a host of others have succeeded because they have latched onto an old myth Americans always itch to apply to themselves in an era when they need one badly. Vietnam grabbed Americans around the neck and shook the daylights out of them. To their rescue came the old Puritan myth of a "Christian America," God's chosen people, who would stand as a bulwark of free enterprise against the threat of world communism. The chief exponents of that vision were not mainline Protestants, as had been true so often in the past, but the fundamentalists who earlier had disclaimed the public forum. Given their virtual monopoly on religious programming on television, fundamentalists got the message through to a lot of Americans. His way prepared by a growing public consciousness among evangelicals, Ronald Reagan roused an army of extreme right supporters for his supply side economics, his communist baiting and bashing, and his New Political Right agenda.

Observers should not underestimate either the appeal or the peril in the nationalistic vision of the New Christian Right. Fundamentalists are onto some real issues, issues close to the soul of American public life, and the fact that they offer a familiar remedy sounds reassuring to a vast number of thoughtful people, people who would again like to believe their country is at least as moral as they are privately.

The line of reasoning runs in this direction: America is God's chosen nation. In the past America has become great because she has been good. But, alas, America is now in peril because that is not longer true. Secular humanists, liberals, "com-symps," and their ilk have seized control of the country and led Americans away from their cherished principles and values. However, it is not too late. If this people, God's people, will repent and change their ways, God will bless America again. The key lies in a moral revolution touching every facet of American life.

Like the Puritans who first framed this vision, fundamentalists tie the moral restoration of the country to revitalization of the family as the chief block in building society. Anything that threatens the family comes under vigorous attack: abortion, ERA, homosexuality, pornography, sex education in the schools. Similarly, they attach great importance to education, especially to those who control it. Because many could not sway educators, fundamentalists created their own schools, designing curricula that would inculcate values they approved. At the same time, though, they have worked zealously to force revamping of public education, undertaking legal action to ban textbooks, prompting state legislatures to require teaching of creationism, coercing school boards to remove teachers who use "liberal" materials in their classes. High on the agenda for moral reform is the issue of prayer in public schools. Unless the children pray, America will never become the godly nation she must become.

To home and school, fundamentalists have added a strange mixture of foreign policy perspectives propounded with the same fanatical zeal as personal ones. Underlying everything is, of course, a paranoia about Communism, America's greatest threat and challenge. America must stand as the last bulwark against world communist takeover. If she is to do so, she must have a strong defense; peace is obtainable only through strength. America must also support Israel, our strategic ally in the Middle East. In the past God has blessed America because America has stood by Israel. Fundamentalists find few right wing governments they would not stamp with their approval. Jerry Falwell gave his blessing to Ferdinand Marcos just before his fall. On a visit to South Africa he lauded the Botha policies and later denounced Bishop Desmond Tutu as a "phony" whose ideas were not representative of blacks in that country. Pat Robertson and an array of others have raised funds for the Contras in Nicaragua.

Widely publicized indiscretions of Jim Bakker and Jimmy Swaggart have eroded confidence in the morality of these erstwhile reformers of American ethics and led to huge drops in their budgets. But the perilous aspect of this movement resides less in ethical inconsistencies than in its extreme nationalism. The political tide carrying American Christian fundamentalism presents some striking analogies to that which swept German Christians along during the

1930's, bewitched by the millenarian rhetoric of Hitler about Germany as a Christian nation.

Jerry Falwell, as a matter of fact, dates the beginning of his political activism from 1967 when he visited Israel just after the Israelis won the "Six Day War." That victory pulled the trigger on fundamentalist expectations that Christ will soon return and inaugurate his millennial reign, for, according to their eschatological scheme, the restoration of the territory of Israel to its Davidic boundaries and the rebuilding of the temple must precede the return. Some of the most ardent dispensationalists among them have proceeded to take the next step, viz. toward restoration of the temple. The Jerusalem Temple Foundation has supplied funds for defense of Jewish terrorists apprehended while trying to blow up the Al Aqsa Mosque and the Dome of the Rock. Ignition of a Third World War and a nuclear holocaust worries some fundamentalists much less than it may bother others, for, according to their reading, scriptures predict that the world will eventually be destroyed by fire anyway. This frightening aspect of fundamentalist thinking is not so well known because leaders have toned it down when their predictions have proven inaccurate. Christ did not return either in 1985 as Falwell predicted or in 1988 as Hal Lindsey did!

Many observers of this movement would like to know how long it will retain its force. A number of recent developments already indicate that, Jerry Falwell's claim of victory notwithstanding, the fundamentalists have not been able to halt the emergence of world-consciousness. New Christian Right candidates did not fare well in the elections in 1988, and a conservative Supreme Court has not shown clear signs of doing their bidding.

Sometimes, however, an illusion is as potent as the reality it is supposed to represent. Where this movement has its greatest potency is in control of the Southern Baptist Convention, the largest single Protestant denomination in the United States. The Convention has become a gargantuan showcase for the nationalistic agenda of the New Christian Right. Even there, however, knowledgeable insiders can see signs that the force which swept this group into power is diminishing as once ardent exponents develop doubts about the rightness of the vision. Rabid commitment to the Bible always poses a threat to the cohesiveness of such movements, for when even unskilled interpreters open and read scriptures for themselves, they will find a variety of answers to the questions they raise. And it could be that God may break through with some new light.

How should other Christians respond to fundamentalism and to the Fourth Awakening? Political experience of the eighties should hoist some caution flags against any inclination to dismiss fundamentalism as unworthy of attention. Quite the contrary, reflective Christians would do well to search for alternative solutions to the serious problems in American culture to which fundamentalists have pointed: the breakdown of the family, devaluation of human life, private and public morality, terrorism, death of political leadership, pornography, dependence on drugs (alcohol, tobacco, as well as hard drugs), and a host of others. What is problematic about fundamentalism is not concern for the problems but overly simplified solutions to serious issues stated with such absolute certainty as to preclude further discussion. Other Christians must view with real alarm, moreover, the nationalistic consciousness which informs so much of the fundamentalist agenda. Christianity is by its very nature a world-conscious religion. To give in to a narrow Americanist outlook would be to violate the most basic Christian convictions, namely, that there is only one God who loves all humankind and that Christ died for all. Americans have never found it easy to look at life in world scope. Recent events in the eastern bloc of nations, however, especially the crumbling of the Berlin Wall, may supply some lenses through which they can see in new ways. Christians should have a vested interest in fostering this awakening to world consciousness, inasmuch as it conforms to their own basic tenets. Even if it did not, they should embrace it out of human interest, for the survival of humankind may depend on it.

FUNDAMENTALISM AND CATHOLICISM

ROMAN CATHOLIC FUNDAMENTALISM: A CHALLENGE TO THEOLOGY

Francis Schüssler Fiorenza

The problem of Roman Catholic fundamentalism raises both historical and systematic questions. Is there a Roman Catholic fundamentalism and what is it? Is it justifiable to label certain movements in contemporary Catholicism "fundamentalism"? Is the label "fundamentalism" equally applicable to Protestantism, Roman Catholicism or to Islam? To what extent is fundamentalism a distinctively Protestant label that should be modified if applied to other religions? Such questions involve complex social and historical issues that need to be addressed before one can discuss the problem of a theological assessment or interpretation of Roman Catholic fundamentalism.

Such a theological assessment is particularly difficult because "fundamentalism" differs in style from traditional theological currents. Modern Roman Catholic theological movements, such as neoscholasticism, modernism, transcendental Thomism, Latin American liberation theology, and feminist theology are distinct movements expressed in theological literature that is clearly identifiable. These movements can be readily analyzed and assessed. Roman Catholic fundamentalism, however, is not so clearly delineated. It is as much a social phenomenon expressing discontent with certain liberal developments in the Roman Catholic church as anything else. Its theological opinions are expressed more in articles, columns, and newspaper editorials than in published books. Its theological polemic is expressed in letters of protest sent to chancery offices rather than in manuscripts sent to refereed theological journals.

The term, "fundamentalism," moreover, is often used indiscriminately. Unfortunately, liberal Roman Catholics often use it as a label for every conservative theological opinion that they do not like. For example, when I had accepted the invitation to write this essay, someone quite seriously asked me, "Why don't you write about Cardinal Joseph Ratzinger as a Roman Catholic fundamentalist? Surely you can write about your former teacher!" Interestingly enough, as we shall see, Cardinal Ratzinger criticizes Catholic fundamentalism and views liberal theologians as responsible for its rise.

Such an indiscriminate use of the term "fundamentalism" is widespread. Many associate the word "fundamentalist" with the Ayatollah Khomeini and his followers. The term "fundamentalist" has even been applied to adherents of the "Green Party"—a European party advocating ecological issues. Against the indiscriminate use of the term David Rausch has wisely cautioned: "If every right-wing fanatic or schismatic is a "fundamentalist," we have irreparably muddied the waters of scholarly analysis concerning this religious movement and phenomenon. We will have defeated our intellectual pursuit before we begin."[1]

To guard against such indiscriminate use, I shall first briefly sketch some diverse methodological approaches to defining fundamentalism. This sketch will provide a framework for assessing some recent Roman Catholic analyses of fundamentalism and Roman Catholicism. These recent analyses often give fundamentalism a theological or doctrinal definition. They then apply this definition to Roman Catholicism—though with some modifications. Such theological deinitions of fundamentalism, when applied to Roman Catholicism, are not as helpful as some assume.

Then, I shall propose that Jürgen Habermas's theory of communicative action and its interpretation of modern society helps to illumine the potential and limits of fundamentalism. The process of modernization, as outlined in theory of communicative action, provides useful categories for understanding not only fundamentalism in general but also that phenomenon within Roman Catholicism labelled "fundamentalism."

Finally, using this interpretive framework, I shall argue that fundamentalism presents a challenge to Roman Catholic theology. Consequently, Roman Catholic theologians should not interpret fundamentalism primarily in negative terms or with pejorative labels. Instead they should view it as a challenge, for fundamentalism is both an expression of modernity and a reaction to modernity.

---

[1]David Rausch, "Fundamentalist Origins," in *Fundamentalism Today: What Makes It So Attractive?*, ed. Maria J. Selvidge (Eligin, Illinois, Brethren Press, 1984), p. 11.

Defining Fundamentalism

In attempting to define fundamentalism, three basic approaches can be clearly delineated: social, doctrinal, and church historical. One can attempt to understand fundamentalism primarily through social analysis as a social movement. One can also interpret fundamentalism primarily in doctrinal terms. Fundamentalism is viewed in relation to a specific set of doctrines and beliefs or as a specific attitude toward religious beliefs. The doctrinal approach can be narrow or broad. It can describe fundamentalism narrowly as consisting of specific beliefs or broadly as consisting of a general attitude. Finally, one can also describe fundamentalism in terms of specific characteristics drawn from the history of American Protestant church life. Each of these three approaches provides a quite distinctive view of fundamentalism. A brief description of each of these approaches can provide a framework for understanding Roman Catholic approaches to fundamentalism.

Social Analysis

The attempt to understand fundamentalism primarily as a social movement interprets it as a premillenarian or revitalization movement. This approach tends to emphasize the "sectarian" characteristics of fundamentalism as opposed to the openness of established mainline Christianity. In *The Social Sources of Denominationalism*, H. Richard Niebuhr distinguishes fundamentalism and modernism on the basis of social experience.[2] Whereas modernism represents the social experience of the urban bourgeoisie, fundamentalism grows out of the social experience of the rural and agricultural population. Niebuhr picks up Max Weber's distinction between urban and rural.[3] The urban experience leads to a practical rationality and an ethics of self-help. The rural experience is closer to nature, more dependent upon nature, and is therefore more inclined to magic. Niebuhr suggests that the symbolism of the Bible, especially of the Hebrew Scriptures drawn as it is from nature, is closer to the rural person than to the urban. He concludes; "Hence the faith of the rural community centers more in the appropriation of the grace of God that men may live in harmony with Him, while urban

---

[2](New York: World Publishers, 1957. 1927), pp. 184–187.

[3]Interestingly, Max Weber himself used the urban/agrarian distinction in reference to the relation between Roman Catholicism and Protestantism.

religion is more concerned with the gain of that same grace that men may live at peace with one another."[4] Niebuhr himself later became skeptical of these formulations.[5] Nevertheless, the contrast between the urban and the rural represents a widespread theme of cultural critique.[6] Recently, Harvey Cox has observed: "For the smalltown and rural poor who appropriated it, fundamentalism expressed their opposition to the powerful modern, liberal, and capitalist world that was disrupting their traditional way of life."[7]

The classic description of fundamentalism with relation to social categories remains Ernest Sandeen's analysis of fundamentalism as a premillennial movement.[8] Sandeen maintains that he has provided a new definition of fundamentalism based upon its continuity with millenarianism. Although he discusses Princeton theology, Sandeen traces the roots of fundamentalism almost exclusively to millenarianism. It is from millenarianism that fundamentalism inherited its anti-worldly biases, its organization and leadership, and its dispensational pre-millennialism.

More recently, the social category of "revitalization movement" has attracted scholarly attention and has been applied to fundamentalism.[9] Frank Lechner has argued that the various revitalization episodes in American history have had fundamentalistic characteristics, and that this helps to explain the anti-modern biases within fundamentalism.[10]

In short, the analysis of fundamentalism as a social movement tends to emphasize its anti-worldly and anti-modern bias. Current social analyses of the growth of fundamentalist churches in the United States interpret fundamentalism as a social reaction to the

---

[4]Ibid., p. 184.

[5]"Fundamentalism" in Encyclopedia of the Social Sciences, ed. E. R. A. Seligman (New York: The Macmillan Co: 1931), Vol. 6, pp. 526–527.

[6]Morton and Lucia White, The Intellectual versus the City (Cambridge: Harvard University Press, 1962).

[7]Religion in the Secular City (New York: Simon & Schuster, 1989), pp. 60–61.

[8]See the debate about defining fundamentalism in relation to social millenarianism, Ernest R. Sandeen, The Roots of Fundamentalism: British and American Fundamentalism 1800–1930 (Chicago: University of Chicago Press, 1970) and the review essay by George Marsden, "Defining Fundamentalism," Christian Scholar's Review 1 (1971): 141–151 and Sandeen's reply "Defining Fundamentalism: A Reply to Professor Marsden," Ibid.: 227–233. Sandeen views the millenarianism as the most decisive element of fundamentalism.

[9]See William McLoughlin, Revivals, Awakenings, and Reform: An Essay on Religion and Social Change in America 1607–1977 (Chicago: University of Chicago, 1978).

[10]Frank Lechner, "Fundamentalism and Sociocultural Revitalization in America," Sociological Analysis 46 (1985): 243–259.

liberal emphasis upon activism to the detriment of a concern for ultimate questions.[11] Moreover, this social analysis tends to emphasize the sectarian characteristics of fundamentalism. It is, however, questionable whether such a view adequately depicts fundamentalism's public influence and its interest in making the United States into a Christian nation.[12] Recent research locates fundamentalism "in relatively homogeneous niches within the larger environment in which the connections between core tenets and life-style can remain implicit."[13]

Theological Definition

Theological definitions of fundamentalism within Christian Protestant theology take fundamentalism in relation to a diverse set of doctrines. For some these induce a wide range of theological issues, whereas others emphasize particularly the doctrine of scripture and the doctrine of dispensationalism.[14]

The broader theological definition of fundamentalism refers to a series of twelve volumes, *The Fundamentals*, published between 1910 and 1915 to reaffirm the "fundamentals" of Christianity. These basic tenets include the divinity of Christ, His virgin birth, salvific death, resurrection, and second coming. The largest portion of the essays, however, focused on the literal interpretation of scripture. The correct belief in Christ's second coming is the test case for belief in the Bible.

Contemporary systematic theological analyses that locate fundamentalism within the history of doctrine emphasize the inerrancy of scripture. Donald Bloesch defines fundamentalism as a synthesis of old orthodoxy and evangelical pietism with a docetic view of scripture. Modern fundamentalism, he argues, uses the category of verbal

---

[11]Dean Kelley, *Why the Conservative Churches are Growing* (New York Harper, 1972). For an explanation of growth in relation to fertility rates see R. Bibby and M. Brinkerhoff, "Circulation of the Saints Revisited: A Longitudinal Look at Conservative Church Growth," *Journal for the Scientific Study of Religion* 22 (1983): 253–262.

[12]Jerry Falwell, *Strength for the Journey* (New York: Simon and Schuster, 1987). See also Frank Newport and Stuart Rothenberg, *The Evangelical Voter* (Washington: Institute for Government and Politics, 1984).

[13]Robert Wuthnow, *Meaning and Moral Order* (Berkeley: University of California, 1987).

[14]The doctrine of dispensationalism was developed in England by John Nelson Darby, in *Evidence from Scripture of a Future Dispensation* (London: G. Morrish, 1834) and *Seven Lectures on the Prophetical Addresses to the Seven Churches* (London: G. Morrish, 1852).

₁ᵥᵥᵤation to talk of the Bible and "thereby unwittingly calling into question the dual authorship of Scripture."[15]

Likewise, James Barr defines fundamentalism in relation to its interpretation of the Bible. Fundamentalism, he argues, is not so much interested in a literal interpretation of the Bible as in the doctrine of inerrancy. For example, fundamentalists will stretch the literal meaning of the bible in order to safeguard its inerrancy or its harmony with those data of modern science that are accepted as true. Therefore, apparent conflicts between science and the Bible are resolved not so much by adhering to the literal meaning of the bible as by stretching the literal meaning so as to guarantee the literal meaning.[16]

American Historical Definition

In addition to definitions drawn from social and doctrinal categories, a third approach analyzes fundamentalism from the perspective of church history, especially American church history.[17] Marsden describes fundamentalism as a "broad coalition" of anti-modernists. In the 1920s and 1940s fundamentalism was used almost synonymously with conservatism. A fundamentalist was basically a theological conservative. A fundamentalist believed in the basic tenets of evangelical Christianity. Because of this belief, he or she was strongly opposed to modernism and to liberal Christianity. Fundamentalism did not imply then, as it does today, either a dispensationalist or a separatist element.[18]

Yet fundamentalism came to be narrowly defined in relation to dispensationalism. Dispensationalism was the most influential anti-modernist doctrine. Its theological view of history offered an inter-

---

[15]*Essentials of Evangelical Theology* (New York: Harper & Row, 1978), p. 74.

[16]James Barr, *The Scope and Authority of the Bible* (Philadelphia: Westminster Press, 1980), especially chapter five, "The Problem of Fundamentalism Today." See also *Holy Scripture: Canon, Authority, Criticism.* (Philadelphia: Westminster, 1983).

[17]See George Marsden, *Fundamentalism and American Culture: The Shaping of Twentieth Century Evangelicalism* (Oxford: Oxford University Press, 1980). Whereas Sandeen had emphasized millenarianism, Marsden's church historical interpretation emphasizes the continuities and discontinuities between fundamentalism and nineteenth-century evangelicalism. See "From Fundamentalism to Evangelicalism: A Historical Analysis," eds. David F. Wells and John D. Woodbridge, *The Evangelicals* (Nashville: Abingdon Press, 1975) and "Fundamentalism as an American Phenomenon, A Comparison with English Evangelicalism," in *Church History*, 46 (1977): 215–232.

[18]George M. Marsden, *Reforming Fundamentalism: Fuller Seminary and the New Evangelism* (Grand Rapids, Michigan: William B. Eerdmans, 1987), p. 10.

pretation of the present and future. The present age or "dispensation" was the sixth dispensation. This disposition marked the great apostasy in the churches before the return of Christ. In short, it was precisely the current modernism and liberalism within the Christian churches that constituted that premillennial apostasy. Consequently, dispensationalism was for fundamentalism the major antimodernist belief because it fixed modernism as the great apostasy. In addition, narrow descriptions point out the degree of fundamentalist separatism from mainline Christian churches, viewed as corruptions of Christianity, and underscore the connection between fundamentalism and superpatriotism.[19]

When fundamentalism is defined primarily with characteristics drawn from American church history, then a dimension emerges not obvious in theological definitions with their emphasis on inerrancy or in the social analysis of fundamentalism as a sectarian movement. This dimension is the development of the theme of America as a "Christian nation." This emerges within American fundamentalism especially at the end of World War I and represents a tension within fundamentalist theology. Insofar as fundamentalists were premillennialists, they rejected modern culture as secular. Insofar as fundamentalists were American evangelicals they urged a national return to Christian principles. They sought to emphasize the Christianization of civilization as the hope for culture. This reformist hope for culture was combined with a strong American patriotism.

In short, the diverse definitional approaches to fundamentalism come up with three diverse images of fundamentalism: fundamentalism as a sectarian antimodern movement, fundamentalism as the emphasis of fundamental doctrine, especially biblical inerrancy, and fundamentalism as a superpatriotism hoping to develop a Christian civilization. It is important to keep these three images in mind in analyzing theological interpretations of fundamentalism within the Roman Catholic Church.

Catholic Theological Definitions of Roman Catholic Fundamentalism

An analysis of recent Roman Catholic theological assessments of fundamentalism within the Roman Catholic Church shows that they predominately interpret fundamentalism from a doctrinal or church

---

[19]See Marsden, *Fundamentalism and American Culture.*

historical approach. These Roman Catholic assessments define fundamentalism narrowly or broadly. Either they identify Protestant fundamentalism with biblical inerrancy and transfer the term to Roman Catholicism or they define fundamentalism as a conservative approach to Christian faith and theology, and see conservative Roman Catholics as fundamentalists.

Roman Catholic theological analyses of the phenomenon of fundamentalism within the Roman Catholic Church take over doctrinal categories used to interpret American Protestant fundamentalism. At the same time they seek to differentiate Roman Catholic from Protestant fundamentalism. They are aware that the notion of fundamentalism cannot be simply transferred on a point by point basis. Nevertheless the modifications they propose need further nuancing.

Gabriel Day defines Roman Catholic fundamentalism by substituting papal authority for biblical inerrancy. For him "authoritarian heteronomy can therefore rightly be seen as the Catholic form of fundamentalism, in that it treats the ecclesiastical magisterium in the same manner as the Protestant fundamentalist treats the Bible."[20] John Coleman interprets Roman Catholic fundamentalism as the integralism that emerged in reaction to Catholic modernism just as Protestant fundamentalism reacted to Protestant liberalism.[21] He takes specific Protestant fundamentalistic doctrines, e.g. the inerrancy of the Bible and the pre-millennialism, and applies them to Catholicism. The distinctive difference between Roman Catholic and Protestant fundamentalism is that Catholicism substitutes the papacy and papal infallibility for scripture. The infallibility of the papacy replaces the inerrancy of scripture. The premillennialism of Protestant fundamentalism finds its parallel in the Marian appearances which Coleman sees as a version of premillennialism. Finally, Protestant fundamentalism and Roman Catholic fundamentalism emerged at the same time and criticized similar modernist theologies.

---

[20]"Catholicism and Modernity," *Journal of the American Academy of Religion* 63 (1985): 794. For a critique of this identification, see Peter Berger, "Secular Theology and the Rejection of the Supernatural: Reflections on Recent Trends," *Theological Studies* 38 (1977): 54—55.

[21]John Coleman, "Who are the Catholic 'Fundamentalists'? A Look at Their Past, Their Politics, and Their Power," *Commonweal* 116 (January 27, 1989): 42—47. Integralism usually refers to the conservative current in Roman Catholic thought in the post-French Revolution period that argued for an integral relation on synthesis between religions and political authority in criticism of the Enlightenment's separation of church and state.

Coleman's suggestion describes in a helpful manner distinctive features of Roman Catholic fundamentalism. Nevertheless, his analysis needs to be modified insofar as it does not sufficiently take into account some significant data. First, the claim that Papal infallibility replaces biblical inerrancy does not take into account the degree to which Roman Catholic fundamentalists criticize modern Catholic biblical studies and biblical scholars.[22] Even if one grants that many Roman Catholic Bible study groups are not biblicist, one still encounters a severe critique of contemporary exegesis. Roman Catholic fundamentalist writings, for example, The Wanderer, often criticize even moderate scripture scholars such as Raymond E. Brown.

Second, the claim that papal infallibility or papalism has replaced biblicism also overlooks the criticisms of the papacy within Roman Catholic fundamentalism. Archbishop Marcel Lefebvre is an obvious example. He strongly criticizes the Pope for departing from tradition.[23] Moreover, the Pope has conservative views on doctrine and sexual morality, but progressive views on social and economic policies. Roman Catholic conservatives such as Michael Novak, and Catholic fundamentalists sharply criticize these policies. Superpatriotism made Protestant fundamentalists critical of American Catholics as foreigners. Where this superpatriotism exists among Roman Catholic fundamentalists, it places them in confrontation with a papacy whose social agenda is not a defense of the American economic enterprise.

Roman Catholic fundamentalists, therefore, face a dilemma in regard to the papacy. They have to deal with the progressive changes of Vatican II, the social doctrines of the Papacy, and the internationalism of the Vatican. Some escape the dilemma in part by sharply distinguishing faith from social and economic moral teachings, and hence set up a kind of hierarchy of truths—a fault for which they criticize liberal Roman Catholics.

Third, Roman Catholic integralism and Protestant fundamentalism are not chronologically parallel. Catholic integralism did not emerge in reaction to theological modernism, but has a longer history. In the modern period, integralism arose primarily in reac-

---

[22]The Philippine Bishops' Conference issued on January 22–24, 1989 a statement critical of biblical fundamentalism within Roman Catholicism, "Philippine Bishops' Statement on Biblical Fundamentalism," Origins 18 (Feb. 23, 1989): 627–628.

[23]See for example the correspondence between Archbishop Lefebvre and the Vatican, "Breakdown of Negotiations with Archbishop Lefebvre" Origins 18 (June 30, 1988): 97–101.

tion to the Enlightenment and the French Revolution. It represented a combination of political conservatism (royalty over democracy), ultramontanism (loyalty to the Papacy over national interests), and the return to Thomistic philosophy.

In short, these three considerations suggest that one cannot simply interpret Roman Catholic fundamentalism as a form of Protestant fundamentalism that substitutes the Pope for the Bible and Marian appearances for premillennialism.

Others attempt to describe fundamentalism theologically broadly as a conservative reaction and a traditional theology that is closed to modernity. It is a form of integralism.[24] Such a broad use of the term "fundamentalism" is exemplified by Stanley B. Marrow's *The Words of Jesus in Our Gospels*. Although subtitled "A Catholic Response to Fundamentalism," the book does not give any specific definitions of fundamentalism. Instead it simply considers fundamentalism to be an antonym of liberalism.[25] Thomas O'Meara in "Fundamentalism and the Christian Believer," links together "charismatics, evangelicals, and every fundamentalist-oriented group" who "share certain characteristics."[26] These characteristics are the localization of God's power in some thing, the possession of a direct line to God, and a God who is not a God of Nature and creation, but one of miracles. He argues that "Fundamentalism is ultimately not a theology but a psychological attitude. Not what it appears, this faith reflects not so much divine power as a human need for religious supports."[27] In addition to this psychological need, he suggests that "the fundamentalist personality tends to be afraid and angry."[28] It is against similar statements that Harvey Cox has rightly cautioned: "When theologians do pay attention to fundamentalism, they often misunderstand it. They tend to examine it as a somewhat bizarre variant of Protestantism."[29]

Such a negative assessment is present in the recent American Bishops' statement on fundamentalism. It paints fundamentalism in broad strokes, though with some reference to definite and explicit

---

[24]See Daniel Alexander, "Is Fundamentalism an Integrism?," *Social Compass* 32 (1985): 373–392.

[25]*The Words of Jesus in Our Gospels* (New York: Paulist Press, 1978), p. 2. Marrow is, of course, very much aware of the inadequacy of such terminology.

[26]"Fundamentalism and the Christian Believer," *The Priest* 44 (March 1988): 39–42.

[27]Ibid., p. 40.

[28]Ibid., p. 41.

[29]*Religion in the Secular City*, p. 40.

characteristics. The Bishops' statement affirms that "Fundamental-ism indicates a person's general approach to life which is typified by unyielding adherence to rigid doctrinal and ideological posi-tions—an approach that affects the individual's social and political attitude as well."[30]

Anne E. Patrick, the current president of the Catholic Theological Society of America, offers a carefully nuanced description. Her analysis contrasts Roman Catholic fundamentalism and what she calls "New Catholic Traditionalism."[31] The latter is called "new" because it takes into account modern discoveries of philosophy, history, the natural and social sciences, etc. It is a traditionalism because it affirms the classic Catholic view of the compatibility between faith and reason, and because it continues the practice of reinterpretation. In distinction to this new Catholic Traditionalism, Roman Catholic fundamentalism has a specific view of theology. It views theology as a static heritage. Moral theology, for example, is a static heritage that contains all the truths necessary for dealing with the ethical problems of life.

Roman Catholic fundamentalism does not take into account the concrete situation of believers. It is convinced that to change or even to question past teaching is to undermine the authority of that very tradition. Therefore, it keeps change to a minimum. Catholic funda-mentalism, consequently, gives theologians a very limited task. They are limited to explaining what the church has taught. They can neither question nor dissent from that teaching. Instead they have only to apply it. Dissent and criticism are limited to academic squabbles.

This suggested contrast between Roman Catholic fundamentalism and the "new Catholic Traditionalism" assesses fundamentalism as a kind of static and conservative faith. Some cautions should be raised about such an assessment. A first caution is whether such a view of fundamentalism as a closed static view of faith corresponds to the reality of fundamentalism. Some recent studies criticize the notion that fundamentalism is a static worldview lacking in change and cognitive differentiations. Fundamentalist attitudes do show a rigidity in regard to some aspects of behavior and belief, but they are quite open in regard to many other points. There is a low correlation

---

[30]"Pastoral Statement for Catholics on Biblical Fundamentalism," Origins 17 (No-vember 5, 1987): 376–377.

[31]Anne E. Patrick, "Conscience and Community: Catholic Moral Theology Today." Warren Lecture Series in Catholic Studies, The University of Tulsa, February 13, 1989.

between fundamentalist beliefs and other personal attitudes. The major link seems to be local custom. The prescribed values, norms, and beliefs rest on local custom.[32]

Second, such a view of fundamentalism tends to identify it in a general way with conservativism or traditionalism, and Catholic faith with modern liberalism. It views fundamentalism as a closed, static, and limited mode of faith opposed to the new Catholic theology seeking to take seriously the challenges of modernity. Does such a view underscore what is distinctive about fundamentalism? Does such a view tend to overlook what it is about fundamentalism that is precisely modern? In a way, one could also label fundamentalism as "new." To affirm that the intellectual discoveries of historical and literary criticism have challenged the fundamentalist understanding of the biblical authority may well be true. Yet it does not sufficiently recognize that the fundamentalist understanding of the Bible is itself an innovative and modern phenomenon.

Third, if theological analyses of fundamentalism see it primarily as a static faith, they might fail to grasp its legitimate impulse. A theological analysis of fundamentalism has to ask the following questions: What is the source of its strength? Do some aspects of fundamentalism have a theological legitimacy? Why is fundamentalism so strong now? Such questions must be central to any theological analysis of fundamentalism.

Modernity as Process of Differentiation

Habermas' theory of communication action and his interpretation of modernity provide categories that can help us to understand fundamentalism.[33] The theory of communicative action seeks to interpret modernity as a process of differentiation. This differentia-

---

[32]Stuart Rothenberg and Frank Newport, The Evangelical Voter: Religion and Politics in America (Washington, D.C. Institute for Government and Politics, 1984); Wade Clark Roof, Community and Commitment: Religious Plausibility in a Liberal Protestant Church (New York: Elsevier, 1978); and Nancy Taton Ammerman, Bible Believers: Fundamentalists in the Modern World (New Brunswick, N.J.: Rutgers University Press, 1987).

[33]The Theory of Communicative Action. Vol. I and II (Boston: Beacon, 1984 and 1987). See also his The Philosophical Discourse of Modernity: Twelve Lectures. (Boston: Beacon, 1987) and Vorstudien und Ergänzungen zur Theorie des kommunikativen Handelns (Frankfurt: Suhrkamp, 1984). Good expositions of Habermas' position are: David Ingram, Habermas and the Dialectic of Reason (New Haven: Yale, 1987) and Stephen K. White, The Recent Work of Jürgen Habermas: Reason, Justice and Modernity (New York: Columbia University, 1987).

tion leads negatively to a split between the institutions of this rationality and the lifeworld of everyday practice.

Max Weber had argued that modernity results from the process of disenchantment and entails secularization. The process of modernization thereby corrodes traditions by splitting life into diverse cultural spheres that increasingly become separate from one another. In Weber's eyes modernization leads to a cultural impoverishment, to an iron cage with a loss of freedom and meaning.[34] In contrast, Talcott Parsons argues that the differentiation of modernity is positive. It provides individuals with freedom from external authority and it enables work, family, law, education, religion, etc. to develop and grow with increasing autonomy from each other. Differentiation leads not so much to a loss of meaning or a loss of values as to a generalization and inclusiveness of values.[35]

The conception of modernity within Habermas' theory of communicative action differs from those of both Weber and Parsons. The ambiguity of this process is central to his interpretation. On the one hand, the differentiation involves an increasing rationalization in each sphere and leads to the growth of a type of expertise in each sphere of knowledge. On the other hand, this rationalization can also lead to a one-sided emphasis on a certain type of rationality, namely, instrumental and functional rationality. It also leads to a split between the rationality of expert culture and everyday life. An uncoupling takes place between the system (economic and administrative system) and the lifeworld of shared meaning. This result of modernization involves an impoverishment of the lifeworld as well as its colonization, that is, the dismantling of traditional values and their replacement with technocratic and monetary values. These two elements of the process of modernization are important for our interpretation of fundamentalism.

Habermas argues that modernization entails a separation of science, morality, and art in autonomous spheres. Each sphere develops its own internal logic. As a result of the institutionalization of expertise, each of these spheres (scientific rationality as the cogni-

---

[34]See Wofgang Schluchter's analysis of Weber, *The Rise of Western Rationalism* (Berkeley: University of California, 1981).

[35]See Talcott Parsons' collection of essays written after the 1950s in *Sociological Theory and Modern Society* (New York: Free Press, 1967) as well as *Societies: Evolutionary and Comparative Practices* (Englewood Cliffs, N.J.: Prentice-Hall, 1966). For a sympathetic analysis of Parsons' work, see the chapter "Successful Modernity," in Jeffery C. Alexander, *Twenty Lectures: Sociological Theory Since World War II* (New York: Columbia University, 1987).

tive instrumental rationality, moral as moral practical rationality, and art as aesthetic expressive rationality) comes increasingly under the control of specialists. These specialists are more adept in the logic and rationality of these specific areas than other people. The result is an increasing distance between the culture of the larger public and the expert culture of these particular spheres.[36]

The process of modernization is not adequately described as simply increasing rationalization and secularization, whereby religion, for example, loses its centrality within the cultural, educational, and political spheres. There is indeed an erosion of traditional values within the lifeworld. However, as Habermas' argues, this erosion results not so much from the differentiation of the distinct cultural spheres of value according to their own logic as from the separation of expert cultures from the contexts of everyday life-practice.[37] The increasing distance between the culture of the larger public and the expert culture of the particular spheres leads to this erosion.

The differentiation of the value spheres of science, morality, and art within modernity leads to a professional analysis of cultural tradition and, consequently, the distance between the expert cultures and the broader public increases. "What accrues to a culture by virtue of specialized work and reflection does not come *as matter of course* into the possession of everyday practice. Rather cultural rationalization brings with it the danger that a lifeworld devalued in its traditional substance will become impoverished."[38]

The result of this process is the transformation of the role of the state. The dynamism specific to the administrative system of the state affects the lifeworld. The process of increasing juridification of life is labelled "inner colonization."[39] The neutral processes of law increasingly are brought to bear on areas of life that were regulated by religious and moral traditions. These areas of life now come under the organization of administrative bureaucracies. Decisions are based upon administrative regulations. Personal needs are met primarily through administrative decision and the distribution of money.

---

[36]Jürgen Habermas, "Modernity versus Postmodernity," *New German Critique* 22 (1981): 3–14.

[37]*The Theory of Communicative Action*, Vol. I, pp. 241–271. See also, Jürgen Habermas, *Kommunikatives Handeln*, eds. Axel Honneth and Hans Joas, (Frankfort: Suhrkamp, 1986), pp. 327–495.

[38]*The Theory of Communicative Action*. Vol. II, p. 326.

[39]See Lechner, p. 257.

One way in which juridification affects traditional values of the lifeworld is evident in the United States in the separation of church and state. Court decisions and legislation attempting to enforce such a separation often abolish completely the presence of religion and can lead to a religious impoverishment of culture and education. West Germany provides a contrasting example. The state provides in primary and secondary schools teachers of religion for the respective denominations as well as instruction in ethical and moral philosophy for those opting out of religious instruction. The fundamentalist critique of the banning of school prayer and religious symbols underscores that the important distinction between church and state can be so interpreted that it leads to an impoverishment of public and civic life. This impoverishment provides the context for the charge that the fundamentalist theologian Francis Schaefer makes that secular humanism is a religion which "the government and courts in the United States favor over all others."[40]

Protest movements emerge within modernity against the modern impoverishment and colonization of the life-world. Such protests can be divided into protests of resistance and protests of withdrawal. Protests of resistance represent forms of protest that incorporate Enlightenment ideals. Protests of withdrawal represent those that do not. Feminism is an example of the former to the extent that it strives to extend bourgeois rights and ideals to women. Religious fundamentalism is in Habermas' view an example of the latter. Such an interpretation of fundamentalism as a protest movement accords with the working definition of the University of Chicago's Fundamentalism Project.[41]

The stress on separation or on withdrawal, however, should not overlook the fact that renewed religious fundamentalism is a motivating force within contemporary protests. "The painful manifestation of deprivation in a culturally impoverished and one-sided rationalized practice of everyday life" is obvious and manifest.[42] It should be obvious not only to fundamentalist groups, but also to others. Religious communities build up communal support for the search for personal and collective identity. The re-evaluation of the

---

[40]Quotation in A. James Reichley, "The Evangelical and Fundamentalist Revolt," *Piety and Politics: Evangelicals and Fundamentalists Confront the World*, eds. Richard John Neuhaus and Michael Cromartie (Washington, D.C.: Ethics and Public Policy Center, 1987), p. 77.

[41]See James L. Franklin, "An Ever-Changing Fundamentalism," *The Boston Globe* (December 4, 1988), p. 432.

[42]Habermas, *The Theory of Communicative Action*, Vol. II, p. 341.

particular, the natural, the local can be interpreted as reactions against the deprivation of modernity.

Rather than label fundamentalists as angry personalities or as believers with a static personality, it is important to underscore that fundamentalism expresses a protest against cultural impoverishment. In religious fundamentalism as well as in other protest movements within modernity, there is evident a genuine concern about the lack of shared moral values in the lifeworld where money and efficiency have indeed taken over. Nevertheless, to locate fundamentalism within protests against the impoverishments of modernity and to acknowledge the legitimacy of the protest of fundamentalism is not to agree with all of fundamentalism. A nuanced theological assessment of fundamentalism is needed.

A theological assessment should take into account that fundamentalism is a phenomenon of modernity.[43] The modernity of fundamentalism relates not only to its existence as a social movement, but also to key elements of its belief systems. Second, a theological assessment has to consider the legitimacy of its protest against the impoverishments of modernity. And finally, theology should consider fundamentalism as a positive and not simply a negative challenge.

Fundamentalism as a Phenomenon of Modernity

That one must interpret fundamentalism as a phenomenon of modernity is usually supported by the social scientific interpretation of fundamentalism as a social movement.[44] Interpretations of fundamentalism primarily under the aspect of a doctrinal definition often overlook this point. Fundamentalism is within a doctrinal perspective often seen as a defense of traditional Christianity. Such a viewpoint needs to be modified both in regard to the emphasis on the literal meaning of scripture and the significance of the papal magisterium.

---

[43]For diverse discussions of fundamentalism and modernity that take a different approach, see James Davidson Hunter, *American Evangelicalism: Conservative Religion and the Quandary of Modernity* (New Brunswick, N.J.: Rutgers University Press, 1983), and Robert Wuthnow, *The Restructuring of American Religions: Society and Faith Since World War II* (Princeton: Princeton University, 1988).

[44]See for example, Frank J. Lechner, "Fundamentalism Revisited," *Society* 26 (January/February 1989): 51–58. Unfortunately, I could not obtain his relevant essay, "Fundamentalism and Sociocultural Revitalization: On the Logic of Dedifferentiation," eds. Jeffrey Alexander and Paul Colomy, *Differentiation Theory and Social Change*. (New York: Columbia University Press, 1988).

The emphasis on the literal meaning of the text and its truth within fundamentalism represents an innovation in the history of theology. The fundamentalist emphasizes the literal meaning of the text to the extent that the literal meaning asserts inerrancy. Likewise, they seek to establish that the literal meaning corresponds to the facts and that inerrancy is especially demonstrated by archaeological facts.[45] Such an approach to scripture does not continue tradition, but departs from tradition. Classic Christian interpretations of the Bible developed the fourfold interpretation of Scripture, going beyond the literal meaning to the spiritual, allegorical, and anagogical meaning. In fact, going beyond the literal meaning was identified with the proper Christian attitude to the Scripture. The Fathers of the Church attacked literal interpretation of Scripture as "Jewish" and "according to the flesh." Christian interpretation should, in contrast, go beyond the flesh, beyond the letter, to the spiritual meaning of the text. Whoever remained at the literal meaning of the text and did not go on to the spiritual meaning of the text failed to grasp the text's true and authentic meaning. While the anti-semitism of this is both patent and embarrassing, it clearly displays the classic Christian rejection of literalism.

Classic interpreters of Genesis, for example Augustine and Origen, attempt to elaborate the theological meaning of Genesis in a way that represents directions, insights, and mentalities that are utterly foreign to a biblicistic or literalist reading. This observation is theologically important. If one views fundamentalists as having a static conception of faith or as wanting to preserve the pristine past, one concedes that the past belongs to a fundamentalist reading of scripture and one overlooks the extent to which a literalist interpretation of scripture contrasts with classical Christian interpretations.

What is needed is a post-critical way of reading the scriptures that is in no way a code name for an uncritical or pre-critical way, but rather a bridge crossing over the gap between the expert culture of historical critical method and popular piety.[46] The classical expositions of scripture with their multiplicity of senses of scripture sought to interpret scripture in a way that related the text's meaning to personal, historical, and communal life. Its pluralism and multi-

[45]Josef Oesch, "Fundamentalismus und fundamentalistische Versuchung ins Spannungfeld vom Archaeologie und Bibel," in Niewiadomski, pp. 111–124.

[46]For perceptive remarks critical both of fundamentalism and of certain presuppositions of historical criticisms, see Joseph Ratzinger, "Foundations and Approaches of Biblical Exegesis," Origins 17 (February 11, 1988): 593–602.

dimensionality contrasts with the one-dimensionality of a literalist interpretation that contemporary hermeneutical theory also seeks to overcome.[47]

The emphasis on a literal interpretation of the Bible is not the only innovation within fundamentalism. Even when Roman Catholic fundamentalists criticize the Papacy and the episcopal magisterium for changes in the practice of liturgy or for changes in social policy, they often overlook that the very notion and practice of the magisterium has undergone major innovative changes within modern times.[48] The concentration of the magisterium almost exclusively to the papacy, the role of the papacy in appointing bishops, and the notion of faith and heresy are just some of the radical changes that have taken place within the modern Roman Catholic Church. The point is that the two major factors that others have labelled as essential to fundamentalism, namely emphasis on literalness of scripture and emphasis on the papacy, represent not so much classic positions of Christianity as modern positions.

Fundamentalism and the Critique of Modernity

Fundamentalism shares characteristics of modernity even in its critique of modernity. Nevertheless, its critique of modernity is also central to fundamentalism. A theological assessment needs to go beyond the observation that fundamentalism is a reaction to the Enlightenment and that Catholic fundamentalism is a reaction to modernism. The crucial theological issue is: How does one assess that reaction? What are the criticisms of the Enlightenment and of modernity that theology should incorporate?

Fundamentalism does not stand alone in its criticism of the

---

[47]Another important contrast between classic and modern historical critical interpretations lies in the significance of spiritual preparation for the understanding of the scriptures. On this point, both the emphasis in hermeneutical theory on pre-understanding and the significance of experience of oppression in liberation theology point to dimensions of interpretation that antiquity grasped and that go beyond the neutrality of a modern objective, scientific viewpoint. The fundamentalist critique of scientific exegesis underscores an important weakness which other movements also grasp.

[48]See Yves Congar, "Pour une histoire sémantique du terme 'Magisterium' " and "Bref histoire des formes du 'Magistère' et de ses relations avec les docteurs," Revue des Sciences Philosophiques et Théologiques 60 (1976): 85–98 and 99–112, John Boyle, "The 'Ordinary Magisterium': Towards a History of the Concept," Heythrop Journal 20 (1979): 380–398 and 21 (1980): 14–29; Avery Dulles, "What is Magisterium?" Origins 6 (1976): 81–88.

Enlightenment and modernity. Diverse political and liberation theologies also criticize modernity.[49] They underscore the degree to
which all First World countries, especially the United States, are
heavily indebted to the Enlightenment and to the progressive traditions of modernity. At the same time they point out that liberalism
and modernity have an "other side"—a side that Third World countries with their oppressed poor vividly experience and see.[50] Even if
the important point has to be made that political and liberation
theologies should take into account the significance of liberalism
and the Enlightenment, their criticisms of the modern world provide
important challenges.[51]

There are three important discussions about modern liberal society that should be related to the assessment of fundamentalism. One
is that the Enlightenment sharply separates questions of right from
questions of the good, questions of a procedural rationality from
questions of the conception of the good.[52] Such a separation, it is
argued, leads to an impoverishment of the public arena. Another
critique, made by a group called the "communitarian critics" of the
Enlightenment, points to the individualism underlying the contract
theory of political society.[53] This individualism envisions the human self as "unencumbered" and hence overlooks the importance
of the situations of humans within particular communities and
traditions. A third critique, articulated by feminist theorists, demonstrates the inadequacy of the separation of the private and public
spheres within liberalism.[54]

[49]See Rebecca Chopp, The Praxis of Suffering: An Interpretation of Liberation and
Political Theologies (Maryknoll: Orbis, 1986).

[50]Gustavo Gutierrez, The Power of the Poor in History (Maryknoll, N.Y.: Orbis, 1983),
pp. 169–221.

[51]Francis Schüssler Fiorenza, "Politische Theologie und Liberale Gerechtigkeits-
Konzeptionen," Eduard Schillebeeckx, Mystik und Politik. Johann Baptist Matz zu
Ehren (Mainz: Matthias Grünewald, 1988), pp. 105–117; "Die Kirche als Interpreta-
tionsgemeinschaft. Politische Theologie zwischen Diskursethik und hermeneneu-
tische Rekonstruction," Edmund Arens, Habermas und die Theologie (Dusseldorf:
Patmos, 1989), pp. 115–144.

[52]See the critique of the Enlightenment by Alasdair MacIntyre. After Virtue (Notre
Dame: Notre Dame Press, 1981, 2nd ed. 1984) and Whose Justice? Which Rationality?
(Notre Dame Press, 1988).

[53]See Michael Sandel, Liberalism and the Limits of Justice (New York: Cambridge
University Press, 1982), and "The Procedural Republic and the Unencumbered Self,"
in Political Theory 12 (1984): 81–96. See the important critical analysis of this
position by Amy Gutmann, "The Communitarian Critics of Liberalism," Philosophy
and Public Affairs 14 (1985): 308–322.

[54]See the essay by Seyla Benhabib, Nancy Frazer, and Iris Young, in Feminism as
Critique: On the Politics of Gender. Edited by Seyla Benhabib and Drucilla Cornell
(Minneapolis: University of Minnesota, 1987). See also Susan Moller Okin, "Justice
and Gender," in Philosophy and Public Affairs 16 (1987): 42–72.

These three critiques raise very central issues. One can be of a divided mind about each of them. Yet they point to the erosion of conceptions of the good, of the community, and of private values from the public and political sphere. They point to a certain impoverishment of modernity. It should not be overlooked that fundamentalism is pointing to similar impoverishments. Even though one might not agree with a specific religious, social, or political option that a fundamentalist group might take, one must acknowledge that their critique of modernity raises legitimate issues and points to significant problems.

Fundamentalism as a Challenge to Modern Theology

The theory of modernity suggests that the differentiation of modern society, with its separation of values and of expert cultures from everyday life-praxis, represent a part of the cultural impoverishment of modernity. This split of expert culture from everyday culture is a phenomenon that should be of concern to theologians and a central task for theology.

In an analysis of contemporary Roman Catholic theology within the present-day situation of the church, Joseph Cardinal Ratzinger raises the issue of fundamentalism. He argues that when theology comes to exercise a similar role in Roman Catholic churches that it has in Protestant churches, then the reaction known as "fundamentalism" in Protestant churches appears also in Roman Catholic churches. He attributes to modern theology the responsibility for the emergence of fundamentalism. Modern theology is, if not the cause, at least the occasion of fundamentalism.[55]

What is that role? According to Ratzinger, theologians and scholars have the tendency to complicate the faith. They place conditions on Christianity. The faithful have a simple "yes" and "no" to faith. The academic theologians, however, have "ifs," "buts," and "maybes." These theologians who complicate the faith accuse the shepherds of the church and the Holy Office in particular of inquisitorial practices, of using power and force to strangle the spirit of faith. The simple faithful, however, take a completely different stance. They criticize the bishops, the shepherds of the faith, of being "mute and cowardly watchdogs that stand idly by under the

---

[55]Joseph Cardinal Ratzinger, *Principles of Catholic Theology. Building Stones for a Fundamental Theology* (San Francisco: Ignatius Press, 1987), p. 324.

pressure of liberal publicity while the faith is being sold piecemeal for the dish of pottage of being recognized as 'modern' "[56]

Ratzinger's judgment views fundamentalism as a product of modernity. Yet it views fundamentalism not so much as a reaction to modernity in general as to modern theologians as liberal skeptics. It sharply distinguishes between the expert culture of theologians and the simple faith of the people. Fundamentalism is not linked with a specific doctrine or with angry personalities. Instead fundamentalism is a reaction to an impoverishment of religious culture within the church today. Because Ratzinger's critique abstracts from the problem of societal differentiation and modernization, it is less an analysis than an indictment. The theologians are primarily responsible for causing fundamentalism.

Such a view correctly grasps fundamentalism as a reactive mode within modernity, but its narrow theological criticism fails to see three elements. First, secularization of the modern world is a modern societal process of differentiation. It does not simply result from arbitrary and voluntary interpretations given by intellectuals. The process of specialization and professionalization is a process that is not specific to theology, but to all disciplines. This specialization— of which theological reflection is a small part—is a general process of differentiation within society itself.

Second, the Christian faithful cannot be adequately described as the simple and naive faithful. In my Cambridge parish near Harvard Square, the faithful in the pew are Harvard professors and students. Though not theologians, they would scarcely fit his description of the "simple faithful." The process of rationalization involves a generalization of levels of education and a move away from adherence based on authority to a consensus that involves communicative discourse and voluntary consent.

These considerations suggest that the impoverishment of the religious lifeworld against which fundamentalism protests cannot be laid at the feet of theologians. Rather theology attempts to deal with religious faith under the conditions of modernity. Nevertheless, the growing difference between the culture of experts and popular religious piety does challenge theology. Two examples from my recent personal experience at a funeral can illustrate this challenge. A relative asked me: "What do you teach about life in heaven in your courses at Harvard? Is the deceased person not talking with her

---

[56]Ibid., p. 324.

mother in heaven?" We were interrupted and I did not answer. Yet I could not help but think that I had just come from a class discussing whether Gadamer was correct in that Dilthey had tried unsuccessfully to overcome the impasses of historicism. Even if I had been teaching eschatology that semester, the discussion would have been about differences between a consistent, a realized, and a futuristic eschatology. The expert culture of the academy often does not deal with the religious question that I had been asked.

At the same occasion, a person referred to a biblical verse around which he had lived his whole life. He was dying and undergoing a long painful illness. His fate seemed to invalidate the biblical verse. How could I answer? Obviously, I couldn't say that the passage was from a controversy dialogue, dealing with the early church's *Sitz im Leben* and expressing Lukan theology. I had to leave aside the world of scientific exegesis and quote another verse in a way he could understand. I was offering a contrary "proof-text."

These two examples illustrate that modern academic expert culture deals with theoretical issues and uses methods that are removed from popular culture. Its method of reading the Bible, even independently of critical issues, represents an approach to the Bible sequestered from popular religious culture. The challenge remains for academic theology to bridge the gap between the issues and methods of academic culture and the religious needs of popular culture.

Third, in addition to both the distance between expert culture and popular religious questions and the impact of modern specialization upon academic discourse, the nature of religious and Christian identity represents a problem within modernity. In the face of modern scientific, social, cognitive, and moral challenges to traditional convictions, Christianity needs to interpret anew its identity. Religious and Christian identity is not simply given as an object. To use Bernard Lonergan's terminology, interpretation of the Christian tradition is not simply a matter of taking a look, as if the Christian tradition existed as an object of naive realism that one can simply look at or intuit. Instead Christians must make decisions about what constitutes Christian identity. Such decisions involve a complex process, moving from experience to understanding, to interpretation, to judgment, and to decision. The process is dialectical because the data and experience can be interpreted differently from diverse viewpoints. The process entails a complex set of judgments about the comprehensiveness of the data, the adequacy of the horizons, etc.[57]

---

[57]*Method in Theology* (New York: Crossroad, 1972). See Vernon Gregson's applica-

Contemporary hermeneutical theology leads to a similar conclusion: Identity is not simply a pre-given but needs to be hermeneutical, reconstructed in relation to relevant background theories and in relation to warrants retroductively drawn from contemporary experience and practice.[58] The notion of Christian identity, not simply as given, but as critically and hermeneutically reconstructed proves frightening to many. It robs them of the absolute certitude they desire. It is on this point that fundamentalists and non-fundamentalists disagree. In part, fundamentalism protests against reconstructions that appear more to deconstruct Christian identity than they appear to affirm Christian identity. In part, it protests against deconstructions as impoverished as the rationalized modern society or that appear intelligible to an elite class of experts who do not confront existential religious questions.

Conclusion

This essay has argued several points. First, in the context of diverse theological definitions of fundamentalism, a theological definition of Roman Catholic fundamentalism does not do justice to the complexity of the phenomenon. A theological analysis of Roman Catholic fundamentalism should not simply take a doctrinal definition of fundamentalism and apply it to Roman Catholicism in a way that fundamentalism appears as totally negative. Second, we must locate fundamentalism in relation to a current analysis of modernity. Consequently, Roman Catholic fundamentalism is not simply a set of conservative beliefs or a conservative attitude but should be seen as a modern phenomenon as well as a protest against modernity. Its theological views are shaped by modernity and are a protest against modernity. Roman Catholic fundamentalism departs from traditional views and practices at the same time that it criticizes such departures. Third, since this fundamentalism contains a legitimate protest against the colonization, impoverishment, and fragmentation of modern society, one should interpret it as a modern phenomenon with a legitimate protest and concern. Fourth, if the protest that

---

tion of Lonergan's method to the issue of fundamentalism in *The Desires of the Human Heart: An Introduction to the Theology of Bernard Lonergan* (New York: Paulist, 1988), pp. 94–95.

[58]Francis Schüssler Fiorenza, *Foundational Theology* (New York: Crossroad, 1984). See also: "Theory and Practice: Theological Education as a Reconstructive, Hermeneutical, and Practical Task," *Theological Education* 23 (1987): 113–141.

fundamentalism incorporates is not to turn into a protest of withdrawal or separation, then the theological task consists in working against the impoverishment, colonization, and fragmentation in conversation with others. Theological differences about the constitution of Christian identity are not abstract theoretical issues but take place within the formation of identity under the conditions of modernity. The theological task increasingly includes bridging the gap between the academic discourse and religious discourse, and clarifying Christian identity.

CATHOLIC FUNDAMENTALISM

William D. Dinges

Naming and defining always have political implications. Language reveals realities of power. The power to name is the power to define, the power to position a group socially and politically. By devising a linguistic category with a specific connotation, one is designing armaments for battle. By having this category accepted and used, one has already scored a major victory.[1]

In accordance with this conviction, I shall address two issues in this presentation. The first centers around the definition of fundamentalism and the appropriate use of this term in reference to certain ideological orientations and social movements that have arisen in the Roman Catholic Church in the wake of the Second Vatican Council. The second concerns the problematic aspects of distinguishing between fundamentalist and conservative Catholicism. I assert that there are important distinctions between fundamentalists and conservatives and that in Roman Catholic context use of the former term should be confined to those movements and orientations associated with self-proclaimed traditionalism.

Fundamentalism and Traditionalism

Fundamentalism is a generic term. The current Catholic analogue to Protestant fundamentalism is found among the Roman Catholic traditionalists who repudiate major reforms of the Second Vatican Council and who continue to adhere to preconciliar doctrinal and disciplinary formulations. The most media visible issue associated with the traditionalist cause is the campaign to save the Latin

[1]Erich Goode, "Marijuana and the Politics of Reality," *Journal of Health and Social Behavior* 10 (1969):83–94, esp. 89.

Tridentine liturgy. Although by no means a homogeneous phenomenon either ideologically or sociologically, traditionalism stands
united in its repudiation of all theology identified as liberal, modernist, or progressive.

Catholic traditionalism is today an international, segmented, and
loosely organized movement. Many, but not all traditionalist Catholics are supporters of French Archbishop Marcel Lefebvre and his
priestly fraternity, the Society of St. Pius X, canonically established
in the Canton of Valais, Switzerland in 1970. The precise number of
participants is difficult to ascertain. The Vatican places the number
of active traditionalists world-wide at around 60,000 to 80,000
thousand. I take this as a conservative figure, and one that does not
include substantial numbers of Catholics sympathetic to the traditionalist cause, but who are only marginally involved. Traditionalism is also understood to be both larger and more militant in Europe
(especially France) than in the United States where the movement
has somewhere between 10,000–15,000 active supporters.[2] There
are currently over 264 unauthorized traditionalist chapel sites in the
United States, nearly half of which are operated by Lefebvre's
Society of St. Pius X.[3] Many of these wildcat parishes were initially
located in homes, motel rooms, and meeting halls until suitable
facilities were found. Traditionalist parishes unaffiliated with organizational structures are often ministered to by individual priests
who are either on leave, or who have been suspended or retired by
their local bishop.

Traditionalist dissent has also found expression through independent publishing initiatives, and through various corporate forms.[4]
One of the earliest organizational initiatives in the United States was
that of Fr. Gommar De Pauw, a canon law professor at Mount St.
Mary's Seminary in Emmitsburg, Maryland, who launched the Cath-

---

[2]*Latin Liturgical Association Newsletter* 32 (March, 1989): 4. An additional clue to
the scope of the movement is the size of Lefebvre's priestly fraternity. As of 1986,
Lefebvre had ordained 250 priests. The Society's "Letter of Superior General" (November 27, 1989) lists 201 active priests. Lefebvre's fraternity operates in 22 countries
and currently has five seminaries with about 280 candidates.

[3]These figures are based on my research on the movement in the early 1980's. See
William D. Dinges, "Catholic Traditionalism in America: A Study of the Remnant
Faithful." Unpublished dissertation, University of Kansas, 1983.

[4]See William Dinges, "Catholic Traditionalism in America: A Study of the Remnant
Faithful." Two principal journalistic efforts on behalf of the traditionalist cause are
Hugh McGovern's *The Voice* (Canandaigua, New York, 1967–1977), and Walter Matts'
The Remnant (St. Paul, Minnesota). Virtually all traditionalist organizations have
their own publications.

olic Traditionalist Movement, Inc., in 1965. The first truly national traditionalist organization, however, was not established until 1973 with the founding of the Orthodox Roman Catholic Movement, Inc., in Bridgeport, Connecticut, by Fr. Francis Fenton and his supporters. By its peak year in 1979, the ORCM had 28 Mass locations and nearly 20 priest members.

The largest traditionalist effort both here and abroad is that of Archbishop Lefebvre's Society of St. Pius X. Marcel Lefebvre was ordained in 1929. Following years of missionary work in French-Speaking Africa where he was eventually appointed Apostolic Delegate, Lefebvre returned to France in 1959 and became bishop of the diocese of Tulle. Between 1960 and 1962, he served on the Central Preparatory Commission charged with producing the schemas presented at the Second Vatican Council. In 1962 he was also elected Superior-General of the Holy Ghost Fathers.[5]

Lefebvre's opposition to new theological currents animating Vatican II was apparent during the Council deliberations.[6] Lefebvre helped found the International Group of Fathers (*Coetus Internationalis Patrum*), an organization of conservative prelates upholding tradition against liberal/progressive elements pushing for change.

In 1968 Lefebvre resigned as head of the Holy Ghost Fathers in a dispute over reform of the order in keeping with the Council directives. He then moved to Rome to retire, but, by his own account, was sought out by a group of young men who were seeking a traditional priestly formation. Lefebvre eventually received permission from Bishop Charrière of Sion to establish a priestly fraternity, the *Fraternité Sacerdotale de Saint Pie X* (the Society of St. Pius X)—named after the pope known as the "scourge of modernists."

During the next three years Ecône's reputation as an orthodox seminary adhering to the Tridentine rite, to Thomistic theology, and to a repudiation of *aggiornamento* spread rapidly. In the fall of 1974, in response to the archbishop's escalating critique of the Council, continuing use of the Tridentine Mass (then prohibited), and in response to pressures from the French bishops who opposed Lefebvre's "rebel seminary", the Vatican announced an Apostolic Visitation of Ecône.

On November 21, 1974, in reaction to the scandal occasioned by

---

[5]See Michael Davies, *Apologia Pro Marcel Lefebvre*, 3 vols. (Dickinson, Texas: Angelus Press, 1979–1988).

[6]See Lefebvre, *A Bishop Speaks: Writings and Addresses, 1963–1975* (Edinburgh: Scottish Una Voce, 1976).

remarks made by the two Belgian priests who carried out the visitation, Lefebvre issued an acerbic "Declaration" denouncing the Council and the new liturgy. Tensions with the Vatican accelerated dramatically from this point on, culminating two years later (July, 1976) in Lefebvre's suspension for failing to disband his priestly fraternity and to cease ordinations.[7] In spite of the archbishop's suspension and public censure for "contumacious insubordination," his priestly fraternity steadily expanded its international network of publishing enterprises, chapels, schools, priories and seminaries. The Society of St. Pius X began its work among American Catholics in 1973–1974 when several of Lefebvre's American seminarians returned to the United States and established chapels in East Meadow, New York; Houston, Texas; and San Jose, California.

In addition to the above organizations and initiatives, there are other traditionalist groups associated with bogus religious orders with no licit canonical status, and with self-proclaimed popes who have ordained priests and consecrated bishops lacking any qualifications whatsoever. Among the latter "sedevacantist" (the see of Peter is vacant) traditionalists are bishops consecrated by Archbishop Pierre Martin Ngo Din-Thuc, the one-time Archbishop of Hue who ordained a group of men in 1975.[8]

While traditionalist groups and organizations that have arisen since the Council are numerous and diverse, the discussion in this paper is derived from the analysis of themes and positions taken by Archbishop Lefebvre and his supporters.

A Catholic Fundamentalism?

There is widespread scholarly recognition that fundamentalism is not a religion or culture specific phenomenon. Nevertheless, use of the term fundamentalism in Catholic quarters has been both restrictive and highly political. Generally speaking, Catholic officialdom and those on the Catholic right use the term narrowly. Fundamentalism, usually preceded by the adjective Biblical, is assumed to apply

---

[7]For a detailed account of the "affaire Econe" from a traditionalist perspective see Davies, Apologia.

[8]Most sedevacantist groups have ties with the unapproved apparitions of the Blessed Virgin Mary at Palmar de Troya, Spain. One of these individuals, Clement Dominique, subsequently consecrated dozens of bishops and went on to declare himself pope. Other bishops consecrated by Thuc also consecrated a number of North American traditionalist bishops. See Michael Davies, "The Sedevacantists," The Angelus 6 (February, 1983): 10–12.

to a distinctively Protestant phenomenon. Collaterally, fears are expressed regarding the large number of "alienated" and "disenchanted" Catholics who have abandoned their faith and affiliated with a fundamentalist Bible Church. Attention is then focused on how Catholics are to meet this **external** challenge.[9] Recent works on fundamentalism by Catholics are typical in this regard, as is a current booklet produced by the NCCB Ad Hoc Committee on Biblical Fundamentalism.[10] Entitled *A Pastoral Statement for Catholics on Biblical Fundamentalism* (1987), the National Conference of Catholic Bishops' publication presents fundamentalism as something Biblically centered, outside the Church, and threatening to it.[11]

In addition to the above usage, John Coleman has recently noted a tendency of some right-of-center Catholics to assert that liberal theologians have invented the term fundamentalism as a means of deflecting attention from their own theological dissent from papal authority.[12] If the Catholic center and right restrict use of the term fundamentalism to denote an exclusively Protestant phenomenon, left-of-center Catholics engage in a more promiscuous use of the term. In his final statement before a Vatican-imposed silence, Matthew Fox decried the current round of "fundamentalist zeal" in the Church.[13] Penny Lernoux, recently deceased Catholic commentator on Latin America, in her exposé on the current Restoration movement in the Church repeatedly uses the phrase fundamentalist Catholic in reference to the Pope, the Vatican, and to groups such as

[9]See, Damien Kraus, "Catholic Fundamentalism: A Look at the Problem," *Living Light* 19 (Spring 1982): 8–16. Also the series of articles on "Fundamentalism" in *New Catholic World* (January/February 1985) and *America* (September 1986).

[10]See Karl Keating, *Catholicism and Fundamentalism: The Attack on Romanism by Biblical Christians* (San Francisco: Ignatius Press, 1988); Anthony E. Giles, *Fundamentalism: What Every Catholic Needs to Know* (Cincinnati, OH: St. Anthony Messenger Press, 1985); Richard W. Chilson, *Full Christianity: A Catholic Response to Fundamenalist Questions* (Mahwah, New Jersey: Paulett Press, 1985); and Edwin Daschback, *Interpreting Scripture: A Catholic Response to Fundamentalism* (William C. Brown, 1985). Also "A Pastoral Statement for Catholics on Biblical Fundamentalism," District of Columbia: NCCB Press, 1987.

[11]The question of whether or not Catholics who believe in the literal inerrancy of scripture are "fundamentalist" remains to be examined. Gallup and Castelli report that 32% of the Catholic population believe that the Bible is the "literal word" of God. See George Gallup and Jim Castelli, *The American Catholic People: Their Beliefs, Practices, and Values* (New York: Doubleday, 1987), p. 21.

[12]John Coleman, "Who Are Catholic Fundamentalists?" *Commonweal* 116 (January 27, 1989): 42–46.

[13]Matthew Fox, "Final Statement" in the *National Catholic Reporter*, December 23, 1988.

Catholics United for the Faith, Opus Dei, and Communion and Liberation that do not fit her own partisan vision of aggiornamento. In short, fundamentalism has become for many liberal Catholics an epithet, a label used interchangeably with conservative, neo-ortho- dox, hard-line, right-wing, as though the words were entirely syn- onymous.[14]

In the very act of labeling, the users reveal as much about their own group interests as they do about the phenomenon of fundamen- talism. Among many Catholics the term fundamentalism has come to denote either something alien or external to the Catholic tradition or a verbal means of symbolically degrading opponents within it.

The questions who is a Catholic fundamentalist and how to distinguish fundamentalism from authentic conservatism in the Church are difficult not only because of the political use of language, but because fundamentalism and conservatism are kindred phenom- ena. As will be seen below, they are not totally discrete. Their relationship is symbiotic. Christian conservatives and fundamental- ists share many ideological, social, and psychological affinities.[15]

Fundamentalism as an Ideal Type

While there is no universally accepted definition of fundamental- ism in the literature, there is an emerging scholarly consensus that certain characteristics, taken together, constitute family resem- blances from which one can construct an ideal type of fundamental- ist orientation. This approach does not assume that all fundamental- ists exhibit every characteristic, or that the presence of any one trait makes an individual a fundamentalist. These characteristics are, however, informing orientations or habits of mind present in a critical and determinative way in a fundamentalist world-view. I shall first summarize these characteristics, and then briefly illustrate how they find expression in the Roman Catholic traditionalist move- ment.[16] There are six of them, namely: fundamentalism's reaction- ary/innovative character, selective basis of authority, cognitive ori-

---

[14]Penny Lernoux, The People of God: The Struggle for World Catholicism (New York: Viking, 1989).

[15]See also, Patrick Arnold, "The Rise of Catholic Fundamentalism," America 56 (April 11, 1987): 297–302.

[16]The difficulties in defining "Catholic fundamentalism" (and the term "fundamen- talism" in its wider application as well) also illustrates a longstanding problem in the "soft sciences"; namely, that of reaching consensus on definitions.

entation, tendencies toward extreme objectifying, elitism/ exclusivism, and conspiracy/action orientation.

Before proceeding, the temporal character of fundamentalism should be noted. Fundamentalism is a profoundly modern movement; it is chiefly about the present, not the past. In spite of its self-presentation as the "Old-time religion" (or that of tradition or eternal Rome in the Catholic case), fundamentalism is a contemporary phenomenon, a religio-cultural response to the dynamics of modernity (pluralism, social differentiation, instrumental rationality, pragmatism, bureaucratic organization, industrialism). However, while fundamentalism is one response to the impact of modernization on any religious tradition, its *form* and *style* are specific to the polity and ideological structure of a particular tradition.

The use of the term fundamentalism to designate an American Protestant movement originates in the fact that Protestantism's engagement with modernity, particularly in the theological (as distinct from the social and political) realm was more vigorous, direct, and decisive than that of Roman Catholicism. Certain anti-modernist trends in Catholic theology and ecclesiology clearly paralleled early Protestant fundamentalist patterns (e.g., the legalism, authoritarianism, verbal dogmatism, and the opposition to evolution and the scientific study of scripture).[17] However, Catholicism's institutional conservatism, its hierarchical and bureaucratic centralization, its early suppression of modernism, and its cultural insularity precluded the development of a full-blown fundamentalist movement.

The fundamentalist impulse in Roman Catholicism did, however, find a cogent sociological expression in integralism, a reactionary

[17]These characteristics are derived from my reading of the standard literature on fundamentalism both within conservative evangelical Protestantism viz., Stewart G. Cole, *The History of Fundamentalism* (New York: Richard R. Smith, Inc., 1931); Norman F. Furniss, *The Fundamentalist Controversy, 1918–1931* (New Haven: Yale University Press, 1954); Willard Gatewood, ed. *Controversy in the Twenties* (Nashville: Vanderbilt University Press, 1969); C. Allyn Russell, *Voices of American Fundamentalism* (Philadelphia: The Westminster Press, 1976); George Marsden, *Fundamentalism and American Culture: The Shaping of Twentieth-Century Evangelicalism: 1870– 1925* (New York: Oxford University Press, 1980), and in the more limited cross-cultural literature on the topic, e.g., Lionel Caplan, ed. *Studies in Religious Fundamentalism* (Albany: State University of New York Press, 1987). The question of whether or not fundamentalist characteristics are indicative of an orientation applicable to politics, nationalism, ethnicity, or other ideologies as Barr asserts remains to be seen. See James Barr, *Fundamentalism* (London: SCM Press, 1977), p. 341. These were motifs expressed in papal anti-modernist documents such as the Syllabus of Errors, *Lamentabili*, *Pascendi Dominici Gregis*. See "On the Doctrines of the Modernists," (Staten Island: Daughters of St. Paul, n.d.).

movement that arose in conjunction with the magisterial condemnation of modernism. This connection between integralism and
fundamentalism has been noted by more than one Catholic
scholar.[18] Integralism was a particular form of Roman Catholic
scholastic theology distinguished by a blanket condemnation of
liberalism, authoritarian heteronomy regarding the Magisterium, the
imposition of uniform belief and theology, and the championing of
Christendom models of the social order. Integralism achieved a static
categorization of tradition, the conversion of doctrine into dogma,
and the construction of heretical conspiracy charges against deviant
insiders.[19]

    While some elements of the Integralist reaction, chiefly Umberto
Benigni's *Sodalitium Pianum* were eventually suppressed (1921),
the fundamentalist orientation to which integralism gave expression
did not disappear from the Roman Catholic Church. In the wake of
the turmoil surrounding the reforms of the Second Vatican Council,
integralism revived as the anti-conciliar traditionalist movement.[20]
However, in both its integralist and traditionalist manifestations,
Catholic fundamentalism, like Protestant fundamentalism, is a very
contemporary response to the impact of modernity on religion.

    1) Fundamentalism is reactionary, that is, it is self-consciously
anti-modernist. Fundamentalism is not a form of first naiveté, nor a
form of emotional religion. As a reactionary ideology, fundamentalism does not stand unaware of a new culture, intellectual, or theological order; *it stands in opposition to it*, defending a world-view
and governing assumptions that have been decisively penetrated by
the theological, cultural, and scientific currents of modernity. Fundamentalism is a reaction against the loss of "the sacred," the loss
of religious identity, the dissolution of social boundaries and the
perception of defilement and penetration.[21]

----

[18]See Daniel Alexander, "Is Fundamentalism an Integrism?" *Social Compass* 34
(1985): 373–392; Gabriel Daly, "Catholicism and Modernity," *Journal of the American
Academy of Religion* 53 (1985): 773–796; Theodore C. Ross, "Catholicism and
Fundamentalism," *New Theological Review* 1 (May, 1988): 74–87.

[19]See Lester Kurtz, *The Politics of Heresy: The Modernist Crisis in Roman Catholicism* (Berkeley: University of California Press, 1986).

[20]It is noteworthy in this regard in the case of Archbishop Lefebvre that as a young
seminarian he studied under and, by his own account, was heavily influenced by Fr.
Le Foche, the monarchist, integralist rector of the French Seminary in Rome. See
Lefebvre, *They Have Uncrowned Him* (Dickenson, Texas: Angelus Press, 1988), pp.
49–50.

[21]Fundamentalism remains to be examined in the context of Mary Douglas's
concept of pollution behavior, especially in terms of its pervasive use of sexual and

   Catholic traditionalism, especially among its intellectual elite, is a repudiation of historical consciousness, the anthropocentric turn, and other hermeneutical, relativizing and *praxis* tendencies that characterize contemporary consciousness and much modern Catholic theology, and that are reflected in one manner or the other in the documents of Vatican II. Traditionalism is not a revitalization movement as is the Catholic Charismatic Renewal; nor is traditionalism a restoration movement concerned with simply recapitulating the cultural and symbolic forms of a previous Catholic identity.

   As a fundamentalist phenomenon, traditionalism militantly opposes modernism while simultaneously manifesting innovative tendencies that are distinct from previous patterns of Catholic ecclesiology and practice. Lefebvre's establishment of a world-wide counter-church infrastructure outside the boundaries of proper juridical authority is one of the more conspicuous expressions of this innovative dynamic within the traditionalist movement.

   2) Fundamentalism is only selectively anti-modernist. While fundamentalism is a reaction against the impact of modernization on religious frames of reference, it is not a categorical repudiation of *all* elements of modernity. Fundamentalism does not turn its back on its own era as do introversionist religious sects; it is selective rather than culturally retreatist.[22]

   In the first place, fundamentalism rejects only *some* aspects of modernity (typically cultural and intellectual value orientations) while uncritically embracing others. For all of their tirades against secularism and the moral depravity of the modern age, Protestant fundamentalist apologists lost little time in utilizing technology, bureaucratic organization, and mass media communications in their own institutional development. Likewise, Catholic traditionalist apologists inveigh against the errors and immorality of the modern experiment while simultaneously utilizing bureaucratic structures and mass media communications technology to further their own organizational initiatives in the battle against the apostates of the conciliar Church.

   Second, fundamentalism entails a highly selective use of its basis of authority. As scholars have shown, Protestant fundamentalists have always been able to make arbitrary use of the scriptures to

medical metaphors (e.g., the description of liberalism as a virus, a poison, an adulterous spirit that infects the purity of the faith). Symbolism of this nature is standard parlance in traditionalist Catholic rhetoric.

[22]Bryan Wilson, *Religious Sects* (New York: McGraw Hill, 1970).

defend their positions while denying or obscuring the role of interpretation. Where inerrantists cannot deal with scriptural problems
such as doublets, mythical elements, and textual inconsistencies,
they ignore them or twist back and forth between literal and non-
literal interpretations.[23]

In the Roman Catholic case, the traditionalist defense of "Tradition"—which is imputed to be a defense of the *total patrimony* of
the Church's orthodoxy—is, in fact, highly selective and focused
almost exclusively on theological and ecclesial orientations derived
from the Council of Trent, from categories of Thomistic scholasticism, and especially from the papal anti-modernist broadsides of
the last century and one-half. This narrow and restricted understanding of "Tradition" is also static rather than dynamic, denying
the authority of the Church's living Magisterium. It is also marked
by a legalistic casuistry which elevates to the core of the faith
historically emergent and socially conditioned doctrinal and disciplinary formulas.

3) Fundamentalism is a highly cognitive form of religiosity in
which correct belief is taken as the primary datum of religion. The
significant feature here is not the content of belief (e.g., pre-Kantian
empirical rationalism, dispensational millennialism, a Newtonian
world-view, or "Princeton theology" in the Protestant case; scholasticism, Thomism, papal anti-modernist pronouncements in the
Catholic), but the *priority and saliency of belief*. Correct doctrine is
taken as the determinative dimension of all aspects of religious self-
understanding.

As Barr and Marsden have noted, for the true fundamentalist
holding right views is normative for all other aspects of religious
identity.[24] From this position it follows that doctrine is not the
historical product of Christian experience, but what determines
Christian experience; religious truth is a fixed and absolute body of
eternally valid propositions; religions are contraposed ideological
entities; and the theological task is strictly apologetic rather than
exploratory and critical.

Catholic traditionalism manifests this same fixation with the pri-

---

[23]Robert Gnuse, *The Authority of the Bible: Theories of Inspiration, Revelation and
the Canon of Scripture* (Mahwah, New Jersey: Paulist Press, 1985), esp. 29–31; See,
also, Kathleen Boone, *The Bible Tells Them So: The Discourse of Protestant Fundamentalism* (Albany: State University of New York Press, 1989); and Barr, *Fundamentalism*.

[24]See Barr, *Fundamentalism*, and Marsden, *Fundamentalism and American Culture*.

ority of correct doctrine. Public perceptions notwithstanding, the traditionalist cause is not first and foremost a nostalgic campaign on behalf of Baroque rituals; it is a battle over correct doctrine and the authority that upholds it. The real traditionalist *casus belli* with the Vatican is the controversy over the distortion of orthodoxy attending the reforms of the Second Vatican Council. The problem raised by *aggiornamento* from the traditionalist perspective is one of maintaining fidelity to the purity and integrity of Catholic orthodoxy in the face of alleged heresy and apostasy.

In essence, traditionalists charge that the Second Vatican Council provoked a crisis of authority in the Church by raising the specter of contradition: The Magisterium now endorses as truth in Catholic theology and ecclesiology what it had once condemned in the most solemn and unequivocal terms as error and heresy. The problem of Vatican II is not, therefore, the problem of abuse and distortion as Cardinal Ratzinger and other conservative apologists have contended; it is the problem of propagating false doctrine. According to Archbishop Lefebvre, the Council assimilated into the Church the false principles of Protestantism, liberalism, and modernism unleashed by the Reformation and the French Revolution and which it had always resisted—directly in documents like "Declaration on Religious Freedom" (*Dignitatis Humanae*), and indirectly through ambiguities and equivocations in other texts.[25] The *Liberté, Égalité* and *Fraternité* of the Revolution have metamorphosed into religious liberty, collegiality, and ecumenism in the postconciliar Church. Catholicism's current self-destruction is the logical fruit of this capitulation to the poison of heresy. The proper response to this situation, therefore, is for Catholics to recognize that the proximate cause of the crisis in the Church is more than a wrong interpretation of the Council, but the Council itself.[26]

This traditionalist fixation with "correct doctrine" is also manifest in the controversy over the reform of the liturgy. The traditionalist repudiation of the *Novus Ordo Missae* is not based primarily on aesthetic or anthropological consideration, nor on the violation of liturgical norms (although these criticisms abound in traditionalist literature). The traditionalist case against the new liturgy is doctrinal. The new Mass is denounced as dangerous and bad because it is

---

[25]Marcel Lefebvre, *Liberalism* (Dickinson, Texas: Angelus Press, 1980. 1975), p. 3.

[26]See, also, by Marcel Lefebvre, *A Bishop Speaks; An Open Letter to Confused Catholics* (Herefordshire, England: Fowler Wright, Ltd., 1986); and *They Have Uncrowned Him*.

theologically polluted, a Protestant and bastard rite that no longer conveys the Eucharistic doctrines of the Church as they were articulated by the Council of Trent. The new *Ordo* presents an entirely new faith.[27]

Implicit in this orientation is a presentation of Catholicism as a fixed and closed tradition composed of propositional revelation constituting definitive, literal, and exclusive truth. Adherence to correct doctrine—under the code name Tradition—defines who is and who is not a member of the true Church. Within this framework, traditionalist institutional initiatives are promoted as the only authentic expression of this true Church because only they teach sound doctrine. Affective modes of religiosity, such as those associated with Catholic Charismatic Renewal, are derided as false and Protestant. Social activism within the Church on behalf of peace and justice and movements of liberation theology are berated as Marxist and the politicizing of Catholicism. For traditionalist Catholics, orthodoxy, not orthopraxis, ensures salvation.

As with Protestant fundamentalism, traditionalism also tends toward a literalistic and dogmatic cognitive style. It should be noted in this regard, however, the Catholic traditionalism is not a movement in defense of the literal inerrancy of scripture, for scripture has not played the same role in Catholic religious self-understanding that it has among Protestants. However, the same ahistorical, objectivist, literalistic and dogmatic orientation operative in the Protestant fundamentalist approach to scripture is recapitulated in the traditionalist approach to magisterial pronouncements. Traditionalists have asserted, for instance, that no episcopal authority has the power to abrogate Pius V's *Quo Primum* (1570) because the document grants an indult to all priests the right to use the Tridentine rite "in perpetuity."[28] Catholic traditionalists share with Protestant fundamentalists the proclivity for approaching sacred texts or pronouncements in a manner that, while selective, tends to absolutize as inerrant or infallible a broad spectrum of doctrine and discipline that could be otherwise taken as contingent.

4) Fundamentalism also manifests extreme tendencies toward objectivication/reification and a heightened sense of supernaturalism in the religious sphere. This orientation presupposes that objectivity in religion means that human persons experience the sacred

---

[27]See, James Wathen, *The Great Sacrilege* (Rockford, Illinois: TAN Publishers, 1971); also, Marcel Lefebvre, *A Bishop Speaks*.

[28]See, Wathen, *The Great Sacrilege*, esp. 36–45.

as something that confronts them exclusively from outside. Eternal truths are deposited in forms that stand apart from any other source of religion. True religion is superimposed, concretized, codified, fixed, and outside the mediation of history or culture.[29] Fundamentalist hermeneutics show little sensitivity toward or awareness of the role of historical and social conditions in the construction of Church doctrine or other aspects of religious identity.

In the case of Protestant fundamentalism, the Bible is the authoritative focus of this objectivist approach to sacred reality. The Bible is ontologically foundational and superimposed; it is without error or imperfection, and is the only true testimony of divine truth. Because the Bible is objective, unmediated, and super-imposed, it is a hermeneutical circle: The Bible interprets itself.[30]

Exaggerated objectivism in Catholic traditionalism is reflected in themes intimating that the Church is essentially unconstructed by human experience. There is nothing in the core of the Church's tradition produced by the human mind or configured by cultural and historical circumstances. According to Archbishop Lefebvre, the truths of the Roman Catholic faith are ready made and come strictly from outside. The human person does not construct or create, but merely receives this faith in the form of absolute and objective truth.[31] Dogma, therefore, cannot evolve, Catholicism cannot change, and all forms of subjectivism in the religious sphere are to be repudiated.[32]

In traditionalist literature and public pronouncements the Tridentine rite is presented as a perfect ritual, a jewel that is essentially devoid of subjective or culturally determined elements—in contrast to the *Novus Ordo* Mass that has been artificially fabricated. Understood in this manner, Catholic ritual has the character of a reified object or sign, a sacred *thing* devoid of human mediation that has been superimposed from the age of the apostles, rather than symbolic presentation of an encounter with sacred reality reflecting the predominance of certain cultural forms over time.

This highly objectivist understanding of the Mass has obvious

---

[29]On objectification see Peter Berger, *The Sacred Canopy* (New York: Doubleday, 1967) and, Barr, *Fundamentalism*, esp. 310–317.

[30]Barr, *Fundamentalism*.

[31]Lefebvre, *They Have Uncrowned Him*, 120–121.

[32]Lefebvre, *A Bishop Speaks*, p. 160. Lefebvre's static understanding of Catholic tradition is symbolized in his 1988 consecration ceremony remark that he merely wished to be remembered as " . . . a postman bringing you a letter." See *The Angelus*, 11 (July, 1988): 31.

parallels with the fundamentalist view of scripture: as the Bible is the timeless and eternal, the Tridentine rite is the Mass of all time; as God's perfection is revealed in the Bible, so it is revealed in the spiritually perfect Tridentine liturgy; as an inerrant scripture propounds Christian life, theology, faith, and morality in a uniform manner, a perfect and universal Tridentine liturgy promotes Catholic doctrinal and disciplinary uniformity; as an inerrant scripture promotes a sense of security and enduring permanence, so does the "Mass of all time"; as the Bible cannot change, neither can the true Mass.

5) Fundamentalism is elitist, exclusivistic, and marked by a categorical distinction between the "true" and the "false" Church. Fundamentalism seeks to monopolize the interpretation of all religious reality, and to deny the legitimacy of all other theologies and ecclesiologies. Only fundamentalists have the pure, and uncorrupted faith. From this position fundamentalist apologists have continually protested that liberalism is not a variety of Christianity, but a generically distinct and mutually exclusive religion. Liberal or modernist theologians therefore can never be viewed as reconciling orthodox Christianity with a new intellectual and cultural era; they are always creating a new and heretical faith. The primary threat to Christianity, therefore, lay not in the external sphere of culture, but, internally, in the person of the modernist, the deviant insider who remained within the Church to corrupt its essence through sophistry and the manipulation of language and doctrine. The charge that all liberalism was subversive of true orthodoxy was a consistently repeated motif during the formative stages of the fundamentalist movement.[33]

Catholic traditionalism manifests this same elitist and exclusive orientation. Traditionalism does not present itself as an alternative in a pluralistic Catholic ecclesiology, but as the *only* authentic expression of the true Church. Traditionalists denounce all forms and vestiges of liberalism as false religion. They attack all ecumenical initiatives and inveigh against the heresy of Protestantism and the errors and falsehood of all other religions.[34] In the broader

---

[33]This was a central theme in J. Gresham Machen's classic *Christianity and Liberalism* (Grand Rapids: Eerdmans, 1946. 1923).

[34]It is noteworthy in this regard that Lefebvre's decision to consecrate episcopal successors was precipitated by the Pope's visit to Assisi in 1986 and the Vatican response to Lefebvre's *dubia* on the matter of religious liberty.

cultural sphere, traditionalists also call for the reassertion of Catholic hegemony over all political and social life.[35]

Traditionalist elitism also combines themes of self-deprecation with motifs of spiritual grandiosity and heroism. Traditionalists are a beleaguered remnant faithful, the little people of God who are holding fast to the pure and unadulterated faith in a time of widespread apostasy. It is they who will save the true Church through their holy resistance. Within this elitist mental structure, a doctrine of double election is at work: Catholicism is the one true religion; traditionalism the one true expression of Catholicism.

7) Fundamentalism is also characterized by a predilection for conspiracy and subversion theories of social causality. Fundamentalists tend not to interpret the sweep of history in mundane terms; they situate historical events, especially where adversity and conflict are concerned, in an eschatological framework of conspiracy, subversion, and the "work of the devil." Sociological explanations of change and/or conflict are taken as too prosaic, portraying a secular bias that lacks insight into the current eschatological dimensions of the struggle between good and evil occurring in the Church and the world at large.[36]

While sharing the conservative view that postconciliar transformations and tensions are the result of bureaucratic insurgency and neo-modernist machinations, traditionalist interpretations of these events are also more extremist in conspiracy and apocalyptic imagery. Such thinking was not initially widespread among those concerned about the conciliar "tampering" with the Sacred Deposit. However, as time-honored patterns and symbols of Catholic identity became de-stabilized in the wake of the Council, and as the traditionalist movement became more marginalized within the Church and subject to disciplinary action, conspiracy theories among traditionalists became more pervasive, eventually culminating in the view that Vatican II was part of a massive plot, the work of enemies (i.e., communists, Zionists, Masons) who had set out to destroy the Church from within.[37]

---

[35]See Lefebvre, *They Have Uncrowned Him.*

[36]See Richard Hofstadter, *Anti-Intellectualism in American Life* (New York: Knopf, 1963).

[37]Examples of traditionalist conspiracy thinking regarding *aggiornamento* can be found in Clarence Kelly, *Conspiracy Against God and Man* (Belmont, Massachusetts: Western Island, 1974); Jacquin Saenz y Arriaga, *The New Montinian Church* (Hawthorne, California: Christian Book Club, 1971); William Strogie, *Pope, Council, and Chaos* (Lebanon, Oregon. n.d.); and Francis Fenton, "The Roman Catholic Church: Its Tragedy and Its Hope," (Stratford, Connecticut: ORCM, Inc., 1977).

With the promulgation of the *Novus Ordo Missae* and its mandatory implementation in 1971, the specter of subversion became a
full-blown part of the traditionalist ideological repertore. In apocalyptic imagery, traditionalist apologists linked the New Mass with
"the final savage onslaught" to destroy the Church, "with the religion of the beast," and with the onset of an apocalyptic era in which
"the forces of hell have broken upon earth and Satan is deceiving
the Nation."[38] For traditionalists, the new *Ordo* liturgy came to play
a role analogous to that played by Darwin's theory of evolution in
the rise of Protestant fundamentalism: it was both the preeminent
symbol of modernist inroads into the Church, and a concrete and
powerful issue around which to crystalize an anti-conciliar movement.

In conjuction with the conspiracy view of history, fundamentalism is also an action-oriented ideology, a *militant* campaign against
the inroads of modernity in the realm of religion. As such, fundamentalism seeks not merely to state a particular religious position,
but to discredit and eliminate all others. **Pure** doctrine necessitates
pure organization. The fundamentalist mentality is, therefore, ag-
gressive, and one dominated by the imagery of spiritual warfare that
situates the fundamentalist cause within the broader framework of a
cosmic battle for truth and righteousness. The impetus to give
doctrine a pure organizational form, combined with the mentality of
Holy War belligerency contributes to the fundamentalist proclivity
for sectarian separatism. When Protestant fundamentalists proved
unsuccessful in purging liberals and progressives from their respective denominations and gaining control of these structures, they
eventually separated to form their own independent Churches and
organizations.

---

[38]*The Voice*, November 13, 1971; Lawrence Brey, "The Final Test of Orthodoxy,"
Pro Multis, 1 (n.d.); Robert McKenna, letter in *The Remnant* (November 30, 1970);
Wathen, *The Great Sacrilege*. The most prominent conspiracy charge to emerge from
within the traditionalist movement centered around allegations of Masonic influences
among the hierarchy. Drawing on Catholicism's long-standing antipathy toward
Masonry as the sworn enemy of the Church (*In Eminenti*, 1738; *Humanum Genus*,
1884), traditionalists opposed to the conciliar reforms saw *aggiornamento* as an
unfolding of a "Masonic plot." In the mid-1970's, accounts began appearing in
traditionalist publications (first in Europe, later in the United States) charging high-
ranking Vatican prelates with membership in Masonic lodges. These charges also
coincided with the mounting tensions between the Vatican and Archbishop Lefebvre.
Throughout the "affair Ecône," Lefebvre and his supporters continued drawing
attention to the alleged "Masonic spirit" of Vatican II and all of its reform initiatives.
See, Lefebvre, *An Open Letter*, pp. 94–96.

While this holy war imagery is not an explicit system of doctrine, it is scripturally-based and serves as an important cognitive mode by which fundamentalists organize their perceptions of religious and cultural crisis and by which they mobilize to do battle against the powers of darkness. Like their Protestant counterparts, Catholic traditionalists present themselves not only as the remnant faithful, but as soldiers of Christ warring against modernism and the manifold demons that have struck at the Church in the postconciliar era. Traditionalists have assailed not only modernist elements in the Church, but have also attacked their own conservative co-religionists and the Church's magisterium itself.[39]

Fundamentalism, then, is a religious response to modernity, a reaction to intellectual and cultural threats to the taken-for-grantedness of sacred reality. Fundamentalism is selective both in its repudiation of modernism, and in its retrieval of the past. Fundamentalism is also an innovative response to change. As a world-view orientation or habit of mind, fundamentalism manifests a highly cognitive, doctrinal form of religiosity characterized by exaggerated objectivism, by tendencies toward literalism and dogmatism, and by an elitist and exclusivistic ecclesiology. Fundamentalism is also animated by conspiracy theories of social causality and an action-oriented ideology with separatist proclivities. Fundamentalism expresses in antithetical form elements of the epistemology and religious views it seeks to depose (emphasizing objectivity in the face of subjectivity; exclusivism in the face of pluralism, certitude in the face of relativism, militancy in the face of tolerance, and so forth). In so doing, fundamentalism reveals the dialectical nature of the social construction of reality and the problems that can arise when one sociology of knowledge is displaced by others.[40]

---

[39]For Catholics traditionalist separatism stemming from militancy and the quest for pure orthodoxy is more problematic than in the Protestant case. This difficulty derives from the nature of Catholic ecclesiology and the role of the Church's magisterium in the Catholic economy of salvation. Much traditionalist ideology, therefore, is taken up with the problem of legitimation. This legitimation is accomplished primarily through historical analogy and conspiracy theories, through Catholic forms of dispensationalism linked with the cultus of Marian apparitions, and through justification based on Canon law grounds of "necessity." I have treated these issues at length in "The Quandary of Dissent on the Catholic Right" in Roger O'Toole, ed., *Sociological Studies of Catholicism* (Lewiston, New York: Edwin Mellon, 1989), pp. 107–126.

[40]Although not the focus of this essay, it should be noted that the causes of Catholic traditionalism *qua* fundamentalism parallel many of the same dynamics that gave rise to Protestant fundamentalism: the logical development and extension of certain theological orientations; the staying power of prior religious identities and orienta-

The Relation of Traditionalist to Conservative Catholicism

In an analysis of postconciliar Catholicism published two years ago, John Deedy noted that in the Roman Catholic experience the word traditionalist has been nearly synonymous with the word conservative.[41] As I suggested at the beginning of this paper, both terms are now being used by some Catholics as though they are synonymous with fundamentalist. However, events in the Church in the last two decades, marked by the emergence of a schismatic traditionalist movement at odds not only with the Church's magisterium but also with conservative Catholic groups and organizations raises new questions about distinctions between conservative, traditionalist, and fundamentalist Catholics. Responsible reflections on the meaning and usage of these terms will need to consider the following:

1) The traditionalist movement did not begin as a discrete or autonomous phenomenon; it emerged out of, not independent of, the conservative Catholic reaction to *aggiornamento*. Gommar De Pauw's "Catholic Traditionalist Manifesto" was not a radical document at the time (1965). Traditionalist initiatives during and immediately following the Council echoed many fears and anxieties widespread in conservative Catholic quarters concerning the resurgence of neo-modernism in the Church and the perceived threat of *aggiornamento* to Catholic identity, stability, and institutional credibility. Nor was Archbishop Lefebvre's opposition to Vatican II initially a categorical repudiation of the Council.[42]

2) Traditionalists and conservatives are both inheritors of the integralist and anti-modernist legacy in the Church. Both give con-

---

tions that were once normative; the reaction against new epistemological and hermeneutical frames of reference that decisively penetrated Catholicism and that found legitimation through the Second Vatican Council. Traditionalism also arose in the context of the weakening of Catholic identity and discipline, and in the midst of a crisis of religious authority marked by the erosion of certitude in matters of faith and morals. Furthermore, the rise of the traditionalist movement must also be situated within the context of widespread cultural turmoil, urban upheavals, and social dislocations in Western industrial societies in the last three decades, as well as within the context of a broad resurgence of political and religious conservatism earmarking the 1970's and 1980's.

[41]John Deedy, *American Catholicism: And Now Where?* (New York: Plenum Press, 1987).

[42]Daniel Mennozi, "Opposition to the Council (1964–1984)" in Giuseppe Alberigo, Jean Pierre Jossua, and Joseph A. Komonchak, eds., *The Reception of Vatican II* (Washington, D.C.: The Catholic University Press, 1987), pp. 325–349.

temporary expression to ideological orientations attending Catholicism's construction as a counter-society. This construction occurred largely in the century and a half between the Congress of Vienna and the close of Vatican II (1815–1965) in response to liberalism and modernism that altered the social and cultural standing and roles of the Church in society.[43]

As inheritors of the Integralist/anti-modernist ethos, conservatives and traditionalist Catholics share many affinities. Both decry the modernist subversion of the faith and the attendant dismantling of the infrastructure of Catholicism's anti-modernist network. Both denounce the desacralization and abuse of the liturgy, and the weakening of Catholic identity, discipline and authority. Both are characterized by an ideology of cultural decline, a cognitive defiance of modernity, and by tendencies toward ethical rigorism and counter-cultural piety. Both advocate Christendom models of the social order. Both display affinities for right-wing political orientations and socio-political agenda condeming homosexuality, pornography, abortion, feminism, socialism, rock-music, and the Supreme Court decision on prayer in school. Anti-communism and Cold War themes are also standard litanies on the Catholic right, as are the virtues of free-market capitalism and concern to diminish issues of race and sexism.[44]

Both conservative and traditionalist apologists have tended to view Church involvement in peace and social justice initiatives as a modernist agenda that reduces salvation to issues of economic and social well-being. Right-wing themes emphasizing authority, social hierarchy and obedience are also prominent in the public pronouncements of both groups.

3) The majority of traditionalist supporters, especially during the movement's formative years in the wake of the Council, were drawn from the ranks of disaffected conservative Catholics.[45] Both groups compete for the same constituency base.

In light of the above affinities and relationships, traditionalist Catholics should not be viewed as a fringe element of antiquarian

---

[43]On Catholicism's political struggle with modernity see, Joseph Komonchak, "Interpreting the Second Vatican Council," Landas 1 (1987): 81–90.

[44]See Michael Cuneo, "Conservative Catholics in North America: Pro-Life Activism and the Pursuit of the Sacred," Pro Mundi Vita 36 (1987): 3–28, and John Coleman, "Who Are the Catholic Fundamentalists?"

[45]See Dinges, "Catholic Traditionalism in America."

malcontents as much as a hard expression of diffuse estrangement on the Catholic right consequent upon the tensions and strain generated by change and reform in the Church. What traditionalist leaders have done is to transform conservative estrangement through the rhetoric of subversion, conspiracy, heresy, injustice and eschatological urgency (and with episcopal authority in Archbishop Lefebvre's case) into a counter-Church schismatic movement. The distinction between conservative and traditionalist Catholic may, therefore, be taken as more one of degree than of kind; what is latent in one is more radicalized and explicit in the other, suggesting the aptness of Harry Emerson Fosdick's observation in the midst of Protestantism's earlier fundamentalist/modernist controversy that fundamentalists were essentially "illiberal and intolerant" conservatives.[46]

The question remains, however, as to whether or not there are any definitive distinctions that differentiate conservatives and traditionalists qua fundamentalists. In an insightful article entitled "Who are the Catholic 'Fundamentalists'?" John Coleman correctly points out that conservatism is an authentic and necessary orientation within any religious tradition. In the Roman Catholic experience, conservatism "cherishes the traditional symbols, rituals, and spirituality that give Catholicism a rich religious heritage." Conservatism is cautious about "trendy fads" or the too quick adoption of new practices without considering their long-term consequences. Coleman goes on to add, however, that conservatives generally respect "the church's need to change and adapt." Conservatives are also less elitist and exclusivistic than traditionalists and are given to being "charitable to those with whom they disagree."

Coleman also argues, however, that Catholic fundamentalism, which he associates with Opus Dei, Catholics United For the Faith, and Communion and Liberation, is characterized by authoritarian heteronomy that treats the ecclesiastical magisterium in the same manner as the Protestant fundamentalists treat the Bible, appealing to a literal, ahistorical, uncritical and nonhermeneutical reading of papal or curial pronouncements. Such an orientation puts a solum Magisterium litmus-test of orthodoxy in place of a traditional Catholic sense of balanced and multiple sources of authority (scripture,

---

[46]Harry Emerson Fosdick, "Shall the Fundamentalists Win?" In H. Shelton Smith, Robert T. Handy, and Lefferts A. Loetscher, eds., American Christianity: An Historical Interpretation with Representative Documents, vol. 2, (New York: Charles Scribner's, 1963),pp. 294–301.

magisterium, human experience, *sensus fidelium*)."[47] Coleman also notes the integralist genealogy of contemporary Catholic fundamentalism in that the former has always been mediated in and through the institutional Church and has maintained its connections within mainstream Catholicism.

To propose, however, that the rallying cry for Catholic fundamentalism is *solum Magisterium* is to miss a critical and distinctive characteristic of the traditionalist phenomenon. While Archbishop Lefebvre and his supporters manifest a type of infallibilist mentality, it is not a recrudescence of 19th century ultramontanism. Lefebvre has repeatedly rejected the sedevacantist position of the most bizarre segment of the traditionalists movement.[48] However, he has also categorically rejected the *Roma locuta est, causa finita est* solution prevalent among other segments of the Catholic right. Lefebvre and his supporters have openly and actively challenged the exercise of hierarchical authority in the name of fidelity to authentic Tradition. The archbishop denounces the false sense of obedience among conservatives and asserts that it has been Satan's "Master Stroke" in the wake of the Council to get Catholics to disobey the whole of Tradition in the name of obedience; nor, he argues, is there any law or jurisdiction that can "impose on a Christian a diminution of his faith."[49] In this particular view of hierarchical authority, it is no small irony that the archbishop is conspicuously closer to the position of the "modernists" he so vehemently denounces than he is to the authoritarian heteronomy espoused by his own conservative co-religionists.

Secondly, contemporary conservative groups have not set up distinct counter-church institutional structures. While conservatives have organized to promote preconciliar piety and their own interest-group agenda related to catechetics, to oppose neo-modernism, or to promote official Catholic teaching (e.g., on abortion or homosexuality), they have generally done so within the parameters of proper juridical authority. And, while sometimes polemic and uninhibited in criticizing individual bishops and episcopal conferences for weak

---

[47]Coleman, "Who Are the Catholic Fundamentalists?" Coleman follows Daly in this. See Gabriel Daly, *Transcendence and Immanence: A Study in Catholic Modernism and Integralism* (New York: Oxford U.P., 1980).

[48]In his "Letter to the Future Bishops" (August 29, 1987) Lefebvre charged that the See of Peter and the posts of authority in the Church were now occupied "by anti-Christs," an accusation that clearly moved him closer to the *sedevacantist* position. (*The Angelus* July, 1988): 38.

[49]Marcel Lefebvre, *Open Letter to Confused Catholics*, pp. 135, 138.

or misguided leadership, conservatives have generally attempted to "think with the Church" (read: Pope) in regard to matters of doctrine and discipline.

In spite of unprecedented Vatican initiatives to contain Lefebvre, the archbishop and his supporters have, by contrast, opted for the classic sectarian mode of protest. Like their Protestant fundamentalist counterparts, traditionalists have separated from an institution they could not decisively influence from within, forming a counter-Church movement that presents itself as something pristine and uncorrupted—implying that they, and they alone, have continuity with the one true faith.

In thinking about the distinction between conservative and traditionalist Catholics, two concepts in social movement theory are particularly helpful. Catholic traditionalism is oriented by values rather than by norms. Value-oriented movements represent more radicalized responses to change and conflict. Such movements are not concerned primarily with normative violations. Instead, they involve a restoration of past values and a fundamental reconstitution of self and society. Norm-oriented movements, by contrast, are primarily concerned with upholding a rule, law, or regulation of duly constituted authority. Norm-oriented movements do not call for the same sweeping changes associated with value-oriented ones.[50]

Thus, while anti-conciliarism can be found in conservative quarters, and while the conservative response to the Council has sometimes been less than enthusiastic, it is not a refusal and repudiation of *aggiornamento*, per se, as is the case of traditionalists. The conservative position is cautious and strict-constructionist in nature.

The traditionalist position by contrast, is a value-oriented (doctrinal) repudiation of the Council and its attendant reforms. This more radicalized and value-oriented dissent is also evident in interpretation of conflict in the Church in conspiracy terms and in the traditionalist perspective on the new liturgy which is riveted on matters of doctrine and authority. Furthermore, where conservative Catholics extol an authoritarian and hierarchical Church, traditionalists also want a counter-revolutionary one.

In the wake of the consecrations of four bishops by Archbishop Lefebvre in June 1988, it has become evident that the cognitive

---

[50]See Neil J. Smelser, *Theory of Collective Behavior* (New York: The Free Press of Glencoe, 1963).

dissonance associated with schism that has previously held funda-
mentalist/integralist tendencies within the Church is no longer operative in all sectors of the Catholic right. The emerging traditionalist
subculture has been able to derive—in large measure from previous
Vatican anti-modernist pronouncements—a self-validating belief
system by which their own position cannot now be disconfirmed.

If conservative and traditionalist Catholics are cut of the same
ideological cloth but distinguished by norm and value differentiations and by the degree of radicalization and separatist militancy,
then any attempt to understand the emergence of a fundamentalist
movement in the Roman Catholic Church (as distinct from a fundamentalist orientation) must address the matter of how this radicalization and estrangement are precipitated. How are those claiming
the high ground of orthodoxy moved to the contradiction of schism?
Or, in the distinction I made above, how are norm-oriented movements transformed into value-oriented ones?

This is a multifaceted issue which cannot be treated here at length.
The radicalization of the Catholic right over the past quarter century
is a product of both the elitist and contentious position taken by
certain elements within that sector, in concert with "excesses" and
"abuses" in interpreting and implementing aggiornamento. Radicalization was also facilitated by ideological and organizational inflexibility on the part of those in leadership positions in the Church.
This volatile combination of factors led to the rapid escalation of
symbolic issues into conflicts of authority, all but insuring the
inevitability of schism and intractable dissension. Liturgical reform
is again instructive in this regard.

As long as the Tridentine rite was permitted as a legitimate
liturgical form within the Church, traditionalist Catholics clinging
to the old liturgy remained integrated into the Church's institutional
life.

Once the Novus Ordo liturgy became mandatory, however, those
who could not or would not give up the old Mass faced the choice
of either openly defying the hierarchy by attending now illicit
traditionalist chapels (where they were exposed to a more radicalized ideology), or of not attending Mass at all—a highly untenable
option for "orthodox" Catholics. With the prohibition of the Tridentine rite (1971), traditionalism attained a deviant status in the
Church. Once this deviant status was conferred and sanctions imposed, traditionalists were further isolated, thereby intensifying
their militancy, their ideological radicalism, and their perception of

conspiracy and persecution.[51] Traditionalists found themselves in open conflict with Church authorities and without an exit option. Ironically, the kind of authoritarianism and hierarchical order many of them extolled by virtue of their religious self-understanding made their manner of resistance and rebellion a zero-sum game.

Conclusion

Religious fundamentalism is a type of schismatic conservatism. It shatters the very community it professes to save and turns against conservatism itself. Fundamentalism divorces dogmatic tradition from religious experience, terminates dialogue by making ideology more important than charity, and denies that humanly acquired truth is always tenuous and imperfect.[52]

As has often been observed, Catholicism has historically expressed itself through inclusiveness and a synthesis of culture and intelligence.[53] In spite of the prominence of its Greco-Roman cultural heritage and tendencies toward Europeanization, the Church has struggled to reproduce itself through assimilation and adaptation (now called inculturation) through the ages in order to give more creative fulfillment to the Gospel. Through its church-like proclivities Catholicism has sought to come to grips with the different intellectual and spiritual needs of different constituencies situated differently within social structures. As the primitive Church opened itself to diverse cultures of the ancient world, so the Church has struggled throughout its history to develop a powerful and credible synthesis of culture and the Gospel that can support and enhance both culture and religion. This process of change and diversification has been necessitated by social, political, and cultural changes, and by new historical contexts. In the process of adapting and diversifying, Catholicism has struggled with the tensions inherent in maintaining the integrity and prophetic stance of the tradition while simultaneously promoting and developing it.

---

[51]Specific issues surrounding the controversy over liturgical reform are examined in William D. Dinges, "Ritual Conflict as Social Conflict," *Sociological Analysis* 48 (Summer, 1987): 138–157.

[52]Nancy C. Ring, "Heresy," in Joseph A. Komonchak, Mary Collins, Dermot A. Lane. eds. *The New Dictionary of Theology* (Wilmington, Delaware: Michael Glazier, Inc., 1987), pp. 459–462.

[53]Ernst Troeltsch, *Social Teachings of the Christian Churches*, 2 vols. (Chicago: University of Chicago Press, 1931); Joseph P. Fitzpatrick, *One Church Many Cultures: The Challenge of Diversity* (Kansas City: Sheed and Ward, 1987).

Traditionalism, by both maintaining and exaggerating the reactionary response that became a prominent feature of Catholicism's institutional life during its troubled engagement with modernity in the late 19th and early 20th centuries, denies this responsibility. The Church is thereby reduced to a sectarian aspect of the broader culture, further removing religion from an axial role in society while, paradoxically, proclaiming the triumph of "The Faith" over it. This is a very different cause from that associated with authentic religious liberalism or conservatism.

A CHURCH WE LONG FOR: THE FUNDAMENTALIST CHALLENGE

Mary Jo Weaver

Gabriel Daly's identification of integralism as "the Catholic form of fundamentalism,"[1] an assertion that has been repeated by John Coleman and others,[2] provides us with a provocative description of Catholic resistance to the accommodations of the second Vatican council. Since fundamentalism is notoriously difficult to define, however, and since its use in Protestant circles has a complicated history, our ability to use that category effectively demands that we start with some reflections on Protestant fundamentalism before talking about its Catholic cousin.

After the national sensation of the Scopes "monkey trial" in 1925 where Clarence Darrow attributed his presence to an attempt to prevent "bigots and ignoramuses" from controlling the schools, and H. L. Mencken did his share to characterize fundamentalists as stupid, sour minded rubes, fundamentalism became a synonym for backwater Bible thumping. Although scholars of religion were not as savage, they, too, defined fundamentalism as a rural phenomenon growing best in those pioneer outposts without access to modern culture. To countermand the view that fundamentalism was a disease best cured by education, Ernest Sandeen interpreted fundamentalism as a long-standing millenarian movment related to end of the world speculation in nineteenth century England.[3] For him, funda-

---

[1]"Catholicism and Modernity" in *Journal of the American Academy of Religion* 53 (1985): 773–796.

[2]"Who Are the Catholic Fundamentalists" in *Commonweal* 116 (27 January 1989): 42–47. See also the essays in *America*, 155 (27 September 1986), and Peter Hebblethwaite, "A Roman Catholic Fundamentalism" in *The Times Literary Supplement*, August 5–11, 1988, p. 866.

[3]*The Roots of Fundamentalism: British and American Millenarianism 1800–1930* (Chicago: University of Chicago Press, 1970).

mentalism was not a product of the twenties, but was a "self-conscious, structured, long-lived, dynamic entity with recognized leadership, periodicals, and meetings."[4] Furthermore, far from being indebted to the "five fundamentals" as has often been claimed, Sandeen saw fundamentalists characterized primarily by pre-millennialism, and so placed them within the context of nineteenth-century speculation about the end of the world and Biblical prophecies about the eschaton.

Sandeen made a genuine contribution to the study of fundamentalism by interpreting it as a movement with coherent beliefs. It is impossible, after reading his book, to believe that fundamentalists will disappear given the proper education, or to continue to identify fundamentalism with a country bumpkin mentality. Nevertheless, the redneck image took hold of the American religious imagination so firmly that fundamentalism became a badge of shame. Television evangelists, direct descendents of early fundamentalists, preferred to call themselves evangelicals and have only recently claimed to be proud of the term "fundamentalist."

American Catholics and mainline Protestants often saw no differences between evangelicals and fundamentalists and so, captive to their own biases about fundamentalism, were not prepared for the media sophistication and technological savvy that began to characterize television preachers during the Carter presidency. The use of computer mailing lists coupled with an ability to sway national political issues bemused and frightened many people and led to a general confusion about fundamentalism. Protests about the mixing of religion and politics, a mixture which did not deter Civil Rights workers and anti-war activists, were hurled at these new fundamentalists in an attempt to undermine their power. In this context, where some fundamentalists identified with empire builders like Jerry Falwell and others did not, George Marsden published his landmark book on American fundamentalism.

Protestant fundamentalism, according to Marsden, is a distinct brand of evangelical Christianity uniquely shaped by the circumstances of early twentieth-century America.[5] Militant opposition to modernism sets fundamentalism apart from other conservative traditions and makes it a "loose, diverse, and changing federation of

---

[4]Ibid., p. xv.

[5]George M. Marsden, *Fundamentalism and American Culture: The Shaping of Twentieth Century Evangelicalism 1870–1925* (New York: Oxford University Press, 1980).

co-belligerents united by their fierce opposition to modernist attempts to bring Christianity into line with modern thought."[6] Marsden's task required him to make sense of theological interpretations like those of Sandeen, and to explain what appear to be widely differing styles of fundamentalist affiliation. Accordingly, he began with the post Civil War dominance of American evangelicalism, traced its early schisms, explained the significance of eminent figures like Dwight Moody and William Jennings Bryan, and demonstrated persuasively that fundamentalism today is not monolithic. At the same time, with Sandeen, he made it clear that fundamentalism is not "a temporary social abberation, but a genuine religious movement or tendency with deep roots and intelligible beliefs."[7]

Marsden's book is most useful, I think, because of his tolerance for ambiguity. He explains why fundamentalists sometimes identify with a majority established culture and other times prefer to think of themselves as separate from the world around them. He uses the tension between old revivalist roots, which require active service in the world, and the "culture-denying, soul-rescuing Christianity" of men like Dwight Moody to show that fundamentalists have not settled the question of worldly involvement for themselves. Similarly, he explains the tension between trust and distrust of the intellect which makes them appear to be, on the whole, anti-intellectual and anti-scientific.

Two things about the modern interpretation of fundamentalism can be especially useful to us as we try to understand the motivation and persistence of "Catholic fundamentalism." First, and here Marsden is quite brilliant, fundamentalists after 1925 were strangers in their own land, internal immigrants distressed by the erosion of the social support for religion and searching for something that would give their movement internal cohesion. Secondly, far from being dismissible as people suffering from "status anxiety," a characterization that would lead to the conclusion that once status was achieved the movement would disappear, fundamentalism is a social, political, and intellectual phenomenon that is here to stay.

Discussion of Catholic fundamentalism ought, I believe, to take shape within these parameters: we will do best by trying to understand the profound motivations of its adherents and by seeing them as members of a coherent movement which has the power to shape

---

[6]Ibid., p.4.
[7]Marsden, cited, p.6.

a particular kind of Catholicism by its criticisms of the post-conciliar church. We may look at the various groups that have been labelled fundamentalist within Catholicism and not like them; but we owe it to ourselves to figure out *why* they are there and we can bet that they will be around for a long time.

The fundamentalist impulse in Catholicism cannot be explained apart from its characters. Who are the Catholic fundamentalists? Are they the Marian apocalyptists discussed by Thomas Kselman in his paper on our Lady of Necedah?[8] If so, then they are often mobilized against what appear to be governments hostile to Catholicism. Mary's appearances in this century have been extrapolated to meet an anti-communist need and have been extremely useful to the present pope as his visits to Fatima have shown. The Marian appearances for the last one hundred and fifty years have upheld papalism and warned the faithful against the dangers of the modern world.

Are fundamentalists what Michael Cuneo calls "conservative Catholics,"[9] searching for a return to a pristine time in which sacred identity was clearly transcendent, moral norms rigorously upheld, papal authority respected, and personal piety rooted in a vertical relationship with the deity? Cuneo identifies James Hitchcock, Monsignor George Kelly, and others as the intellectual wing of this group and locates the sources of popular appeal in *The Wanderer*, *Fidelity* magazine, and Catholics United for the Faith (CUF). If these are our fundamentalists, then we should note that they appear to be attracting scores of young people and have the potential to become a specific branch of Catholicism. Pro-life activism is, for this group, a ritual expression of their need for absolutes since it enables them to find "an unimpeachable locus of ultimacy."[10]

Are Catholic fundamentalists Lefebvrist traditionalists, rightly interpreted by William Dinges as those involved in a power struggle with the Vatican?[11] Far from being grounded on an essential respect for the present leadership of the church, traditionalists reject the second Vatican council and directly challenge the authority of the pope. Lefebvre is not unschooled in Catholic ecclesiastical politics:

---

[8]"Our Lady of Necedah: Marian Piety and the Cold War" in Charles and Margaret Hall Cushwa Center for the Study of American Catholicism: Working Paper Series 12 #2. (Notre Dame, IN: 1982).

[9]Michael W. Cuneo, "Conservative Catholicism in North America: Pro-Life Activism and the Pursuit of the Sacred" in *Pro Vita Mundi Dossiers* 36 (January 1987): 1–30.

[10]Ibid., p. 28.

[11]"The Vatican Report on Sects, Cults and New Religious Movements," *America* 155 (26 September 1986): 145–147, 154.

he knows that a pope acting with a council holds an unassailable position and that the only way to counteract Vatican II is to refuse to accept it. Unlike conservatives who believe that the council has not been *interpreted* properly, traditionalists reject the council altogether and identify themselves primarily by way of Trent and Vatican I. Where they might be called fundamentalists is in their intrepid claim to define real or true Catholicism against any attempt to find religious identity in collegiality, pluralism, or ecumenism. Whether traditionalists appeal mostly to those over forty and so can be expected to pass away eventually is not clear to me.

Are Catholic fundamentalists members of Opus Dei identified by Peter Hebblethwaite as having major influence at the Vatican?[12] If so, does that mean that Catholic fundamentalism, besides having popular levels of support, also can claim an elite corps of right wing political activists? What is at stake in Latin America where Catholic fundamentalists might belong to an elite cadre like Opus Dei, or, more likely, might have actually joined a Protestant fundamentalist church? If Opus Dei is especially active in Latin American countries, and if the common people there identify more directly with Protestant fundamentalism, what does that say about our attempts to define Catholic fundamentalism?

Following Marsden's understanding of fundamentalism as a flexible alliance that resists efforts to conform to a universal description, I am willing to live with some ambiguity of definition. At the same time, I believe we can find some clarity of motivation and some continuity with the past. Gabriel Daly connects modern Catholic fundamentalists with those people who opposed modernism either as a crypto "movement" or as any impulse to threaten the integrity of a Catholicism built upon a strategic alliance of scholastic methodology, Canon Law, and magisterial control over ecclesiastical structures. With the dismantling of scholasticism by the council and the reform of Canon Law, integralists have become strangers in their own land threatened, Daly says, with "cognitive misery," and constrained to take a stand on the battlefront of moral and administrative authority. His description is not unlike that of Michael Cuneo who finds parallels between Roman Catholic and Protestant fundamentalists in a profound sense of disinheritance: conservative Catholics who are most at home in a triumphalist, exclusive, world-transcending church are homeless in the modern, pluralistic context.

---

[12]*Times Literary Supplement.*

Since Catholics in general are not eschatologically minded, it is not surprising that millennialism is not a major aspect of Catholic fundamentalists as opposed to their Protestant cousins. At the same time, the fears of all the groups I mentioned do have resonances in the apocalyptic plot as outlined in the Bible: there is a sense that the church is at war with the powers of darkness, that the faithful are being tested by way of terrible suffering, and that Catholicism, real Catholicism, demands conscious resistance and heroic action. The anticipated reward changes somewhat from group to group, but takes the general form of a return to the past where transcendence, mystery, supernaturalism,[13] and moral absolutes characterize a society with real power to persuade and to unify religious people. I am a little reminded of Wilfrid Ward's dream of the perfect resolution to the disorienting battles of the late nineteenth century. He hoped that the church would relinquish its needs to meet the modern world with the spiked palisades of anathema and retreat and dreamed that the church would then be constituted by a grateful and obedient people under the direction of a wise and benevolent pontiff.[14] The difference between Ward's hopes and those of modern Catholic fundamentalists is this one: however fondly he entertained this fantasy, Ward knew it to be a "medieval dream," whereas Catholic fundamentalists perceive their paradise as the only realistic choice for the future of the church.

I want to link the fundamentalist dream to my assertion that Catholic fundamentalists, like their Protestant cousins, have the power to become a specific and influential movement within the church. I admit that I am more persuaded that such an outcome can occur with Cuneo's conservative Catholics than with the Lefebvrist traditionalists, and I do not believe the political Marian appearances will be a significant factor. I do, however, believe that Opus Dei and other types of communitarian groups will continue to play a role in the future of Catholicism.

How can this collection of dissident groups challenge and enhance a post-conciliar understanding of Catholicism? Michael Cuneo's suggestive analogy can clarify my question. Catholic fundamental-

---

[13]One of the best descriptions of the supernaturalistic dimension of Catholicism is in Langdon Gilkey, *Catholicism Confronts Modernity* (New York: Seabury Press, 1975).

[14]See my *Letters from a "Modernist"* (Shepherdstown, WV: Patmos Press, 1981), or read Wilfrid Ward's epilogue to his *Life and Times of Cardinal Wiseman* (London: Longmans, Green, and Co., 1900), II, pp. 533–583.

ists might function in the church as Orthodoxy has done in Judaism. Jacob Neusner characterizes Orthodox Judaism as a reactive movement meant to restore tradition to its rightful place.[15] Whereas Reform Jews accommodated to the modern world by relinquishing practices that separated them from others in order to define Judaism in ethical terms based on the prophets and intellectual terms based on reason, Orthodox Jews insisted that the Torah was the fundamental sounding board against which modern culture could be judged and found wanting. Orthodox Judaism, therefore, appealed to what Neusner calls "the natural conservatism of religious people." Additionally, Orthodoxy, in claiming to represent the "true Judaism" kept the historical linkage between ancient and modern times alive and attracted people who were prepared to make sacrifices for the faith. Orthodox Judaism, therefore, "came to offer a security and certainty unavailable elsewhere."[16]

The conversion rate from modern secular Judaism to Orthodoxy, especially among young, upwardly-mobile Jews today, is an indication of the power of this alternative within the broader spectrum of Judaism. Orthodoxy offers, if I may put it this way, a place to be Jewish for those who cannot cope with a purely secular society or who see no alternative except secularity. Because Orthodoxy represents a highly traditional Jewish option, it has become a dialectical partner of Reform Judaism and helped to produce yet another alternative, Conservative Judaism. Each of these varieties, along with Reconstructionism, is a venue in which Jews can develop ways of being religious. Furthermore, it is hard to imagine Judaism without this range of alternatives.

If Catholic fundamentalism can function as an alternative to post-conciliar Catholicism, how will its questions shape our own view of Catholicism? I find no universal answer. Catholics who have converted to Protestant fundamentalist churches, as William Dinges has argued, call the forms of worship and ministry of contemporary Catholicism into account.[17] Dinges means that the Vatican must examine its "institutional credibility," but his argument applies as well to the ways any of us teach and practice Catholicism. Catholic integralists, says Daly, long for a return to a time of innocence which he takes to mean a pre-scientific worldview. Although we cannot deny that we live in the modern world with its scientific skepticism,

---

[15]*The Way of Torah* (Belmont, CA: Wadsworth Publishing Co., 1988).
[16]Ibid., p. 128.
[17]"The Vatican Report," p. 147.

we can, says Daly, learn something from fundamentalist desire, and from their resistance to a religion that appears to have lost its power to attract and to satisfy. If fundamentalists tend to be literal minded, whether toward the Bible or toward tradition, perhaps we can learn to be more clear about the ways in which contemporary Catholicism engages the imagination in ways that opens pathways to religious experience. If Catholic fundamentalists make common cause against the political mission of the post-conciliar church and its enthusiasm for a socially transformative ethic, perhaps we can show more clearly how those goals relate to divine transcendence and personal sin.

A year before he died, George Tyrrell wrote to a friend, "God will not ask us: What sort of church have you lived for? but What sort of Church have you longed for?"[18] He longed for a church of the people with a theology based on experience, and he was passionately against authoritarianism because it smothers the Spirit and ignores the religious life of ordinary people. His concept of revelation proceeded not from a fixed deposit, but from the spirit of Christianity as it was continually being embodied and realized in the particular lives of Christians. Roman Catholic fundamentalists embody part of the spirit of Catholicism along with post-conciliar Catholics. What happens to subsequent generations depends very much on the ways we respond to those particularities in Catholic fundamentalists.

---

[18]Maude Petre, editor, *George Tyrrell's Letters* (London: Fisher, Unwin, 1920), p. 31.

Newman's *Sensus Fidelium* and Papal Fundamentalism

Edward Jeremy Miller

In a recent *Commonweal* article John A. Coleman has noted the curious affinities between Protestant fundamentalism and a phenomenon in Roman Catholicism which he terms "integralism" or "Catholic fundamentalism" and which Gabriel Daly has called "papal fundamentalism."[1] Although I have chosen Daly's term for reasons I shall presently describe, Coleman provides an ideological backdrop to the purposes for which I see Cardinal Newman making a most important contribution.

This particularly Catholic version of fundamentalism, argues Coleman, does not rest so typically in scriptural inerrancy as with Protestant fundamentalism but rather in a literal, ahistorical and uncritical reading of papal or curial teachings. It seeks in papal teachings a sure bulwark against relativism, the claims of science, and other influences of modernity. From this attitude certain tendencies proceed: a forgetfulness that there is a hierarchy of truths in what the Catholic magisterium proclaims; a lack of appreciation for the varying levels of authoritative papal teachings; an "infallibilist" mentality that wants to elevate all papal and curial statements into their most solemn implication, namely, a teaching that Catholics must accept on divine faith.

Whereas Coleman's analysis then moves in the direction of the affinities between this Catholic integralism and Protestant fundamentalism (coping with modernity—read "modernism" for turn-of-the century Catholics—preserving the authority of the Bible against

[1]J. A. Coleman, "Who are the Catholic 'Fundamentalists'?" *Commonweal*, 116 (January 27, 1989):42–47; Gabriel Daly, "Catholicism and Modernity," *Journal of the American Academy of Religion* 53 (1985): 773–96.

movements of historical and textual criticism, seeking sure sources of authority during times of cultural and social transformation),[2] my point of departure is simply one of Coleman's themes: the "fundamentalistic tendency" to consider all papal teachings as inerrant and therefore final. Such a tendency invites seeing in the papal magisterium, in all of its various expressions, the same authoritative imperative that Protestant fundamentalists would have for the inerrant biblical text. "If you do not accept the authoritative word, simply because it is given you and under whose judgment you need to stand, you are not a true Christian." "The matter is not open for question since the teaching is clear." These two statements could equally have been made by a Protestant fundamentalist or a papal fundamentalist. For this reason papal fundamentalism, Daly's term, attracts me.

From a Catholic perspective, and with the interest in preserving legitimate Catholic liberties and the contributions of the laity, I am concerned with the distinctions that need to be made. So, too, was Cardinal Newman, as shall be seen. There are different kinds of papal teachings, all of them "authoritative" but not all of them commanding the submission of faith.[3] Furthermore, one must also distinguish the teaching moment from its ultimate reception and appropriation by the community. This is crucial, and I will consider it subsequently under its more exact theological term, "ecclesial reception." Lastly, one must distinguish mentalities. There is a mentality that says, "Rome has spoken, the matter is ended. Either accept it or withdraw from the Catholic body." Against this is a mentality that both respects authority and holds for the rightful role of discernment that is lodged in the depths of personal conscience and in the value of lived experience. There is another mentality, one that has little respect for Church authority, and with that mentality I am not concerned here.

Certain teachings of Newman would caution one against tendencies to papal fundamentalism. He would provide a counterpoint to it, which is instructive because at the same time Newman is a

---

[2]For an analysis of these crises and Protestant fundamentalism, see George M. Marsden, *Fundamentalism and American Culture* (New York: Oxford University Press, 1980).

[3]The Vatican II document, *Constitution on the Church*, #25, describes a "religious submission of mind and will" to the noninfallible yet authentic teaching of the pope, but this carefully worded phrase does not preclude certain forms of dissent nor imply that such a teaching can never be changed. I am concerned with the flexibility contained in the nuanced phrase.

champion of the role of authority in the Catholic Church, rightly understood and practiced. To situate his contribution, I wish to use an example of papal teaching he never considered. The example touches intimately the lives of the Catholic laity, and the example cuts across mentalities. For the papal fundamentalist it is a closed case. For others, who do not consider themselves disloyal and uncommitted Catholics, it is an open case. It is, by design, an instance of papal teaching that was not issued as a solemn infallible pronouncement, though in the minds of some it had the same practical effect. When later I have Newman speak for himself about the role of the laity, he will be illustrating with two matters of dogma, and my example is not dogma. Yet if what he says about dogma holds, then all the more can one draw certain inferences about my example, as I shall do by way of conclusion.

The teaching of the Roman Catholic magisterium on sexual morality and contraceptives is a helpful example. Rome's teaching on the immorality of using artificial contraceptives within married life has been consistent. There was a time when it went generally unchallenged, both by theologians and by laity. Those married Catholics who used contraceptives either abstained from communion, or would make frequent confessions, or would simply drift away from the community because they "accepted the groundrules" of what it meant to belong or not belong. Nor did theologians challenge the groundrules. Rome had spoken, and people listened.

That situation has changed. Statistics tell us that most married Catholics practice some form of contraception, at some time or other.[4] These Catholics do not feel they need to quit the Church, and contraception is rarely if ever mentioned in the confessional, as one hears from parish priests. Many theologians do not think that contraception, in every instance and in any situation whatsoever, is intrinsically immoral. The present pope teaches that it is, as did his predecessors, as does any curial document on the matter.[5] Are the

---

[4]Andrew M. Greeley, *The American Catholic: A Social Portrait* (New York: Basic Books, 1977), p. 142.

[5]The papal teaching on conjugal morality has very much to applaud: the dignity of the human person and especially the dignity of women; the non-hedonistic valuation of sexual love; the placing of coitus within the larger and more important framework of the married relationship; the need for altruism; the openness to begetting children as belonging to the Christian view of marriage. These features need to be preached to the modern world, and Pope John Paul II is rightfully champion of them. The essential orientation of *Humanae Vitae* is gospel-grounded. My example only turns on the question whether contraception can ever be countenanced within a life-long Christian marriage. An analysis of the encyclical can be found in *Contraception: Authority and Dissent*, ed. Charles E. Curran (New York: Herder and Herder, 1969).

majority of married Catholics who do not agree with the teaching and do not follow it simply persons of so-called bad will? Or are their conscientious instincts truer? In whatever event, does their experience of trying to live a Christian life, as married persons, as sexual persons, *count*? Is their experience a *fact* to be reckoned with, and if so, how is the fact to be interpreted? Does the formulation of an authentic and authoritative teaching on marital sexuality need to deal with that fact?

John Henry Newman formulated his theological positions by dealing with uneasy facts. It was his appreciation for the upshot of these facts that enabled him to have a nuanced understanding of the manner in which ecclesiastical authority was to understand its role and to formulate its positions. He was not in principle against authority and therefore he was not against papal pronouncements rightfully understood. But he did not think that a papal authoritative decree, in and of itself, was where the matter should begin or should terminate. Further, if the experience of people, which gives rise to uneasy facts, counts—and it does for Newman—then a caveat to papal fundamentalism is found in his understanding of the *sensus fidelium* and in its complement, the *consensus fidelium*.

Sensus Fidelium *and* The Rambler *Article*

Newman's teaching on *sensus fidelium* was occasioned by the uneasy fact that between the general councils of Nicea and Constantinople I in the fourth century it was the laity more than the episcopacy who witnessed to the orthodox understanding of the nature of Jesus Christ. It was the laity who were repelled by the Arian understanding of Jesus. How Newman came to articulate this position in the famous *Rambler* article of 1859 and what he advanced in it merit brief recollection. The *Rambler*, begun by Anglican convert John Moore Capes in 1848, was a journal of religious opinion run by the laity.[6] In the issue of February 1958, Scott Nasmyth Stokes contributed an unsigned article, "The Royal Commission on Education," which criticized Catholics and especially

---

[6]Episcopal pressure to terminate the magazine occurred in late 1858. Sir John Acton, by then a co-editor with Richard Simpson, published a book review in which he argued that no Catholic is as perfect as Catholicism itself, for did not St. Augustine plant the seeds of Jansenism. A storm ensued, and Acton asked his former mentor, Ignaz von Döllinger, to provide documentation. Döllinger's letter, "The Paternity of Jansenism," appeared in the December issue, and the letter was sent to Rome for censure.

the bishops for refusing to cooperate with a government commission examining education for all English youths. Unused to criticism, the English bishops threatened to censure the magazine. They and the magazine's editors appealed to Newman to mediate, which led to Newman's assuming editorship as of the May issue. In this issue he wrote an unsigned commentary on the Royal Commission, part of which read:

> Acknowledging, then, most fully the prerogatives of the episcopate, we do unfeignedly believe, both from the reasonableness of the matter, and especially from prudence, gentleness, and considerateness which belong to them personally, that their Lordships really desire to know the opinion of the laity on subjects in which the laity are especially concerned. If even in the preparation of a dogmatic definition the faithful are consulted, as lately in the instance of the Immaculate Conception, it is at least as natural to anticipate such an act of kind feeling and sympathy in great practical questions.[7]

Editor J. H. Newman began receiving critical letters on this anonymous observation, especially from Dr. John Gillow, professor of dogmatics at Ushaw College, who characterized as *haeresi proxima* the idea that the episcopacy consult the laity in anything bearing on dogmatic definitions. Newman's own Ordinary, Ullathorne of Birmingham, informed Newman of continuing discontent with the *Rambler*; Newman offered to resign, and Ullathorne asked him to make the next issue his last.[8] Newman decided to make a full statement in the July issue and wrote the famous article, "On Consulting the Faithful in Matters of Doctrine." What has subsequently become a theological legacy on *sensus fidelium* was delated to Rome by Bishop Thomas Brown of Newport, a censuring process about which Newman was never informed, and he remained under a cloud of suspicion at the Vatican for years.

Newman's article posed two key questions. Is it correct to say the laity can be consulted? The word *consult* can mean both asking for advice and asking for factual matter. In the former sense the laity are not consulted in dogmatic matters, according to Newman, for that would make them judges of orthodoxy. In the latter sense, and analogous with consulting a barometer, the belief of the laity can be

---

[7]Quoted in *Letters and Diaries of John Henry Newman*, ed. C. S. Dessain (New York: Thomas Nelson, 1961-), vol. 19, pp. 129–30, n. 3.

[8]Newman's May 22nd memorandum of the meeting is in *Letters and Diaries*, 19, p. 141.

sought as a "testimony to that apostolic tradition, on which alone any doctrine whatsoever can be defined."[9] Second, can such consultation be a preliminary to a dogmatic definition? Yes, Newman claims, because the laity as a group is one voice of the apostolic revelation, and he mentions that the laity were consulted in the recent case of the dogma of the Immaculate Conception. There can be many witnesses to revelation: scripture primarily, the teachings of the early Church doctors, episcopal teaching, theological schools, the liturgy, and, argues Newman, the laity themselves. Although discerning the tradition may be the role of the magisterium, it may not disregard any witnessing source in ascertaining the tradition.

While some stress one or another of these witnesses, Newman chose to underline the "sense of the faithful" since certain doctrines in their earliest stages of development have a clearer basis there than in other sources, such as synodal decrees. Newman offered various ways to understand this witnessing gift of the laity. It is a sort of instinct, or *phronema*, deep within the Christian community. It is the impulse of the Holy Spirit—one notes here that Newman gives full play to baptismal grace. It is a jealousy of error, an error the laity at once feels to be a scandal. The fourth century experience of the church provided Newman with an uneasy fact. Note his unminced words: "In that very day the divine tradition committed to the infallible Church was proclaimed and maintained far more by the faithful than by the episcopate," and "the body of the episcopate was unfaithful to its commission, while the body of the laity was faithful to its baptism."[10]

Newman's unsigned essay drew two further conclusions from the uneasy fact of the fourth century that unsettled his conservative antagonists, the ultramontane party. During that intra-council Arian period, bishops taught inconsistently, leading Newman to say that "there was a temporary suspense of the functions of the 'Ecclesia docens,' " and furthermore the councils of that period "said what they should not have said, and did what obscured and compromised revealed truth."[11] Professor J. B. Franzelin of the Gregorian University objected particularly to these contentions.[12] Newman waited

---

[9]*On Consulting the Faithful in Matters of Doctrine*, ed. John Coulson (London: Chapman, 1961), p. 55.

[10]Ibid., pp. 75–76.

[11]Ibid., pp. 77, 76 respectively. Newman offers many examples of doctrinal confusion among the hierarchy after Nicea.

[12]Johann Baptist Franzelin (1816–1886) was a distinguished theologian of the day who was later to be influential at Vatican I. His objections were never published but were expressed in lectures at the Roman College.

until he reedited *Arians of the Fourth Century* in 1871 to answer Franzelin. He reiterated evidence from the *Rambler* essay to show that in the period between A.D. 325 and 381 a clear and consistent teaching from the bishops was lacking, and in this sense the *Ecclesia docens* faltered. During this same period large episcopal synods simply erred in their teachings about the divinity of Christ. These conflicting episcopal voices were the uneasy facts with which theological reflection had to deal. It was never Newman's purpose to undermine the authority of the magisterium, a fact evident from his defense of authority in his *Essay on Development*. However, his vision of the laity as an actively contributing, personally involved, and even doctrinally testifying force in the social fabric of Christianity simply touched raw nerves among those accustomed to view the church from the top down.

Consensus Fidelium and the Vatican I Decrees

There is another uneasy fact, drawn from Newman's own day, that extends the notion of *sensus fidelium* to its full breadth and which I term *consensus fidelium*.[13] When the first Vatican Council adjourned,[14] Newman was unsure that its decrees carried the authority of an infallible conciliar teaching. A moral unanimity was necessary, in his opinion, to evidence the presence of the Holy Spirit in the solemn teaching moment. Although 533 conciliars voted in favor of the decree on papal infallibility on 18 July 1870 and two bishops opposed it, the uneasy fact was the 60 conciliars avoided voting by leaving the council the previous day. This was a sizable minority party, and Newman wondered whether this fact undermined the necessary moral unanimity a conciliar decree required. Earlier, on June 6, Newman had written Ullathorne that a moral unanimity was indispensable, "for how could we take as the voice of the council, which is infallible, a definition which a body of Bishops, of high character in themselves, and representing large masses of the faithful, protested against?"[15]

---

[13]In the *Rambler* essay Newman had used the terms "sensus" and "consensus" of the faithful somewhat interchangeably; see Coulson, p. 55. More precisely, "sensus" refers to the gift of discernment, and "consensus" refers to the collective voice of Christendom, which Newman calls the infallible voice of the Church; Ibid., p. 63. I am faithful to Newman in using the term to analyze Vatican I.

[14]The Council never officially ended. September 1, 1870 turned out to be the last meeting day. A week later troops of the new Italian government invaded the Papal States, and on October 20 Pius IX suspended the council indefinitely.

[15]*Letters and Diaries*, 25, pp. 138–39.

When word of the minority party walkout reached Newman, he raised three suppositions. If these bishops (practically the entire episcopate of Hungary, and large numbers of the French, German, Austrian, and American hierarchies) maintained their protest as a *body*, there would be serious reason to think the decree invalid. If the protest did not remain corporate, then isolated and individual protest would not undermine the moral unanimity necessary for a valid decree. Finally, if the definition of papal infallibility was eventually *received* by the body of the faithful, "it will claim our assent by force of the great dictum (of Augustine), 'Securus judicat orbis terrarum.'"[16]

This third supposition, which is the Newmanian expression of the theological category *ecclesial reception of doctrines*,[17] sums up the other two suppositions, and it leads us into Newman's notion of *consensus fidelium*. It also underlines the uneasy fact on which Newman reflected: there was sizable protest to the decree on papal infallibility. What was to be made of it? Reception is not equated with majority vote, and though moral unanimity was difficult to gauge, it was Newman's best way to judge the harmony of an official teaching with the universal church's instinct for the true faith, its *sensus fidei*. As Newman wrote to his Oratorian friend, Ambrose St. John, "till better advised, nothing shall make me say that a mere majority in a Council, as opposed to moral unanimity, in itself creates an obligation to receive its dogmatic decrees. This is a point of history and precedent."[18]

The objection could be raised that bodies of bishops had wrongfully protested earlier decrees and had gone into schism: Donatists, Nestorians, Monophysites. Mere corporate protest, of itself, could not automatically invalidate doctrinal decrees. This fact forced Newman to articulate another dimension that was grounded in his organic metaphor for genuine developments of doctrine: What is true will make its way forward, and what is false will decay. Error has the seeds of its self-destruction within it. As Newman observed, the Arians came to nought, as did the Donatists.

Save for the Old Catholics of Holland and Germany, a group Newman considered marginal, corporate dissent following Vatican I

---

[16]Ibid, p. 165.

[17]One of the finest studies on reception remains Yves Congar, "La 'réception' comme réalité ecclésiologique," *Revue des Sciences Philosophiques et Théologiques* 56 (1972):369–403.

[18]*Letters and Diaries*, 25, p. 165.

never sustained itself. The bishops of the minority party, either individually or in regional synods, came to accept the decree and promulgate it in their dioceses.[19] As the opposition to the decree melted away, the decree was assuming conciliar force in Newman's mind. This feature might be called the first phase of *securus judicat orbis terrarum*, its judgmental moment. The wider church is not a judge of papal or conciliar teachings in that strictly Gallican sense which makes the local or universal church the arbiter of any teaching; rather, ecclesial reception by the community is an active and thoughtful process of *conspiratio*—Newman's term—between the magisterium and the laity. Seen in this view of acting together in a deeper spiritual unity, the laity's contribution is somewhat judgmental; it is not simply automatic obedience to the *dictum* of authority.

The second phase of *securus judicat* is an interpretative moment, and it represents the radicalness of Newman's thinking, radical in the sense of how a teaching operates deeply within the soul of the faithful, and radical in Newman's utterly serious valuation of the faithful themselves. The secure judgment of the whole church is both a reception of a teaching and simultaneously an interpretation of it. The wider church assimilates a teaching by *understanding* it. What Bernard Lonergan calls *integrated knowing* as opposed to a "taking a look" theory of knowledge is intended here.[20] To teach that God is love is to invite understandings of it, insights into it, and in this sense the teaching is received and embraced by those being taught it.

Wanting to maintain that a true teaching will be received and that it will be correctly understood in its essential ramifications, Newman attributes an active power to the mind of the community. Although he calls the process "passive infallibility" under what I think is his wish to avoid unnecessary trouble, *passive* is misleading because it suggests total determination from without.[21] Reception of a teaching and the rightful understanding of it are surely active powers of the whole community in the very way that an "instinct for the truth" is

---

[19]Cuthbert Butler, *The Vatican Council: 1869–1870* (London: Collins, 1962), pp. 417–38, provides a moving account of this period and its struggles of conscience.

[20]Taking a look is "elementary extroversion," a knowing people share with animals. But fully human knowing is a dynamic pattern of experiencing, inquiring, reflecting, and judging. See B. Lonergan, *Insight* (New York: Harper and Row, 1978), pp. 372, 415–16, 425, 582–83, 635.

[21]Newman uses the distinction active/passive infallibility, itself already a classical distinction. He does not want to confuse ecclesial reception with the teaching office. The magisterium remains the active teacher, the possessor of active infallibility.

an active effect of baptismal grace. There are no words, ever so clear, Newman says, that do not require some interpretation of them. The Gospel teaches that God is love, but suppose some few persons conclude that there is no future punishment for the wicked. "Some power then is needed to determine the general sense of authoritative words—to determine their direction, drift, limits, and comprehension, to hinder gross perversions. This power is virtually the *passive infallibility* of the whole body of the Catholic people. . . . Hence the maxim 'Securus judicat.' "[22]

Sensus fidelium and *consensus fidelium* represent coming full circle on how the authentic teaching process works, where the starting point and ending point for Newman are the baptized faithful. The magisterium's role is to teach, that is to say, to put Christian faith into the form of words. The teaching must come from somewhere, and it can only be from the living faith of a community. Even the Scriptures, normative though they be, are but the living faith expressions of the first community. From the uneasy fact of the fourth century Newman retrieved the 'sense of the faithful' as a most important entry for church teachers into this living faith. Formulating Christian truth into language never expresses perfectly the content of belief, as language carries inherent ambiguities. Language, however, if rightly chosen, can express adequately the content of faith, but the adequacy always involves the dialectical relationship between what is being said and those who are invited to understand it. It is, after all, some aspect of their faith that is being put into the form of words. The magisterium then addresses the teaching back to the very soil in which the faith lives, the community of the faithful. This teaching, if it truly captures the faith imperfectly yet adequately, is received by the wider church, which in assimilating it, understands it in the way it needs to be understood. One has come full circle.[23]

This dialectical movement occurs at the level of grace, and the process can be described in terms of the original unity of revealed truth that is the Holy Spirit. It is helpful to recall an example when rejection of a teaching occurred, when, in other words, the original

---

[22]*Letters and Diaries*, 27, pp. 337–38.

[23]David Tracy approaches the dialectical relationship of which I speak in terms of *conversation*. "We converse with one another. We can also converse with texts [doctrines in my sense]. . . . Just as there is no purely autonomous text, so too there is no purely passive reader. There is only that interaction named conversation." *Plurality and Ambiguity* (San Francisco: Harper & Row, 1987), p. 19.

unity of the spirit was inadequately (and even falsely) expressed. The wider church came to eventually reject the Gospel of Thomas, though that text was authoritatively professed in certain portions of the early church; this, too, is an uneasy fact and underlines the importance of the judgmental and interpretative moments in Newman's *securus judicat* that is exercised by the wider church, the *orbis terrarum*. It must be said again that Newman does not intend the Gallican notion of a separate act of ratification by the wider church subsequent to a promulgation from the magisterium. That would rupture the unity within the dialectical process. In my opinion Newman means the assimilative process that is simultaneously a process of understanding. The translation I would offer for *securus judicat orbis terrarum* that captures Newman's non-Gallican intention is, "the teaching ends up being understood correctly." One may call it a passive infallibility to avoid confusion with the active infallibility attributed to magisterium. Nevertheless, it is an active instinct for the truth of the Gospel, and for Newman it belongs to the whole church: clerics and laity, men and women, married and celibate, the rich and the poor, and, though Newman does not mention it, maybe especially the latter, God's *anawim* when one considers the teachings of Jesus in Matthew's gospel.

The Historical Context of Sensus Fidelium

Newman did not make use of *sensus fidelium* in a vacuum. The reality existed in the Church long before the term was coined. Although already in use, it is important to understand how Newman might have come to the term. Let us briefly consider the reality and the term itself.

In the New Testament the knowledge of the faithful is described as a discernment of God's revelation. The faithful recognize Christ's voice (Jn. 10:4). They are able to distinguish between Christ and antichrist (1 Jn. 2:18–27). In Pauline thought the faithful interpret spiritual matters (1 Cor. 2:10–16). In the liturgical texts of the early centuries, especially those dealing with sacraments of initiation, Christians are anointed and thereby made prophets (Didascalia, c.9). Such anointed ones can even scrutinize the teachings of their appointed shepherds! "On those who have a right faith, the Holy Spirit bestows the perfect grace of knowing how those who are at the head of the Church must teach and safeguard all things."[24] Yves Congar

---

[24]Hippolytus, *Apostolic Tradition*, chap. 1.

has collected the testimony of the third and fourth century theologians concerning the "faith of the universal ecclesial community."[25]

Various terminologies have been employed to service this fundamental reality of Christian ecclesial life.[26] *Sensus fidelium, sensus ecclesiae, sensus fidei,* etc., are terms belonging to different moments of Church history, but all of them have a common thread: the personal dimension of faith relates to the community's faith and supports its indefectibility. In the analysis developed by the scholastics of the Middle Ages, personal faith is depicted as having an instinctive ability to adhere to its proper objects (God and God's revelation).[27] If the ecclesial context was more assumed than developed in the High Middle Ages, certain theologians of the second half of the Sixteenth Century applied the "sense of the faithful" to its fuller ecclesial extent. It became, for someone like Melchior Cano and his school, a witness to revelation and thereby a "locus theologicus," that is, a kind of "instrument" for working out theological insights, especially under the aspect of their warrants. At this stage, *sensus fidelium* enters the theological vocabulary as a working term.

The term will come to Newman by way of Giovanni Perrone (1794–1876), a Jesuit professor in the Roman College. One must note, however, that Perrone had been influenced himself by Johann Adam Möhler. Against an excessive stress on the role of the hierarchy in the post-Tridentine ecclesiologies, Möhler emphasized the pneumatological aspect of the Church in his *Die Einheit der Kirche,* arguing that the community created by the Spirit precedes authoritative structures. His later thinking, especially in *Symbolik,* was more incarnational and sought the working unity between authoritative structures and the faith of the community, but he remained committed to the notion that the community as a whole (laity and bishops) were the guardians of the faith.[28] Möhler's developed thought in *Symbolik* exercised a direct influence on Perrone.

In considering Newman and the term *sensus fidelium,* an imme-

---

[25]Y. Congar, *Lay People in the Church* (Westminster, MD: Newman Press, 1967), Appendix 2. Congar faults the Reformers for elevating the personal witness of Christians into an ecclesiastical structure and setting church authority under the judgment of the laity. See p. 279.

[26]See M. Seckler, "Glaubenssinn," *Lexicon für Theologie und Kirche* (Frieburg: Herder, 1960) vol. 4, pp. 945–48.

[27]See especially Aquinas, *Summa Theologiae,* II-II, q. 1, article 1 and 3.

[28]For the teachings of Möhler and his influence on the Roman theologians, see Y. Congar, *L'Eglise de s.Augustin à l'époque moderne* (Paris: Cerf, 1970), pp. 417–34. See also the important work by W. Kasper, *Die Lehre von der Tradition in der Römischen Schule* (Freiburg, 1962).

diate distinction must be made. From his study of the early Church and especially of the Arian controversy, Newman was already aware as an Anglican of the role the laity played in doctrinal matters. What was lacking to him was an explanation of a difficulty he had sensed in accounting for certain doctrines taught by the Church. In Newman's 1837 *Lectures on the Prophetical Office* he used Vincent of Lerin's rule that doctrines should be based on what was taught "everywhere and by everyone," but he knew that certain doctrines of the later Church lacked such pervasive warrants. It was Perrone who introduced to Newman a way of seeing the testimony of the laity as an "instrument" of revealed tradition when other sources were unclear.

Newman met Perrone while Newman was studying in Rome in 1847. Newman had recently published his *Essay on Development*, and he wished Perrone's support for the Essay's main contentions. For Perrone's better comprehension, Newman outlined his position in a Latin document.[29] Richard Penaskovic has argued, quite persuasively, that this Newman-Perrone Paper has been overlooked by scholars, yet it provides the link between Newman's 1845 *Essay* and his 1859 *Rambler* article.[30] Perrone's influence, formed through the many conversations the two men had, can be detected in Newman's Latin exposition, and central to my point is Perrone's decisive influence on the question of the laity's witness to the faith. From Perrone, who himself took it from Möhler, Newman was led to see that the silence of "authorities" (e.g., synods, doctors of the Church) about a particular doctrine could be compensated for by the *sensus fidelium*. At this very time Perrone had been working on a book about Mary's Immaculate Conception, and in tracing the historical roots of the doctrine, he stressed the local Marian feasts, liturgical texts, and pieties of the laity that honored Mary under this aspect. He argued that this *sensus fidelium* was a legitimate expression of the doctrine's centuries-long rootedness.[31] Newman, however, does far more with this notion than Perrone would countenance. For Perrone, the laity witness by being exact reflections of what they were taught by their bishops, whereas Newman envisions their

---

[29]This treatise, "De catholici dogmatis evolutione," was published in *Gregorianum* 16 (1935): 404–444.

[30]R. Penaskovic, "Open to the Spirit: The Notion of the Laity in the Writings of J. H. Newman," Ludwig-Maximilians Universität, Munich: unpublished dissertation, 1972.

[31]J. Perrone, *De Immaculato V. Mariae Conceptu* (Rome: Marini et Morini, 1847), p. 139.

witness in a less passive fashion. The word of God penetrates the minds and hearts of the Christian community and has a vitality within the laity that is measured not simply by what they had been taught but by what they understand their faith to mean. This more active understanding of *sensus fidelium* will enable Newman, in the later *Rambler* article, to envision the laity as champions of orthodoxy in the face of Arian teachings by their bishops.

In the *Rambler* article Newman calls upon Perrone's recognized authority in defending himself against the charge that he is placing too much stock in the laity's role.[32] Newman falls back on the tradition that Perrone had used in the latter's book on the Immaculate Conception. Newman also makes reference to Möhler as justification for saying that the laity are possessed of an instinct (*phronema*) that enables the laity to discern religious truth from error. It is likely, however, that Newman did not know Möhler's *Symbolik* directly but rather knew the text through Perrone.[33]

The distinction that governed this excursion into the historical roots of the term *sensus fidelium* bears repetition lest an important point be lost. Newman's appreciation of the laity's role in doctrinal matters came from his own study of Church history. It was not a borrowed idea. What he took from Perrone, and from the tradition to which Perrone's book introduced him, was a theological warrant which enabled Newman to attribute to the laity's "sense of the faith" (*sensus fidei, sensus ecclesiae*) a level of theological authority that could function when other "authorities" were lacking.

Applications to a Contemporary Problematic

I began with the example of contraception, and I wish to end with a few proposals about it, informed from the observations above. To formulate teaching about Christian family life and especially sexual relationship in it ought, if anything ought, to invite "consulting the faithful" in that area. This does not imply that unmarried persons cannot teach about marriage any more than it implies that Jesus could not teach about marriage. It simply implies that Christian married persons have a great deal of personal experience, and within that experience are "instincts for the faith" as it pertains to their

---

[32]Coulson, p. 65 ff. See also Newman's letter to Gillow, *Letters and Diaries*, vol. 19, pp. 135–36.

[33]See Coulson, p. 74, and Perrone, p. 142. Newman's 1859 correspondence listed many supports for his contentions; nowhere is Möhler mentioned.

sexual experience. There were very few laypersons invited to the Vatican committee deliberations which preceded the encyclical *Humanae Vitae*, but significantly they were all signatories to the majority report that was not adopted by Paul VI.[34] Following the encyclical, many priest confessors were wizened and humbled by the struggles conscientious married Catholics had with the teaching. It is also noteworthy that the presbyterium in direct contact with the voices of the laity had much more pliant viewpoints on the encyclical's prohibition against contraception than did the episcopate. All this is another set of those uneasy facts.

The encyclical has been promulgated and its teaching reiterated frequently by the Vatican. Has there been an ecclesial reception of the teaching? Let it be understood that much of the encyclical and much of the subsequent teaching is gospel grounded: the valuation of women, the integration of sexuality into the wider marital relationship, the place of children not as an afterthought to marriage nor as a counter-thought but as a central thought, and so forth. But has the absolute prohibition of artificial contraception for each and every conjugal act *been received*? A number of things are clear. Statistical surveys indicate that most American Catholics practice some form of contraception at some time or other. Parish preachers never mention contraception from the pulpit. Most confessions never have that topic mentioned, this according to priests who gather and talk about "trends." Nor is it a topic at pre-marriage Cana conferences. The defense of the teaching does not even seem to be anywhere met in the theological journals. Where, then, is the issue? Whose issue is it? I suspect that some aspects of the teaching on sexuality are being received by the faithful—here I particularly mean the laity—and the aspect on contraceptives is not. Ultimately,the Holy Spirit is handling this matter, for that is what Newman basically intends when he mentions *securus judicat*. The pope needs to reiterate what he in conscience feels impelled to teach. Newman supports that. Whether all aspects of that teaching are returning receptively to the soil from whence the teaching ought to have arisen remains to be seen. Newman supports that too. The laity, in their consciences under God, have the last word, even when confronted by the papal prohi-

---

[34]For the text of the encyclical, the texts of the majority and minority reports, and for the statements of episcopal conferences following the promulgation of the encyclical, see *The Birth Control Debate*, ed. Robert G. Hoyt (Kansas City: National Catholic Reporter, 1968).

bition against artificial contraception. And the ultimate responsibility of personal conscience is more than just Newman's position, although he was even ready to drink a toast to the fundamental truth of that responsibility before toasting the pope's authority.[35]

---

[35]Newman's famous text on toasting conscience first and the Pope afterwards is found at the very end of his chapter on conscience in his *Letter to the Duke of Norfolk*. The letter is printed in *Difficulties of Anglicans*, Uniform Edition (London: Longmans, Green & Co., 1910) vol. 2.

FUNDAMENTALISM IN CURRENT CATHOLIC RELIGIOUS LIFE: GUIDELINES FROM THOMAS MERTON

Thomas McKenna

It is no surprise to anyone that the fundamentalist worldview which has had its progressing impact on the Roman Catholic Church in the years after Vatican II should have made its appearance in the religious orders and congregations which have played so prominent a part in Catholic history.[1] What might come as a revelation, if only a soft one, is that there has been considerable thought given by theologians and sociologists of religious life as to how one might react to the pressures which tend to bring out the fundamentalist response. Even though the explicit category has not been much referred to, various commentators and congregational bodies have worked on strategies to face the harsh cultural shock which so jolted the orders in the last twenty years. Inasmuch as I understand fundamentalism to be one reaction to just such trauma, it is my contention that some of the lessons learned by the congregations might well have value for the rest of the Church. And interestingly enough, a theologian who died shortly after Vatican II and long before fundamentalism became a significant public issue had as keen an insight into the issue as any. Thomas Merton's writings on Cistercian reform draw the general lines of a sound approach.

In this essay, I first describe briefly how fundamentalism as a style of believing has appeared in certain sectors in the religious congre-

---

[1]While there are distinctions of structure and spirit among religious orders, congregations and institutes in the Catholic church, I use the terms interchangeably to refer to their common thread of official recognition in church law as groups giving communal public witness in lifestyle and service to the transcendent dimension of faith.

gations as well as offer some reasons why that is so. Then I introduce Thomas Merton's thought on a similar development in monasticism during the early days of the conciliar reform movement. Finally I draw out some of Merton's generic renewal formulae, mainly through the writings of Gerald Arbuckle, a cultural anthropologist who from within that discipline has published considerably in recent years about the theology and development of religious life.[2] He can expand on Merton but in at least one useful respect also learn from him. Finally, I rejoin the larger issue, how the experience of renewal efforts in the congregations might shed some light on avenues of approach to the fundamentalist challenge in the wider church.

In its most extensive sense, I understand fundamentalism to be a religious style of reaction to convulsions brought on by major shifts in a culture. When cherished symbols which have carried the under-lying patterns of meaning in a given world no longer hold, the self-perceptions, securities, wisdoms, and identities of that universe begin to unravel and a world unease sets in.[3] The more cohesive and self-contained the culture, the more agitation and trauma there is at the break up. Reactions span a whole range, from glee at getting out from under the old, to cries for help from some outside Messiah/expert, to hyper-organization of the infrastructure, to withdrawal, to malaise, to splitting into various monads of private interest, to a militant reaffirmation of the correctness of certain symbols from the preceding age. The fundamentalist response is this last. The method for handling cultural upheaval is first to set into sharp relief and then defend symbols of the previous culture.[4] Among their strata-gems can be found rejection of emerging truth models and herme-neutical approaches, insistence that certain writings have fixed meanings which can be called "literal," and attack upon others within the same fold who have accommodated to modernity.[5]

The upheaval for Catholicism, of course, came at Vatican II whose

---

[2]See Gerald Arbuckle, "Innovation in Religious Life," Human Development 6 (Fall, 1985): 45–49; Strategies for Growth in Religious Life (New York: Alba House, 1987), pp. 1–3; Refounding Religious Congregations: Out of Chaos (New York: Paulist Press, 1988); and "Refounding Religious Community: Roots in the Past, Seeds for the Future;" Origins 18 (September 22, 1988), pp. 231–35.

[3]William Dinges, "Fundamentalism," The New Dictionary of Theology, J. Koman-chak et al., eds. (Wilmington, Delaware: Michael Glazier, 1988), pp. 411–414.

[4]Gerald Grace and Steven Bosso, "The Language of Fundamentalism: A Language of the Past or a Reality of the Future?," Proceedings: The Catholic Theological Society of America 42 (Louisville: Bellarmine College, 1987), pp. 125–128.

[5]William Dinges, "Quo Vadis, Lefebvre?" America 158 (June 11, 1988): 602–606.

new and competing images jostled so many of the foundational myths of the post-Tridentine Church. The wave which crested over the Catholic edifice had all the more impact both because of the height of the anti-modernist wall thrown up at roughly the time when early twentieth-century Protestant groups were scrambling to face modernity, and also because of the remarkable cohesiveness of the Catholic subculture inside that barrier.

If symbols of the Catholic Church as a whole were losing some anchorage at this time, the pivotal myths of the religious congregations were cast even further adrift. For centuries, as an instance, much of the orders' accepted wisdom has been premised on an adversarial stance to the world; i.e., transcending it by distancing from it.[6] The injunctions of the Council to seek out the good in creation, to ally with the seekers of truth outside the cloister, and to go beyond the world by transforming it, were felt even by sympathizers as an about-face. Equally shaking were the reinterpretations of the institutes' originating spirit. Vatican II mandated that each order reappropriate the charism of its founding person. This not only implied that its prevailing birth myth might not square with the historical record, but also invited the religious to step off onto a yet uncharted line of march along which even group identity stood the possibility of being reconfigured.

Little wonder that all the predictable reactions to culture shock should appear. Departures, malaise, disorientation, spiritualities of disengagement, intensive restructuring, "cargo cultism," denial—all of these surfaced and to greater or lesser extents are still with us.[7]

The fundamentalist impulse also made itself felt. Some have taken the road of return to the Golden Age, "golden" referring not to the era of the first generation but to the very stable and prosperous one of the decades before Vatican II.[8] In this so called "reverse nativism,"[9] symbols of that earlier world are assigned unchanging value and adherence to them becomes the litmus test for what is and what is not authentically religious. The previous interpretations of the congregations' founding documents enter reluctantly and even intractably into conversation with newly emergent meanings. There are some who argue that criticisms given by the Vatican Congrega-

---

[6]See Sandra Schneiders, New Wineskins, (New York: Paulist Press, 1986), p. 25.
[7]See G. Arbuckle, Strategies, pp. 15–32.
[8]See Patrick Arnold, "The Rise of Catholic Fundamentalism," America 156 (April 11,1987): 297–302.
[9]G. Arbuckle, Strategies, p. 16.

tion on Religous Life to sections of renewed constitutions of certain orders are in some measure instances of such resistance, even though arising from outside the congregations. Institutes who envisioned governance structures other than a hierarchical chain of command appear to have received the most pointed challenges. In addition, involvement in civil political process for reasons of justice is faulted as extraneous or secondary to the original spirit of the order. Rather than regard commitment to the marginalized as an inner moment of the religious charism, some perceive issues of freedom and equality in society as potentially disruptive of the contemplative project and therefore in the concrete often enough the enemy of the deeper goal of religious life.[10]

Finally, other community members are attacked for diluting the purity of the religious state by their introduction of secular innovations and for throwing over, in their rush for relevancy, that which gave the order its distinctiveness in the church. The contestation between the Leadership Conference of Women Religious and the Institute Perfectae Caritatis over who is to represent American nuns to the Roman authorities is a recent case showing the disparate inner bearings of American religions. Also, some reactions to the Vatican document, *Essential Elements in the Church's Teaching on Religious Life*, pointed out how certain ingredients listed there, especially the items concerning the exercise of authority, represent a pullback to an essentialist approach which attempts to fence in by earlier descriptions something which by its eschatological pedigree is straining to move beyond those definitions.[11]

The result naturally is tension between different factions in the whole religious establishment and breakdown of cohesiveness within many congregations. While the temperature of conflict seems to have moved from the heat of direct confrontation to the cool of pragmatic toleration, the rifts run deep and many groups search for ways to span the gulf between traditional and emerging perspectives.[12]

II

Well over twenty years ago, Thomas Merton sensed the unrest brewing at the edges of monastic life. Especially alert to nascent

---

[10]See Albert DiIanni, "Faith and Justice: A Delicate Balance," *America* 161 (July 15, 1989): 32f.

[11]See Joan Chittister, "Rome and American Religious Life," *America* 156 (November 1, 1986): 257 ff.

[12]See George Aschenbrenner, "Quiet Polarization Endangering the Church," *Human Development* 7 (Fall 1986): 16 ff.

meaning in the mid-century culture and having his hunches borne out by the young entrants to Trappist life with whom he was working, Merton caught the shape of the coming conflict. Many novices were coming to the monastery because they supposed it to be the best place to pursue the monastic vocation. But to their chagrin and Merton's, much of what they met was instead an encrustation of the ancient ideal maintained through righteous adherence to certain forms which were in fact the products of an age much later than the founding one.

He analyzed the building tensions extensively and indeed did not forget to direct some of his most scathing criticism at what he saw to be faddist and utopian excesses of the left.[13] But it is to his handling of our myth of the Golden Age that we presently turn. His sense of the issues and his prescriptions for facing them outlast the particular points he addressed in his day.

Those familiar with Merton's writings know the axis of his thought to be the pursuit of the genuine self. The title of Anne Carr's book, *A Search for Wisdom and Spirit: Thomas Merton's Theology of the Self*,[14] well captures this unrelenting quest for that mystical juncture at which his own best self meets its ground in the selfhood of God. In his arresting imagery: "If we enter into ourselves, find our own true self and then pass beyond the inner 'I,' we sail forth into the immense darkness in which we confront the 'I Am' of the Almighty."[15]

But what concerns our topic is the way in which this spiritual pursuit gradually validated Merton's choice to be a monk. He became convinced of the rightness of his calling as he steadily realized that his highly personal journey was cousin to that of the founders of monasticism. The more his own inner quest took hold of him, the more he came to know theirs. And the more he read of their spiritual experience, the more language he received for his own. Merton's life-journey was a trip back into the sacred spaces and times when his type of religious life first appeared. And when in touch with that originating encounter which he discovered to be his and theirs, he looked out with a critical and relativizing eye on all succeeding

---

[13]See Thomas Merton, "Notes on the Future of Monasticism," *Contemplation in a World of Action* (Garden City, New York: Doubleday, 1965), p. 238. This book will hereafter be referred to as *CWA*.

[14]See Anne Carr, *A Search for Wisdom and Spirit: Thomas Merton's Theology of the Self* (Notre Dame, Indiana: University of Notre Dame Press, 1988).

[15]See Merton, "The Inner Experience," p.11; cited in Carr, p. 44.

forms which that experience had taken in history.[16] This very much included the so-called "accepted spirituality" of the order, in his judgement actually an ideology constructed from forms of the recent era and absolutized into the touchstone for monastic authenticity.

But another of his insights is needed to round out the process. He noticed that his ability to draw near that privileged moment of founding was given through his contact with the contemporary culture.[17] While historical studies had their necessary place, of themselves they could not lead a person into the myth time. Only when joined to the struggle for meaning on the part of real people in the twentieth century could information about the founders reveal what of grace had happened in those third-century Egyptian waste-lands. And did not the process stand to reason since those desert fathers and mothers were seized by the Spirit precisely as they engaged the spiritual issues of their world? The paradigmatic spiritual journey for primitive monasticism, for instance, that of St. Anthony of the desert, was pursued at the extreme edges of civilization. Anthony sensed that society's deeper meaning could no longer be found at its center but only off in those forgotten places where the power of its self-congratulatory justifications did not prevail.

For Merton, the doors of entry to the founding vision were the faith struggles of twentieth-century believers.[18] Those thirsting for justice in a racist and militaristic society and those lining up with the poor in a materialistic world were among the special ones who caught his attention as modern purveyors of the ancient insights. To write off the bulk of the culture by standing behind the fiercely defended structures of an earlier one led only to illusion. On the contrary, only by sympathetic interchange with the future-oriented groups in society—in Merton's designation, those anonymous monks in the world, the monastery's natural allies—could the monk gain access to the spiritual force of the founders.[19]

And thus Merton's renewal formula: proceed with one foot in the authentic tradition of the order and the other in the stream of modern North American culture. Standing in both streams simultaneously, catch the relativity of any historic form as well as the suitability of any proposed form to carry the primal impulse. Even though difficult because more ambiguous than following only one of

---

[16]See Merton, CWA, p. 28.
[17]See Merton, "Marxism and Monastic Perspectives," CWA, p. 327.
[18]See Merton, CWA, p. 261.
[19]Ibid., p. 13.

the paths, this approach disallows absolutizing any practice or behavior whether past or present.[20] More to the point, it opens a way beyond polarizations since it points to the common ground out of which all structures spring.

To the extent opposing factions allow themselves to be converted by reimmersion in the saving waters of the originating grace, can they get past the hurt, fear, and anger generated by shifts in symbols. The moment for conversion for the liberal is to be put into communion with the wealth of the past. The transformation of the traditionalist—here read "fundamentalist"—is to glimpse even a little of the wisdom coming from the monastery's partners in the culture. Both contacts are needed to draw near that inner energy which funded the Order throughout all its ages.

III

The move from Thomas Merton, a theologian of monastic life in the 1960s, to Gerald Arbuckle, a cultural anthropologist of the late 1980s, is a surprisingly easy one. With his expertise in the processes by which cultures rise, die and can rise again, Arbuckle sketches out much the same dynamics of religious renewal. When faced with the breakdown of its meanings, a society responds with the whole range of reactions noted above: i.e., denial, anomie, privatism, structural rigidity, etc. For rebirth, a certain rare type must enter the scene. This is the "change agent" or "change master," a cultural angel who performs the heroic task of bridging the gap between the best of the past and the promises of the future.[21] He or she spearheads the only kind of change which is lasting for group identity, that which reinculturates the vision which gave rise to the group in the first place. In religious life, the gifts of this individual are to have relived personally the founding myth and to have discerned insertion points for that vision in the current social fabric.[22] This is the refounding person, the one who has reentered the timeless experience of the first generation and while standing there has, with a stubborn faith, devised and implemented socially relevant expressions for its release.[23] The Hebrew prophets are Arbuckle's paradigm personalities. Touched as they were by the living remembrance of

---

[20]See Jean LeClerc, "Introduction," CWA, p. 12.
[21]See Arbuckle, "Innovation in Religious Life," pp. 45ff.
[22]See Arbuckle, Out of Chaos, p. 111.
[23]Ibid., p. 28.

God's gracious deeds, they were able to make the connections between the Exodus encounter and their needy present. Religious today who combine a prophetic imagination with a creative touch for initiating new works and discovering new symbols are their successors in the orders. They lead the rest across the alien land between the older securities and the newer openings for unleashing the power of the originating experience.

Central to Arbuckle's process are the different ways in which groups read the chaos swirling around them in cultural change. Like all deep symbols, this key Biblical one of chaos is double edged, evoking feelings of confusion and loss of meaning as well as indeterminacy and potentiality.[24] The change agent is more taken by the glimmers of light in the crises than with the darkness therein. His or her regenerative journey back to the chaotic beginnings has converted the ways in which he or she perceives the new and alien. Transported again to the present, this refounder invites others to see in the midst of the confusion a call to fill up what is lacking of God in society.[25] The nothingness and rootlessness which struck terror before are now felt as opportunity and even vocation. In sum, the essential conversion is away from fear of the culture to service of it. And Arbuckle thinks this service to be envisioning new strategies to fill in the valleys between the gospel and modern society.[26]

While Arbuckle is more detailed than Merton in his analysis of response to cultural crisis, the main direction is similar—save in one respect. Both counsel return to the founding encounter and both prescribe that saving experience as the only base from which to engage culture in a non-polarizing manner. But Merton is more insistent that solidarity with eschatological elements in the wider world is the high road back to the constitutive period. To be sure, Arbuckle does not deny this, but his thrust is ministry to the places which the founding vision has revealed as godless. Merton concurs, but goes the extra step of bonding with the contemporary mediators of the originating impulse. The class of "unpropertied intellectuals,"[27] people in faith crises, the riders of human transcendence everywhere[28]—they are the pathfinders who can act as guides to the wellspring.

---

[24]Ibid., p. 62.
[25]Ibid., p. 111.
[26]Ibid., p. 87.
[27]See Merton, CWA, p. 235 ff.
[28]Ibid., p. 200.

Both Merton and Arbuckle, in a qualified sense, are "culture friendly." Their basic desire is to engage the ethos and not retreat from it. At the same time they hardly regard all of it with an approving uncritical eye. Arbuckle leans toward bringing the primordial spirituality of the orders to the broken places in the world. Merton would select out the future-oriented groups in the culture and pay special attention to what of God's inbreaking they are proclaiming to the monastery.

Each in his own way calls for a twofold conversion in the congregations: first to interpret cultural upheaval as call, and second to search for signs of the best of their traditions in the midst of the "brave new world." Together they suggest that the fundamentalist challenge can best be met by an invitation to go beneath any particular historical form to that divine vitality which suffuses all the forms, past and future. Arbuckle would personify that invitation in the refounding change agent; Merton would enlarge it, asking the fundamentalist to let down his or her guard ever so slightly in order to recognize the Lord coming in the guise of some of the strangers who inhabit the culture.

Conclusion

Possiblities for strategies in the wider church are apparent. To the extent that the church holds open a way into the "sacred times," into the felt memory of the Lord Jesus Christ, it can hope to contextualize the structures and symbols onto which the fundamentalist so firmly holds. Only such a spiritual experience allows a person to know the difference between the expressions of a life and the life itself, granting that some expression or other is always needed. Catching this difference, one lessens the fear of letting go one set of rules for another. Disrupting parties are also less prone to move to exclusionary positions because they are more immediately aware of the common ground on which each one stands. And if a final step could be made of celebrating the presence of the God one pursues as living in the midst of the enemy camp, unease with what seems alien in the age diminishes still more.

Such lessons are learned when standing simultaneously in the two streams of founding event and emerging culture. It is only when both nourish the individual or the group that ideological adherence to either past or present is overcome. For the past is only accessible through the present and yet the present loses its depth when not anchored in the primitive vision. More to the point for these present reflections, such a strategy within the religious orders speaks intrinsically to the issues raised by the fundamentalist challenge.

Immersed in the first stream, the church gives its witness from a fuller and more fleshed out experience of the Spirit. Testimony of this kind shows itself both in a tenacious hold on Christian identity and in a certain unpredictableness in the church's reaction to its age. This community is not easily labeled as either for or against the culture because its disputes with society revolve around the deeper non-negotiables of discipleship and not simply the differences with the preceding age. It will be counter-cultural but only for foundational reasons. Even though its range of issues is more select than the fundamentalist agenda, its willingness to do battle on these fewer fronts undercuts accusations that the church is selling its inheritance for the tainted blessing of relevance.

In a more positive vein, an ecclesial body which struggles to reappropriate the content of its witness is inherently sympathetic to the intent to preserve the fundamentals. Following the lead of faith, this group is less liable to write off fundamentalist believers simply as reactionaries, empty of Gospel conviction. Hard-won contact with the Lord of the early church fosters such a dialogical style.

Wading in the second stream, the meanings being born in the present age, the church can pursue a complementary strategy. It acknowledges that the cultural elements being introduced and especially the rate of their introduction have disturbed the equilibrium of believers, many to the point of trauma. It recognizes that at least in part, the fundamentalist agenda springs from this type of mistrust which severely pinches the possibilities for seeing good in the wider society.

Paralleling the religious strategy, the church would strive to brighten these darker perceptions by searching out the revelations in the present age. It would consider the potentials more than the dead ends in society, have a sharper eye for inculturations rather than distortions of the Gospel, and in general would tend to give benefit of the doubt to the new. Such a tactic encourages alliances with the anonymous bearers of the Kingdom. Clearly identifying distrust of the culture as the rawest and more damaged nerve, it nonetheless prescribes an immediate (though selective) contact with the present ethos as the only access to the healing powers incarnated within it.

The challenge for the church is to embody the advantages of being not so much culture-friendly as culture-hopeful. For it to look upon social upheaval as the time in the desert, a threatening wilderness indeed but more so the enticing dwelling place of the divine lover, is to grapple with the underlying reason for the fundamentalist move. *Mutatis mutandis*, some renewal strategists in the religious orders such as Thomas Merton and Gerald Arbuckle can help point the way.

"LEAVE OUT THE POETRY"
REFLECTIONS ON THE TEACHING OF SCRIPTURE

J. P. M. Walsh, S.J.

An elderly parishioner, talking with the parish priest about "all the changes in the Church," gave lengthy expression to confusion and dismay, and ended the lament by saying, "Father, I know you say the Holy Spirit is behind all these changes. And I believe that. It's just that . . . well, I don't think the Holy Ghost would approve."

Since I am a teacher of Scripture and of college freshmen, it is fitting, I think, that I use a narrative method in discussing fundamentalism and the Catholic church. I have some stories and some reflections on them—and a text to end with.

The first story comes from a discussion some theology majors at Georgetown University had with faculty members several years back. One particularly perceptive student observed that, although we all lay great importance on the ability to enter generously and with sympathetic imagination into different religious traditions—trying to give an authentic account of the experience of Hindus or Buddhists or Muslims, reading their scriptures as if from within the tradition—"There is one tradition," he said, "that you can't and won't 'enter into' in the same way: Fundamentalism."

We had to allow that that was so. Why is that so? I have no clarity on the question, but I do sense that the "Thou art the man" principle can be helpful in answering it. What is our reaction to fundamentalism? Harsh scorn, exasperation, eye-rolling. It is a good rule of thumb, of course, that when we react to others so sharply and negatively, it is a way of denying within ourselves something that is there, or that we fear is there, and that we don't want to face. I will be suggesting that in fact the adherence to "modernity" that enables us to refute the presuppositions and interpretive procedures of fundamentalism is of a piece, historically and epistemologically, with fundamentalism itself. Precisely because we are children of the modern era, there is something of the fundamentalist within each of us.

Some more stories first, though, to help make the argument clearer.

In April of 1968 I was visiting a Jesuit seminary, and watched the funeral of Martin Luther King on television with the Jesuits there. The first reading at the service was taken from Wisdom 2, the speech of the wicked who persecute the just man. It included the following lines:

> Let us lie in wait for the righteous man,
> because he is inconvenient to us
>   and opposes our actions; . . .
> He professes to have knowledge of God,
> and calls himself a child of the Lord. . . .
> Let us see if his words are true,
> and let us test what will happen at
>   the end of his life;
> for if the just man is God's son,
>   he will help him,
> and will deliver him from the hand
>   of his adversaries.
>   (Wisdom 2:12a-13, 17–18 RSV)

One of the Fathers expressed bemusement that this reading was used in the funeral service: "Why are they reading that for *that* fellow? That's about Our *Lord!*"

It would have been a simple matter to explain that in fact the passage was "about" the generalized figure of the just one whose life the wicked seek; that it dates from (probably) a generation before the crucifixion; that Matthew (27:40, 43) applies the text to Jesus on the cross; and that the persons who selected it for use at Doctor King's funeral were making yet another application of it, one consonant with the dynamic of violence and persecution the text sets forth. I did not presume to explain all this, but I noted the instinctive reaction of my Jesuit brother: Wisdom 2 is about Jesus.

A second story. A colleague told me of a classroom exchange on the poem "Simon the Cyrenian Speaks," by Countee Cullen (1903–1946). Cullen, a poet of the Harlem Renaissance, has Simon tell the story of being made to carry the cross of Jesus. Simon at first refuses to let the cross be placed on his back: "He only seeks to place it there / Because my skin is black." Gradually Simon accepts the burden because of what he sees in Jesus. The beginning of this transformation comes in Simon's words, "But He was dying for a dream."

A student seized on these words, "dying for a dream." This is a poem about Martin Luther King, he said: there it is, "dying for a dream." My colleague was consoled that the student was acquainted with the life and words of Doctor King, but dismayed at the connection the student was making in disregard of the plain meaning of the text. Obviously, the poem reflects the passage in Matt 27:32 (Mark 15:21; Luke 23:26); Cyrene is in North Africa, so Cullen makes Simon a black man, and imagines Simon's experience in order to comment on the black (Cullen would have said "Negro") experience in this country nineteen centuries later. And in the poem, the one who "was dying for a dream" was Jesus, not Simon. In any case, when Countee Cullen died, Martin Luther King was only seventeen years old—and that was nine years before Rosa Parks, the Montgomery bus boycott, and the beginnings of the Civil Rights movement. These exegetical observations made no matter: the student was adamant. The poem was about a man who died for "a dream." It was about Martin Luther King.

Notice that these two stories are, in effect, one. A piece of writing, with its own history and integrity, is heard as applicable to someone; an identification is made; the poem is "about" that other person. The fact that that other person is someone the author did not have, and could not have had, in view is beside the point. The intent of the author, and the historical setting or settings the words envision, is simply ignored. What is primary is that the words remind the listener of something, and that something becomes their meaning.

The last example comes from a piece in a right-wing Catholic newspaper some years ago. In seeking to refute the historical assertion that auricular confession, as a form of the sacrament of penance, emerged only towards the end of the first millennium A.D., the article claimed to find the practice recorded in the Old Testament. The story in Joshua 7 tells how the hapless Achan, having violated the law of herem, is discovered and (in v. 19) urged "My son, give glory to the Lord, the God of Israel, and make confession." There it is: "confession!" Of course, it is the Hebrew term tôdah that is in question, and the word does indeed mean confession, but in its root sense of declaration or profession; it can also be translated "thanksgiving" or "praise." In Josh 7:19 *tôdah* is used in parallelism with *kabôh*, "glory." Even if we allow that the word in its context of wrongdoing and admission of guilt has the nuance of "confession" in the narrow (modern) sense, the argument that Joshua's exhortation to Achan reflects the practice of what we call auricular confession is based on a purely equivocal usage. The word reminded someone of something, and that something comes to be the meaning of the word.

What is going on in these cases? We are dealing with interpretation that is uncritical of itself and indifferent to what might be the intention of the author. Meaning is what pops into the listener's mind, based on how the listener understands words and usages in his or her own cultural and historical and experiential context. The listener does not consider that another meaning is possible. Neither, of course, does the listener envision the possibility that the meaning he or she takes from the words—what pops into the mind—might be different from what the speaker or author means by them.

We might understand this phenomenon as a failure or incapacity of imagination. One hears words and seizes on what they remind him or her of. There is no interest in trying to take them any other way. The listener or reader is locked into a certain world of discourse, with its associations and usages. In effect one is locked into one's own world. One cannot leave it, to enter another world—even the world of discourse from which, or in terms of which, the writer or speaker is in fact trying to communicate. One is incapable of imagining, not only another way of taking the words, but even the possibility that there might be another way of taking them. One is wholly occupied with one's own "agenda": what I am now hearing *must* be aimed at my preoccupations and questions and experience. The speaker *must* be addressing herself to me as I am, in terms of what I know and how I use words.

In practice, of course, all this is unthematized. I am trying to articulate the kind of self-understanding and way of imagining reality that underlie what we call fundamentalism. I am also describing the way I often deal with people (ask my friends). When I miss the point, or grow restless and distracted when someone is talking, that involves a failure of imagination, an inability to enter into *their* experience, on *their* terms.

The best example I know of this way of reading or hearing—making words or text or discourse fit one's own procrustean agenda—comes in a story Anais Nin tells in her diary.[1] She had

---

[1] *The Diary of Anais Nin 1939–1944*, ed. Gunther Stuhlmann (New York: Harcourt, Brace & World, 1969), p. 58.

undertaken to produce "erotica a dollar a page" for the delectation of a wealthy client: it was a way of paying for rent and groceries. But since she was a careful writer, with a reverence for language, what she wrote was not without literary merit. She was soon told that that was not what her patron expected. "Today," she wrote in her diary, "I received a telephone call. 'It is fine. But leave out the poetry and descriptions of anything but sex. Concentrate on sex.' "

A failure of imagination indeed. Her client had an agenda, and everything else—nuance, suggestion, image, art—was beside the point. None of all that was what he was paying for. But the failure of imagination, the lack of interest in what can be expressed only by indirection and subtlety, took a specific form. There was an agenda in his agenda, and I want to suggest that it is an agenda that largely defines the epistemology at the heart of what we call modernity. I refer to our culture's bias toward fact as what defines reality and truth, as the only worthy object of mind. At least since the Enlightenment reality has been understood as verifiable fact; knowing is understood as mental correspondence with that fact; language is understood as expressive of that correspondence. An event occurs and an account of that event is true or not depending on whether or not it represents it "as it really happened" (von Ranke's famous phrase has thus been misconstrued).

Examples are not hard to come by. Journalists are disgraced because their reports of complicated human situations are found not to correspond point-by-point to what they are describing; using composite characters and something like poetry (in Nin's patron's usage) they fall victim to the reading public's extreme literal-mindedness. "That's made up! That's not true!" A recent TV series, "The Monocled Mutineer," was attacked in the English press as a " 'great big BBC lie' because many of the shocking incidents it portrays never took place" (as the Washington *Post* [May 4, 1989] reports the outraged criticism of the London *Daily Mail*). TV commercials run the caption SIMULATION, lest anyone think they are seeing the real thing. And "docudramas" are severely criticized, not because they use characterization, background music, camera angles, and other artistic means to tell their story, but because these means of story telling supposedly interfere with rendering a "literal" account of the "true" (or "unvarnished") "facts."

There are signs that this disjunction of fact and poetry—the former real or true, the latter a lie or at best expendable—is being seen through. E. L. Doctorow has said, "There's no fiction or nonfiction now, there's only narrative";[2] but that sort of monism only proves the hold on our imaginations the disjunction has.

My argument so far, then, has been that fundamentalism is one form of something pandemic in, and foundational to, our culture: a certain understanding of reality and truth as a matter of fact, one that makes the mastery of fact the only agenda worth pursuing; and that this agenda shapes a more general failure of imagination, the inability to enter into the world and experience of another—especially when that other speaks from a different culture and/or time— on the other's own terms. The resultant literal-mindedness, cultural blindness, and inflexibility, it seems to me, go a long way towards explaining both the operation of our legal system and the formation and conduct of our foreign policy.

What remedies are there? In teaching Scripture these many years I have worked out a format for the discussion of passages that does an end run around these presuppositions and introduces, or at least makes possible, a certain amount of nuance in the way students think about the biblical stories. I offer it here as being pedagogically helpful and, more especially, serving to lay out the dynamics of biblical—and indeed all—narrative.

I make them draw time lines. On one time line I put the event (the promise to Abraham, for example, or Samuel's warning against monarchy). On another I put the narrative: the story teller and the audience to whom the story was told. Our tendency is to focus on the event. That's not helpful for understanding the text. What is helpful, and interesting, is to study the interaction between the narrative and its audience, in their historical situation, with their questions and preoccupations and experience. The promise to Abraham as recounted to a tenth-century B.C. audience reminded them of David and the traditions of divine election associated with him; that double focus, Abraham as a type of David, is part of the meaning of the story. The two historical situations—that of Abraham and that of the tenth-century audience at the beginning of the Davidic dynasty—come together in the J narrative. Similarly, Samuel's warning against the institution of monarchy (1 Samuel 8), heard through the ears of the audience it was written for, does not give information about the late eleventh-century political situation in Israel. It provides a devastating critique of the way royal power was exercised under Solomon: it itemizes, and presents as rejection of Yahweh, the characteristic features of Solomonic rule.

---

[2]Quoted by Gordon S. Wood, *New York Review of Books*, August 12, 1982, p. 8.

The distinction between the two time lines—the two historical situations that can be distinguished in most biblical narratives—helps students to develop a historical sense. It also instills an awareness that narrative is addressed to a particular audience, and takes its meaning not so much from any correspondence to the event it purports to recount as from the light it sheds on the audience's situation and experience. The audience is brought to re-imagine their own lives and choices, by entering into the lives and choices depicted in the story. I would argue further that, in a real sense, narrative constitutes the event it portrays: that while (of course) events occur, the shape and pacing and intelligibility of the events is a function of the narrative that brings them alive for the hearer; and that that intelligibility is indissolubly linked with the experience and sensibility, the preoccupations and interests of the audience for whom the narrative was originally intended. But now we have gotten into deep and murky epistemological waters I cannot hope to navigate here.

At the end of last semester a student, reviewing for the final exam, expressed puzzlement at my suggestion that what Samuel was deploring was Solomonic rule. "Wasn't Samuel a hundred years before Solomon? So how could he be talking about Solomon?" A golden question: it went to the heart of the method. So in the final I asked some time-line questions, not about biblical material but about the TV show "M*A*S*H." Step one: Place the Korean War on the event time line, and date it 1950–53. Step two: place the series "M*A*S*H" on the narrative time-line, and date that to the late sixties and early seventies. Now discuss what the following statement might mean: "Though 'M*A*S*H' is set in the Korean War it is really about Vietnam." Though the students had no real recollection of Vietnam, they knew enough about that war—and from reruns certainly knew the TV series well enough—to write a plausible answer to the question. Some even threw in Watergate.

The time-line method is merely one way of anatomizing the dynamics of event and narrative, but what I use it to explain is central to biblical scholarship—at least non-fundamentalist scholarship. In coming semesters I will probably begin the course with the "M*A*S*H" example, and others as well. Here is another example (I owe it to my colleague Thomas Pauly of the University of Delaware). Fifty years ago two works appeared that captured the imagination of the American public, *Gone With the Wind* and *The Grapes of Wrath*. Though on the event line separated by seventy or so years, and put in very different settings (Georgia, the Dust Bowl), the movie and the book had the same appeal to their audience. People found in them a reflection or embodiment of their own experience, and a source of hope as well. Both stories showed people's lives crashing down about them, their ordinary world destroyed while they watched and suffered helplessly. After ten years of the Great Depression Americans could relate to these stories. In a real sense, both were about Depression-era America. They helped people come to terms with, name, imagine the disaster they were going through. And they helped people to re-imagine their plight as well, in the characters' ability to pick up the pieces and get on with their lives, whether in Scarlett's "Tomorrow is another day" or in Steinbeck's homilies about the life force and the human spirit.

Another example. Robert Bolt's Thomas More is a existentialist hero whose self-understanding and rationale for his choices would have been abhorrent to the sixteenth-century believer More: the way Bolt's narrative presents the historical character reflects the post-war existentialist *Zeitgeist*. Bolt's purpose is not to give information about Thomas More but to communicate a sense of how we are to give life meaning.

Once we see this interaction between the event and the narrative, and learn to listen with the ears of the audience the narrative is addressing, and see how the event is not so much reflected in narrative as constituted by it, stories (in literature, in movies, in historiography) take on new meaning, and the reader or listener or viewer is brought beyond the impasse of the positivistic obsession with fact, definitive of modernity, that locks us into our own experience and world of discourse. We cease to look for mere information and learn to listen for meaning: the meaning the story had for its audience and—to the extent we can enter into that audience's experience and hear the story through their ears—the meaning it can have for us.

Now the text I promised. On October 26, 1979, Pope John Paul II addressed the International Theological Commission. Here is my translation of part of his address (*AAS* 71 [1979] 1430–1431).

The christological faith that, under the lead and with the confirmation of grace, the universal Church professes relies on the experience of Peter and the other Apostles, as well as the Lord's disciples, who were in Jesus' company [qui cum Iesu conversati sunt], who "looked upon" and whose "hands handled of the Word of Life" [cf. 1 John 1:1]. What is this way they had experienced, thereafter, in the light of the Cross and Resurrection, as well from the movement of the Holy Spirit, they interpreted. From this there arose that first "synthesis" that appears in the confessions and hymns of the apostolic letters. Thereafter, in the course of time, the Church, continually calling herself back to these testimonies and experiencing them in her life, expressed her faith in words ever more precise [verbis semper accuratioribus], in the articles of the great councils.

You as theologians of this Commission have bent to the study of these councils—in a special way the councils of Nicaea and Chalcedon. For the formulas of these universal synods have lasting force [vim habent permanentem]; not, indeed, that one should leave out of account historical circumstances [adiuncta historica] and the questions that were posed in those times in the Church, [the questions] to which she [the Church] by conciliar definitions responded. In fact however the questions put forward today are connected with the questions of earlier centuries, and the solutions suitable then are carried forward into new responses [in novas responsiones ingeruntur]; indeed the responses of today presuppose always in a certain way what Tradition has pronounced [enuntiata Traditionis], although they [today's answers] cannot in every respect be reduced to those things [what Tradition has pronounced]. This lasting force of dogmatic formulas is the more easily explained because they are expressed in common words used in ordinary life [verbis communibus, quae in vitae usu et consuetudine adhibentur edictae sunt], even though sometimes expressions [locutiones] occur that are specifically philosophical. It does not thereby follow that the Magisterium has adhered to any particular school, since the same expressions [locutiones] signify only what is found in all human experience.

You have also investigated how these formulas can be brought back [referantur] to the revelation of the New Testament, as the Church understands this.

This long quotation has many interesting features. I mention two. Notice the description of the process by which the New Testament writings came into being: the experience of Peter, the Apostles, the disciples was interpreted, and that inspired post-Easter interpretation came to expression in confessions and liturgical materials, and these materials (presumably the Pope is thinking of oral materials) took written form, eventually to be included in the writings we call the New Testament. That is, the events of the New Testament writings are a matter of experience interpreted and expressed by and for the early Christian community. The Holy Father has drawn both time lines.

The second point is that, in giving an account of the development of dogma, the Pope's address depicts the process as continuous with the way the New Testament writings emerged, and in doing so draws a necessary hermeneutical conclusion: conciliar statements must be understood in the context of the historical circumstances and questions they were meant to address. To put it in terms accessible to freshmen: don't just take the words as they stand and make them mean whatever comes into your mind; enter into the world and experience of the people who asked these questions, and understand the conciliar answers in terms of what they meant to *them*, back *then*. Look to the narrative time line, not just the words. Don't "leave out the poetry."

It has been observed that Catholics have not always avoided fundamentalism, but it is our own kind of fundamentalism, one that is operative not so much in reading the Bible as in reading pronouncements of councils and popes. It might be called "dogmatic fundamentalism": it comes into play in the area of dogma, that is, in construing dogmatic formulas. Pope John Paul's statement, it seems to me, offers a valuable and authentic way to counteract the influence of this fundamentalism. Together with the similar remarks of Pope Paul VI in *Mysterium ecclesiae* (*AAS* 65 [1973] 116–117), John Paul's 1979 teaching on hermeneutics presents us with an instrument that can allow a dialogue to begin with our fundamentalist brothers and sisters—and even with the fundamentalist that lurks within the psyche of each of us. I think the Holy Ghost would approve.

APPENDIX I

A Pastoral Statement for Catholics on Biblical Fundamentalism

This is a statement of concern to our Catholic brothers and sisters who may be attracted to Biblical Fundamentalism without realizing its serious weaknesses. We Catholic bishops, speaking as a special committee of the National Conference of Catholic Bishops, desire to remind our faithful of the fullness of Christianity that God has provided in the Catholic Church.

Fundamentalism indicates a person's general approach to life which is typified by unyielding adherence to rigid doctrinal and ideological positions—an approach that affects the individual's social and political attitudes as well as religious ones. Fundamentalism in this sense is found in non-Christian religions and can be doctrinal as well as biblical. But in this statement we are speaking only of Biblical Fundamentalism, presently attractive to some Christians, including some Catholics.

Biblical Fundamentalists are those who present the Bible, God's inspired Word, as the only necessary source for teaching about Christ and Christian living. This insistence on the teaching Bible is usually accompanied by a spirit that is warm, friendly and pious. Such a spirit attracts many (especially idealistic young) converts. With ecumenical respect for these communities, we acknowledge their proper emphasis on religion as influencing family life and workplace. The immediate attractions are the ardor of the Christian community and the promises of certitude and of a personal conversion experience to the person of Jesus Christ without the need of church. As Catholic pastors, however, we note its presentation of the Bible as a single rule for living. According to Fundamentalism, the Bible alone is sufficient. There is no place for the universal teaching Church—including its wisdom, its teachings, creeds and other doctrinal formulations, its liturgical and devotional traditions. There is simply no claim to a visible, audible, living, teaching authority binding the individual or congregations.

A further characteristic of Biblical Fundamentalism is that it tends to interpret the Bible as being always without error, or as literally true, in a way quite different from the Catholic Church's teaching on the inerrancy of the Bible. For some Biblical Fundamentalists, inerrancy extends even to scientific and historical matters. The Bible is presented without regard for its historical context and development.

In 1943 Pope Pius XII encouraged the Church to promote biblical study and renewal, making use of textual criticism. The Catholic Church continued to study the Bible as a valuable guide for Christian living. In 1965 the Second Vatican Council, in its *Constitution on Divine Revelation*, gave specific teaching on the Bible. Catholics are taught to see the Bible as God's book—and also as a collection of books, written under divine inspiration by many human beings. The Bible is true—and to discover its inspired truth we should study the patterns of thinking and writing used in ancient biblical times. With Vatican II we believe that "the books of Scripture must be acknowledged as teaching firmly, faithfully and without error that truth which God wanted put into the sacred writings for the sake of our salvation" (*Constitution on Divine Revelation*, no. 11). We do not look upon the Bible as an authority for science or history. We see truth in the Bible as not to be reduced solely to literal truth, but also to include salvation truths expressed in varied literary forms.

We observed in Biblical Fundamentalism an effort to try to find in the Bible all the direct answers for living—though the Bible itself nowhere claims such authority. The appeal of such an approach is understandable. Our world is one of war, violence, dishonesty, personal and sexual irresponsibility. It is a world in which people are frightened by the power of the nuclear bomb and the insanity of the arms race, where the only news seems to be bad news. People of all ages yearn for answers. They look for sure, definite rules for living, and they are given answers—simplistic answers to complex issues—in a confident and enthusiastic way, in Fundamentalist Bible groups.

The appeal is evident for the Catholic young adult or teenager— one whose family background may be troubled; who is struggling with life, morality and religion; whose Catholic education may have been seriously inadequate in the fundamentals of doctrine, the Bible, prayer life and sacramental living; whose catechetical formation may have been inadequate in presenting the full Catholic traditions and teaching authority. For such a person, the appeal of finding *the answer* in a devout, studious, prayerful, warm, Bible-quoting class is easy to understand. But the ultimate problem with such Fundamentalism is that it can give only a limited number of answers and cannot present those answers on balance, because it does not have Christ's teaching Church, nor even an understanding of how the Bible originally came to be written and collected in the sacred canon or official list of inspired books.

Our Catholic belief is that we know God's revelation in the total gospel. The gospel comes to us through the Spirit-guided Tradition of the Church and the inspired books: "This sacred Tradition, therefore, and Sacred Scripture of both the Old and New Testament are like a mirror in which the pilgrim Church on earth looks at God" (*Constitution on Divine Revelation*, no. 7).

A key question for any Christian is: Does the community of faith which is the Lord's Church have a living Tradition which presents God's Word across the centuries until the Lord comes again? The Catholic answer to this question is an unqualified "yes." That answer was expressed most recently in the *Constitution on Divine Revelation* of the Second Vatican Council. We look to both the Church's official teaching and Scripture for guidance in addressing life's problems. It is the official teaching or *magisterium* that in a special way guides us in matters of belief and morality that have developed after the last word of Scripture was written. The Church of Christ teaches in the name of Christ and teaches us concerning the Bible itself.

The basic characteristic of Biblical Fundamentalism is that it eliminates from Christianity the Church as the Lord Jesus founded it. That Church is a community of faith, worldwide, with pastoral and teaching authority. This non-church characteristic of Biblical Fundamentalism, which sees the Church as only spiritual, may not at first be clear to some Catholics. From some Fundamentalists they will hear nothing offensive to their beliefs, and much of what they hear seems compatible with Catholic Christianity. The difference is often not in what is said—but in what is not said. There is not mention of the historic, authoritative Church in continuity with Peter and the other apostles. There is no vision of the Church as our mother—a mother who is not just spiritual, but who is visibly ours to teach and guide us in the way of Christ.

Unfortunately, a minority of Fundamentalist churches and sects not only put down the Catholic Church as a "man-made organization" with "man-made rules," but indulge in crude anti-Catholic bigotry with which Catholics have long been familiar.

We believe that no Catholic properly catechized in the faith can long live the Christian life without those elements that are had only in the fullness of Christianity: the Eucharist and the other six sacraments, the celebration of the Word in the liturgical cycle, the veneration of the Blessed Mother and the saints, teaching authority and history linked to Christ and the demanding social doctrine of the Church based on the sacredness of all human life.

It is important for every Catholic to realize that the Church produced the New Testament, not vice-versa. The Bible did not come down from heaven, whole and intact, given by the Holy Spirit. Just as the experience and faith of Israel developed its sacred books, so was the early Christian Church the matrix of the New Testament. The Catholic Church has authoritatively told us which books are inspired by the Holy Spirit and are, therefore, canonical. The Bible, then, is the Church's book. The New Testament did not come before the Church, but from the Church. Peter and the other apostles were given special authority to teach and govern before the New Testament was written. The first generation of Christians had no New Testament at all—but they were the Church then, just as we are the Church today.

A study of the New Testament, in fact, shows that discipleship is to be a community experience with liturgy and headship and demonstrates the importance of belonging to the Church started by Jesus Christ. Christ chose Peter and the other apostles as foundations of his Church, made Simon Peter its rock foundation and gave a teaching authority to Peter and the other apostles. This is most clear in the Gospel of Matthew, the only Gospel to use the word church. The history of twenty Christian centuries confirms our belief that Peter and the other apostles have been succeeded by the Bishop of Rome and the other bishops, and that the flock of Christ still has, under Christ, a universal shepherd.

For historical reasons the Catholic Church in the past did not encourage bible studies as much as she could have. True, printing (the Latin Bible was the first work printed) was not invented until the mid-fifteenth century, and few people were literate during the first sixteen centuries of Christianity. But in the scriptural renewal the Church strongly encourages her sons and daughters to read, study and live the Bible. The proclamation of the Scriptures in the liturgical assembly is to be prepared for by private bible study and prayer. At the present time, two decades after Vatican II, we Catholics have all the tools needed to become Christians who know, love and live the Holy Bible. We have a well-ordered Lectionary that opens for us the treasures of all the books of the Bible in a three-year cycle for Sunday and Holy Day Masses, and a more complete two-year cycle for weekday Masses. Through the Lectionary the Catholic becomes familiar with the Bible according to the rhythm of the liturgical seasons and the Church's experience and use of the Bible at Mass. We have excellent translations (with notes) in The New American Bible and The Jerusalem Bible. We have other accurate translations with an imprimatur. We have an abundance of commentaries, tapes, charts and bible societies.

We Catholics have excellent bible resources and scholars of international repute. Our challenge now is to get this knowledge into the minds, hearts and lives of all our Catholic people. We need a Pastoral Plan for the Word of God that will place the Sacred Scriptures at the heart of the parish and individual life. Pastoral creativity can develop approaches such as weekly bible study groups and yearly bible schools in every parish. We need to have the introduction to each bible reading prepared and presented by the lector in a way that shows familiarity with and love for the sacred text (cf. Foreword to the Lectionary: No. 15, no. 155, no. 313, no. 320). In areas where there is a special problem with Fundamentalism, the pastor may consider a Mass to which people bring their own Bibles, and in which qualified lectors present a carefully prepared introduction and read the text—without, however, making the Liturgy of the Word a bible study class. We need better homilies, since the homily is the most effective way of applying biblical texts to daily living. We need a familiar quoting of the Bible by every catechist, lector and minister. We have not done enough in this area. The neglect of parents in catechetics and the weakness of our adult education efforts are now producing a grim harvest. We need to educate—to reeducate—our people knowingly in the Bible so as to counteract the simplicities of Biblical Fundamentalism.

In addition to that, we Catholics need to redouble our efforts to make our parish Masses an expression of worship in which all—parishioners, visitors and strangers—feel the warmth and the welcome and know that here the Bible is clearly reverenced and preached. The current trend towards smaller faith-sharing and bible-studying groups within a parish family is strongly to be encouraged.

We call for further research on this entire question. We note that the U. S. Center for the Catholic Biblical Apostolate (1312 Massachusetts Avenue, N.W., Washington, D.C. 20005) will maintain an updated listing of available resources for Catholic bible study. Any individual Catholic or parish representative may write to learn the many available helps for developing bible study and bible teaching in accord with our long and rich Catholic tradition.

Ad Hoc Committee on Biblical Fundamentalism

The Most Reverend John F. Whealon
Archbishop of Hartford, Chairman

The Most Reverend Alvaro Corrada del Rio, SJ
Auxiliary Bishop of Washington

The Most Reverend Theodore E. McCarrick
Archbishop of Newark

The Most Reverend Richard J. Sklba
Auxiliary Bishop of Milwaukee

The Most Reverend J. Francis Stafford
Archbishop of Denver

The Most Reverend Donald W. Trautman
Auxiliary Bishop of Buffalo

APPENDIX II

"Toward Your Happiness"
Catholicism and Fundamentalism:
A Contrast
A Pastoral Letter to Catholics in
Mississippi and Alabama*

1. The quest for happiness in human history is a powerful force that touches individuals and, through them, all of society. Our successes and failures in succeeding generations show that happiness cannot be found apart from order and harmony. In a variety of ways order and harmony emerge as natural needs for all people. To live lives in balance with others around us, free from fear and unpredictable change, is the dream and longing of every person. But as we here in Alabama and Mississippi approach a new millennium, all too often we seem to experience anything but calm and stability.

Certain rapid change in so many areas of our lives is a major contributor to these unsettling feelings. We Catholic bishops of Alabama and Mississippi want to take this opportunity to share with you some observations about our times and to offer some historical and faith insights about various movements which have sought to meet the challenge of change. We also desire to reflect with you upon the richness of our Catholic tradition. Finally, we would like to indicate some directions that we believe the church can take to help us move with a vision of hope into the 21st century.

2. Alongside the many wonderful advances in science, technology and medicine in the last century, we must note that there have arisen certain pressures in our nation and world which have adversely affected people. Today's youth tell us that they feel the pressure of

*The letter is printed with the permission of Oscar H. Lipscomb, Archbishop of Mobile. It was issued on June 29, 1989 and signed by Archbishop Lipscomb, Bishops Joseph Howze of Biloxi, William Houck of Jackson, and Raymond Boland of Birmingham.

living under the threat of nuclear holocaust. They can cry, "No more war," but they still must live with the worldwide presence of nuclear weapons poised for destruction. Social and economic upheavals have often come too swiftly for the individual to make some comfortable adjustment. For many, life in general seems so complex that they feel they have lost control. In short, many increasingly sense the absence of a firm anchor of security in their lives.

We see the symptoms of this pressure all about us—a weakening of family life which threatens both personal security and the stability of marriage itself; a growing distrust of, and disrespect for, civil authority; a quest not for lasting fulfillment, but for instant gratification. The effect is to turn us inward, to encourage us to be more selfish and self-centered in "doing our own thing." Even in our ancient and sure anchor of security, the church, many fear an erosion of authority, suspect a watering down of doctrine and detect a weakening of moral resolve. Truth itself seems to have become relative and shifting, leaving not a few to wonder just what is true anymore. There is, in the minds of many, little or no certitude about absolute moral values; we hear this expressed in cliches like, "If I think it's OK, it's OK for me" or "If it feels good, do it." Too many people sense no black and white answers . . . just a vast, frightening sea of gray.

3. This discomfort of feeling adrift brings to the surface a natural religious and political hunger. We want to be part of a nation that is strong and purposeful. We need firm political authority to assure our protection from economic chaos and social violence. We need the clear authority of religion to give us certainty about forgiveness and salvation and God's will. We want to be certain about the truth of Sacred Scripture. Surrounded by a complex and often confusing world we want simple, clear answers even if our problems and questions are difficult. But, as history and personal experience teach us, there are no simple answers to complex problems.

Such lessons even in our own century are well within the memory of many who read these words. Nations after World War I were under pressure to realign. A fragile effort to establish world community could not compete with protectionist nationalism. The economy of the world was shaken by banks collapsing and markets crashing. Depression and insecurity were the hallmarks of the times. Then there rose up a man who offered security as a result of rigid authority, racial purity through genetic manipulation, certitude founded on Teutonic superiority. Thus, Nazism was spawned by

Adolph Hitler. Various terrorist organizations throughout the world have from time to time sought to correct the perceived wrongs of their nation or of the larger globe with one simple method—violence. Even some radical religious movements today, like that which engages the followers of the Ayatollah Khomeini, guarantee salvation by embracing the fanatical demands of their cause leaving no room for questions, doubts or dissent. While somewhat different, all three of these examples share one thing in common—the guarantee that there is a simple and singular solution to complexity, a solution that harkens back to a past and supposedly less complicated age.

For better or for worse, we are privileged to live in one of those complex and important times in human history—a time of great change. As bishops of Alabama and Mississippi, we want to assert that it is not the present time which is bad. It can be an opportunity for good or for evil, but the important thing is how we respond to the times. After all, the same age that produced Khomeini produced Mother Teresa of Calcutta. Similar times have occurred before and undoubtedly will occur again. It is to ensure that we Catholics cooperate in making this a good time, a time of blessing and spiritual opportunity, that we your bishops address a movement which we see as offering a false security to our people—fundamentalism.

4. In order to understand fundamentalism in our day, it is necessary to look back at its beginnings.[1] Around the turn of this century there began a Protestant movement in our country which fostered a return to the real basics of Christianity, a return to the "good old days" when there had been simple and certain answers. This was in large measure a reaction to liberalism, which in part sought to cast off the yoke of rigidly structured scientific theory and religious thought.

In the last century, Charles Darwin had proposed his theory of evolution. While scientific in its scope, the theory seemed to religious people to attack the heart of some of their most firmly held beliefs. Such new "truth" seemed totally opposed to the Bible's account of creation. A newer understanding of German schools of biblical criticism, was threatening traditional scriptural interpretation. Sigmund Freud's theories of psychoanalysis had suggested that some human behavior was due to the unconscious mind rather than

---

[1]Bill J. Leonard, "The Origin and Character of Fundamentalism," *The Review and Expositor: A Baptist Theological Journal* 79 (1982): 5–17. For a more popular presentation, see Anthony E. Gilles, *Fundamentalism: What Every Catholic Needs to Know* (Cincinnati: St. Anthony Messenger Press, 1984).

to free choice. The Social Gospel movement was calling churches to a new agenda. Some saw the church's response to the human and social ills of a newly urbanized and industrial society as a dangerous retreat from its spiritual mission. Many Protestant leaders sought to accommodate religious teaching to these "new" insights, thus giving rise to liberalism.

Such wide-ranging complex changes posed challenging questions. Is the Bible true? Am I responsible for my actions or is my unconscious determining my behavior, thus weakening or destroying my own free will? In an environment of uncertainty and doubt a number of Protestant theologians at Princeton Theological Seminary[2] and the participants of the various Niagara Bible Conferences[3] drew up what they considered to be the basic, non-negotiable fundamentals of the Christian faith. Although the number of these items sometimes varied, the list commonly included: 1) the inspiration and absolute inerrancy of Scripture (often referred to as literal interpretation of Scripture); 2) the virgin birth and the divinity of Christ; 3) the substitutionary atoning death of Jesus; 4) the bodily resurrection of Jesus; 5) the literal second coming of Jesus to rule this earth.

At the very core of fundamentalism lies the doctrine of strict and literal individual interpretation of Scripture and the absolute inerrancy of every word in the Bible. For those who now called themselves *fundamentalists*, this is the key to defending what they perceive as traditional orthodox truth against any threat to it. By setting forth and emphasizing the absolute basics of Christianity as they saw them, the fundamentalists were looking for simple solutions to the increasingly complex problems of life.

5. We are not saying that there is not much that is sound in some of these principles nor that as Catholics we do not share some of the same beliefs. For, after all, we are a church of basics—basic beliefs grounded in Scripture and our tradition developed over almost 20 centuries. But we do see certain tenets of fundamentalism as contrary to Catholic belief. While we have always been a church of fundamentals, we are not a church of fundamentalism. As bishops of these Deep South dioceses we note that while modern fundamentalism is of rather recent origin, its roots are a part of our American religious experience, especially within the southern Bible Belt.

Do these roots of modern fundamentalism pose a temptation and

---

[2] Eric W. Gritsch, *Born Againism: Perspectives on a Movement* (Philadelphia: Fortress Press, 1982), pp. 37–38.

[3] Leonard, p. 5.

a danger to our people? We think so. The fundamentalist stance of literal interpretation of scripture by each believer violates the history and tradition of Scripture itself. That is the danger. We also believe that fundamentalism constitutes a grave temptation in our two states, for it offers:

a) An unreasonable certainty about the meaning of Scripture texts regardless of their context.

b) An overly simplistic certainty of salvation, achieved instantaneously upon acceptance of Christ as savior.

c) A deep sense of personal security, in often identifying the "American way" with God's call and will.

d) Intimacy with God in a relationship so personal that it effectively excludes others.

Such attitudes are too readily accepted by those who equate the "American way of life" with rugged individualism and self-sufficiency.

6. If our history helps us to understand the appeal of fundamentalism, its danger must be assessed in the light of the faith. The true fundamental understanding of Scripture for Catholics is that Scripture cannot stand apart from the community. God in Old and New Testament times called people to himself and revealed himself to every generation: "In times past, God spoke in fragmentary and varied ways to our fathers through the prophets; in this, the final age, he has spoken to us through his son, whom he has made heir of all things and through whom he first created the universe."[4] It was the task of the community to hand on this sacred revelation from God to each succeeding age. This they did in human language and ideas, and manners and customs. Sometimes the community spoke, at other times it wrote; always the community had a care to pass on the word it had received.

This community, the church, has always recognized the divine authorship of the Bible and its central, divinely directed role in her life, but it is important to remember that the church existed before there was a New Testament. Before the New Testament was composed and assembled, generations of Christians had lived heroic lives of faith and missionary zeal, and had even given the ultimate witness to their faith in martyrdom. God inspired members of the early

---

[4]Heb. 1:1–2.

Christian church to produce the New Testament. It was those early Christian communities who preserved the sacred text, copied it by hand and then passed it on to successive generations of Christians. Under the guidance of the Holy Spirit, the leadership of the church decided upon the 27 books of the New Testament.[5] We can only ask those who claim the authority of Scripture alone as expressing the divine will, who only want a "religion of the book," where in the Bible is the list of its inspired books? There is no such list. It was a teaching religion, the church, which decided, under the guidance of the Holy Spirit, which books were inspired and which were not to be a part of the Bible. That same teaching continues in the Second Vatican Council:

"Sacred Scripture is the speech of God and it is put down in writing under the breath of the Holy Spirit. And tradition transmits in its entirety the word of God which has been entrusted to the apostles by Christ the Lord and the Holy Spirit. It transmits it to the successors of the apostles so that, enlightened by the Spirit of truth, they may preserve, expound and spread it abroad by their preaching. Thus, it comes about that the church does not draw her certainty about all revealed truths from the Holy Scriptures alone. Hence, both Scripture and tradition must be accepted and honored with equal feelings of devotion and reverence. Sacred tradition and Sacred Scripture made up a single, sacred deposit of the word of God, which is entrusted to the church."[6]

7. Since Scripture is the possession of the church community, we take this opportunity to praise those members of the church who have rediscovered or discovered for the first time this essential foundation of our faith. Because God expressed his sacred word not only in human language, but entrusted it to the living context of a believing community, we have always recognized that it is the church's vocation, led by the Holy Spirit, to proclaim with confidence the true meaning of Sacred Scripture. The Bible is not just "mine," it is of its own nature and origin "ours." The inerrancy of the Bible arises from the fact that the Holy Spirit guided the church in producing Scripture to begin with and continues to guide new generations of Christians in understanding its meaning by guiding the leadership of that community—as has happened in the past—in interpreting it.

---

[5]This was firmly and finally fixed at the Council of Trent in 1546, although the earliest councils of Hippo in 393 and Carthage in 397 issued like decisions.

[6]Dogmatic Constitution on Divine Revelation, 9–10.

It is from our 20 centuries of Spirit-led life experience, and in union with the church universal, that we your bishops offer you Christ's "way and truth and life" for our times. Our vantage point enables us to accept the very much that is good in "the American way" but reject exaggerated and selfish values. Hence, in recent years our National Conference of Catholic Bishops in the United States has issued clear and careful statements on racism,[7] on peace[8] and on the economy.[9] It is this experience which has led the church in America and abroad to condemn injustices in society and to speak on behalf of those who are not allowed to speak, to seek a world of truth, justice, love and peace. The church has always sought to heed Paul's admonition that we not conform ourselves to this world, but rather be transformed by the renewal of our minds in Christ Jesus so that we "may prove what is the will of God, what is good and acceptable and perfect."[10]

8. Fundamentalists, because of their literalist mind-set, have often led others, by using brief Scripture quotations taken out of context, to world views and judgments very much opposed to our Catholic understanding. They set up an exaggerated contrast between the world (evil) and the kingdom (good). While it is true that Scripture talks about the antagonism between the world and the kingdom, it does not condemn our basic creation. The Bible teaches that we often take the good things God has created and misuse them. It is we who can be evil, not the universe. For Catholics, biblical teaching has always maintained that our world is good and has been entrusted to our care by God. We do not see it as something evil to escape, rather we embrace our world without embracing the sin within it.

The fundamentalist approach often leads one to an unbalanced spirituality. Holiness, in this view, comes from fleeing the world; Perfect holiness will only be achieved when the world is destroyed. This gives the lie to the incarnation. Christ Jesus entered the world and began the process of its conversion and transformation. What Adam undid through sin, Christ redoes, and more, through the grace of his redeeming death and resurrection.

From the beginning, Christ has promised to be with us all days and has sent us the Holy Spirit to instruct and guide us.[11] We have

---

[7]"Brothers and Sisters to Us," 1979.
[8]"The Challenge of Peace: God's Promise and Our Response," 1983.
[9]"Economic Justice for All," 1986.
[10]Rom. 12:2.
[11]Mt. 28:20; Jn. 16:13.

recognized that it is not only as individuals, but especially as a community of believers that we make his kingdom present.[12] It is as a community that Christ nourishes us with both his word and his flesh and blood in the eucharist. We profess that in baptism we are adopted by God as his children and are engrafted onto Christ's living body, the church. We profess that it is from the very person of Christ always present among us through his Holy Spirit that our community life and sacramental nourishment flow. We live with confidence in our teaching church and with hope because we know our Lord came that we might have life to the fullest and that we might share his joy here and now as well as forever in heaven.[13]

9. As a community we have come to understand that the Bible is not a mere answer book for every problem. It is rather the record of God's loving and saving presence among his people. It is his call to us to become a loving, saving presence to one another in the community that is the church. We are called by the church and God's word to a fullness of life that develops the community and its members as people of God. That is why we cherish the sacraments so much and celebrate them with unparalleled joy. That is why the eucharist, the greatest sign of our unity in sharing God's life, is the sun and center of our lives.

The presence of uncertainty and doubt, of hardship and human suffering, does not mean that God is not with us. While he often leads us out into the desert, he also feeds us and brings us to the promised land. With Christ we experience Good Friday, with Christ we rise on Easter Sunday. He is our God, we are his people. That is why we are people of hope who do not fear the complexity or insecurity of discipleship. It is a part of our faith journey.

10. These reflections urge us to make some recommendations for all who are serious about their journey of faith. We believe that those who follow them will avoid the temptations and dangers of fundamentalism and at the same time discover that confidence and hope to which the Lord calls all true disciples. "Come to me, all you who are heavy laden, and I will give you rest. Take my yoke upon you and learn from me, for I am gentle and lowly in heart, and you will find rest for your souls."[14]

We call all to become more acquainted with the word of God as it is embodied in the richness of our Catholic tradition. We encourage

[12]Jn. 18:20–26; Mt. 18:20.
[13]Jn. 10:10, 15:11.
[14]Mt. 11:28–29.

all to read it daily. We recommend the establishment of courses of biblical study in every parish or among groups of parishes in our dioceses so that all, especially the adults, can become more familiar with Sacred Scripture.

We recommit ourselves as bishops and remind priests and deacons of our ordination call to be teachers of God's word. This is one of our most important ministries, to prepare well-ordered and biblically sound homilies. We also call the faithful to be attentive listeners to the biblical faith that is communicated as Scripture is proclaimed and God's word is preached.

We encourage all undertakings among our people that lead to a spiritual development flowing from Scripture and community. We call our parishes to become more and more communities of God's love. We must work at this using various biblically-centered programs and processes that can help bring this about and sustain it. We recommend, for example, the Rite of Christian Initiation of Adults, Cursillo, prayer groups, retreat movements, social ministry.

We commend, in particular, the work of the Catholic charismatic movement. Avoiding the biblical fundamentalism we have noted above, it has often provided much-needed leaders in biblical studies and community building and service.

Remembering that it is the community of the church, with its teaching, its sacraments, its signs and symbols which lifts us up and nourishes us, we offer the Catholics of our two states the challenge to become more involved in our parish and diocesan life and programs. Ultimately, we will not find peace and joy in a simplistic manipulation of biblical texts or in some instantaneous and emotional religious experience. Rather, we are assured of Christ's peace when we take on that gentle yoke of discipleship which is based upon the paschal mystery: The Lord died and rose for our salvation. In turn, our death to self, sin and such consequences of sin as racism, materialism and consumerism will bring to birth in us, and around us, that happiness which the world cannot give. May our dying and rebirth in Christ show us truly to be the light of the world. Then, because of loyal and persevering discipleship, the Lord will find us waiting when he comes.

APPENDIX III

The Fundamentalist Project
The American Academy of Arts and Sciences

Introduction

On September 28, 1987, the Council of the American Academy of Arts and Sciences authorized a multi-year study of Fundamentalism(s) around the world. The President of the Academy with the consent of the Council, then appointed a Steering Committee and named Martin E. Marty of the University of Chicago chairman of this Committee.[1] The project is supported by a substantial grant from the John D. and Catherine T. MacArthur Foundation.

Hypotheses

Have we any hypotheses as we begin the study? There were certain common expressions which can be systematized as very tentative theses. They include:

1. Fundamentalisms emerge as movements of reaction of modernity. This reaction has a selective character; for example, most such movements are quite at home with technology if not with the scientific world-view that produced it. Fundamentalism seems to arise when conservative, traditional, or orthodox groups react against threatening erosive forces such as secularism, pluralism, relativism, or a self-indulgent individualism which strains or severs previously cherished familial and communal ties. These erosive forces bring with them certain ideological threats, including "toler-

---

[1]The document is printed with the permission of The Fundamentalist Project of the American Academy of Arts and Sciences. It should be read along with the more recent statement of Martin E. Marty "Fundamentalism as a Social Phenomenon," *Bulletin of the American Academy of Arts and Sciences* 42 (November 1988): 15–29.

ance," an evolutionary view of history, and the tendency to "spiritualize" or "symbolize" formative events in the movement's past.

2. We hypothesize that leaders of such movements and their followers then select those "fundamentals" from the past, especially from the documentary or textual past, which will best serve as defenses. The process of selection ordinarily requires an authoritative text—a canon of scripture, a code of law, an approved philosophy—which can be insisted upon and administered authoritatively. Of course, there will be disagreements within all intense movements, but there must be a presumption that these could at least in theory be settled by authority, as in an inerrant Bible for Protestants, or in Shariah, the code of law, for some Muslims.

3. These stirrings take new social form when the people who react take steps to prevent erosion and in many cases to permit aggression. Some fundamentalisms, at least in certain stages, are quite passive. The people who hold them, in other words, have the faith that they can endure the vicissitudes of history and must simply remain pure, an elect people, as it were. At another stage, the same people may grow dissatisfied with "sectarian" formation, with building figurative walls to protect themselves and their way of life. Also, new groups may form, originating from the shared desire actively to protect a valued way of life. In both cases, people seek to reform society on their own terms, and organize in order to inconvenience others around them, to convert them, or to seek dominance over them. This belligerent stage may find them content with persuasive means, though in some circumstances there may also be resort to arms in order to effect their way.

4. Are there common themes among Fundamentalisms? We further hypothesize that in either active or passive forms, most such movements have to have confidence that history has a direction and that they have a knowledge about the direction. Messianisms and millennialisms typify such movements. The people must be chosen or elect, agents and instruments of a transcendent will—usually seen as divine—which is moving history. It is not possible to see the particular substance of each Fundamentalism paralleled by "doctrinal" elements in others. Thus the Protestant Fundamentalist will insist on Jesus' Virgin Birth, blood atonement, physical resurrection, and literal Second Coming. All of these beliefs are, of course, repudiated in ultra-Orthodox Jewish Fundamentalism which, in turn, harbors no sympathy for the laws or interpretations of law in

Islamic Fundamentalism. One looks elsewhere, then, for common features.

As hypotheses, these are not final, conclusive statements, but starting points which await further investigations and possible revision during the course of the project.

Cautionary Words

1. Because of the controversial character of the movements to be studied, it is important to treat them fairly, summoning the scholarly objectivity and concern for fairness present within the academic community. Thus a suitable attitude toward the study of fundamentalism is expressed in Spinoza's words: one comes not to laugh, not to cry, but to understand.

2. Participants in the formative stages of this project voiced concern that if fundamentalism is to be understood, its possible positive aspects must be considered. Some witnessed not only to ways they had been victims of fundamentalism, but also to features they had come to admire. What values do fundamentalists respect—in the family, neighborhood, traditional society, religion? Do fundamentalist reactions against selected features of modernity benefit outsiders who might not otherwise engage in such a critique?

3. There should be as much preoccupation with what movements have in particular as with what they have in common. While a comparative study will likely produce helpful observations about what is common if not universal across the spectrum of Fundamentalisms, it would be incomplete without scrutiny of the factors distinct to each movement. One cannot proceed to public policy discussions without an accurate description of particulars, and interest in the "thickness" of separate experiences and cultural expressions, and a dedicated attention to historical and environmental contexts.

4. There must be great care in the use of terms. Not all religions and cultures have cognate terms for reactionary fundamentalisms. There is danger of misclassification, of "clumping," of creating resentment if uncongenial movements are too formally clustered and compared. But there cannot be complete linguistic precision, especially when one studies inchoate, volatile, dynamic movements. Just as there are many kinds of radicalisms, liberalisms, conservatisms, so there will be many kinds of fundamentalisms.

5. The study will have little effect if the people being described

are not consulted or, in some instances where possible, participants in formulating and to some extent executing the study. Fundamentalists may not agree with what "outsiders" study, precisely because they resist description as being itself relativizing. But there should be efforts to assure that they would recognize themselves in the emergent descriptions, that they would see that the describers made every effort to be fair and accurate. There will be special attempts to include scholars from various Fundamentalist communities, whether as contributors, critics, or consultants.

6. There is interest in the ways fundamentalisms pose challenges to the modern academy in the West, to scientific world views, to disciples of progress, to those who had envisioned a single form of rationality developing along the trajectory of modernity. Sometimes the assault is entirely external, as in the creationist movements, or in obscurantisms which induce the academy to "get its collective back up." But an object of study ought also to be how fundamentalisms cause reexamination of cherished philosophies of history, academic conventions, and perhaps unreflectively held world views which fundamentalist assaults serve to revitalize.

The Disciplines of Inquiry

It is also clear that various disciplines can make rather precise contributions; indeed, it is hard to think of subjects that demand the attention of more disciplines than does this one, if it is to be treated fairly and with some comprehension.

By pointing to some of the disciplines and approaches, we may seem to suggest that the list is exhaustive, that other disciplines are to be overlooked. But this is not the case. This list is for illustrative purposes only.

History: Both the longer "pre-history" and the more recent history of movements need to be studied by historians. Thus there must be a background in Jewish Orthodoxy before modern fundamentalist Ultra-Orthodoxy makes sense; one must know about classic Islamic attitudes toward the Koran as a completely authoritative book before the particulars of reactive anti-modernism's use of law codes comes into clear view; it will be important to know the long history of EuroAmerican Protestant evangelical conservatism in order to see how modern Fundamentalism developed. There is the need to keep the historical contexts of all the movements in the forefront.

What role do memory and nostalgia play, and what part does

critical history have to contribute? Fundamentalisms seem to be motivated in part by grief and mourning over what was lost or presumed to have been lost. There is reference to a pure time of origins during which the "fundamentals" were stated and set, a golden age from which societies have fallen and which can be recovered by proper tactics, steadfastness, or millennial and apocalyptic interventions.

Are there fundamentalisms beyond those regularly called such? Is there, for example, Catholic Fundamentalism? Are there fundamentalisms on the soil of Asian religions and philosophies? Is there a secular fundamentalism, a scientific fundamentalism?

Philosophy: Philosophers are interested in seeing terms used with conceptual propriety, in criticizing hypotheses, in providing clarifications in the use of language, in defining. They have much to say in a field where there has necessarily been much blurring and confusion. They may also help make public policy proposals and refine those brought by others.

Theology, Philosophy of Religion, "Religious Studies": Many participants voiced concern lest the study be simply reductionistic; that is, in order to understand phenomena one often "reduces" them into something analogous or compatible. But such reduction can turn to reductionism, an a priori suggestion that complex religious phenomena are "nothing but" this or that (such as expressions of personality, class interest, and the like). Theologians and scholars of religion should be expected to keep pressing the search for distinctively religious responses and claims.

Psychology: There was some expression of interest in studying whether there is such a thing as a "fundamentalist personality" or predisposition. Is there something in the makeup of some individuals within a pluralist society who choose to be fundamentalist when many options are present? Social psychologists will be interested in the study of mass movement fundamentalism. They may choose to inquire where quasi-religious movements like ultra-Marxism, "scientism" and various hyper-nationalisms may be expressive of fundamentalist temperaments. Social psychologists might well ask why young people are so often attracted to fundamentalisms (in Israel, in Islamic societies, in North America) while they repudiate moderating, tolerant religions and movements? Are there common elements in their leadership? Can it be ascertained why some gain power and others are rejected? What are the attracting features in fundamentalist leadership?

Sciences: In societies like our own, many scientists with full academic credentials are fundamentalist; that fundamentalism tends to be a movement among scientific or technological elites elsewhere; that fundamentalisms often make claims concerning cosmology or earth sciences or human sciences which directly challenge scientific methods, world views, perceptions and practices. Scientists from many disciplines will be called forth to study these challenges, including the well-known "creationism" movements in America. Such a study may also be a mirror held up by scientists leading to a reexamination of their methods and assumptions. Scientists might also help understand how and why technology is so much prized by many fundamentalist movements which react against scientific assumptions and endeavors that helped produce them.

Literary and Other Arts: With some frequency, participants stressed the need for inquiry concerning artistic implications. Do fundamentalists have iconoclastic tendencies? Is there an iconography characteristic of such movements? Why are there no major novelists with fundamentalist outlooks? Are there none such? (Certain possible examples come to mind.) What about the use of music in fundamentalist movements? An aesthetic critique and accounting is in order.

Political Science, Law, and the Like: Most fundamentalisms move rather rapidly toward actions and intentions that have a bearing on public policy, public order and polity. In almost every case they rely upon a legal framework and challenge existing ones. Because legal systems are rooted in the past, they tend to be involved in, and affected by, the conflict between those who see the past as mandatory or normative for the political community, and those who advocate reform and look elsewhere for impetus. Thus jurisprudence can be a powerful instrument of change or, conversely, a bulwark of the status quo. While not all fundamentalisms intend to be explicitly political, most of them turn to politics as a means of extending influence, so political scientists and legal scholars will be consulted.

Committee members urged that there be study of how modernity and technology empower fundamentalisms. They may well take advantage of democratic polities to advance, an option unavailable to them in earlier hierarchical societies. Or they may be able to form mass movements thanks to cassette recorders (as in Iran), computers and television (in the United States), skillful use of mass media (as in Israel). Modernity does not simply take away; it also gives to astute fundamentalists.

Economics: Since most fundamentalisms do have views about polity and since polities often exist in part to help preserve or extend differing economic orders and approaches, fundamentalisms become economic entities. The practices they induce may undercut existing economic patterns; they may become large economic movements on their own.

Anthropology and Sociology: Many concerns of anthropologists when they study modern movements are well-directed toward fundamentalisms. A study of the role of their rites of passage and rituals in general; the mytho-symbolic frameworks with which they work; the implications for family and kinship; the development of social patterns—all these come into the scope of various schools of anthropology, each of which will be making some contribution. The appropriateness of sociology as providing instruments and "handles" is equally obvious, for fundamentalism issues in forms of social behavior concerning which sociologists develop expertise.

Public Policy

The MacArthur Foundation extended the grant and the Academy accepted it chiefly for what it might have to say for public policy comprehension and strategy. This means that the panels and symposia will not concentrate so much on what could be done and is already being done by isolated scholars in various disciplines as in coordinating efforts and featuring aspects that have a bearing on public policy. This is first of all a "study," and there may never be direct recommendations, but there should certainly be a consistent eye on public policy implications. Thus such a study, which is not likely to cause its readers to underestimate Fundamentalism in the future, might well teach them not to overestimate it or misidentify its various expressions. A study has public policy implications if it teaches discrimination among movements, provides accurate assessments concerning the size, motivation, and intention of movements, and the like.

Possible Topics

The following sequence may be used for heuristic purposes:

1. Fundamentalism observed: Phenomenological and historical studies of the longer backgrounds to, the immediate contexts of, and the present appearances of fundamentalist movements. This would

be an international, interreligious, interdisciplinary effort simply to bring the movements into view.

2. Impact of fundamentalism: Several participants stressed that for a public policy study an early volume should set forth understandings not only of the genus of fundamentalism but of particular effects. What bearing does it have on economies, on national strategies, on military conduct, on legislation, on religious organizations, on cultural expressions, and the like?

3. Fundamentalism as a social phenomenon: There would here be room for the psychological study of "the fundamentalist temperament" or inclination, the various factors which motivate individuals who join and contribute to fundamentalist movements. For a public policy study there would be even greater interest in the social expression of fundamentalism than what is held privately. Here one would wish to study the different "active" and "passive" forms, those that coexist with democratic politics and those that would replace them or have done so.

4. Fundamentalism comprehended: This means not that one has a full comprehension of the movement but that the scholars begin at this stage to coordinate their studies, integrate their findings, analyze and criticize what was presented about particular movements. There would be no interest in straitjacketing, but much interest in trying to find coherent ways to speak of the varied phenomena.

5. Public policy consequences: Some hope that we would move beyond public policy study to public policy proposal. It is too soon to predict what the Steering Committee, the Executive Committee, and the working groups will decide to do about proposals. But they will certainly be studying the implications for public policy of what they have turned up. There should be careful attention given to the ways these findings can be used by mass communicators, politicians, religious figures, and others.

Possible Outcomes

1. A description of possible outcomes would include concrete objects such as books, reports, findings, reference works; it might also include the holding of working conferences and some sort of public events in which the scholars would confront each other and a public with their theses and findings. Out of such conferences, which include in the audience other scholars who may not be formally part of the inquiry, there can be a "ripple effect," an

encouragement of scholarship beyond the Academy's original project, a stimulus to continuing work. This is how one hopes scholarly inquiry has effects far beyond its own constraints and scope.

2. The "concrete objects" referred to above ought to include at least five annual volumes which will bring forth the theses and disseminate the tentative findings of companies of scholars who participate. One would hope that these volumes would become widely-recognized assets as data banks and sources of reflection for other scholars, mass communicators who deal with Fundamentalisms, public policy experts and responsible administrators and officials, and, most of all, the general public. Beyond these volumes, one can envision working with the editor of *Daedalus* to produce issues or parts of issues dealing with the subject, bibliographies, inventories of scholars and scholarly centers devoted to the subject, and the like.

APPENDIX IV

The Chicago Statement on Biblical Inerrancy

Preface

The Authority of Scripture is a key issue for the Christian church in this and every age. Those who profess faith in Jesus Christ as Lord and Savior are called to show the reality of their discipleship by humbly and faithfully obeying God's written Word. To stray from Scripture in faith or conduct is disloyalty to our Master. Recognition of the total truth and trustworthiness of Holy Scripture is essential to a full grasp and adequate confession of its authority.

The following Statement affirms this inerrancy of Scripture afresh, making clear our understanding of it and warning against its denial. We are persuaded that to deny it is to set aside the witness of Jesus Christ and of the Holy Spirit and to refuse that submission to the claims of God's own Word which marks true Christian faith. We see it as our timely duty to make this affirmation in the face of current lapses from the truth of inerrancy among our fellow Christians and misunderstanding of this doctrine in the world at large.

This Statement consists of three parts: a Summary Statement, Articles of Affirmation and Denial, and an accompanying Exposition. It has been prepared in the course of a three-day consultation in Chicago. Those who have signed the Summary Statement and the Articles wish to affirm their own conviction as to the inerrancy of Scripture and to encourage and challenge one another and all Christians to growing appreciation and understanding of this doctrine. We acknowledge the limitations of a document prepared in a brief, intensive conference and do not propose that this Statement be given creedal weight. Yet we rejoice in the deepening of our own convictions through our discussions together, and we pray that the Statement we have signed may be used to the glory of our God toward a new reformation of the Church in its faith, life, and mission.

We offer this Statement in a spirit, not of contention, but of humility and love, which we purpose by God's grace to maintain in any future dialogue arising out of what we have said. We gladly acknowledge that many who deny the inerrancy of Scripture do not display the consequences of this denial in the rest of their belief and behavior, and we are conscious that we who confess this doctrine often deny it in life by failing to bring our thoughts and deeds, our traditions and habits, into true subjection to the divine Word.

We invite response to this statement from any who see reason to amend its affirmations about Scripture by the light of Scripture itself, under whose infallible authority we stand as we speak. We claim no personal infallibility for the witness we bear, and for any help which enables us to strengthen this testimony to God's Word we shall be grateful.

—THE DRAFT COMMITTEE

A Short Statement

1. God, who is Himself Truth and speaks truth only, has inspired Holy Scripture in order thereby to reveal Himself to lost mankind through Jesus Christ as Creator and Lord, Redeemer and Judge. Holy Scripture is God's witness to Himself.

2. Holy Scripture, being God's own Word, written by men prepared and superintended by His Spirit, is of infallible divine authority in all matters upon which it touches; it is to be believed, as God's instruction, in all that it affirms; obeyed, as God's command, in all that it requires; embraced, as God's pledge, in all that it promises.

3. The Holy Spirit, its divine Author, both authenticates it to us by His inward witness and opens our minds to understand its meaning.

4. Being wholly and verbally God-given, Scripture is without error or fault in all its teaching, no less in what it states about God's acts in creation and the events of world history, and about its own literary origins under God, than in its witness to God's saving grace in individual lives.

5. The authority of Scripture is inescapably impaired if this total divine inerrancy is in any way limited or disregarded, or made relative to a view of truth contrary to the Bible's own; and such lapses bring serious loss to both the individual and the Church.

Articles of Affirmation and Denial

Article I. We affirm that the Holy Scriptures are to be received as the authoritative Word of God.

We deny that the Scriptures receive their authority from the Church, tradition, or any other human source.

Article II. We affirm that the Scriptures are the supreme written norm by which God binds the conscience, and that the authority of the Church is subordinate to that of Scripture.

We deny that Church creeds, councils, or declarations have authority greater than or equal to the authority of the Bible.

Article III. We affirm that the written Word in its entirety is revelation given by God.

We deny that the Bible is merely a witness to revelation, or only becomes revelation in encounter, or depends on the responses of men for its validity.

Article IV. We affirm that God who made mankind in His image has used language as a means of revelation.

We deny that human language is so limited by our creatureliness that it is rendered inadequate as a vehicle for divine revelation. We further deny that the corruption of human culture and language through sin has thwarted God's work of inspiration.

Article V. We affirm that God's revelation within the Holy Scripture was progressive.

We deny that later revelation, which may fulfill earlier revelation, ever corrects or contradicts it. We further deny that any normative revelation has been given since the completion of the New Testament writings.

Article VI. We affirm that the whole of Scripture and all its parts, down to the very words of the original, were given by divine inspiration.

We deny that the inspiration of Scripture can rightly be affirmed of the whole without the parts, or of some parts but not the whole.

Article VII. We affirm that inspiration was the work in which God by His Spirit, through human writers, gave us His Word. The origin of Scripture is divine. The mode of divine inspiration remains largely a mystery to us.

We deny that inspiration can be reduced to human insight, or to heightened states of consciousness of any kind.

Article VIII. We affirm that God in His work of inspiration utilized the distinctive personalities and literary styles of the writers whom He had chosen and prepared.

We deny that God, in causing these writers to use the very words that He chose, overrode their personalities.

Article IX. We affirm that inspiration, though not conferring omniscience, guaranteed true and trustworthy utterance on all matters of which the biblical authors were moved to speak and write.

We deny that the finitude or fallenness of these writers, by necessity or otherwise, introduced distortion or falsehood into God's Word.

Article X. We affirm that inspiration, strictly speaking, applies only to the autographic text of Scripture, which in the providence of God can be ascertained from available manuscripts with great accuracy. We further affirm that copies and translations of Scripture are the Word of God to the extent that they faithfully represent the original.

We deny that any essential element of the Christian faith is affected by the absence of the autographs. We further deny that this absence renders the assertion of biblical inerrancy invalid or irrelevant.

Article XI. We affirm that Scripture, having been given by divine inspiration, is infallible, so that, far from misleading us, it is true and reliable in all the matters it addresses.

We deny that it is possible for the Bible to be at the same time infallible and errant in its assertions. Infallibility and inerrancy may be distinguished, but not separated.

Article XII. We affirm that Scripture in its entirety is inerrant, being free from all falsehood, fraud, or deceit.

We deny that biblical infallibility and inerrancy are limited to spiritual, religious, or redemptive themes, exclusive of assertions in the fields of history and science. We further deny that scientific hypotheses about earth history may properly be used to overturn the teaching of Scripture on creation and the flood.

Article XIII. We affirm the propriety of using inerrancy as a theological term with reference to the complete truthfulness of Scripture.

We deny that it is proper to evaluate Scripture according to standards of truth and error that are alien to its usage or purpose. We further deny that inerrancy is negated by biblical phenomena such as a lack of modern technical precision, irregularities of grammar or spelling, observational descriptions of nature, the reporting of falsehoods, the use of hyperbole and round numbers, the topical arrangement of material, variant selections of material in parallel accounts, or the use of free citations.

Article XIV. We affirm the unity and internal consistency of Scripture.

We deny that alleged errors and discrepancies that have not yet been resolved vitiate the truth claims of the Bible.

Article XV. We affirm that the doctrine of inerrancy is grounded in the teaching of the Bible about inspiration.

We deny that Jesus' teaching about Scripture may be dismissed by appeals to accommodation or to any natural limitation of His humanity.

Article XVI. We affirm that the doctrine of inerrancy has been integral to the Church's faith throughout its history.

We deny that inerrancy is a doctrine invented by scholastic Protestantism, or is a reactionary position postulated in response to negative higher criticism.

Article XVII. We affirm that the Holy Spirit bears witness to the Scriptures, assuring believers of the truthfulness of God's written Word.

We deny that this witness of the Holy Spirit operates in isolation from or against Scripture.

Article XVIII. We affirm that the text of Scripture is to be interpreted by grammatico-historical exegesis, taking account of its literary forms and devices, and that Scripture is to interpret Scripture.

We deny the legitimacy of any treatment of the text or quest for sources lying behind it that leads to revitalizing, dehistoricizing, or discounting its teaching, or rejecting its claims to authorship.

Article XIX. We affirm that a confession of the full authority, infallibility, and inerrancy of Scripture is vital to a sound understanding of the whole of the Christian faith. We further affirm that such confession should lead to increasing conformity to the image of Christ.

We deny that such confession is necessary for salvation. However, we further deny that inerrancy can be rejected without grave consequences, both to the individual and to the Church.

Exposition

Our understanding of the doctrine of inerrancy must be set in the context of the broader teachings of the Scripture concerning itself. This exposition gives an account of the outline of doctrine from which our summary statement and articles are drawn.

Creation, Revelation and Inspiration

The Triune God, who formed all things by His creative utterances and governs all things by His Word of decree, made mankind in His own image for a life of communion with Himself, on the model of the eternal fellowship of living communication within the Godhead. As God's image-bearer, man was to hear God's Word addressed to him and to respond in the joy of adoring obedience. Over and above God's self-disclosure in the created order and the sequence of events within it, human beings from Adam on have received verbal messages from Him, either directly, as stated in Scripture, or indirectly in the form of part or all of Scripture itself.

When Adam fell, the Creator did not abandon mankind to final judgment but promised salvation and began to reveal Himself as Redeemer in a sequence of historical events centering on Abraham's family and culminating in the life, death, resurrection, present heavenly ministry, and promised return of Jesus Christ. Within this frame God has from time to time spoken specific words of judgment and mercy, promise and command, to sinful human beings so drawing them into a covenant relation of mutual commitment between Him and them in which He blesses them with gifts of grace and they bless Him in responsive adoration. Moses, whom God used as mediator to carry His words to His people at the time of the Exodus, stands at the head of a long line of prophets in whose mouths and writings God put His words for delivery to Israel. God's purpose in this succession of messages was to maintain His covenant by causing His people to know His Name—that is, His nature—and His will both of percept and purpose in the present and for the future. This line of prophetic spokesmen from God came to completion in Jesus Christ, God's incarnate Word, who was Himself a prophet—more than a prophet, but not less—and in the apostles and prophets of the first Christian generation. When God's final and climactic message, His word to the world concerning Jesus Christ, had been spoken and elucidated by those in the apostolic circle, the sequence of revealed messages ceased. Henceforth the Church was to live and know God by what He had already said, and said for all time.

At Sinai God wrote the terms of His covenant on tables of stone, as His enduring witness and for lasting accessibility, and throughout the period of prophetic and apostolic revelation He prompted men to write the messages given to and through them, along with celebratory records of His dealings with His people, plus moral reflections on covenant life and forms of praise and prayer for covenant mercy. The theological reality of inspiration in the producing of biblical documents corresponds to that of spoken prophecies: although the human writers' personalities were expressed in what they wrote, the words were divinely constituted. Thus, what Scripture says, God says; its authority is His authority, for He is its ultimate Author, having given it through the minds and words of chosen and prepared men who in freedom and faithfulness "spoke from God as they were carried along by the Holy Spirit" (1 Pet. 1:21). Holy Scripture must be acknowledged as the Word of God by virtue of its divine origin.

Authority: Christ and the Bible

Jesus Christ, the Son of God who is the Word made flesh, our Prophet, Priest, and King, is the ultimate Mediator of God's communication to man, as He is of all God's gifts of grace. The revelation He gave was more than verbal; He revealed the Father by His presence and His deeds as well. Yet His words were crucially important; for He was God, He spoke from the Father, and His words will judge all men at the last day.

As the prophesied Messiah, Jesus Christ is the central theme of

Scripture. The Old Testament looked ahead to Him; the New Testament looks back to His first coming and on to His second. Canonical Scripture is the divinely inspired and therefore normative witness to Christ. No hermeneutic, therefore, of which the historical Christ is not the focal point is acceptable. Holy Scripture must be treated as what it essentially is—the witness of the Father to the incarnate Son.

It appears that the Old Testament canon had been fixed by the time of Jesus. The New Testament canon is likewise now closed inasmuch as no new apostolic witness to the historical Christ can now be borne. No new revelation (as distinct from Spirit-given understanding of existing revelation) will be given until Christ comes again. The canon was created in principle by divine inspiration. The Church's part was to discern the canon which God had created, not to devise one of its own. The relevant criteria were and are: authorship (or attestation), content, and the authenticating witness of the Holy Spirit.

The word *canon*, signifying a rule or standard, is a pointer to authority, which means the right to rule and control. Authority in Christianity belongs to God in His revelation, which means, on the one hand, Jesus Christ, the living Word, and, on the other hand, Holy Scripture, the written Word. But the authority of Christ and that of Scripture are one. As our Prophet, Christ testified that Scripture cannot be broken. As our Priest and King, He devoted His earthly life to fulfilling the law and the prophets, even dying in obedience to the words of Messianic prophecy. Thus, as He saw Scripture attesting Him and His authority, so by His own submission to Scripture He attested its authority. As He bowed to His Father's instruction given in His Bible (our Old Testament), so He requires His disciples to do—not, however, in isolation but in conjunction with the apostolic witness to Himself which He undertook to inspire by His gift of the Holy Spirit. So Christians show themselves faithful servants of their Lord by bowing to the divine instruction given in the prophetic and apostolic writings which together make up our Bible.

By authenticating each other's authority, Christ and Scripture coalesce into a single fount of authority. The biblically interpreted Christ and the Christ-centered, Christ-proclaiming Bible are from this standpoint one. As from the fact of inspiration we infer that what Scripture says, God says, so from the revealed relation between

Jesus Christ and Scripture we may equally declare that what Scripture says, Christ says.

Infallibility, Inerrancy, Interpretation

Holy Scripture, as the inspired Word of God witnessing authoritatively to Jesus Christ, may properly be called *infallible* and *inerrant*. These negative terms have a special value, for they explicitly safeguard positive truths.

Infallible signifies the quality of neither misleading nor being misled and so safeguards in categorical terms the truth that Holy Scripture is a sure, safe, and reliable rule and guide in all matters.

Similarly, *inerrant* signifies the quality of being free from all falsehood or mistake and so safeguards the truth that Holy Scripture is entirely true and trustworthy in all its assertions.

We affirm the canonical Scripture should always be interpreted on the basis that it is infallible and inerrant. However, in determining what the God-taught writer is asserting in each passage, we must pay the most careful attention to its claims and character as a human production. In inspiration, God utilized the culture and conventions of his penman's milieu, a milieu that God controls in His sovereign providence; it is misinterpretation to imagine otherwise.

So history must be treated as history, poetry as poetry, hyperbole and metaphor as hyperbole and metaphor, generalization and approximation as what they are, and so forth. Differences between literary conventions in Bible times and in our time must also be observed: since, for instance, nonchronological narration and imprecise citation were conventional and acceptable and violated no expectations in those days, we must not regard these things as faults when we find them in Bible writers. When total precision of a particular kind was not expected nor aimed at, it is no error not to have achieved it. Scripture is inerrant, not in the sense of being absolutely precise by modern standards, but in the sense of making good its claims and achieving that measure of focused truth at which its authors aimed.

The truthfulness of Scripture is not negated by the appearance in it of irregularities of grammar or spelling, phenomenal descriptions of nature, reports of false statements (e.g., the lies of Satan), or seeming discrepancies between one passage and another. It is not right to set the so-called phenomena of Scripture against the teaching of Scripture about itself. Apparent inconsistencies should not be ignored. Solution of them, where this can be convincingly achieved, will encourage our faith, and where for the present no convincing solution is at hand we shall significantly honor God by trusting His assurance that His Word is true, despite these appearances, and by maintaining our confidence that one day they will be seen to have been illusions.

Inasmuch as all Scripture is the product of a single divine mind, interpretation must stay within the bounds of the analogy of Scripture and eschew hypotheses that would correct one biblical passage by another, whether in the name of progressive revelation or of the imperfect enlightenment of the inspired writer's mind.

Although Holy Scripture is nowhere culture-bound in the sense that its teaching lacks universal validity, it is sometimes culturally conditioned by the customs and conventional views of a particular period, so that the application of its principles today calls for a different sort of action (e.g., in the matter of women's headgear/coiffure, cf. 1 Cor. 11).

Skepticism and Criticism

Since the Renaissance, and more particularly since the Enlightenment, world views have been developed which involve skepticism about basic Christian tenets. Such are the agnosticism which denies that God is knowable, the rationalism which denies that He is incomprehensible, the idealism which denies that He is transcendent, and the existentialism which denies rationality in His relationships with us. When these un- and anti-biblical principles seep into man's theologies at presuppositional level, as today they frequently do, faithful interpretation of Holy Scripture becomes impossible.

Transmission and Translation

Since God has nowhere promised an inerrant transmission of Scripture, it is necessary to affirm that only the autographic text of the original documents was inspired and to maintain the need of textual criticism as a means of detecting any slips that may have crept into the text in the course of its transmission. The verdict of this science, however, is that Hebrew and Greek texts appear to be amazingly well preserved, so that we are amply justified in affirming, with the Westminster Confession, a singular providence of God in this matter and in declaring that the authority of Scripture is in no way jeopardized by the fact that the copies we possess are not entirely error-free.

Similarly, no translation is or can be perfect, and all translations are an additional step away from the *autographa*. Yet the verdict of linguistic science is that English-speaking Christians, at least, are exceedingly well served in these days with a host of excellent translations and have no cause for hesitating to conclude that the true Word of God is within their reach. Indeed, in view of the frequent repetition in Scripture of the main matters with which it deals and also of the Holy Spirit's constant witness to and through the Word, no serious translation of Holy Scripture will so destroy its meaning as to render it unable to make its reader "wise for salvation through faith in Christ Jesus" (2 Tim. 3:15).

Inerrancy and Authority

In our affirmation of the authority of Scripture as involving its total truth, we are consciously standing with Christ and His apostles, indeed with the whole Bible and with the mainstream of church history from the first days until very recently. We are concerned at the casual, inadvertent, and seemingly thoughtless way in which a belief of such far-reaching importance has been given up by so many in our day.

We are conscious too that great and grave confusion results from ceasing to maintain the total truth of the Bible whose authority one professes to acknowledge. The result of taking this step is that the Bible which God gave loses its authority, and what has authority instead is a Bible reduced in content according to the demands of one's critical reasonings and in principle reducible still further once one has started. This means that at bottom independent reason now has authority, as opposed to scriptural teaching. If this is not seen and if for the time being basic evangelical doctrines are still held, persons denying the full truth of Scripture may claim an evangelical identity while methodologically they have moved away from the evangelical principle of knowledge to an unstable subjectivism, and will find it hard not to move further.

We affirm that what Scripture says, God says. May He be glorified. Amen and Amen.

CONTRIBUTORS

R. SCOTT APPLEBY is associate director of The Fundamentalist Project of the American Academy of Arts and Sciences. A church historian and research associate at the University of Chicago, he is co-author of *Transforming Parish Ministry: The Changing Roles of Catholic Clergy, Laity, and Women Religious*, and author of several articles on American religious history.

CHRISTOPHER CHAPPLE received his Ph.D. from Fordham University and is now associate professor of theology at Loyola Marymount University, Los Angeles. He has published several articles on classical Sanskrit texts and modern applications of Indian ethics, as well as the book *Karma and Creativity*.

ANNE M. CLIFFORD, C.S.J., assistant professor of theology at Duquesne University, received her Ph.D. in theology from The Catholic University of America. Her dissertation is entitled "The Relations of Science and Religion: Theology in the Thought of Langdon Gilkey." An earlier article, "Women Missioned in a Technological Culture," appeared in *Claiming Our Truth*, edited by Nadine Foley.

CYNTHIA S. W. CRYSDALE received her Ph.D. in Theology from the University of St. Michael's College, Toronto, in 1987. She is currently an assistant professor in the Department of Religion and Religious Education at The Catholic University of America. Her research interests include moral and religious development, conversion, and method in Christian Ethics.

WILLIAM D. DINGES is an associate professor in the Department of Religion and Religious Education at the Catholic University of America. He received his doctoral degree from the University of Kansas. His research interests include religion and culture, religious movements, methods in religious studies, and Roman Catholicism. Dr. Dinges is currently working on a book on the conservative and traditionalist reactions to the Second Vatican Council.

JOHN L. ESPOSITO is professor of religious studies and Director of the Center for International Studies, the College of the Holy Cross. He is currently President of the Middle East Studies Association and of the American Council for the Study of Islamic Societies. Among his publications are *Islam: The Straight Path, Islam and Politics, Women in Muslim Family Law,* and *The Iranian Revolution: Its Global Impact.*

FRANCIS SCHÜSSLER FIORENZA formerly taught at Catholic University of America and the University of Notre Dame, and is presently the Charles Chauncey Stillman Professor of Roman Catholic Theological Studies at Harvard University's Divinity School. He is a former president of the Catholic Theological Society of America. In 1984 he published *Foundational Theology: Jesus and the Church.* He has recently co-edited a two volume compendium of Roman Catholic systematic theology entitled *Systematic Theology, Catholic Perspectives.*

ROBERT GNUSE received his M.Div. and S.T.M. from Concordia Seminary in Exile and his Ph.D. from Vanderbilt University. Since 1980 he has taught at Loyola University of the South in New Orleans. He has authored six books, most recently *Heilsgeschichte as a Model for Biblical Theology* (1989). Articles of his have appeared in *Zeitschrift für die alttestamentliche Wissenschaft, Biblische Zeitschrift, Revue Biblique, Novum Testamentum,* and *Biblical Theology Bulletin.*

SAMUEL S. HILL has been a Professor of Religion at the University of Florida since 1972 and publishes in such fields as religion in the South, religion in American culture, and comparative religious movements. Educated at Georgetown College (Ky.), Vanderbilt University, and Duke University, he was briefly a Baptist pastor. From 1960 to 1972 he was a member of the Religion Department faculty at the University of North Carolina at Chapel Hill.

E. GLENN HINSON is David T. Porter professor of church history at the Southern Baptist Theological Seminary, Louisville, Kentucky. He received his Ph.D. from that seminary and his D. Phil. from Oxford University. He has taught as well at St. John's University Collegeville, The Catholic University of America, and the University of Notre Dame. He has published a dozen books in church history and historical theology, and numerous articles in academic journals.

He has taken a leading role in ecumenical contacts between Southern Baptists and other Christian communities.

JOHN P. MCCARTHY is an assistant professor of theology at Loyola University of Chicago. Presently he serves as Chairperson for Research and Publication for the College Theology Society. He holds his Ph.D. from the University of Chicago. His essay, "The Density of Religious Reference," was published last year in the *International Journal for the Philosophy of Religion*.

THOMAS F. MCKENNA, C.M. is a member of the Vincentian Community. He holds an M.A. in philosophy from St. John's University, N.Y., and a Th.M. and M. Div. from Mary Immaculate Seminary, Northampton, Pa. He received his S.T.D. from the Catholic University of America in systematic theology. He is presently assistant professor in the theology department at St. John's University, N.Y. where he teaches courses in both spirituality and systematics. He has had articles published in *Spirituality Today, The Bible Today, The Priest, The Merton Annual*, and *Review for Religious*.

EDWARD JEREMY MILLER is professor of religious studies at Gwynedd-Mercy College, Gwynedd Valley, PA. Prior to that he was professor of systematic theology at Emory University and was also officer for higher education programs at the National Endowment for the Humanities. He received the Ph.D. and S.T.D. from the University of Louvain. He has recently published *John Henry Newman on the Idea of Church*.

LANCE E. NELSON (Ph.D., McMaster University) is lecturer in the Department of Theological and Religious Studies at the University of San Diego. He is the author of a number of articles including "Madhusudana Sarasvati on the 'Hidden Meaning' of the *Bhagavadgita: Bhakti* for the Advaitin Renunciate." He is currently completing a book on the place of devotional religion in Hindu nondualism.

PETER C. PHAN has his S.T.D. from the Salesian Pontifical University and Ph.D. from the University of London and has published in *Salesianum, The Heythrop Journal, The Irish Theological Quarterly, The Thomist, The Living Light, Ephemerides Liturgicae* and *Sobornost*. He has written four books, one of which, *Eternity in Time*, was given the 1988 Best Book Award by the College Theology Society. Currently he is professor of systematic theology at The Catholic

University of America and is the editor of an eight-volume series on systematic theology published by Michael Glazier, Inc.

BERNARD L. RAMM is professor emeritus of theology at the American Baptist Seminary of the West in Berkeley, California. He has authored over a half dozen books concerned with the problem of faith and modernity, including *After Fundamentalism: The Future of Evangelical Theology* (1983).

WILLIAM M. SHEA (Ph.D., Columbia University) is Chairperson of the Department of Theological Studies, St. Louis University. He was president of the College Theology Society (1984–86) and resident fellow at the Woodrow Wilson International Center for Scholars (1986–1987). In 1984 he published *Naturalism and the Supernatural*, and has contributed essays and reviews to *Horizons, The Thomist, Journal of Religion, The American Journal of Education, Journal of the American Academy of Religion,* and *Commonweal.*

TERRANCE W. TILLEY (Ph.D., Graduate Theological Union, Berkeley) has published articles in *Journal of American Academy of Religion, Theological Studies, Horizons, Modern Theology,* and other journals. He has also written *Talking to God: An Introduction to Philosophical Analysis of Religious Language* (1978); *Story Theology* (1985) which won the CTS Book of the Year Award in 1986; and *The Evils of Theodicy.* He is now associate professor of religion at the Florida State University.

JAMES P. M. WALSH, S.J., is associate professor in the department of theology at Georgetown University, where he has taught biblical studies since 1973. He received his doctorate in near eastern languages and civilizations from Harvard University. His book, *The Mighty from Their Thrones: Power in the Biblical Tradition,* was published in 1987.

MARY JO WEAVER is a professor of religious studies at Indiana University where she is also an adjunct member of the Women's Studies faculty. She teaches courses on contemporary Roman Catholicism and on various aspects of women and religion. She has just revised her textbook, *Introduction to Christianity,* and her last book, *New Catholic Women,* is now out in paperback.She is currently working on a book on women in Judaism, Christianity, and Islam. She is a long-time member of the College Theology Society and on the editorial board of *Horizons.*